Child Care and Health

FOR NURSERY NURSES

Third Edition

Jean Brain, Cert. Ed. and Molly D. Martin, R.G.N., H.V.Cert.

Stanley Thornes (Publishers) Ltd

First published in 1980 by Hulton Educational Publications Ltd
This edition published by
Stanley Thornes (Publishers) Ltd
Old Station Drive
Leckhampton
CHELTENHAM GL53 0DN
ENGLAND

First edition 1980
Revised and reprinted 1981
Reprinted 1982
Second edition 1983
Reprinted 1984, 1986
Third edition 1989
Reprinted 1990
Reprinted 1991
Reprinted 1992

British Library Cataloguing in Publication Data

Brain, Jean
    Child care and health: for nursery nurses.
    —3rd ed.
    1. Children, to 7 years. Home care, — For
    nursery nursing
    I. Title   II. Martin, Molly D.
    649'1

    ISBN 1-871402-13-1

Typeset by Tech-Set, Gateshead, Tyne & Wear.
Printed and bound in Great Britain by Butler and Tanner Ltd, Frome.

Contents

Foreword

During recent years, caring for young children has been elevated to the status of a profession which employs tens of thousands of people. One branch of child care in particular, that of nursery nursing, requires its practitioners to be able to care for the whole child; his physical, intellectual, emotional and social development.

There are thousands of child care students training to a high level in Colleges of Further Education throughout the country, so it is particularly welcome that Jean Brain and Molly Martin have produced this revised version of their book *Child Care and Health for Nursery Nurses*. Already a favourite in a large number of colleges, this book will be a valuable addition to libraries and the bookshelves of students following a variety of courses.

The revised edition includes all the basic information for an understanding of the so-called 'normal' child being brought up in the traditional two-parent family, but also current thinking on child abuse, changing social patterns incorporating single-parent families, multiculturalism and equal opportunities for all. Changes in welfare benefits and the public sector, developments of family centres and combined nursery centres are also explored, as well as the role of those who choose to work with individual children as nannies and child-minders. The section on children with special needs has been updated and the scope of the book has been extended to cover the early school years in more detail.

Jean Brain was a tutor on one of the best-known and most widely recognised courses in child care, the two-year Certificate course of the National Nursery Examination Board. She was a Co-ordinating External Examiner for the Board and a prolific writer on child care topics. Molly Martin has also tutored NNEB courses and is a qualified health visitor who worked for many years in the community.

Students, practitioners in all branches of child care, and parents, too, will find much of value in the pages of the revised edition of this book.

David Peck
Publisher, *Nursery World* magazine.

July 1988

Introduction

The National Nursery Examination Board was formed in 1945, conferring a nationally recognised qualification (NNEB Certificate) to fit people to work with young children up to the age of five. This was later extended to seven.

From the start, it was an imaginative and enlightened scheme, designed to continue the students' education as well as train them for their chosen career.

Most courses are conducted within colleges of further education, although one is housed separately. There are also a very few independent colleges; the majority, however, form part of the state education system.

Students usually train for two years, at the end of which time they will take a national examination. Students must be sixteen or over when they embark on the course. The NNEB does not dictate academic entry qualifications, but fluency in written expression is a great advantage as, at the time of writing, the Board requires each student to produce sixty pieces of child observation work at an acceptable standard in order to pass the course. There will also be numerous projects to be completed, a three-hour essay paper, and a one and three-quarter hour multiple choice question paper. Some individual courses set their own entry requirement of between two and four GCSE grades A–C.

Training varies with the centres, but the NNEB lays down a minimum amount of time over a 2/3-year period; 1260 hours must be spent in college-based study, and similarly a minimum number of 140 days must be spent in approved practical training establishments. Depending on areas and opportunities, practical training will take place in day nurseries, nursery centres, nursery schools, nursery classes, infant schools, hospitals, schools and units for children with special needs. In recent years, more emphasis has been placed on preparation for private

work (nannying), and practical experience with a family and child/children of under school age is now a compulsory element of the course.

Eventually the award of a qualification will not be tied to any one training course. All child care students will attain various levels of competence, for which performance evidence will be required. This evidence will be assessed either direcly in placement or indirectly by projects, assignments and examples of work.

Theoretical training comprises vocational studies, all linked with child development and care of children, and complementary studies, a wide range of creative and communication subjects. It is the former which this book sets out to encompass but, wherever possible, this is linked to students' day to day practical experience of working with children.

The role of the nursery nurse has reflected the many changes in society which have come about since our original book was published in 1980, and revised over the succeeding years.

In this book we have tried to update both theory and practice in the light of current issues and today's society. We hope that it will be of use for students in any field of child care from GCSE upwards.

Readers should appreciate that what follows is *our* interpretation of the NNEB syllabus and, in places, this may differ from other tutors' interpretation or emphasis.

The emergence of male students in recent years, although numbers are not increasing as fast as we would like, has made a valuable contribution to this traditionally female world. Our continued use of the female sex when writing of nursery nurses should not be seen as dismissive or outdated: it is merely less clumsy than the s/he hers/his terminology. In the same way, we have always referred to the child as 'he', in order to be succinct and consistent, and to distinguish the child from the carer. 'He' should be taken to mean *any* child, regardless of sex, colour, or ethnic group. We do not always distinguish between children of different nationalities when talking about the care they need because such basic care is universal.

We would do well to hold the universality and relative timelessness of good practice in child care uppermost in our minds: this much will remain consistent, despite forthcoming changes in syllabuses, names of training courses or validating bodies.

Readers may notice that in this edition there is no separate chapter on child observation, although suggestions for child observation work are given at the end of each chapter. This is because it is such an important topic that it requires greater space than can be afforded within the scope of this book.

Inevitably, any text book which attempts to cover the vocational study content of a course cannot deal fully with the knowledge required on every subject. Further investigation, reading, discussion and guidance are strongly recommended. Our suggestions for follow-up work may be used as the basis of seminars, class exercises, starting points for discussion, or projects undertaken by individuals or pairs. We would also recommend that they be used whenever students have time in research or private study periods, or when tutors may be unexpectedly prevented from teaching them.

We hope that this book also conveys our wholehearted confidence in the intrinsic worth of training to care for children, and an essential spirit of service to children and their families.

The Family

From very early times people have lived in groups, mainly for protection and food gathering, but also because human beings are gregarious creatures and like to be with others. People with similar characteristics and aims tend to stay together.

Human babies, unlike other animals, need a long period of protection and training before they are able to fend for themselves. The family setting, within a larger group, is ideal for this task. Historically, men acted co-operatively to obtain food and protect the women and children. The women were then able to nurture their children in a safe environment.

The family is the basic unit of society; it comprises people who relate to one another by blood, marriage or affection.

The family unit has undergone many changes through the centuries. We cannot begin to do justice to this fascinating subject here, but there is a wealth of literature available for further study.

In order to appreciate the changes in recent times which have had a dramatic influence on family life in Britain today, we need to look at British families a hundred or so years ago.

FAMILY LIFE IN THE NINETEENTH CENTURY

The nineteenth century saw a huge growth in numbers of the British middle class. This came about through Britain's prosperity and influence in the world, built on industrialisation, trade and colonisation.

In general, the middle class imitated the ways of the rich and aristocratic, and this affected many aspects of family life.

The middle-class family of Victorian times

This would have consisted of mother, father, and possibly ten or more children. Several children may have died at birth or in infancy.

Father was often an autocratic, remote figure, whose word was law. He was the provider, and mother had no need to work. She would preside over the household and several servants, who may have been residential. A governess would care for the children, teach them in infancy, and possibly continue the education of daughters through their teens.

This education at home would include drawing, embroidery and playing the piano. Daughters would be expected to make a 'good' marriage (that is, a financially advantageous one) at an early age. If they remained single in their twenties, daughters were considered to be 'old maids' and had to find worthy occupations, inside and outside the family, to fill their lives. Financial provision for them would probably be made by their fathers or brothers.

Women were considered to be inferior to their husbands, and had no property, legal, voting or other rights. Once married, their own property became their husbands' property. Divorce was scandalous, and would have been financially impossible for a woman.

Religion was a mainstay of family life. Church attendance was generally obligatory for family and servants. Leisure activities on Sundays had to be quiet, decorous and solemn.

The Church traditionally taught that children were conceived and born in sin. Baptism began the process of redeeming them, and was urgently sought for delicate babies who might pass into the next world in a sinful state.

Children were expected to be 'seen and not heard', and to obey their 'elders and betters' implicitly. Spontaneity and individuality were not encouraged. Mother/child relationships, however, were notable for their sentimentality, as can be seen in Victorian paintings and literature.

Open displays of affection or, worse, passion between adults was taboo; between young people it was unthinkable. The sex act was held by genteel women to be an unavoidable necessity in the procreation of children. Yet prostitution records in large cities prove that many respectable Victorian men indulged their sexual appetites away from home.

Without easy access to transport and communication systems, people's lives tended to be narrow, both geographically and mentally. Men worked near their homes, and usually remained in the same locality all their lives. Consequently, grandparents, aunts, uncles and cousins – the extended family – played an important part in family life.

The lower-class family of Victorian times

For the very poor family, having relatives close by was vital at times of failing health or unemployment.

The husband was the chief breadwinner but wives usually worked too, in light industry, domestic service, seasonal agricultural work such as lifting potatoes, or laundry work which might have been done in their own homes ('taking in washing').

The working day, week and year were long and hard. Babies and children were often taken to work by working mothers, to the fields, for example. Holidays were almost unknown. A bank holiday *day* out at the nearest seaside resort, or a children's Sunday school outing in a charabanc were highspots of the year.

Families had little leisure to spend together or apart; all their time and energy went on eking out a frugal subsistance. For those undeterred by warnings of hell-fire and damnation, there were the temporary escape routes offered by ale or gin ('mother's ruin').

Traditional remedies such as rhubarb leaves or bags of warmed salt to cure earache, were used to treat the sick because doctors' fees, before the National Health Service was set up, were out of the question. Epidemics of measles, whooping cough and dysentery raged in towns from time to time, accelerated by lack of sanitation and poor housing.

Large families were the norm because methods of contraception were so primitive.

After 1880 education was compulsory and free for all but many children left school at the earliest possible moment, by the age of thirteen, to begin work. In areas where there was seasonal work many children would be kept away from school to help parents by earning extra money. Apprenticeship to a trade, at a very low wage, was virtually the only further training/education available. College education was beyond the reach of most people.

FAMILY LIFE IN THE TWENTIETH CENTURY

Since the late nineteenth century there have been far-reaching social and economic changes which have profoundly affected the family unit and family life. Listed here are the main areas of change:

- Health and life expectancy
- Educational opportunities
- Working conditions
- Equality of opportunity
- Status of men and women
- Sexual attitudes
- Contraception
- Child rearing
- Multicultural society
- Divorce
- The Welfare State
- Poverty and unemployment
- Housing
- Mobility
- Family networks
- Leisure
- Influence of religion

Health and life expectancy.   Health has improved dramatically and life expectancy has increased with greater prosperity and the adoption of good public health measures such as sanitation and better housing. Research leading to a better understanding of the factors that produce a healthy life style and the application of this knowledge have also contributed. Infant mortality is vastly reduced, although it is still not as low in Britain as it is in countries such as Finland. A death in the family is no longer such a common occurrence as it once was. Each individual life, from the antenatal period onwards, is more precious. For the parents, a baby will be a great responsibility and the focus of high hopes.

Paradoxically, now that death, suffering and acute illnesses, such as fevers which used to work up to a crisis, have passed out of our lives, with them has gone much drama. Some students of social behaviour believe that present-day problems of depression and boredom stem largely from this lack of real life drama.

Because people live longer, marriages which are theoretically undertaken for life, last much longer and may be exposed to more stress.

As older people remain active, the traditional picture of a white-haired old granny in a rocking chair, 'spoiling' her grandchildren may be replaced by that of a lively career woman with an active social life.

Increased life expectancy has serious implications for the balance of the population and the national economy in the near future. Will there be enough young people to earn money and care for the older generation?

Educational opportunities.   The repeated raising of the school-leaving age reflects the enhanced status of the child in society, but it also increases the dependancy years. Life in a complex, technological age has made higher education and further training necessary for large numbers of young people, which has further extended the years of dependancy.

Greater educational opportunities, however, have not been matched in recent years by greater employment opportunities and unemployment has become a major social problem. In 1983 the Government introduced a training scheme in an effort to help the situation, to provide paid training and experience for all sixteen and seventeen-year-olds who have no job to go to.

Working conditions.   A series of political reforms ended sweated labour of women and children and improved working conditions. In more recent times, working hours have steadily decreased and holidays increased, so creating leisure for the masses.

Equality of opportunity.   Women were given the vote in 1928, mainly as a result of their contribution in the First World War and agitation by the suffragette movement. Subsequently, aided by legislation such as the Equal Pay Act and the Sex Discrimination Act, women have, in theory, secured equal rights and opportunities in education and work. In the last twenty years, much lip-service has been paid to 'Women's Liberation' and equal rights. In terms of paid employment however, although 48 per cent of the people who work are women, their average earnings are only the equivalent of 75 per cent of men's income, sometimes even when they are doing almost the same job.

On the subject of representation in government, we should remember that at the beginning of this century even male suffrage (one man–one vote) had not long applied to Britain. This century has seen a steady increase in direct participation in government by the people, and also in the influence of the trade union movement and other bodies. Consequently family considerations are used by political parties to woo the support of voters.

Status of men and women. With a secure position in society, a good education and often career training too, many women now choose to return to a former job, or take up a new career after spending a comparatively short time on child-rearing. In Chapter 22, we shall look at how society provides for the young children of such women.

When both parents work they are more likely to share the household chores. Few modern families can afford to employ servants. In any case, the idea of working as another person's servant is often distasteful today. It is now possible for a woman to take a short maternity leave and plan to return to work, knowing her job should be kept open for her. Many fathers are happy to be involved with the upbringing of their children, from birth onwards. In some countries and in some jobs in Britain, fathers can claim paternity leave.

Single women now enjoy a status and a freedom in society unknown to their Victorian forebears, and the grim-sounding name 'spinster' has almost vanished. Consequently, many women choose to remain single, especially if they are in a well-paid professional job.

A subtle change has taken place in the status of father within the family. As the sole breadwinner he used to experience an authority and a definite status within his family. Now this is no longer so. Children educated to question past assumptions may not automatically respect him just because he is their father. This situation, coupled with taking a greater share in the household tasks, can lead to dissatisfaction and an unclear idea of his role in life.

The relaxation of social restraints has led to many couples cohabiting rather than taking on the commitment of marriage. In some cases this is really a trial marriage but in others it signifies a rejection of formal marriage in society.

Sexual attitudes. Enlightened attitudes towards the study of the human body and the development of psychology as a science, have helped to free sexual behaviour from traditional inhibitions. Sexual problems can be openly discussed and receive skilled and sympathetic help so that sexual relations can be fully enjoyed by both partners.

Contraception. Improved family planning methods and legalised abortion have enabled parents to plan ahead and limit their families to a chosen number. In recent years this has usually been one or two children. Effective contraception has resulted in a sharp decline in the birth rate since 1966 as economic pressures have led to many more women planning to return to work. Every child could and should be a wanted child. With such power of choice, some parents find the responsibility too onerous. The decision to defer parenthood for a while, though sensible, is sometimes hard to accept, especially by women in their early twenties who are at their most fertile time. However, many more women are now having their first baby after the age of thirty, and sometimes forty.

Another choice, in this context, is the service of a fertility clinic for a couple who are having difficulty in conceiving a baby. In the past the couple might have remained childless or tried to adopt, but modern technology may enable them to have their own baby.

Child rearing. The findings of child psychologists and educationalists are published in the press and discussed on radio and television. Parents are now expected to keep abreast of the latest ideas on child rearing and personal relationships.

Multicultural society. Since the beginning of recorded history different peoples have settled in Britain so that the population is a mix of many different groups who have been gradually assimilated. More recently the break-up of the British Empire brought about a new wave of immigration. People who lived in the Commonwealth and Colonies were British citizens and therefore had right of entry to Britain. In the 1950s, Britain had a labour shortage and recruited labour from the colonies. For example, British Rail and London Transport advertised for staff in West Indian newspapers and subsidised the cost of travel to Britain. The families of those that came will be second and third generation British. More recently people from the Indian sub-continent, Hong Kong and Vietnam have settled in Britain. In addition, since Britain joined the European Economic Community, nationals of other member countries have used their right of entry to come and work in this country.

All of these people have brought a richness and a diversity to the British way of life, but differences in culture can cause problems due to a lack of understanding.

Divorce. Easier divorce proceedings are often blamed for the rising divorce rate and the difficulties for some children who are being brought up in single-parent families. (See Chapter 2.) Many experienced people, however, agree that it may be more damaging for a child to live within a loveless marriage where partners stay together 'for the sake of the children'.

The Welfare State. The concept of the Welfare State which came into being after the Second World War was to prevent 'want, disease, ignorance, squalor, and idleness'. Various Acts of Parliament were passed to form a basis of protection for people in distress. (See Chapter 21.)

Poverty and unemployment. The possibility of attaining a comfortable and happy life in our society has developed to a point where most possessions and opportunities are seen as instantly obtainable. Television has played an important part here and many advertisements are aimed at children.

Domestic appliances can greatly reduce drudgery; holidays abroad are widely enjoyed. Paying for such items can be deferred by credit and the popular use of the plastic card. But, sadly, despite the signs of affluence so tantalisingly close, in Britain today there are about twelve million people living on or below the poverty line. About nine million people, including increasing numbers of families with children under sixteen, live with one necessity of life, maybe heat or adequate diet, permanently missing. These statistics are, of course, linked to the high figures of unemployment and vary throughout the country.

For the effects of poverty, unemployment and homelessness on families, see Chapters 2 and 18.

Housing. Housing and sanitation have become steadily better this century, thereby improving standards of both physical and mental health. Families expect to have their own homes, and although local authorities cannot keep pace with demand, this is the goal they strive to achieve. After the Second World War, during a period when the birth rate was rising and the availability of building land was diminishing, many authorities built high-rise flats to meet the demand but these have since proved unsuitable and are frequently sources of discontent, depression, isolation and vandalism. They are particularly harmful to mothers of young children.

Recently many more council house tenants have been encouraged to buy their own houses at an economic price. Often this is a successful move. Sometimes it is not; owners may fall behind in mortgage payments and then become homeless. In the private sector, there has been a great increase in the number of people who succeed in buying their own homes, and achieve high standards of comfort and amenities. By contrast again, the low paid live in rented accommodation which is often not properly maintained by either the local authority or private landlords. Deterioration of the property and despair often follow.

Mobility. The upheaval of two World Wars extended the horizons of a whole generation and led to greater occupational and social mobility. Motorised vehicles and good public transport made travel, for work and leisure, a practical possibility.

In more recent years, limited job opportunities, centralisation of resources such as shops, schools, health centres and hospitals, and reduced local transport have made travel more difficult and the ownership of a car a virtual necessity in rural areas.

Family networks. Greater mobility, changing outlooks, a desire for a healthier life style, slum clearance, and bomb devastation in the Second World War, led to the growth of suburbs and new towns. As grown-up children moved away from their roots, however, family and community networks broke up, and the typical family unit today is a nuclear family; that is, it consists only of parents and their child or children. Contact between the nuclear family and other relatives now is a matter of choice, and depends on concern for relatives' well-being. Formerly, life in an extended family meant that contact was unavoidable. Today, greater in-dependence and more privacy in the personal lives and child-rearing patterns of the young mother and father are ensured. But children can be denied valuable contact with grandparents, peer cousins, and other relatives who might enhance the sense of belonging to a strong, distinctive unit. For the parents, particularly young mothers, this can lead to a sense of isolation, lack of support and depression.

Economic independence – thanks to the Welfare State – is welcomed by the older generation, but they, too, can feel lonely, abandoned, and deprived of the rejuvenating company of their grandchildren. The fact that people live to a greater age now means that the years of retirement, which in many cases can mean years without a useful role, accentuate this sense of isolation. On the other hand, improved health and freedom from poverty with universal state pensions can make retirement a period for the pursuit of interests and pleasures.

Leisure. Women's equal right to a social life has been recognised and whole families tend to enjoy leisure pursuits together, where once mother and children would have been left at home while father enjoyed his chosen hobby.

Gardening, decorating and watching television are now said to be the most popular pastimes in Britain, implying equal participation by both partners, and pride in creating and enjoying a pleasant home.

Influence of religion. In general there has been a move away from the influence of religion in everyday life. Many thousands of Christians call upon the services of the church only a few times in their lives, usually to sanctify and add comforting ceremony to births, marriages and deaths. As we live in a multicultural society the influence of other religions such as Islam makes itself felt.

The reduction of the influence of religion is sometimes linked to a general 'moral decline' in family life and elsewhere. Yet however unbelieving a family appears to be, the inheritance of ethics and a moral code has descended from religious thinking. Inner convictions and guiding principles are still passed on from one generation to the next.

INTERACTION WITHIN FAMILIES

Let us take a closer look at the invisible forces at work within families, especially those which most affect the child. His position in relation to other family members is of great significance.

The small family with one child is common in society today. The traditional view that the only child must be a spoiled child may be partly true, for he will be the sole focus of his parents' love and attention, which may include material over-indulgence. On the other hand, many parents, aware of this danger, may even be over strict. They usually make special efforts to secure companionship for the child. He will probably develop social skills early in life; because he has no ready-made companions, he must win and keep them. He may become, of necessity, self-sufficient and prefer his own company to that of other people. He may well be more advanced in conversation, through adult company. His parents' expectations will probably be high, and they may over-protect or cling to him when he should be allowed increasing independence. He will miss the hurly-burly of family life with brothers and sisters – teasing, rivalries, shared jokes, 'ganging up' against parents or each other, and the deep affection, often well hidden, expressed at Christmas, birthdays, and in times of stress. Sharing, taking turns, having to wait with other children are not quite the same if they only happen at school.

(This topic is covered in more detail in *An Examination Guide For Nursery Nurses, Volume 2* by the same authors.)

Families with three or more children are comparatively rare today. Traditionally, they are happy, loving groups in which to grow up, and indeed many undoubtedly are. Others, however, are found in unhappy circumstances due to poverty and other social problems. Sometimes the large number of children is the result of ignorance and carelessness rather than choice. If the parents are not reasonably well off and are not good copers, each new baby will increase their problems. Undoubtedly, such children learn to share, give and take at an early age. Older children gain valuable experience in helping with younger ones. But the youngest may go short of adult attention and language stimulation. Material benefits have to be spread thinly. 'Hand me down' clothes and toys may be the usual lot of the youngest. There will be little privacy. Many people who have grown up in such a family feel that these disadvantages are, however, far outweighed by the experience of family solidarity, the development of resourcefulness, and the choice of particular closeness with one or more sibling, all of which may continue and afford great joy well into adult life.

The middle child out of three or five is often thought to be in an unenviable position; not for him the privileges and status of being the eldest, nor the babying and special treatment of the youngest. He may resent this, and resort to jealous or spiteful behaviour.

Twins often have to fight for their individuality to be recognised. Parents and teachers sometimes reinforce the image of the pair by dressing them alike, referring to them as 'the twins' and so on. At times they may enjoy and even encourage this attention, but at others they long to make their mark as individuals. Sometimes their early language development is slow, for they evolve their own private means of communication. Later, enforced closeness can accentuate differences in academic attainment, social success etc., and lead to rivalry and resentment.

The child born to older parents (in their late thirties to fifties) is a common feature of family life today. Such parents may be wiser and more patient, owing to greater life experience and maturity, but may be less physically energetic, more aware of dangers and pitfalls, and more cautious and protective. They may not be familiar with contemporary child-rearing practice, or, later, the fashions and freedom enjoyed by most teenagers today. This can be a particularly fraught period for the teenager, who will be aware that his parents are different from those of his friends.

The child born after an interval of years may experience some of these effects, possibly coupled with those of being an only child. On the other hand, he may receive fond treatment from older brothers and sisters, and enjoy the company of contemporary nephews and nieces.

Readers can doubtless call to mind many other instances of how positions and relationships within families affect both their own functioning and the developing personality of the children.

THE FUTURE OF THE FAMILY

There are pressures within and outside today's small family units. It is not easy to be a good mother, father, son, daughter – good in everyone else's eyes as well as one's own. In such a small and self-contained setting, each family member's role is constantly in the limelight. It is almost impossible to have an 'off' day, or disappear temporarily from the scene, without others noticing, and being materially and psychologically affected. This situation can lead to stress and discontent.

Some of the traditional functions of the family –

protecting the very young, or the old and weak members, for instance – have been, at least in part, taken over by the Welfare State.

People no longer feel the need to get married in order to enjoy sex and, with contraception effectively separating sex from producing babies, we may well ask whether there is any need for marriage at all?

Marriage in some societies still has an aura of romance. However, some people appear to manage very well by tackling it as a practical, economic arrangement. Should we not then, in Western countries, look seriously for alternative approaches to family life, or even change the whole concept of marriage, and the family as society's basic unit?

While young people and others search in communes and kibbutzim for an alternative, superior unit, marriage becomes more and more popular. Despite increased life expectancy, people marry earlier. Most divorced people remarry within a few years. Clearly then, the high divorce rate does not reflect a rejection of the institution of marriage, but it may be an assertion by individuals of the right to change partners.

In the USSR, which has undergone revolution, civil war and a great sweeping away of traditional values, and where the State wields far more power over the individual than in Britain, marriage and family life still thrive, despite assumptions that they would fade out. We know from irrefutable evidence that the family is infinitely preferable as a setting for the child's development to the impersonal, multi-staffed institution.

Surely these facts strongly suggest that marriage and the family still fulfil the deep-felt needs of human beings.

IN CONCLUSION

As human beings, we need to care, and be cared for by others. To do this we need a few – comparatively speaking – close, lasting relationships, rather than many superficial ones.

We need to matter to others, and how much we matter largely depends on how much we contribute to their well-being. We need a degree of stability in our environment. We need to create surroundings of our choice, and unless there is some guarantee of the future of those surroundings, all our efforts are wasted. We want our lives to be more than a mere speck in the universe, a chance interval of time. We like to feel a sense of continuity – handing on the baton in life's relay race, rather than merely sprinting the hundred metres.

In a world where our daily work may be frustrating or uninspiring, we can derive deep satisfaction from life within a family. In a world of changing values, we feel we belong to one safe, steadfast unit. Helped by this inner security, most parents do their utmost to fulfil their family roles.

In many ways more, rather than less, is asked of parents today. They are expected to decide how many children to have, and at what intervals, depending on economic and other circumstances. They are expected to keep informed about all the institutions – clinics, schools, government agencies and so on – which will affect their children's development and education so as to derive as much benefit as possible from these. Catering for their children's physical, social, emotional and intellectual needs, parents must equip their children for a society which is itself constantly changing. A family which succeeds in this task contributes immensely to the community and is rewarded with status, prestige, reinforcement of its solidarity, and recognition of its identity.

Benefits to the child
Experience shows that the most favourable climate in which a child can develop is within the family group.

Intimate knowledge of and interaction with loving parents who also love one another, gives the child a secure emotional base, where he *knows* he is loved and valued. He has no need to resort to attention-seeking behaviour, then or later. Building on shared experiences and memories, and emerging tastes, talents and characteristics, he gradually forms a clear picture of himself as an individual and feels at ease with that self. Text books call this 'self-image' or 'concept of self'. He will model his future conduct on that he sees in the home. He grows up with a clear idea of male and female roles in marriage, family and society. In moments of stress, he seeks refuge, comfort, reassurance from the family, and good moments are crowned by shared pleasure and pride.

As the years pass, he uses the family as a sounding board, punchbag, haven, anchor, cushion, and springboard. He learns to cope with failure and success, conflict, frustration, his own strengths and weaknesses and those of others. He learns loyalty to a group, and the safe feeling and confidence of belonging. He learns how to give as well as accept support. He contributes to the strength of the family and in doing so becomes stronger himself. Having received love, he can give it, wholeheartedly and wisely, without restraint, resentment or hopes of reward. In short, he can play his part in creating the next generation of good families.

EXERCISES

Investigation
If you are in touch with a grandparent, ask him or her about their childhood. Compare and contrast this with that of your parent(s) and yourself. Do you think your grandparent's experience was better or worse than yours?

Observation
If possible, observe the interaction of siblings at school, perhaps in the playground or garden. In your evaluation, try to identify what attitudes to each other are discernable in their words and actions.

Project
Subject for debate: Why get married?

SUGGESTIONS FOR FURTHER READING

D.W. Winnicott, *The Child and the Family*, Tavistock Publications Ltd
David Kennedy, *Children*, B.T. Batsford Ltd
Edward Shorter, *The Making of the Modern Family*, Fontana
Eleanor Allen, *Victorian Children*, A. & C. Black Ltd
Khalil A. Khavani and Sue Williston Khavani, *Creating a Successful Family*, One World
Helen Bethune, *Positive Parent Power*, Thorsons Publishing Group
Dana Breen, *Talking with Mothers*, Free Association Books
Dulan Barber (Ed.), *One Parent Families*, Hodder & Stoughton Ltd
V. George and P. Wilding, *Motherless Families*, Routledge & Kegan Paul Ltd
P.L. Selfe, *GCSE Sociology*, Pan Study Aids
Audrey Sandbank, *Twins and the Family*, Arrow Books Ltd
Faber and Mazlish, *Siblings Without Rivalry*, Sidgwick and Jackson Ltd
P. Mansfield, J. Collard, *The Beginning of the Rest of Your Life?* Macmillan Ltd
Ann Mitchell, *Families*, Chambers Ltd
Paul Lawless and Frank Brown, *Urban Growth and Change in Britain*, Harper and Row Ltd
Gerard O'Donnell, *Mastering Sociology*, Macmillan Ltd
J. Nobbs, B. Hine, M. Flemming, *Sociology*, Macmillan Ltd
Angela Holdsworth, *Out of the Doll's House*, BBC Books

2 Different Life Styles

Such is the diversity of family life in Britain today that it is impossible to cover all the different life styles, and very difficult to choose examples which will give students all the knowledge they need to work with various groups of children. No longer can we use the 'typical' family beloved of the television advertisements – the breakfast cereal family of two white, middle-class parents, one son and one daughter. It is doubtful whether it was ever typical anyway.

Britain contains many people of different cultures. It is a multicultural society and in this chapter we look at family compositions, circumstances, and life styles. There is always a danger when studying different peoples of losing sight of their similarities. The important thing to remember is that all people have the same basic needs, although they may interpret them differently according to their class, religion or culture.

In addition, it is extremely difficult to generalise about people's life styles. Even families from the same background differ. Children unconsciously absorb their parents' values and their attitudes to life. As they grow up they may rebel and try a different way of life or, perhaps, change their social class or religion but, when mature, most people tend to base their lives on the values of their parents because it has become an integral part of them. This is not to say people do not change at all – human beings are adaptable and in each generation some modifications occur.

Members of a society share knowledge, beliefs and activities; this is their culture. Passing this on to their children is known as socialisation and is an on-going process throughout life. The traditions and rituals of a society's culture give people a feeling of security and the common standards which bind them together add to their sense of identity.

In different cultures things which are important in one society will not matter so much in another. For instance, traditionally, Muslim men and women are expected to cover the whole body from neck to ankles in a modest way. In practice, this might be slightly modified to Western styles of dress.

People living in a multicultural society should respect other people's culture.

It is fairly common for children to have two sets of behaviour – one for school and one for home use, but children coming from a minority group often have to adapt to several very opposing sets of values.

When working with families, it is very important for nursery nurses to try to understand the attitudes and beliefs of the family and not to make judgements based on their own values. This respect is particularly important for the nursery nurse who becomes a nanny as she will be living in the home of people who may be completely different from her own family.

One person's experience as a nursery nurse student will vary from another person's, depending on the area in which she does her practical placement. One area can be very different from another, even within the same town or city.

For instance, most inner city areas with poor housing tend to contain the poorer section of the community (those in the lower socio-economic groups), whereas the spacious leafy suburbs are inhabited by the more wealthy middle classes. Muslim communities, for example, tend to concentrate in certain areas because they like to be within walking distance of their mosque. Everybody is aware of the so-called north/south divide in Britain where the 'haves' are said to congregate in the south and the 'have-nots' in the north.

These are all generalisations of course, but they do serve to illustrate some of the variations in Britain and show how essential it is for students to get to know the groups which predominate in their areas.

When researching types of families and different life styles, sociologists divide people into socio-economic groups for the purposes of comparison.

This is known as the Registrar-General's classification and uses the occupation of the head of the household as the key. The classes consist of:

A Professionals such as doctors, lawyers and accountants
B People like managers, teachers and nurses
C Secretaries, shop assistants and skilled tradesmen such as carpenters etc.
D Agricultural workers, bus conductors, postmen etc.
E Labourers, cleaners, dock workers etc.

The following section looks at different families and their life styles on the basis of how this may be affected by their culture and by their circumstances, e.g. single-parent families. Such categorisation is for simplification and is generalised. Obviously there will be some overlap where the life style is affected by both culture and circumstances.

ASIAN FAMILIES

Many people of Asian extraction live in Britain today. They include people from China (mainly Hong Kong), Vietnam and the Indian sub-continent. Since their culture is largely based on their religious faith it is helpful for the student to have some knowledge of the different religions and how they affect their way of life.

Muslims

Britain's Muslims originally came mainly from Pakistan, Bangladesh, East Africa, and Gujerat in India.

They are followers of the Prophet Muhammad who was the founder of the Islamic faith. Many aspects of their daily life are written in the Koran, and are regarded as direct commands from God. The Koran stresses the responsibilities and obligations of each individual within his/her own family, and the value of the family as a source of support, love and security.

Muslim families are often large. They are usually extended families and grandparents are active in rearing children.

Pregnancy is seen as a crucial time for both mother and baby. Women prefer women doctors. In their country of origin, babies would usually be breast-fed for up to two years, and then weaned quickly onto family foods.

Ageing and sick parents are visited regularly, if they are not already living with grown-up sons.

Sexual morality among Muslims is strict and extra-marital activity is forbidden. The sexes are segregated after puberty, boys and girls attending single-sex schools. Education is very highly regarded.

Women's bodies must be covered modestly. Traditional Muslims regard purdah (the physical seclusion of women) as a measure designed to protect them, although this is not practised in Britain.

Roles of men and women are clearly defined. The woman is the home-maker but in matters outside the home the woman has to obtain the man's consent.

Adolescence can bring pressure and conflict between traditional values and customs, and those of the host society. Marriages are arranged, often with the agreement of the couple.

Traditional Muslims regard the birth of babies as the will of God, so a strict Muslim family would not practise contraception.

Divorce is permitted in Islam but the Koran advises the husband and wife to get the help of relatives to solve their discord.

Practising Muslims pray five times a day (Salah), and give a set proportion of their income to welfare (Zakah). They also fast for the Islamic month of Ramadan, between dawn and dusk. Pregnant and nursing mothers, the old and infirm, and children under fourteen are exempt. Muslims practise strict rules of hygiene in their daily toilet, and in preparation for prayer.

Sikhs

Sikhism was originally a breakaway movement from the Hindu and Muslim faiths. Sikhs rejected the traditional caste (social group) system. The giving of the second name 'Kaur' to all females, and 'Singh' to all males, was intended to reinforce this rejection. Also Sikh first names are not gender based, so Ranjit Singh is male and Ranjit Kaur is female.

Most Sikhs in this country come from the Punjab in India, or East Africa. Traditionally, Sikhs have been great travellers and brave warriors.

Religious life centres round the Gurdwara, the Sikh temple, where prayers, singing and recitation take place, under the guidance of the priest. Teachings have been handed down by gurus (religious teachers).

Sikhs wear the five symbols of Sikhism: a bangle; a comb; a pair of shorts; a sword, sword brooch or pendant; the hair uncut and turban.

Great importance is attached to the evening meal with the whole family.

It is within the Sikh tradition to be active family members. They often live in an extended family situation, and retain strong family obligations to relatives still living in the Indian sub-continent.

Men and women are regarded as having been born equal, and freedom and authority are vested in each as parents. Sons are responsible for ageing parents.

Sexual morality is very strong. Men and women mix socially, but unmarried women will be chaperoned.

While adolescent, Sikhs would be expected to keep parents informed of their whereabouts and companions in the evening, and to respect a set time for coming home.

Divorce is permitted but rare in Sikh communities.

Hindus

Hinduism is the oldest and the third largest religion in the world.

Most of Britain's Hindus come from East Africa, and the rest mainly from India and Pakistan.

Traditionally, the caste (social group) system was built into the Hindu religion, ranging from the Brahmins (priests) to the untouchables, who did all the most unpleasant work. In practice, the caste system is gradually changing but caste is still important when choosing a marriage partner and, in some cases, when seeking a job.

Another tradition was that sons were important (for example, they light the funeral pyre at their father's burial), and families would continue to produce children until a son was born.

Family life is important to the Hindu faith. Family roles and duties are carefully delineated, and the elderly are held in great respect. As they age, some old people, such as Brahmins, may withdraw into a more spiritual life.

Modesty in dress is practised, and divorce is rare.

Hindus do not need to visit a temple to worship and most important rituals are performed in their homes. There are several festivals, the most widely known one in Britain being Diwali, the New Year Festival of Lights.

AFRO-CARIBBEAN FAMILIES

There have been families of Afro-Caribbean extraction living in Britain for many years. But in the late 1950s, when Britain was experiencing an economic boom, British politicians of the day urged people of the West Indies (at that time very much part of the British Commonwealth) to come to Britain and find employment since there was a shortage of labour in Britain. At first they settled in cities where jobs, often unskilled and low-paid, were plentiful.

Characteristics of Afro-Caribbean families vary enormously.

Traditionally, the role of the grandmother in caring for the children is very important, because in the Caribbean most mothers work and there is almost no child-care provision. In Britain, children of working mothers may be looked after by child minders.

The pressing housing, educational and leisure needs of dependents and youths in inner cities have clearly not been met for any sector of the population. Successive government Reports have found that racism and inappropriate teacher expectations have contributed substantially to the under-achievement of young people at school.

Some Afro-Caribbeans may belong to one of a variety of non-conformist churches, such as Pentecostal or Seventh Day Adventist. The church and church worship is the focus of family life, and children are brought up in a strict code of behaviour.

In recent years, there has emerged a religious movement from Jamaica called Rastafarianism. Its followers identify with Ethiopia as the home of their religious leader, Haile Selassie. The hair of a Rastafarian is uncut and plaited into dreadlocks to represent the mane of the lion of Judah. Children's hair should be covered by a hat. Rastafarians use marijuana as a sacrament which frees their minds to see life more clearly.

This religion is part of a wider desire among black people to identify with their African roots, and to celebrate and affirm their colour and culture. Alongside this, however, now that many Afro-Caribbean families have been living in Britain for several generations, it is increasingly found that families have similar aims, values, tastes, life styles and problems as their white neighbours.

TRAVELLING FAMILIES

Travellers comprise many different groups of people and have lived in Britain for about a thousand years.

They are found in largest numbers in south-east England, the Lincolnshire Fens, Hereford and Worcester, the West Midlands, and the North East.

There are fully mobile families, using both authorised and unauthorised sites, semi-settled families who remain on authorised sites for most of the year, housed families who live as travellers for seasonal work e.g. fruit picking, migrant farm workers who are usually caravan-dwellers, families of showmen (fairground), circus families, and housed families who remain true to their traveller/gypsy identity.

In recent years, various disaffected groups have adopted a gypsy life style. They are also sometimes known as the 'peace convoy' or 'hippies'. Their philosophy of life and life style may be at variance with the traditional travellers who do not necessarily want to be identified with them.

Most travellers are self-employed and desire to remain so. Besides seasonal work in the fields, occupations include scrap-metal dealing, tarmac laying, roofing, tree felling, bagging and selling bulk manure, second-hand car sales, selling bric-à-brac, antiques, and carpets. Sale of traditional craft items has been largely replaced by plastic goods. Since unemployment has encouraged the black economy, some of these occupations have been taken over by settled members of the community. Being forced to depend on state benefits has been a great blow to many travellers' self-respect, although there is a wide range of economic circumstances among travelling families.

Their vehicles are vital to them and their earning ability. Many families have two trailers; sometimes one is for the extended family, or one may be a kitchen trailer and one is for 'best'. Standards of hygiene and observance of domestic customs are usually very high within the trailer home although different from those of settled families. But their transitory existence and the trappings of a trade such as scrap-metal often involves a lack of concern for the environment and surroundings where they encamp.

Since 1968 local authories have been required to provide up to fifteen official sites but most authorities have been very slow to do so. Often, where a site is provided, amenities are not based on a real knowledge of the travellers' life style and requirements. Local opposition is frequently aroused when travellers use roadsides and unauthorised sites. The passing of the Public Order Act relating to criminal trespass in 1987 has resulted in further harassment.

Travellers live in an extended family situation, and children are usually very secure and well-adjusted – a fact that sometimes surprises, or even annoys, others. Children are expected to take part in domestic chores and earning the family's living from a very early age. Consequently, toys and playthings may be regarded as a waste of time and unreal. Children are looked upon as trainee adults, but parents are often extremely protective of them.

Great importance is attached to birth, marriage and death, and family members will travel great distances to attend such celebrations which may last several days.

Formal education may be not only fragmented but also seen as irrelevant. A proportion of travelling adults are illiterate.

Consistency of health care can also cause problems. A system of client-held record cards has been working well in Manchester, Sheffield and elsewhere.

In the last ten or fifteen years, real efforts have been made by some local education authorities to take schooling and services to travelling families. Better still, children are encouraged to integrate within local schools, for however short a time.

But the fact remains that travellers are still one of the most discriminated against groups in this country. It is still quite usual in some localities to see 'No Gypsies' notices in pubs and launderettes.

SINGLE-PARENT FAMILIES

More than one in five families today is a one-parent family. Seven out of eight of these are headed by a woman. In the main it is not the single parent status that brings problems to parents and children alike, but the attendant money problems. Less than half of single parents earn their main income; the rest live on social security benefits. Only one in eleven such families can survive on benefits alone, yet maintenance by the other parent is difficult to obtain and may not be reliable. Our present tax system tends to disadvantage single women parents, who often work part time for low wages and live in low-grade housing. In addition, lone parents may find themselves in a child-care trap – they cannot work because they need to care for the child and, because they are poorly skilled, they cannot earn enough to pay for child care. This illustrates the gaps in state care, and the lack of adequate, sufficiently flexible child-care provision.

Single parents include:

- Unsupported mothers
- Deserted, separated and divorced parents
- Widows and widowers.

Unsupported mothers

Most vulnerable of all are the unsupported mothers, many of them under the age of twenty and some even under sixteen. Despite relatively freely available sex education and contraception, every year thousands of single women become pregnant. Many of these pregnancies are accidental but there is evidence to suggest that some young girls see pregnancy as an alternative to unemployment. Also, if a young girl is very unhappy at home, she may make the mistake of confusing a man's sexual demands as a sign of affection. In this situation she may not have the foresight to use any form of contraception, and pregnancy can be the result. The consequences for the baby can be a cause for concern. Early in the pregnancy, the girl has to decide whether or not she is going to have the baby or have the pregnancy terminated. Termination is now available if two doctors agree that it is necessary and it can be arranged before the twenty-eighth week of pregnancy. Unfortunately shame, ignorance or fear of parental reaction may cause the girl to leave it too late for there to be any choice in the matter. Some young girls effectively hide the fact of their pregnancy until the birth itself, sometimes with tragic consequences.

A counselling service is available to help the mother to arrive at the best solution for her particular circumstances. There are many factors to take into consideration. For instance: what is the attitude of the baby's father? Is she likely to get any financial or moral support from him? How will she support the child financially? Who will care for him? Where will she and the baby live? What is the attitude of her parents? What about her disrupted social life and chances of finding happiness with another partner? Is she capable of giving the child a good start in life and providing the unselfish care he needs?

If circumstances at home are difficult she may be able to go to a mother-and-baby home for a few weeks before the birth. In some cities there are mother-and-baby units for schoolgirls where she can continue her studies up to the time of the birth, while also learning child care. Afterwards, she can remain there until her sixteenth birthday, keeping the baby with her, and caring for him under the guidance of nursery nurses and teachers. Regular antenatal care is vital for these mothers, as statistics show them and their babies to be greatly at risk.

There is a great shortage of babies free for adoption, so, in the unlikely event of a single mother deciding to part with her baby, there will be no problem in finding suitable and delighted parents. The mother will have to give final consent when the baby is a few weeks old.

If she keeps the baby, it will be a hard struggle for her to do her best for him, and retain much life of her own. If she stays at home, her mother may still have a full-time job and not be willing to resume baby rearing at this stage of her life. Her father, too, may resent the constraints on his freedom and his money. If she sets up her own separate home the sense of social isolation, the added responsibilities and the insistent demands of a baby can become too much for the young mother, leading to ill-health. Worse, she may neglect and ill-treat the child which would eventually lead to the child being taken into care. However many girls cope very well in this situation and are well supported by their extended family. To be fatherless no longer carries the social stigma it once did.

In contrast, some women make a definite decision to have a baby without marriage or a stable partnership. These mothers, who are single by choice, may well be more mature and established, both emotionally and economically. Although they may experience some of the difficulties besetting other single parents, it is probable that they will have thought through, and be prepared for, the implications of their chosen course of action, at least in the early stages. Also many of them are well qualified and have good jobs and therefore can earn enough to avoid the problems of the poverty trap.

Deserted, separated and divorced parents

Parents who find themselves in this position, committed to coping with a child or children, have some immediate decisions to make. A time of shock, anger, grief or hurt is not the best time to take decisions which will set patterns for the future, but many of these decisions cannot wait.

There are often pressing financial considerations: whether the remaining parent and child/children can afford to stay in their present home, and whether he or she will opt to try and live on state benefits (very minimal) or work full or part time. These are often the two biggest decisions to be taken. A residential housekeeper, or full-time nanny will be out of the question for many families, and most pre-school establishments do not offer full day care. These facts, too, must be reflected in any financial equations.

At home, the parent may feel isolated and depressed. At work, the parent may feel guilty or anxious about child-minding arrangements which will add to fatigue and not enhance time spent with the child.

Holidays, outings and social life may have to be curtailed, denying the family any break from dreary routine and everyday strains.

Anxiety over the effects this situation may be having on the child is never very far away, and having to make all parenting decisions alone is an added worry.

Employers vary greatly in the degree of acceptance and understanding they show to parents in this situation. They may be unsympathetic at times of children's illness and their employee's unavoidable lateness or absence. Chances of working overtime, on shifts or for bonuses, and perhaps promotion if it involves a move away from neighbours' support, for example, may have to be passed up by the lone parent, increasing feelings of resentment and lost opportunities.

Society is often more sympathetic to a man in this situation than a woman, apparently expecting a woman to be able to cope automatically with two full-time jobs.

Christmas and birthdays can be particularly stressful times for single-parent families.

However, now that so many families are headed by a single parent (the majority of whom are women), parents need not feel so isolated or different. There are many formal and informal support systems and organisations to meet many of the needs of parents and children in this situation.

The effects of family break-up on the children. These effects can be many and varied, but the great increase in divorce in recent years has meant that at least a child need not feel alone in his situation today. In fact, the very terms 'break-up', 'broken marriage', etc. may in time be replaced by phrases without these overtones of failure and regret, as changing partners becomes more accepted. This has come about since the 1969 Divorce Reform Act, where, in divorce proceedings matrimonial *offences* were replaced by the concept of irretrievable breakdown of marriage.

Immediate effects on the child will depend greatly on what has preceded the break; prolonged bitter conflict may leave the child shaken and insecure. The end of conflict can bring relief, but also guilt about the relief. In most cases there will initially be sorrow at the departure, bewilderment, hurt, a feeling that in some way the departure was the child's 'fault'. He will need much physical contact and reassurances of love from the remaining parent. He will also need to know that there are other adults who love him and would care for him if the remaining parent, too, were removed from the scene.

Behaviour disturbances may arise; at home, or at the nursery or school he may become 'wild', clinging, or start wetting or soiling himself, become withdrawn, suffer nightmares, do less well at school work, lack concentration, present minor physical ailments, or refuse to go to school. Sometimes these symptoms do not appear until some time after the initial event, when the adults wrongly assume that he has 'settled down'. However, it is a mistake for any adult to *expect* the child to show any of these signs of disturbance, or to label him 'a single-parent child', or worse, 'a typical single-parent child'.

If the family home has to be sold, there may be an accommodation problem.

At home, the degree of closeness to the remaining parent and involvement in more household tasks and similar activities may bind the child in an intense emotional situation. If the absent parent has access to the child, such visits may be fraught with difficulties, such as one parent's anger, resentment and possessiveness. A father may not have money or means to take the child anywhere suitable, and the visits may become arid stretches of time, with the child feeling disorientated. He may be 'wooed' with gifts. He may ask unanswerable questions about the reasons for the marriage break-up, court decisions on custody, the date of the next visit and so on. There may be tearful partings, leaving the child in an upset state for the coming week. Division of loyalties can be very painful. On the other hand, children are often far more resilient than we give credit for, and may seem to take in their stride this divided state of affairs, and some feel a great relief that the stress at home is settled.

Widows and widowers

Although sad, the death of an old person is easier to accept than that of a marriage partner and young parent. We have come to think of death as happening mainly in old age, in hospitals or old people's homes. This puts death outside our everyday experience, where it happened at one time. Death as shown on television is not 'real' and is no preparation for the death of someone we know. The first death we encounter at close quarters is always traumatic.

When a husband or wife dies, the remaining partner may turn in on himself in his grief and become isolated. He may, with the best of intentions, wish to protect the child or children from the harsh facts and from the rituals of burial and evidence of grief. It is now generally believed that this is unwise and that grief should be shown and shared, not suppressed.

Young children will watch the surviving parent and other adults to see how they are reacting. They should not sense that death is a taboo subject, and if they ask bald questions such as 'Where is she?' 'When will she come back?' they should be given answers that are true to what the parent knows and believes. To raise false hopes, or evade the facts will bring uncertainty, confusion and heartbreak. It is not easy to give answers that satisfy, especially as research tells us that children under three cannot understand death at all, children of five to seven can understand it only as a temporary event, and that it is not until children are approximately seven and upwards that they begin to appreciate the finality of death and its connection with illness, hospitalisation, accidents and so on.

Adults with religious convictions will probably give answers of reassurance and the expectation of eventual reunion with the loved one. In all cases, the person who has died should be spoken about and remembered positively, with thankfulness for past happy times. Grief is a normal process that seems to follow a set pattern of shock, disbelief, denial, anger, guilt, self-recrimination, depression, idealisation of the dead person and finally acceptance. These same stages of grief may follow other serious losses in people's lives, such as miscarriage, desertion, robbery, removal by imprisonment. Many societies have set rituals and accepted periods of mourning, which help people come to terms with their loss.

When a parent dies, the key role he or she played in the child's whole world has ended, so besides sorrow and bewilderment, there is often the need for great readjustments all round. If death was preceded by prolonged illness the surviving partner is also probably exhausted and suffering great strain.

If children meet with death in the keeping of pets, this will in some measure help them to understand the inevitability of the birth, life, death cycle, and sensitive handling of this experience will influence attitudes in the future.

RECONSTITUTED FAMILIES

This is the name given to families made up of children by two or more sets of natural parents, in other words, when a man and a woman come together, bringing with them the offspring of a former partnership.

There is usually strong motivation on the part of the parents for the new family to succeed and be happy, and hard work to this effect often brings rewards.

However, it is not possible to *force* children to love, or even like one another. The situation may be compounded by jealousy at having to share a parent, unequal treatment, resentment of the new parent, grief for the past. The child may feel anger at his changed life style when possibly he was unaware of causes of former dissatisfaction. He may feel that he was to blame for the break-up.

Parents have to cope with a great deal from their own children; step-parents find it less easy.

Sometimes the new-found happiness of the couple blinds them to the great confusion the child may be feeling, and the adjustments he has to make. These may include a change of home and school, a totally changed family unit, maybe even a different name which is a fundamental part of his sense of identity.

Against this, we are constantly seeing evidence of children's amazing adaptability, especially while they enjoy the care and security of one constant loving figure. Where siblings can support each other in this changed situation, there is less sense of desolation.

COMMUNITY LIVING

In the last forty or so years, many experiments have been made in living in a more communal way than the sometimes isolated family unit.

Communes, or co-operatives, are groups of people who voluntarily come together to share certain

aspects of their lives, and are conscious of themselves as a group.

The shared aspects may include living accommodation, economic activities and income, and child rearing.

There are many different kinds of community. For some, self-fulfilment of individuals is the motive. Others desire mutual support and brotherhood. Some are activist communes, where members are committed to political and social activity. Some are practical communes, where saving on living costs is the aim. Some are therapeutic communes, where people thought to be in particular need of care and attention can be looked after by founder members and house workers. Some are religious communes, subscribing either to a traditional belief in God, or some other divine power. 'The Brethren' are an example of a religious community who settle in a particular locality round an active church focus. Houses will be bought for church members, who will pay rent, live in a communal way, and possibly hold worship in one of the rooms.

There have been some successful ventures, too, where groups of people, possibly a mix of professionals and others, buy a large country estate and divide it into apartments i.e. one family will live in the coach house, another in the porter's lodge, and so on. Thus they combine a degree of privacy, the retention of their 'main' jobs, while at the same time indulging their interest in the land and livestock. Some attain a large measure of self-sufficiency.

Care of the children in these groups is often communal, ranging from casual day care (parents taking it in turns to look after all the children), to a day nursery run by professionals, to the system used in the old-style kibbutzim in Israel where the children lived separately and were cared for by professionals.

Opinions and research differ widely on whether or not it is advantageous for small children to relate equally to several adults. But in the kibbutzim there has been a move back to child rearing by the natural parents, with day care facilities.

Those who practise an alternative life style are sometimes identifiable by their mode of dress and appearance, and an approach to cooking and household chores which may be very different from conventional ones.

The selection of suitable community members should be thorough and unhurried, for the benefit of all concerned. A sustained willingness by each individual to play his/her full part in shared tasks is critical. Often a period of a year or so spent in a community seems to serve its purpose for the individual concerned. Sometimes the desire by a couple for more privacy in their life together, and/or their child rearing, is the signal to change.

COHABITING PARTNERS

The illegitimacy rate has more than doubled in the past ten years, reaching 21.4 per cent of all live births in 1986. However two-thirds of these births were jointly registered by both parents and, as this is taken to indicate that the babies were born into stable relationships, shows that many couples are choosing to live together without being officially married. This rejection of marriage is a new phenomenon in British society and some people see it as a welcome change from the hypocrisy of the past. Indeed, when divorce is easily obtainable many people can not see the need for a marriage certificate. They feel that true commitment can only come from within and many such couples form very stable family units.

Apart from couples who reject marriage for ideological reasons, others do so for a variety of other reasons. One or both parties may not be free to marry. They may be waiting until they can afford a 'proper wedding'. Some couples want a trial marriage first before deciding to stay together. Others may have had a traumatic first marriage and not be prepared to risk another. Many choose to formalise their commitment after a child is born for the child's sake.

Where children are concerned, the need for responsible attitudes and consistent commitment to the child's well-being is far more important than a marriage certificate. Constant changing of partners and instability in their early years, whether their parents are married or not, is surely far more damaging.

ROLE REVERSAL

For some couples, the man is the partner happiest to be with babies and young children. Until comparatively recently, society would have regarded this as bizarre and even unnatural. Nowadays, there is a much more open and tolerant attitude about personal choice and self-fulfilment.

Some couples are happy for the woman to do a full-time job, while the man stays at home to look after the children. The woman may stand a greater chance of getting a job, and/or may have a greater earning capacity than the man. Male unemployment has had a part to play here.

Present tax arrangements mean that the working partner can claim the marriage allowance as well as their own personal allowance.

If role reversal is complete, then this situation works well for all concerned. The children derive great benefit from having more of their father's company than usual. They also see their parents working together and hopefully will grow up without the usual fixed attitudes to men's and women's roles. Unfortunately there may be some drawbacks, especially if the mother is still expected to do most of the housework as well as coping with her job. Some women feel they must become 'super mums' or they may resent having to do all the work.

Another way for both parents to be equally involved in providing financially for the family and caring for the children is for each of them to do a part-time job. Now that job-sharing is more widespread this is quite possible too.

For addresses of organisations which can help some of the families described in this chapter, see page 279.

EXERCISES

Investigation
1) Working in pairs, find out all you can about the different religious festivals which are celebrated in schools today. As a group, do a presentation about it, illustrating your information as much as possible, and including any personal experiences.

2) Find out what permanent site facilities, health and welfare, and education facilities are provided for travelling families in your area. Are these facilities fully used?

Project
Is Britain's multicultural society sufficiently reflected in books and play materials available to young children?

Through discussion with fellow students plan a nursery classroom where the resources and approaches truly reflect cultural diversity.

SUGGESTIONS FOR FURTHER READING

E.E. Cashmore, *Having To – The World of One-Parent Families*, Unwin Paperbacks
P.J. North, *People in Society*, Longman Group Ltd
Elsa Ferri, *Stepchildren – A National Study*, National Children's Bureau
Anthony D. Smith, *The Ethnic Origins of Nations*, Basil Blackwell Ltd
Ron Ramdin, *The Making of the Black Working Class in Britain*, Wildwood House Ltd
Glenda Banks, *Helping Your Child Through Separation and Divorce*, Dove Communications
Divorce and Children (Pack containing leaflets on the effects of divorce on families.) Available from The Children's Society.
A. Henley, *Caring for Hindus and their Families*, (also available for Sikhs and Muslims), available from the National Extension College

3 Planning a Family

Today marriage in the West is a voluntary commitment to share one's life with a chosen partner and although many Eastern marriages are arranged by the family, it is still hoped that the couple will agree voluntarily to the union. Some couples choose to live together without a formal marriage ceremony. This is often known as a 'common law' marriage because in Britain at one time it was only necessary for a couple to state in front of witnesses that they were married for the marriage to be recognised.

As far as children are concerned, a marriage licence doesn't matter as long as their parents are committed to staying together and to caring for them. It is very traumatic for children when their parents separate, and this can sometimes lead to lifelong problems.

Everyone has preconceived ideas about marriage or partnerships. These are mostly derived from our own families. For instance, statistics show that if parents split up then the chances of their children's marriage breaking down are far greater than if they had remained together.

On the bright side is the fact that children who grow up in a united and loving family become mature adults capable of making close relationships and stable marriages.

Popular ideas on marriage are often unrealistic and glamorised. Young people should understand that a gleaming kitchen, with every latest appliance and refinement is not essential to a good marriage. Nor are the sex and family roles in real life stereotyped, as they often appear in the media. It is not unmanly to change nappies or take a turn with the saucepans, and it is not unwomanly to find home-making unfulfilling. And the stereotype mother-in-law, fierce and formidable, is often far from the truth.

People marry or live together for a variety of reasons. Physical attraction is an overwhelming, yet superficial, part of it. Practicalities like loneliness, unhappiness at home, proximity and availability can all play a part, as can social pressures and a wish to conform. Complex emotional factors are also involved. Many people seek in their partners a quality they feel themselves to be lacking. This may work – if both partners are not seeking the same quality, or if the quality was not perceived from too slight an acquaintance. A good marriage can transform the personal development and emotional well-being of both partners. Gaps and wounds remaining from former less happy relationships can be filled in, or healed. But as personalities grow, needs and expectations change. The good marriage, allowing for this, grows and changes accordingly.

Such a close relationship, must produce ambivalent feelings and conflict. It is often only with the person with whom we feel most safe that we are confident enough to be aggressive and reveal our innermost selves, not all of which is lovable. The value of communication cannot be overstressed. If this breaks down, the marriage is doomed. Where there is genuine affection and – very important – a sense of commitment, communication resolves most difficulties and problems of adjustment.

These are a few of the deeper implications of marriage. But marriage should not be presented in too sober or depressing a light. Although it involves surrendering a certain amount of personal freedom, the partners should ideally exchange this narrow freedom for a deeper one within which each can grow.

PREPARATION FOR PARENTHOOD

Many schools offer instruction and discussion in parentcraft. Opinions vary about how and when this should be done. Sadly, often only the less academic pupils are given this opportunity, and sometimes only the girls. Statistics shows that young parents are most likely to come from this group but *all* prospective parents could undoubtedly benefit from learning how to handle a baby. The utter dependency of the newborn can thus be understood. The parents' role in ministering to his needs can be shown, with practical demonstrations in bathing, nappy changing, making up feeds, etc. Most young people respond well to such sessions, and on this physical level education in parentcraft is probably most effective at this stage.

Later, when a baby is on the way, antenatal classes can offer a more detailed preparation including advice on how the mother-to-be can prepare her body for the birth. Both parents can take part in discussions covering subjects such as the general care of a young baby and child, and his normal growth and development.

At this stage, committed to parenthood, the young couple are usually receptive to advice on a deeper level. They can be made aware how, by performing these tasks for the baby, they will also fulfil other needs – for close contact and emotional security. Foundations will be laid for relationships and the means of communication. The need for mental stimulus can also be stressed and both partners shown the importance of suitable equipment, play materials, making an environment safe and introducing stories and books at an early stage. Such topics will provide the themes for meetings of mother and toddler clubs later on in the child's development. In recent years there have been several excellent television series about this stage in a family's life.

Preparation for parenthood is not, of course, confined to formal sessions. An awareness of all the many reasons *why* people have babies is important;

it is not always to crown a happy marriage – a joint adventure in 'person making'. Some girls see pregnancy as a means of escape from an unhappy home life, lack of success at school or socially. Some see it as a way to force the pace of a relationship. Some single women choose to be unmarried mothers for personal fulfilment. Sometimes pregnancy is a desperate bid to save an ailing marriage. Sometimes, even with contraception widely available and accepted, it is a half-deliberate 'mistake' because a couple feel that planning babies is too cold-blooded. It may be that it is a genuine accident. Contraception, after all, is not a natural phenomenon. Biologically, women are designed to produce babies even though it may not be convenient.

In matters of timing, the head must often rule the heart. Most people believe that a baby is entitled to a start in life of economic and financial security – otherwise he will be affected physically. Emotionally too, he will suffer if, for instance, parents are harassed by money worries, or his arrival has curtailed either parent's training or career, or ended hopes of coping with a large mortgage. Timing also involves awareness of the couple's adjustment to each other, and their emotional stability. It often takes a little while for a couple's sexual relationship to settle down satisfactorily, or gradually change from being their main preoccupation. Parenthood is bound to cause a little disruption here, so it is important that a mutually satisfactory and balanced approach has been achieved.

The fact must be faced that a baby will bring some restrictions. Money will almost certainly be shorter and have to stretch further. This will affect social life, hobbies, holidays, and many of the small pleasures of our materialistic society. Sleep and privacy may be affected. Many demands will be made on both parents. Although today there is a much more relaxed approach than formerly about babies happily fitting into parents' lives, it is still true to say that expectations of a cuddly bundle who will bring only light, joy and love into his parents' lives may be quickly followed by disillusionment and resentment. A new mother may not immediately experience a great surge of maternal feelings towards her baby. Apparent 'failure' here can bring reactions of guilt and anxiety. The attitudes of her mother and mother-in-law and the advice they give her during her pregnancy may be critically influential – for good or bad – as she will be extra sensitive, and very anxious to do the right thing. As parents, the husband and wife will be the targets of much conflicting advice; even the 'experts' differ. Skill at picking one's way through such advice takes time, tact and maturity.

Parentcraft is not something that is learned once and for all. Parents go on learning all their lives, until the role merges into that of grandparent.

In the early days, many different individuals and agencies will play a part – the midwife, doctor, health visitor, baby clinic and above all, the young parents' own families. Besides information, advice and expertise, all these people should give reassurance and support, dispel alarm, discourage comparison with other babies, and help the parents to enjoy the whole procedure, grow in self-confidence and reap the maximum rewards.

REPRODUCTION

All animals and plants reproduce in order to continue their species, and pass on characteristics to the next generation. Human beings are mammals and their reproduction is sexual; one male and one female together can produce offspring by each contributing one cell – a spermatozoon from the male and an ovum from the female.

Although the reproductive system is complete at birth, it is not mature, and boys and girls only become capable of producing babies at puberty which takes place some time between the ages of nine and eighteen years. The changes from girl to woman and boy to man are very gradual processes; the time taken varies with each individual. The physical changes needed to mature the reproductive system are determined by the pituitary gland which lies at the base of the brain in both sexes. At puberty the pituitary gland produces secretions known as hormones which travel through the bloodstream to all parts of the body, causing the production of sperm in boys and ova or eggs in girls, and changes known as secondary sexual characteristics in both sexes. These physical changes are usually completed before a person becomes mentally or emotionally mature. This can lead to problems. For example, a baby can be produced by juvenile parents who lack the maturity to devote the necessary amount of time and energy to his upbringing.

The male reproductive system

Secondary sexual characteristics which develop at puberty:

- broadening of shoulders and development of muscles
- growth of hair in the pubic region, on the chest and under the arms
- change of voice from a high pitch to a low pitch due to growth and development of vocal chords
- production of sweat which has a characteristic odour (intended to attract the opposite sex) by the opocrine glands in the skin
- increase in size of penis
- production of semen (fluid containing spermatozoa) which may be emitted.

The male reproductive system consists of:

Scrotum – a loose bag or sac of skin outside the body containing the testes. The sac is retracted towards the body when cold and away from the body when hot to enable the sperm to stay at the optimum temperature, which is slightly below normal body temperature.

Two testes – produce spermatozoa.

Vas deferens – a tube leading from each teste upwards to loop under the bladder and join up with the urethra, which carry spermatozoa.

The urethra – a tube leading from the bladder through the penis to the outside of the body.

The seminal vesicles – these produce fluid which joins the spermatozoa in the vas deferens.

The prostate gland – also produces fluid which joins the spermatozoa in the urethra.

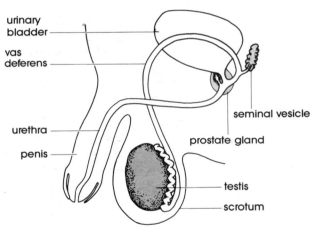

The male reproductive system

The fluid containing spermatozoa is known as semen and it collects in the top part of the urethra and vas deferens ready to be released during sexual intercourse or masturbation. The penis is made of erectile tissue which means that during sexual stimulation the tissue is suffused with blood which enables it to become firm and erect and therefore capable of entering the female vagina. During the climax of the act semen containing millions of spermatozoa is ejected and deposited in the vagina. The spermatozoa are shaped like minute tadpoles, with a head and a long flexible tail which enables them to move rapidly into the female uterus and up into the fallopian tube to meet the ova.

The female reproductive system

Unlike that of the male, the female reproductive system is inside the body and is completely separate from the urinary system. The organs lie between the bowel and the bladder and urethra, and consist of:

The vagina – a narrow corrugated passage which leads from the exterior of the body to the uterus.

The uterus (or womb) – a hollow pear-shaped organ, size 7.5 cm × 5 cm × 2.5 cm and which protrudes into the vagina at the lower end, forming a cervix or neck.

The Fallopian tubes – two narrow tubes which lead from the upper two corners of the uterus.

The ovaries – two small almond-sized glands which contain ova, or eggs. Approximately every twenty-eight days during a woman's reproductive life, one of the ova 'ripens' and is released into the Fallopian tube.

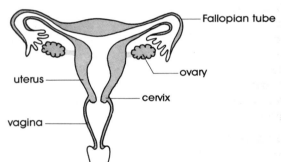

The female reproductive system

Secondary sexual characteristics which develop at puberty:

- rounding of hips
- enlargement of breasts
- growth of hair in the pubic region and under the arms
- production of sweat, which has a characteristic odour, by the opocrine glands in the skin
- beginning of menstruation.

The menstrual cycle is the name used to describe the regular preparation of the uterus to receive a fertilised egg (ovum), and the subsequent discarding of the uterine lining if the egg is not fertilised. For most women this occurs during a period of twenty-eight days but it may vary between twenty-five to thirty days.

The cycle is controlled by hormones produced by the pituitary gland, which, in turn, stimulate the ovary to produce further hormones called oestrogen and progesterone. At the beginning of the cycle oestrogen produced by the ovary causes the lining of the uterus to thicken. This continues for about ten days until the ovum is released from the ovary and is wafted into the Fallopian tube. With the liberation of the ovum the ovary begins to produce progesterone as well, which causes the uterine lining to become even thicker and more ready to receive the fertilised ovum. This continues for another fourteen days but then, if the ovum is not fertilised, progesterone ceases to be produced. This 'cut-off' of progesterone causes the lining of the uterus to deteriorate and to be shed for three to seven days. This is known as the menstrual period.

Two days after the period is completed, the entire cycle begins again. However, if the ovum is fertilised, about six days after its release it becomes implanted in the uterine lining. The fertilised ovum produces another hormone which causes the ovary to continue producing progesterone. This prevents the uterine lining from being shed, therefore there is no menstrual period.

Incidentally, the hormone produced by a fertilised ovum is called chorionic gonadotrophin and this hormone is excreted in the urine, where it can be detected and used as confirmation of pregnancy a week after fertilisation has taken place.

PREGNANCY

Conception takes place when a spermatozoon reaches the ovum in the fallopian tube and penetrates it. This is when pregnancy begins and it continues until the birth of the baby. Immediately after the sperm and the ovum unite, they begin dividing, first into two, then into four, then into eight cells, and so on. These cells will eventually become the baby and the placenta (or afterbirth).

At the same time as this cell division is taking place the fertilised egg (or morula, as it is called at this stage) is being wafted down the Fallopian tube into the uterine cavity. Then, at about the sixth day after conception, the morula will embed itself into the lining of the uterus (or womb).

The development of the fertilised egg is very rapid. Soon the morula will separate into two halves that will become the foetus and the placenta and, by about the twelfth week, the foetus will be recognisable as a baby.

The foetus obtains nourishment and oxygen from its mother via the placenta, which is attached to the wall of the uterus. Between the placenta and the foetus is the umbilical cord which acts as a lifeline carrying food and oxygen to the foetus and removing waste products. Food, oxygen and the waste products are exchanged through the walls of the placenta and uterus and the mother's bloodstream.

The foetus is surrounded by a bag of membranes which contain fluid in which the baby floats. The fluid acts as a cushion, protecting the baby from any blow. It also enables the baby to have free movement and exercise which aids its physical development. Most of the baby's development occurs during the first three months of pregnancy; during the remaining six months the baby will grow and mature until he is ready to cope with the outside world. Because of the rapid development, the foetus is very vulnerable to any damage in the early weeks of pregnancy. At one time it was thought that the placenta acted as an impenetrable barrier to anything which could harm the developing foetus but we now know that certain viruses can get through to the baby, and some drugs too. Smoking can also be harmful to the baby's development. The degree of damage suffered by the foetus will largely depend on what stage it has reached. For example, if the mother has German measles (rubella) at the time the baby's ears are developing, then the baby will probably be born deaf. On the other hand, if the damage occurs very early in pregnancy, there may be such a distortion of development that the foetus is unable to survive and the pregnancy will end in abortion.

HEREDITY

The hereditary factors passed to a baby by its parents are contained in the twenty-three chromosomes present in both the ovum and the spermatozoon. When the ovum and the spermatozoon combine to form a single cell, each of the twenty-three chromosomes from the ovum unites with a matching chromosome from the spermatozoon and twenty-three distinctly different pairs are produced. These forty-six chromosomes form the blueprint for the new individual and, as the cell divides and sub-divides, each new cell will contain an identical set of chromosomes.

At the moment of conception the sex of the baby is decided in the following way. One particular pair of chromosomes are known as the 'sex chromosomes', and the sex chromosome from the ovum is always an 'X' one. But the spermatozoon may contain either an 'X' or a 'Y' chromosome. If the sperm contains an 'X' chromosome then the baby will have 'XX' chromosomes, and will be female. If the sperm contains a 'Y' chromosome then the baby will have 'XY' chromosomes, and will be male. This means that the sex of a baby is always determined by the father's sperm. It is probably a matter of

random chance whether a sperm containing an 'X' chromosome or one containing a 'Y' chromosome reaches the ovum first. But, nevertheless, more boys are conceived than girls. The ratio is fairly constant at 106 boys to 100 girls. However, boys are more vulnerable to injury and disease and this causes the ratio eventually to even out.

Each chromosome carries thousands of genes and each gene contributes to the general make-up of the child. For example, a gene from one chromosome determines eye-colour, another will determine the shape of the eye, and so on.

Because the chromosomes are in matched pairs, it follows that every individual has two genes for each characteristic, one from each parent. Although genes look alike, they can carry different instructions. For instance, a person could have a gene from his mother containing instructions for a round chin, and a corresponding gene from his father containing instructions for a pointed chin. He may be born with the round chin but, because he also carried the gene for a pointed chin, he could pass the pointed chin characteristic on to his future children.

In many cases it is not known why one gene of a pair is used in preference to the other; indeed it may be accidental. But in some cases a gene can be 'dominant' or 'recessive'. Dominant genes always take precedence over other genes so that if one parent contributes this type of gene then the child will always inherit that particular characteristic. Recessive genes, on the other hand, always allow other genes to take precedence. A good example of

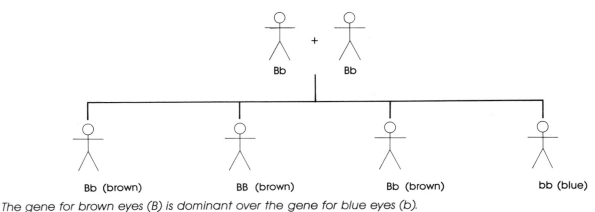

Bb   Bb

Bb (brown)   BB (brown)   Bb (brown)   bb (blue)

The gene for brown eyes (B) is dominant over the gene for blue eyes (b).

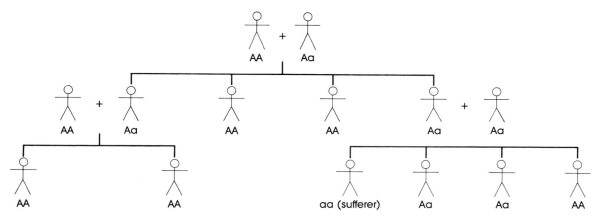

The gene for sickle cell anaemia (a) is recessive.

this is with genes that determine eye-colour, because the genes controlling dark colours are dominant. If a child has a blue-eyed mother who has passed on her blue-eyed characteristic, and a brown-eyed father who has passed on his brown-eyed characteristic, then the child will have brown eyes. However, the child will also carry the gene for blue eyes inherited from his mother, so that when he becomes a father he could pass either the blue gene or the brown one. In some families it is possible to see certain characteristics carried down through each generation in this way, for example, a cleft chin.

Defects in chromosomes or genes, or the absence of crucial ones are the way in which hereditary diseases are caused or passed on. For instance

children with Down's syndrome have a chromosome abnormality; cystic fibrosis is caused by a defective gene carried by both parents.

If the 'bad' gene happens to be located on the 'X' chromosome then the disease is said to be sex-linked – this means that if it is passed on by the mother then only her sons will be affected, since they will have a single 'X' plus a 'Y' chromosome. Of course, daughters could be carriers but as they have a second 'X' chromosome which can counteract the effects, they are very rarely sufferers.

There is also evidence to suggest that the tendency to certain diseases, such as diabetes and rheumatoid arthritis can be inherited which would

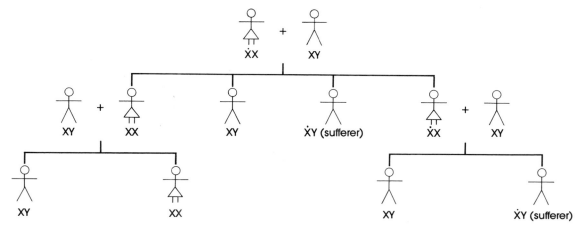

Example of a sex-linked disease, Duchenne muscular dystrophy. (Ẋ shows the gene carrying the disease.)

explain why a disease might appear in several members of the same family, although it is not strictly genetic.

As each chromosome carries about 15 000 genes, it can readily be seen that the possible combinations of genes are endless, even when children have the same parents – hence every child is a different individual. An exception is identical twins, which are formed when the fertilised ovum divides into two, and so they have the same chromosomes and genes. But differences in people can also occur because of environmental effects, so that even identical twins may show some variation in characteristics and development if they are brought up separately.

In addition, changes can occur in chromosomes and genes in individuals in a process known as mutation.

CONTRACEPTION

For thousands of years people have sought ways of controlling their own fertility, but it is only in the past thirty years that this has been universally possible with any degree of certainty.

Several methods of contraception are now available and many general practitioners give advice on family planning. Family planning clinics exist in the majority of health centres and most of the contraceptive devices can be obtained free of charge. The following are used in Great Britain:

1.   The sperm can be killed by the use of *spermicides* in the form of foams, creams, pessaries or jellies. These are inserted into the vagina just before intercourse. Although fairly efficient, it is recommended that this method is used with a mechanical barrier such as a cap or a sheath. Another method of using spermicides is in a specially prepared foam rubber sponge. This can be inserted into the vagina for up to thirty hours where it will release the spermicide gradually, giving protection for the first twenty-four hours of use.

2.   A temporary or permanent *barrier* can be placed

between the egg and the sperm to prevent them meeting:
a) a rubber diaphragm cap which is inserted into the vagina and prevents sperm entering the cervix. When used with spermicidal cream this is very effective.
b) a condom; this is a rubber sheath which encloses the penis, after erection, but before penetration, so preventing sperm entering the vagina. When used with spermicidal cream it is very effective.
c) *female sterilisation* (this is permanent). The fallopian tubes are cut and the cut ends are tied so that the egg cannot travel to the uterus.
d) *male sterilisation* (this is permanent). Both vas deferens are cut and the cut ends are tied so that the sperm cannot travel through the tube. This is called a vasectomy.

3.   The egg can be prevented from being released. This is the most effective method at present. If a woman is taking the 'combined' pill containing a mixture of synthetic female hormones, oestrogen and progestogen, then ovulation does not occur. The action of the 'mini' pill which is progestogen only is somewhat different – it does not always prevent ovulation but causes changes which make it difficult for sperm to enter the womb, or for the womb to accept the fertilised egg.

Progestogen can also be given by injection (e.g. Depo-provera) which is effective for up to twelve weeks.

4.   The conditions inside the uterus can be made unsuitable for implantation of a fertilised egg. This is caused by inserting an intra-uterine device consisting of a loop or coil of plastic wire into the uterus.

5.   Use of the safe period. Since ovulation occurs only at monthly intervals, then it is possible for a woman to work out when this happens and avoid intercourse within two to three days of this date. If a woman has a regular cycle of menstruation, it should be simple because ovulation usually occurs fourteen days before a period. However, it is by no means foolproof because ovulation can occur haphazardly. Accurate record-keeping is essential, and any woman using this method will need medical advice in order to work out her own personal 'safe period'.

Some authorities recommend that a woman using this method should learn to analyse her cervical mucus, taking note of the changes during her menstrual cycle, to ensure greater accuracy. This is known as 'the Billings Method'.

Statistically the 'safe' period is not at all safe yet many mature couples manage to plan their families this way.

6. The 'morning after' pill should also be mentioned here. This is a high dosage of hormones given within three days of unprotected intercourse which will in most cases prevent pregnancy, although this method is not of use as a long-term method of contraception.

THE DANGERS OF PROMISCUITY

Human beings have always had taboos about sexual behaviour, many of which were based on the fear of pregnancy, so that when a relatively reliable method of contraception became widely available (the pill in the early 1960s) it was followed by a relaxation of these rules. However it soon became obvious that unwanted pregnancies were not the only problems arising from promiscuous behaviour.

1.   Widespread promiscuity threatens the stability of society as a whole as family life is the traditional mainstay of civilisation. Frequently changing partners can result in confused and insecure children.

2.   There is the danger of the spread of diseases. Sexual contact is physically close and conducive to the spread of infection. Obviously, the more partners people have, the more likely they are to become infected. Diseases include:

a) Pelvic inflammatory disease (PID): germs can enter the female pelvic cavity via the uterus and fallopian tubes; when the tubes are infected the resulting scar tissue can block the tubes, leading to sterility.

b) Venereal diseases: gonorrhoea, syphilis, non-specific urethritis, genital warts, herpes, thrush, trichomoniasis.

c) Cancer of the cervix: there is evidence to suggest that this can be caused by a virus infection, passed on during sexual contact. Also, the chance of developing the disease appears to be greater, the younger a girl is when she begins to have sexual contacts and the more partners she has. Women who are not promiscuous are less likely to develop this cancer.

d) AIDS (Acquired Immune Deficiency Syndrome). This disease is caused by a virus which attacks the body's natural defence system. The virus is called HIV and people who are infected by it do not all develop AIDS. Even if the disease does develop it may not do so for many years after the initial infection. However, infected people are able to pass on the virus during sexual intercourse. Consequently a promiscuous person can un-knowingly infect many people during this in-cubation period. The only other ways in which this virus is transmitted is from a mother to her baby via the placenta and by inoculation (through a break in the skin) with blood or body fluids from an infected person. There is no evidence that the virus is transmitted by any other non-sexual contact with an infected person.

When people have AIDS they lose their ability to fight any other infection so they can become seriously ill and die.

Unfortunately, as yet there is no cure. The best protection is to prevent the spread of the virus and that can be achieved by a reduction in pro-miscuous behaviour. On a personal level indivi-duals can protect themselves by limiting the num-ber of sexual partners they have and using a sheath or condom during sexual activity.

3.   Emotional problems arise: many women need sex to be part of a loving relationship whereas many men find they can enjoy sex without much emotional involvement. Consequently, some women may be disappointed by their experience of sex, sometimes blaming themselves for their inability to enjoy a sexual affair. Men may reinforce this if they do not understand the woman's need for a complete relationship. Some women mistake the male's sexual urge for love and are then devastated

when the affair comes to an end. Certainly for many people a relationship is meaningless if based on sex alone rather than friendship and affection, because of the transitory nature of sexual pleasure.

EXERCISES

Investigation
Find out about the facilities for family planning in your area, including any provision for publicising the services to

a) people who cannot read or write,

b) people whose first language is not English.

Project
Subject for discussion: should all children have education for parenthood? If so, at what age should this take place, and what subjects should it cover?

SUGGESTIONS FOR FURTHER READING

Geraldine Lux Flanagan, *The First Nine Months of Life*, Heinemann Ltd

Dennis Fox, *Facts for Life*, Macdonald Educational Ltd Granada Television

Kenneth Rudge, *Relationships*, Macmillan Education Ltd

Jacky Gillott, *Connexions – For Better for Worse*, Penguin Books Ltd

Joy Groombridge, *Connexions – His and Hers*, Penguin Books Ltd

Ellen Peck, *The Baby Trap*, Heinrich Hanam Publications

Diagram Group, *Mothers* (*One hundred mothers of the famous and infamous*), Paddington Press Ltd

Stephen Parker, *Life Before Birth*, Cambridge University Press

Dr Miriam Stoppard, *The Pregnancy and Birth Book*, Dorling Kindersley Ltd

Joanna Roeber, *Shared Parenthood*, Century Paperbacks

4

The Baby and the Family

SIGNS AND SYMPTOMS OF PREGNANCY

- Menstruation ceases – there is no period
- Early morning sickness – this may vary between slight nausea and actual vomiting
- Lassitude and tiredness
- Frequency in passing urine and/or constipation – this is due to alterations in muscle tone caused by the hormonal changes
- Chemical test of urine for pregnancy is positive by about the fifth day after conception.

ANTENATAL CARE AND ADVICE

Although pregnancy is usually confirmed by a simple urine test within about four weeks of conception, many women wait until they have missed their second period before consulting a doctor for confirmation of a pregnancy and the beginning of antenatal care. However, some authorities feel that women should be examined earlier than this, perhaps even before pregnancy begins. This is because a healthy woman will have fewer problems during her pregnancy and has the best prospect of producing a healthy baby. Also, as the foetus is at its most vulnerable during the first twelve weeks of pregnancy, the mother-to-be, if seen early, could be warned of the possible dangers to the baby of smoking, drug-taking or exposure to any infectious disease.

Antenatal care is mainly preventive medicine – detecting potential problems and either stopping them developing, or minimising their effects on the mother or baby. The aim of good antenatal care is a fit mother and a fit baby at the end of pregnancy. It is of little use to deliver a healthy baby if the mother is not in a fit state to take proper care of him.

Usually the mother-to-be will first visit her own family doctor (general practitioner). Some doctors do not undertake antenatal care, and if this is the case they will refer the mother to another doctor in the same health centre or to a maternity hospital.

On the first visit, a full examination is made of the mother's general health, as well as confirming that she is pregnant. The date of delivery is calculated by adding nine calendar months and seven days to the date on which the last menstrual period began. This last date is used because it is the one which is easily remembered. It is not usually possible to ascertain when conception actually took place, as there are no visible signs. Taking an average of thousands of pregnancies, it was found that the commonest length of pregnancy varied between thirty-eight and forty-two weeks, so that the average was forty weeks from the first day of the last menstrual period. The date of birth given to the mother is referred to as the estimated date of delivery, or EDD. The doctor will ask the mother for details of any family illness or past personal illness which may affect her pregnancy. A full examination is carried out to determine the present state of her health. This will include the following:

1. The mother's heart function is tested, because pregnancy can be a burden to a woman with a defective heart.

2. The blood pressure is measured because an abnormal blood pressure is an indication that disease is present; investigations and treatment at this stage may prevent future problems. Also the blood pressure may rise during pregnancy because

of 'toxaemia of pregnancy', so it is necessary to know the mother's normal blood pressure for purposes of comparison.

3. The urine is tested for the presence of abnormalities:

a) sugar – which may mean the mother is a diabetic needing treatment;

b) albumen – which usually means that the kidneys are not working as efficiently as they should;

c) pus – which indicates an infection is present in the urinary tract.

4. The blood is also tested:

a) to determine the blood group, which is recorded so that if the mother should need a blood transfusion the correct blood can be given quickly;

b) to determine the rhesus factor, because if the mother is rhesus negative she could produce antibodies which could affect her baby's blood, causing him to need an exchange blood-transfusion at birth. This condition more commonly affects second or subsequent babies but, if a mother is found to be rhesus negative early in her first pregnancy, it is possible to protect her future babies by giving her an injection within forty-eight hours of the birth, which will prevent her forming any antibodies;

c) for anaemia – this can affect both mother and baby if not treated early in pregnancy;

d) to check whether the mother is suffering from syphilis, because the baby will be affected unless treatment is started early in pregnancy.

e) for sickle cell anaemia and thalassaemia. People of African descent, and people from the Caribbean, Mediterranean, Middle East and Far East may carry the gene for these diseases. If this is suspected a test is usually carried out as they can affect a woman and her baby adversely.

5. A check is made for varicose veins, as these tend to become worse during pregnancy.

6. Teeth are examined and the mother is advised to go to the dentist for a check-up.

7. The size of the pelvis is checked and any abnormalities noted.

8. The mother is weighed and measured.

Arrangements for the birth are discussed at this early visit. At present about 99 per cent of births take place in hospital although, if all is normal and her doctor agrees, the mother can choose to have her baby at home with a community midwife in attendance. Some mothers may choose to go into hospital for the delivery only and come home within twenty-four hours of the birth, provided the doctor agrees and all is well with the mother and baby. In this case, in many areas, the community midwife and doctor will go into the hospital to attend to the delivery and then the same midwife will visit the mother daily at home until the baby is fourteen days old. The choice of home delivery or a shortened hospital stay will obviously depend on there being adequate domestic help in the house, as the mother should not be doing housework.

Other mothers will go into hospital when labour begins and will stay for about six to ten days after the birth. The decision about the place of birth depends not only on the mother's choice, but also on various medical factors, because certain groups of mothers have a slightly higher risk of complications at the delivery. These mothers should be in hospital where there are facilities to deal with any problem promptly. Examples of women 'at risk' include women over thirty years of age having their first baby and diabetic mothers. In other cases, warning signs of complications such as a raised blood pressure may occur during pregnancy, indicating that this mother would be best to have her baby in hospital.

The mother-to-be usually attends the antenatal clinic monthly until the sixth month of her pregnancy and then more frequently for the last three months. At each visit checks are made on the mother's health. She is weighed, her blood pressure is taken and her urine is tested. Any abnormality in one or more of these tests can indicate problems needing further investigation. One of the hazards of pregnancy is the development of pre-eclamptic toxaemia which, if left untreated, can lead to fits in the mother and death of the foetus. Although a lot of research has been and still is being carried out on this condition, little is known of the cause. However, if a mother shows any of the signs of the disease – raised blood pressure, albumen in the urine and excess weight gain due to water retention – rest in bed and the use of sedatives can prevent her condition deteriorating.

During the course of pregnancy tests can be carried out to check for specific abnormalities in the baby. A maternal blood test at sixteen to seventeen weeks may reveal an excessive amount of a substance called alphafeta protein (AFP). This could mean that the baby has spina bifida or another neural tube defect. If a second blood test also shows a high result, then an amniocentesis is performed. This involves taking a sample of the fluid surrounding the baby and gives a more definite diagnosis. Amniocentesis is also performed if there is a higher than normal chance of the baby having a chromosome abnormality such as Down's syndrome. Other tests, involving taking a sample of the placenta, can ascertain whether the baby is suffering from an inherited disorder such as muscular dystrophy. All these tests are available to all pregnant women but as there is an element of risk of causing a miscarriage, they are only carried out if there is a history of disease in the family and after the couple have had counselling and have agreed that they will proceed with an abortion if the foetus is affected.

As the baby grows in the uterus the doctor or midwife can, by palpating the mother's abdomen, determine the position of the baby and listen to his heart with a foetal stethoscope. His size and rate of growth can also be monitored. An ultrasonic scanning machine can be used to check the position of the baby in the uterus and gauge its size and maturity. It will also show the position of the placenta and whether there is more than one baby. Another test used to show whether the baby is growing is an estimation of the amount of oestriol in the mother's urine over twenty-four hours. A low result can indicate that the placenta is failing and treatment is necessary.

Nearer to the estimated delivery date the midwife will check that the baby is in a good head-down position ready for birth and the head is 'engaged'. This means that the head has passed through the bony pelvis. If this is so, then the baby can be born normally, as the head is the largest part of the body.

At this stage the mother may be given an activity chart (commonly known as a 'kick chart') to record the number of times the baby moves over a period of time. This gives an indication of the baby's activity and health.

Expectant parents practise methods of relaxation at antenatal classes

All expectant parents may attend and participate in parentcraft classes held in health centres and maternity hospitals. These classes explain the process of pregnancy and birth, advise parents on the care needed during pregnancy and how to look after the baby. They usually take the form of weekly discussion groups over periods of ten to twelve weeks. Each week a different subject is discussed and this is followed by a demonstration and practice of various exercises and methods of relaxation which will help the mother to co-operate in the birth of her baby. The birth is described in detail and films are shown, so that both parents know what to expect. This is very important, and helps lessen the fear of the unknown which can cause tension, leading to increased pain in labour and birth.

In the past it was difficult to include women of differing cultural backgrounds in these groups, especially if their English was poor. In response to this many schemes have sprung up in various parts of the country to offer help to individual parents. For example: Bristol's Maternity Links, set up for Asian women, 'provides support, understanding and, if desired, English tuition for non-English-speaking antenatal and postnatal women who, when communicating with health service staff, experience difficulty in receiving vital medical information necessary for a healthy pregnancy and birth'.

During classes and at antenatal examinations, the mother is advised about the care of her health. Some topics discussed during the antenatal period are:

Diet (see Chapter 6 on food).   The mother must eat a good mixed diet containing protein, calcium, iron and vitamins. She should not increase her consumption of carbohydrates, because this is unnecessary for the baby and will make the mother put on weight. During pregnancy the mother should not put on more than 20 lbs (9 kilos) in weight, otherwise there may be problems at the birth and the mother may have difficulty in regaining her figure afterwards. On the whole the baby will take the nutrients he needs at the expense of his mother, so if her diet is poor her health will be affected first. Iron is especially important, because in the last two months of pregnancy the baby stores enough iron to last him until he is about six months old. Consequently if the mother is already anaemic, she will become more so at this time. If, on top of this, she loses more blood than usual at the birth, she will be in a poor state of health to care for her baby. Because of this, iron tablets may be prescribed to boost the mother's diet. Vitamin A, C, and D tablets are also advised and sometimes vitamin B12. However, all pregnant women should consult their midwife or doctor before taking any supplements as many are unnecessary and some can even be dangerous. For instance many Asian food shops sell a mineral supplement for pregnant women called Sikor (other names are Mithi, Khuri, Kattha, and Patri) which contains lead and arsenic, both of which are harmful to people.

Clothing. Clothing should be loose and comfortable, preferably hanging from the shoulders rather than the waist, which usually disappears early in pregnancy. Breasts should be supported by a well-fitting bra, which should be checked for size at intervals because the breasts enlarge as pregnancy advances. Shoes should have medium heels and be comfortable so that the mother stands up straight.

Exercise and rest.   Exercise is necessary and will not harm the baby, provided it is regular and the mother does not get over-tired. Cycling, swimming, horse-riding and walking are all beneficial in moderation. Rest is also important – a rest during the day with the feet up and a regular reasonable bedtime all help to keep the mother-to-be healthy and happy.

Care of teeth.   Dental care is free for all pregnant women and they should make full use of this facility. During pregnancy the baby takes calcium for his bones and teeth. This may leave the mother short, so affecting her dental health.

Smoking.   This should be avoided because strong evidence suggests that smoking affects the baby's rate of growth. Babies born to mothers who smoke are often smaller than the average. If the mother is a chain-smoker and finds it very difficult to give up, she should be persuaded to reduce the number of cigarettes she smokes to under ten daily.

Drugs.   No drugs of any description should be taken by a pregnant woman, unless they are prescribed for her by a doctor who is aware of the pregnancy.

Maternity benefits and services are available to pregnant women. They are as follows:
a) free antenatal care
b) free hospital care
c) free services of doctor, midwife, obstetrician, paediatrician and health visitor
d) free prescriptions until the baby is one year old
e) free dental care until the baby is one year old
f) home help services for a small charge
g) maternity payment (if she qualifies for income support or family credit)

h) free milk and vitamins (if she qualifies for income support or family credit).

If a mother is working and can satisfy the relevant conditions, she has the following rights:
a) paid time off work for antenatal care
b) not to be dismissed from her job because of pregnancy
c) to return to work after pregnancy
d) statutory maternity pay or maternity allowance.

If a mother is not entitled to d) she may qualify for sickness benefit instead.

The layette and equipment. Planning and preparing the baby's room and buying clothing and equipment can be an enjoyable part of pregnancy which both parents can share. Shopping is best carried out during the middle months of pregnancy before it becomes too tiring for the mother. Many shops catering for babies' needs will send catalogues on request and these can be a great help. Books on baby care usually list suggested clothing and equipment. Generally it is best to buy only the minimum and then add more when the size of the baby is known. New babies are often given presents of clothing, which may duplicate clothes already bought. Babies grow very rapidly in their first few months, so that most clothing is usually outgrown rather than outworn.

There are several points to remember when buying clothing for a baby. Firstly, the materials used for the clothing should have the following qualities for comfort and safety:
- warmth
- softness
- lightweight
- absorbent
- easy to wash
- non-irritating to baby's sensitive skin
- non-flammable.

Natural fibres such as cotton and wool are usually found to be the most comfortable fabrics to wear because of their absorbent qualities, but cotton is not very warm and wool needs very careful washing. Some babies' skins may be sensitive to wool and find it irriating. A wool/cotton mixture, such as Viyella or Clydella, combines the good qualities of both fibres and is ideal for comfort. Man-made (synthetic) fabrics, such as nylon, Terylene, Courtelle and acrylic are popular because of their cheapness compared with natural fibres. They have many advantages, being hard-wearing, warm, soft and light. They are also easily washed, and quickly dried, and need little or no ironing. However, their big disadvantage is that they do not absorb moisture and this makes the clothing uncomfortable, especially in hot weather. They should not be worn next to the skin because of the discomfort and also because some children develop an allergic rash from contact with synthetic fibres. But fabrics which contain a mixture of synthetic and natural fibres, such as wool and cotton, overcome many of these disadvantages. The material is absorbent and easily washed and dried, requiring little or no ironing.

Clothing for a baby should have the following qualities:

- simple design, so that it is easy to put on and take off
- easy to fasten – no fiddly ties
- easy to wash and iron
- allows free movement
- flat seams, so there are no uncomfortable ridges
- suitable for the climate.

A basic list of clothing and equipment
Either disposable nappies or 24–36 terry nappies, 3 pairs plastic pants and 4 nappy pins (safety type)
3 vests
3 day dresses, rompers or all-over suits
3 nightdresses or all-over suits
3 cardigans or jumpers
3 bonnets
3 pairs mittens
3 pairs bootees
2 pram suits or sleeping bags
3 bibs or feeders
tray, bag, basket or box for toilet requirements
cotton-wool balls in plastic container with lid
soap
talcum powder
baby shampoo
2 flannels (if used)
brush and comb

nail scissors
simple baby cream, such as Vaseline or zinc and castor oil
3 towels
apron for carer
pail with lid for soiled terry nappies
bath and stand
6 cot sheets
4 cot blankets
1 cot spread
pram
pram mattress with waterpoof cover
4 sheets (but the same sheets and blankets could be used for cot and pram)
3 blankets
1 pram cover
crib and mattress, sheets and blankets (if wanted)
cot
cot mattress with waterpoof cover
'bouncy' chair
changing mat
sun shade (canopy)
cat net
safety harness

Nappies

Nowadays many parents opt for disposable nappies. They consist of a pad of absorbent material with a plastic outer covering which does away with the need for pants. Instead of safety pins, small sticky tapes hold the nappy in position. These nappies are available in various sizes to ensure a snug fit. Disposable nappies are satisfactory in use, provided the manufacturers' instructions for disposal are carefully followed. They are invaluable when travelling or on holiday because of the time saved by not having to wash, dry and fold nappies. They are also hygienic because there is no need to carry soiled nappies home to wash. Disposables seem expensive, but if the cost is compared with the cost of conventional nappies, washing powder and electricity for washing machine and dryer, it will be found that there is very little difference. Moreover, if the time saved is spent with the baby, then the baby will derive considerable benefit.

100 per cent cotton terry towelling nappies consist of a large square which can be folded into a triangular or kite shape and pinned on the baby like a pair of pants. An alternative version now on sale is the padded triangular shape, which fits better but is more difficult to wash and takes longer to dry than a flat square. Cotton terry towelling is ideal for nappies because it absorbs a large quantity of fluid. It also washes easily and can be sterilised by boiling. It is possible to buy terry towelling nappies made of Terylene, or of 50 per cent cotton and 50 per cent viscose. These are not suitable because of their poor absorbent qualities, although they wash and dry easily. When the baby passes urine, it is not absorbed into the fabric, but remains on the skin causing the nappy to rub, and results in a sore bottom.

The baby will need at least six clean nappies every day, so if they can be washed daily then twenty-four will be enough. However, if the mother's washing and drying facilities are poor, more will be required.

Nappy liners. There are several types of liner available:
a) Disposable tissues may be put inside the terry towelling nappy, to prevent it being badly soiled. The tissue and excreta can be shaken down the lavatory and flushed away, leaving only a wet nappy to wash.
b) One-way liners may be washable or disposable. They allow urine to soak through to the outer nappy, whilst remaining dry themselves, so that the baby has a dry surface next to his skin. They are very useful at night because when the baby stops his night feed, he will sleep through and not be disturbed by a wet nappy. They are also useful if the baby has a sore bottom owing to his concentrated urine affecting his skin.

Plastic pants

If terry nappies are used, plastic pants will be needed, otherwise, clothing and bedding become saturated every time the nappy is wet. They should be chosen with care, making sure that the leg holes are loose enough to allow some ventilation. The more expensive ones with adjustable side fastenings are best, not only for comfort, but also because the better-quality plastics are softer and can be washed many times without deteriorating.

Vests

As vests are worn next to the skin, they should be made of cotton or a wool/cotton mixture for comfort. The easiest ones to put on are those with an envelope-shaped neck which goes over the head.

Dresses, rompers, nightdresses

These can be obtained in various fabrics, and choice depends on time of the year and climate. Cotton, wool/cotton mixture or cotton/synthetic mixture are all suitable. The clothes should be easy to put on and fasten. Sleeves should be wide-fitting, preferably raglan, and seams should be flat to avoid rubbing the skin.

All-over suits

These are very popular with mothers and have the advantage of being all-in-one. However if they are used there are three important points to consider:

- They must be big enough. The 'stretch' should only be used to allow a reasonable fit, because the baby will not be able to stretch the fabric himself – instead he will be restricted by the elasticity in the suit. If he cannot move freely he will lack exercise and can become very cold. He will also feel very frustrated. A baby's bones are very soft and a too-tight garment could cause deformed feet in the same way as badly fitting shoes or socks.
- They should be made from cotton or a cotton/nylon mixture for warmth and absorbency. All-nylon suits are not at all comfortable.
- They should not be used day and night, as the skin needs ventilation. So if they are worn during the night then a dress should be worn during the day, or vice versa.

Cardigans or jumpers

These may be hand-knitted or bought. Again, a wool/nylon mixture or cotton is better than an all-synthetic material. They should be knitted into a firm, close fabric rather than too much openwork, as the baby's fingers can get caught in the wool. Raglan style sleeves are easier to put on.

Sleeping bag/dressing gown

These are very useful garments, as they can be put on like a coat and closed like a bag at the bottom. They can be used in the pram and at night so that it does not matter if blankets are kicked off – the baby will remain covered and warm. They are usually made of a brushed synthetic material and are satisfactory when worn over natural fabrics.

Bonnets, mittens and bootees

These can be hand-knitted or bought and should be made from wool or wool/nylon mixture.

Bibs and feeders

These are best made from cotton terry towelling. Plastic is not suitable because a plastic bib can easily flap up over the face and form a seal, causing suffocation.

Toiletries

These should be as plain as possible. There are many bath-time products on the market and all the advertising claims may cause confusion. As a general rule, a baby needs nothing other than a good baby soap for his skin, and this should be used sparingly and always well rinsed off. Baby shampoo is useful for hair washing, but again should be very well rinsed. Baby powder may be used for a light dusting after the bath. If the baby develops a dry skin, sore bottom or any other skin problem, medical advice should be sought before buying any of the preparations in the chemist's shop. A baby has very sensitive skin and can easily develop an allergy to an ingredient in a new product. Once an allergy develops, it may cause problems for the rest of his life. Some lotions, oils and creams even though promoted as being good for baby's skin, may contain complicated ingredients about which little is known of their effect on the human skin.

Cribs and cots

A crib is a small cot which may be used for the first two months of a baby's life. It is not essential and nowadays many babies go straight into a big cot. Some people use a carrycot placed inside the big cot for the first few weeks to make the baby feel secure.

Cots are covered by the British Standards Institution BS 1753 and there are several points which must be observed if the cot is to carry the 'kite' mark of the Institution.

- Spacing of bars – these should be not less than 7 cm (2¾ in) and not more than 7.6 cm (3 in) apart to prevent a child jamming his head between them.
- Cot sides should be 50 cm (20 in) high measured from the top of the mattress.
- Dropside fastening should be safe, so that the child cannot undo it.
- Paintwork should be lead free.
- Mattress should be firm, so that the baby cannot bury his head.

A mattress with a waterproof covering is a good buy, as it saves having to use waterproof sheets. The sheets can be of cotton/polyester in summer and cotton flannelette in winter. Fitted cot sheets which fit over the mattress are very convenient and easy to use, so worth the extra cost.

Blankets can be of wool or a wool/synthetic mixture. Cellular blankets are good because they are lightweight and warm. The warmth is due to the fact that the tiny holes trap air which acts as an insulator. Many shops sell baby duvets, but these are not suitable unless they have flaps which can be tucked under the mattress. Otherwise they can easily slip over the baby's face and cause suffocation. Similarly, 'baby nests' are not suitable for use in a cot or pram where the baby is left alone to sleep.

The pram

The type of pram chosen will depend on how it is to be used. There are many different sorts on the market from the very large to very small. If the pram is to be used for long shopping expeditions and walking out, then a large one, which is well sprung, would be the best choice. On the other hand, the type of pram which divides into a carrycot and folding wheels would be a better choice for taking the baby in the car.

'Buggies' are not suitable for young babies because they are not very comfortable. They do not have springs to enable them to adapt to uneven paths and do not offer the same protection from cold and wet weather as a pram.

The British Standards Institution has various regulations about prams:

- Material used should be physically and chemically free from substances harmful to the child.
- Materials used should be resistant to normal weather conditions and use.
- Materials should be reasonably non-flammable.
- Brakes should be on at least two wheels and should be out of reach of the child.
- Wheels should be strong and well attached.
- Provision should be made for fitting a safety harness.
- Padding should be firm to prevent suffocation.
- Hood should be positioned to deflect rain.
- Inside depth should be at least 19 cm above the mattress.
- Design of the pram should ensure maximum stability.
- Soft-body prams should have fittings which are safe and will not become detached from the chassis or allow the body to fold up during use.

In addition, a shopping tray which fits under the pram, across the axles, is safer than one fixed to the handlebars, as the weight is distributed more evenly. A cat net is necessary to prevent a cat getting into the pram to sleep and so smother the baby. In summer a fitted canopy will protect the baby from direct sunshine.

The pram mattress should be firm and waterproof. Sheets and blankets are necessary, the same type as those needed for the cot. As a general rule three covers are needed over the baby, as well as a sheet, so that two pram blankets and a coverlet are sufficient. In the early days a baby does not need a pillow at all, but from about four months he will like to be propped up when awake to see what is going on in the world. A special 'safety' pillow can be used for this. He will need a safety harness from about eight weeks of age, because of his increasing mobility.

The baby's room

When planning the room, allowance should be made for the baby's growing interests and future activity. If possible, it should be a bright, sunny room with adequate space for play.

Walls – can be decorated with bright, colourful and washable materials; one area can be set aside for pictures, including the child's own paintings later and another area at child level can be painted with blackboard paint when he is old enough to use chalk.

Ceiling – a white ceiling will reflect light; a mobile can be hung within the child's field of vision.

Floor – cork tiles, plastic or linoleum are all easy to clean and provide a good surface when the child is learning to walk; a colourful, washable rug can be added.

Windows – to provide adequate ventilation; window locks can be fitted for safety; curtains can be made from light, washable materials and lined to keep out light when the baby sleeps.

Heating – if possible a steady background heat is best. Safety factors are important here. The following methods are listed in order of preference:
a) central heating radiators
b) oil-filled electric radiators
c) fan heater
d) open coal fire with an adequate safety guard.

Lighting – a central light and a bedside lamp for reading.

Furniture – this should be both sturdy and washable, as the child will pull himself to his feet by holding on to it. It should include the cot, bath on stand, low chair, a chest of drawers and hanging cupboard for the baby's clothes, a low cupboard for the baby's toys and a low table and chairs which will be useful later. If the room is draughty a screen could be used to protect the baby – this can be improvised by covering a two-winged clothes airer with material.

THE BIRTH OF A BABY

By the thirty-eighth week of pregnancy the baby is usually in the head-down position ready for birth and the mother will have already experienced minor contractions and relaxations of the muscles of the uterus. Like all muscle fibres, the uterine ones shorten (contract) and lengthen (relax) in use, but in labour these fibres gradually shorten altogether because when they relax they do not lengthen as much as before. The process of birth consists of the gradual shortening of the muscle fibres which cause the cervix to 'thin' out and slowly open to enable the baby to pass through. At the same time the baby's head is being pushed down into the vagina by the pressure of the contractions and later in labour by active pushing by the mother. The birth of a baby is a long, slow process, and may be painful for the mother, although the amount of pain varies. The birth of a first baby takes on average fourteen hours and for a second and subsequent child it could take about eight hours.

Labour is described as being in three stages:
a) first stage – this is the longest part and lasts until the cervix is open
b) second stage – the baby is pushed out
c) third stage – the placenta or afterbirth is expelled.

First stage. There are three possible ways in which labour begins and a mother is advised to contact her doctor/midwife or hospital when any of these occurs:
a) contractions start to happen at regular intervals and gradually become more frequent
b) a 'show' – a small plug or blood-stained mucus which blocks the cervix comes away as the cervix opens (this is not always noticed)
c) the membranes rupture ('breaking of the waters') and some of the fluid surrounding the baby gushes out of the vagina.

During this stage the mother will experience some discomfort as the contractions become more frequent. At first it helps if the mother moves around, but towards the end of this stage she will probably place herself in the most comfortable position.

Discomfort varies from mild cramp to real pain and emotional support from her partner will help the mother to cope with it. He can also encourage her to use the relaxation techniques she learned at antenatal class which may relieve the pain. Otherwise various drugs can be given, including gas and air administered by the mother herself. Sometimes a local anaesthetic is injected into the space around the spinal cord to block off the pain messages. This is known as an epidural.

Second stage. At the end of the first stage, when the cervix is fully dilated (open), the mother usually experiences a great urge to push down with her abdominal muscles when each contraction occurs. The vagina gradually stretches as the baby's head is pushed down the canal and outside the mother's body. After the head is born, there is a pause and then with another contraction and push from the mother the rest of the baby is born. This second stage may take about twenty minutes. The baby usually cries immediately. The midwife will clean his eyes and mouth with swabs and separate him from the placenta by tying the umbilical cord in two places with catgut (or synthetic material) and cutting

between the ties, or she may use a clip. He is very quickly examined, wrapped up and given to his mother to hold.

Third stage. There is a slightly longer pause and then the mother feels another contraction and the placenta is pushed out of the vagina. Sometimes the midwife or doctor will help this by pulling gently on the umbilical cord. There may be some bleeding at this stage from the raw area in the wall of the uterus left by the placenta. The uterus rapidly contracts, which prevents further bleeding. Sometimes a drug is administered to the mother to accelerate this contraction.

After the birth is completed the baby's condition is assessed at one minute, five minutes and ten minutes, using the Apgar score. Then he is weighed and measured and examined for any defects. He is labelled with a bracelet which gives his name, sex, date and time of birth. A label is also prepared for his cot which will be ready and waiting for him. His mother and father are encouraged to cuddle him and check that the label is correct and that he is a normal, healthy baby. This is very important for 'bonding' to begin. Not only does a baby need to

Apgar Score	Score 0	Score 1	Score 2	Score at		
				1 min.	*5 min.*	*10 min.*
1. Heart rate	absent	below 100	over 100			
2. Respiratory effort	absent	irregular, slow or weak	lusty cry, good chest movement			
3. Muscle tone (in all four limbs)	limp	poor tone, some movement	active resistance, strong movement			
4. Reflex irritability (response to flicking soles of feet)	no response	slight withdrawal	vigorous withdrawal of leg, strong cry			
5. Colour	blue or pale	body pink, extremities blue	completely pink			
			Total scores			

The Apgar Score: an assessment of the condition of the newborn baby based on normal expectations.

The maximum score is 10 and if the score is less than 7 at 1 minute, less than 8 at 5 minutes, or less than 10 at 10 minutes, it will indicate the need for special care and a close follow-up during the baby's early years.

'know' his mother, but she needs to get to know her baby. The father is usually present at this time even if he chose not to be there at the birth.

Depending on the circumstances, various methods can be used to aid the birth.

Induction. Birth can be induced by rupturing the membranes around baby, or by giving the mother an artificial hormone which stimulates contractions of the uterus. This is done mainly for one of three reasons:
a) The baby is overdue – more than a week after the EDD.
b) The mother has toxaemia so the birth is induced early (from 3–8 weeks) to avoid complications.
c) The placenta is beginning to fail.

Episiotomy. A small cut, called an episiotomy, may be made in the mother's vagina to ease the birth and prevent tearing. It has to be stitched under local anaesthetic after the birth.

Forceps delivery. If progress is slow in the second stage of labour, or if either baby or mother is showing signs of distress, the doctor may decide to use forceps – a pair of large blades which can be put around the baby's head. The doctor can then guide the head and ease it out of the vagina. This is usually performed with an epidural, or under a general anaesthetic, and an episiotomy is needed before inserting the forceps.

Caesarean section. If, for some reason, the baby cannot be born through the vagina, then under an anaesthetic an incision is made through the mother's abdomen and the wall of her uterus and the baby is extracted. The placenta is also removed and then the incision is stitched up. The mother is usually in hospital some days longer and the baby may need special care for a short time, but usually both recover reasonably rapidly. Reasons for Caesarean births vary, but the most common reason is that the mother's bony pelvis is too small for the baby's head to pass through. Another reason is that the placenta may be positioned in the lower part of the uterus, preventing the baby's head from advancing.

Breech birth. Sometimes a baby does not settle in the head-down position, but instead 'sits upright' in the uterus so that his bottom is ready to be born first. Usually this can be diagnosed in the middle months of pregnancy and the baby may be turned by pushing him through the mother's abdomen. If the mother goes into labour with a breech baby, there may be complications because when the body is born the baby may take a breath before his head is out of the vagina. Other complications, such as early separation of the placenta or compression of the umbilical cord, may cause brain damage by starving the baby of his oxygen supply. In many cases the obstetrician decides to perform a Caesarian section, rather than risk these complications.

Appearance of the newborn baby

It is important to know the ethnic group of the parents because there are several conditions which are initially diagnosed from observations of the colour of the baby, e.g. jaundice. For instance, the Apgar Score which was devised by an American doctor, Virginia Apgar, for Caucasian babies has to be adapted for babies of other ethnic groups by substituting 'oxygenated' for 'pink'. Caucasian babies are usually rather red at birth due to the normally high haemoglobin content of the blood which shows through the light-coloured skin. Babies of Afro-Caribbean origin appear fair at birth apart from the mongolian spot (a bluish patch usually at the base of the spine which looks rather like a bruise). They sometimes look rather greyish at first and this can be mistaken for mild asphyxia by the inexperienced. Within twenty-four hours the skin darkens as the pigment reacts to light. Other dark-skinned babies may look a greyish colour at birth but will also darken later.

Most babies appear to have blue eyes, but the darker their final colour, the sooner they will start to change. The skin is usually covered in very fine hairs which vanish fairly soon after birth. There is often vernix present in the folds of skin – this is a thick whitish cream which covers and protects the skin from the amniotic fluid in the uterus before birth. If the baby is overdue then the skin is often dry and peeling due to the fact that the vernix has been absorbed. The amount of hair varies and does not necessarily indicate its future nature and colour.

A newborn baby often appears beautiful only to his parents because he is sometimes rather crumpled in his early days. He usually has a very large head in proportion to his body. In addition the head may be an odd shape due to moulding during the birth. Sometimes there is a swelling on one or other side of the head (known as a caput) or there may be a hard lump (cephalhaemotoma). This is due to the pressure on the baby's head during the birth and soon subsides.

All babies are born capable of certain reflex actions (see pages 114–15), the most important of these being 'rooting' and sucking which enable them to feed efficiently. In addition they are able to make their wants known by crying vigorously.

THE POSTNATAL PERIOD

Although most mothers appear exhausted at the time of the birth, because it is a period of hard work, the majority recover almost immediately. They see their baby – and it has all been worthwhile! However, a period of rest is necessary and usually the baby is placed in a warm cot whilst his mother is given a blanket bath and then a cup of tea. She is left to rest and if she is too excited to sleep a sedative may be given.

The following day she can begin to care for her baby, whilst she herself is being cared for by the midwife. During the next six to ten days the mother and baby get to know one another. The mother's uterus gradually contracts to its original size and the raw area of the placental site heals up. There is a small vaginal loss which gradually ceases. A watch is kept for any fresh bleeding which indicates that the healing process is not taking place. A check is also

kept on the mother's temperature, as a rise could indicate infection entering the raw area in the uterus. Strict hygiene measures are practised to prevent such infection which can have serious consequences for a mother.

The mother is encouraged to practise postnatal exercises to 'tone up' her muscles and help her regain her figure. Breast-feeding begins with the help and supervision of the midwife. The baby is weighed at regular intervals and, after a small initial loss, should begin to gain about 28 g (1 oz) a day if feeding is adequate.

Also during this period, mothers are shown how to care for their babies. Bathing, changing and topping and tailing, sterilising bottles and making up feeds are all demonstrated. As soon as the mother is able and confident, she is encouraged to change her baby and look after him. The baby's umbilical cord gradually shrivels up and usually falls off between the fifth and seventh day. In the meantime it must be kept dry to prevent infection so a special powder is used, and, in some hospitals, the baby is not bathed until the cord is off.

Before being discharged from hospital or care of the midwife, the baby is given a complete examination to ensure that there are no defects, because many of these can be put right at this early stage. The mother is also examined and given an appointment for a postnatal examination six weeks after the birth.

Any creative process is hard work. Not only has the mother created a new baby who has brought awesome responsibilities, but her body has undergone a tremendous change.

Following the long period of expectation, it is understandable if she should now experience a sense of anti-climax. The hormonal changes, as her body goes back to normal, cause mood swings which may make her suffer from depression. Both she and her partner may fail to understand the physical origin of these feelings, especially as the common belief is that her prevailing mood should be one of elation. Relatives and visitors tend to concentrate on the loveable baby and seldom ask the mother how she is.

Few people realise what is in store for them. The physical demands of the baby can be exhausting. He will need four-hourly feeds round the clock at first, and as each feed takes at least half an hour, this is a large proportion of the day. There is the additional housework – washing, ironing, etc. – besides the usual cleaning and meal preparation. Some parents feel overwhelmed at first by the amount of work involved. There is little energy left for the mother to treat her partner as she did before. It requires a mature man to accept this and realise that it is a temporary state of affairs. Satisfactory sexual relationships may not be resumed immediately and again, he will need to exercise tolerance and understanding.

He may have to overcome jealousy and resentment at this small creature taking over the home. Some men find it hard to adapt, and react by abdicating their responsibility as a parent and resuming their former social pastimes. The mother, at this stage, is wary of baby-sitting arrangements, and in any case, lacks the energy to join her partner. This can lead to further tensions.

Fortunately most parents do adapt. The pleasure from having created a family more than counteracts the problems. If the relationship was good to begin with, the child can cement it.

The traditional roles of mother and father are now blurred and it is accepted that the father will want to be involved in all aspects of the antenatal preparation, birth and ensuing care of the baby. Fathers involved in this way are thought to have a much closer bond with both wife and child, leading to a close family relationship. It is important that the mother does not become so wrapped up in the baby that she excludes the father from these activities. However the mother of the family remains the pivot around which the family revolves, and from now on her attitudes will help to chart the family's future. If the mother is unsupported, this responsibility will be even greater.

The mother's physical health is of prime importance. If at all possible, help should be provided for her during the first weeks of the baby's life. Sometimes a relative is able to help. More often the father has to use some of his annual leave entitlement. Some firms are beginning to copy the Scandanavians, allowing fathers to take paternity leave. Failing this, the social services department of the local authority can provide a home aid on a doctor's recommendation. Payment is according to family income. This help relieves the mother of some of the housework so that she can concentrate on the baby, and both she and her partner can enjoy him to the full.

The health visitor will visit after the tenth day to give advice on the care and health of mother and baby. She is a trained nurse with midwifery experience and special training in the care and development of children and the promotion of good health. She is usually attached to the practice of the mother's family doctor and visits all babies and children on his list. By law all births must be notified to the local health authority which informs the health visitor responsible, so that she can visit the mother as soon as the midwife's role ends. In many cases she will already be known to the mother because she has paid antenatal visits or been involved in parentcraft classes. When she calls, the health visitor will invite the mother to attend the local child health clinic to have the baby's development assessed. During the next five years she can, if needed, be a great source of support to the family.

Six weeks after the birth, the mother should attend a postnatal clinic where she is given a physical examination to ensure that her body has returned to its pre-pregnant state. Her doctor may check for anaemia, which is often the cause of tiredness after childbirth. This is an ideal time for the mother to be given family planning advice so that she can space her family.

Most doctors recommend a two-year gap between babies, but of course this is largely a matter of personal preference, and the mother's ability to cope. Other factors affecting parents' decisions here include the economic circumstances of the family, whether the mother is planning to return to her former career, the ages of the parents, and the ultimate size of the family they hope to have.

THE GROWING FAMILY

Another period of adaptation for the family occurs when the second baby is born. Wisely and sensitively handled, this can be a happy and rewarding time for all concerned. It must be remembered, however, that for the first child it could be traumatic. From being the focus of all the parents' love and attention, he has to adjust to being one of a pair.

With a young child (under five) lengthy explanations about the coming baby are unnecessary. Once the pregnancy has been established at about three months, casual references to babies can be brought into conversation with both parents. There are many children's books dealing with the subject, but they should be carefully chosen to suit the child's age and understanding. Opportunities to admire babies seen on shopping expeditions, outings to the park, etc., can be used. Wise parents will not mention the new baby as though he will be a ready-made playmate. This can lead to deep disappointment. The child can be involved in practical preparations for the baby. If any equipment used for the child is to be passed on, the transfer should be done well in advance – for example, the change from cot to bed. Any other major changes in the child's future life – for instance, starting playgroup or nursery school – should also be planned in advance so as not to coincide with the actual birth. Arrangements for the care of the child during the mother's confinement should be carefully considered, especially if the child is to leave his home. The inevitable separation from his mother can be made easier by accustoming him to short periods in other homes without her.

The ideal arrangement for the birth is that the baby is born at home and the older child can remain in his own home with a familiar adult. However, most doctors prefer the baby to be born in hospital, even if the mother comes home within forty-eight hours. In any case, for the child it is best to stay in his own home. If this is not possible, then the home he goes to should be one he knows.

As soon as possible after the birth of the baby, he should see his mother. Nowadays hospitals are aware of the bond between mother and child and allow unrestricted visiting. The reunion of mother and child is most important to establish the relationship; time together is needed before the introduction of the baby. Some parents like to present the child with a special gift at this time. A doll can be particularly useful in preparing the child for sharing later in the care of the real baby.

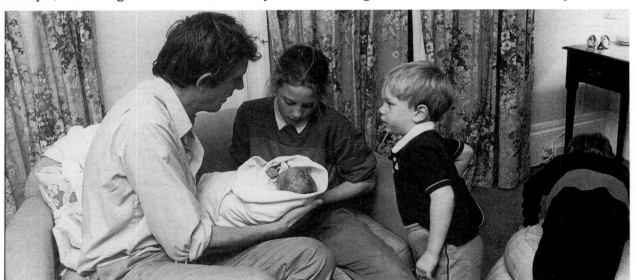

The new baby is introduced to the rest of the family

Many children find it hard to cope with their jealous feelings on seeing the closeness between mother and baby, particularly during breast-feeding and bathing. This may lead to difficult behaviour and is commonly seen in children under stress. A reversion to baby ways, such as wetting, soiling, refusing food and bedtime mutiny, may occur. This is known as regressive behaviour and can be exceedingly trying, both to the harassed parents and staff at the nursery, who frequently see children undergoing this stress in the family. The child strives by any means to gain extra love and attention. Understanding adults will realise that this is a normal and transitory stage. The child should be helped to overcome his feelings, not by punishment or projecting guilt feelings on to him, but by making time to give him complete individual attention. In the home, the father can help a great deal by showing the child the delights of being the older one. With care and forethought, the baby can to a large extent be fitted into the existing routine of the family, thus minimising disturbance to the older child. Visitors to the family can assist by showing attention to the child before going to the baby and by refraining from comments and criticisms of the child's behaviour. Great tolerance, self-control and understanding are required of all concerned adults at this time. When the child makes himself most unlovable that is when he most needs love. Physical contact, cuddles and spoken assurances of love will go a long way to counter his temporary insecurity. So will the continuation of a 'special' bedtime routine with stories, etc., difficult though it may be to keep going. Play materials which lend themselves to expressed aggression and anger, such as dough, woodwork, sand, earth, hammer toys and so forth are also beneficial as they healthily channel the anger and resentment away from baby. Even so, it is not wise to trust the child alone with the baby. Mothers often deceive themselves that *their* child feels only love towards the new baby; even if this is so, the young child has no idea of how to express that love safely. Violent rocking, and embracing which is more akin to throttling are common; so is the 'sharing' of wildly unsuitable play materials. Fortunately babies are tough creatures and, happily, survive much rough handling, but it is sensible to avoid situations which could give rise to anxiety and tension on the parent's part, and guilt and feelings of rejection on the child's.

A nursery nurse seeking a position as nanny will often be taken on by a family at this very time. She would do well to remember that the child is being expected to accept another new face at this critical stage, and moreover will be 'forced' into her company for long periods, when he would probably much rather be with Mummy or Daddy. She may also have to cope with the expectations of grandparents, and possible tension between adults in the family. She must remember the need for consistent handling of the child and must realise how badly he needs frequent contact with his mother, and assurances of what a valued member of the family he is. The baby will not suffer from a little 'neglect' at this stage; her prime concern should be the well-being of the older child. Extra trouble taken and understanding shown now will pay dividends in terms of adjustment and happiness of the whole family in the months to come.

EXERCISES

Investigation
1) Study a family you know well, during the period before and after the arrival of their second child. Note:
   a) the domestic arrangements at the time of the birth
   b) the older child's reaction
   c) the part played by all adults who helped the family at this time.

2) Visit your local shops and choose suitable clothing and equipment for a baby's first six months. Give reasons for your choice of each item, including the cost and factors such as safety and design.

Project
Collect leaflets from the DSS concerning payment made to antenatal mothers. Work out when a woman should fill in the required forms, and when is the most advantageous time for her to stop work.

5 Care of the Young Baby

ATTENDING TO A BABY'S NEEDS

A newborn baby's needs are simple, but they are urgent and of vital importance. They appear to be mainly physical but, in keeping him clean, fed and comfortable, other basic needs are also fulfilled.

To achieve and maintain physical and mental health, all human beings, whatever their ages, have certain basic needs:

Physical
- food
- cleanliness
- rest
- exercise
- fresh air
- warmth
- medical care
- protection from infection and injury

Mental and emotional
- security
- affection
- stimulation
- social contacts
- independence

Obviously, these will sometimes overlap, and during babyhood and childhood the emphasis may move from one aspect to another, but the basic needs will remain the same throughout life. So, when we plan the daily care of a baby, we must ensure that all his needs are covered. This planning is especially important in busy nurseries where a 'good' baby could easily be overlooked.

In practice it is difficult to separate the physical care from the mental and emotional needs but, for the sake of clarity, each will be dealt with separately, remembering that they all contribute to the proper care of the baby.

Food

Most babies will want to be fed approximately every four hours and, even when a baby is breast-fed completely 'on demand' he will eventually settle into a regular feeding pattern which will enable his mother to plan her day. It is important to be flexible but also necessary for the baby's security and the mother's peace of mind to have a framework for a daily routine.

The main problem with feeding on demand is to know whether the baby is crying because he is hungry or for some other reason and, as only experience can tell you this, it is usual to have some guidelines. The commonest pattern of feeding is to feed at 6 a.m., 10 a.m., 2 p.m., 6 p.m. 10 p.m., and at 2 a.m. only if the baby wakes. As a general rule, if the baby is awake and crying three hours or more after his last feed, he should be given another. If it is less than three hours, then he is probably thirsty, or he may need attention. He should be offered cool, boiled water, and be picked up and comforted. Should this early waking and crying occur often, then it would be wise to increase his milk by 25 ml (1 oz) if he is bottle-fed or by breast-feeding more frequently.

On the other hand, if the baby sleeps for more than five hours after a feed (except in the middle of the night) then he should be woken and offered his feed, because sleeping for such a long period may be an indication that he is ill. (See also Chapter 6 on Food.)

Cleanliness

Cleanliness is very important to the health of a small baby because he is vulnerable to infection. He has not had time to build up his own resistance to infection, and the resistance inherited from his mother is by no means complete. Therefore, he needs to be protected from as many germs as possible. Germs live on our skin and all around us, especially in dirt, so cleanliness of the baby and his surroundings will help to reduce the risk of infection. The skin also needs to be kept clean to enable it to carry out its function to excrete waste products.

A high standard of personal hygiene is necessary in a person caring for a young baby, as germs can easily be passed on by dirty hands and dirty habits. It is even more important when babies are in nurseries, because infection can also be spread from one baby to another via the hands of the nurse. Handwashing by carers before handling the baby, before preparing his feed, and after changing his nappy is essential and should become an automatic action.

The baby's surroundings should be kept clean:

- His room should be cleaned daily and well ventilated because sunlight kills some germs and fresh air will dilute their numbers.
- His cot and pram should be cleaned regularly, and the bedding changed frequently.
- Clothes need to be changed morning and evening.
- His nappy should be changed whenever necessary, and at least every four hours.
- Clothing and terry nappies should be washed daily and rinsed well and, if possible, dried in the open air.
- Care must be taken with discarded soiled or wet nappies. They should never be left lying on the floor as they are a source of infection. Disposable nappies should be put into a bin-liner inside a bin with a lid. They can then be removed without having to be handled separately. Washable nappies need to be boiled or treated with a sanitising preparation to kill germs.
- Special care is needed with feeding equipment which must be cleaned and sterilised after each use.

Cleanliness for the baby should be incorporated in his daily routine.

Bathing a baby. He will need a bath or all-over wash at one end of the day, and a 'top and tail' at the other end. This can be fitted in with the mother's (nursery nurse's) preference. Some mothers prefer to bath their babies in the morning before the 10 a.m. feed. Others may prefer the evening if Dad is only available at this time of day. If the baby is restless and miserable in the evening, a bath may soothe him and can be a good preliminary to bedtime. When the baby gets older and begins to crawl, the evening is probably the best time for his bath, because he can get so dirty playing on the floor that this is the best way to clean him. Whenever the bath is given it is best to choose a time just before a feed, rather than after, because he needs peace and sleep following the feed to enable digestion to take place.

Bath time has other values as well as cleanliness. It is a time of contact between mother/father and baby when affection is shown and there is much shared enjoyment. It is also an opportunity for exercise as the baby is able to kick and splash the water.

If the baby has a dry skin an oil-based emollient can be added to the bath water or the baby can be massaged with baby oil. Many Afro-Caribbean, African and Asian mothers do the latter as a matter of routine. Not only does it help a dry skin, but it also gives sensual pleasure to both mother and baby.

There are many variations in methods of bathing a baby, and most young mothers are shown at least one way. Some adults prefer to stand up to bath a baby, so the bath is placed on a table and a changing-pad is used beside the bath to undress the baby. Others prefer to use the floor in this way. Another method is for the carer to sit in a low chair with the bath on a stand in front of him or her. The baby is undressed on his or her lap. This latter method gives the close contact that the baby needs and is more natural. However, many new parents feel very unsure of their ability to hold the baby on their knees and, if this is the case, they may feel safer in using the table method.

Sitting method:

1. Ensure room is warm – close windows and check the temperature. It should be about 21 °C (70 °F).
2. Collect all the equipment needed:
   low chair
   bath on stand
   bucket or bin with lid for soiled nappy
   container for other washing
   set of clean clothes, including nappy
   apron
   towel
   soap
   cotton-wool swabs in covered container
   bin for used swabs
   shampoo
   talcum powder (if wanted)
   brush and comb
   nail scissors.
3. Have baby's feed ready, if bottle-fed.
4. Wash hands.
5. Put some cold water in the bath.
6. Add hot water to make the bath water the correct temperature. Either use a thermometer 38–40 °C (100–105 °F), or test with bare elbow when water should feel pleasantly warm.
7. Put on apron.
8. Undress the baby to nappy.
9. Wrap baby in towel, keeping his arms inside.
10. Using first a swab dampened with bath water, then a dry one, wipe each eye separately from the nose outwards. Discard each swab after one wipe.
11. Wash face with a damp swab. Wipe around nose and ears but do not probe into them.
12. Dry face with corner of towel.
13. Hold the baby under the neck and shoulders with one hand, and tuck his legs under your arms so that you can hold his head over the bath. Using your other hand, scoop up bath water to wet his hair. Add a small amount of

shampoo, then wash head thoroughly by rubbing this in. Then rinse well.
14. Move baby back on to your lap and dry his hair with the corner of the towel. NB: The shampoo should only be used once or twice a week because it tends to dry the scalp.
15. Unwrap towel around baby and remove nappy.
16. Place nappy in bucket or bin with lid.
17. If nappy is soiled, clean baby's bottom with swabs.
18. Soap both hands and massage all over the baby's body, making sure the lather reaches all the creases – neck, under-arms, groin and between fingers and toes.

19. Grasping the baby securely by putting one wrist and hand under his neck and shoulders and holding the arm furthest away, use the other hand to hold his legs. Lift him into the bath, releasing his legs when he is fully in the bath so that he is in a half-sitting position.
20. The free hand can then be used to splash and rinse off all the soapy lather.
21. If the baby is happy in the bath, let him kick and splash for a few minutes – this time should be increased as he gets older.
22. Lift him out on to your lap and wrap loosely in the towel.
23. Pat, rather than rub, him dry, making sure that he is dry in the creases.
24. Discard damp towel.

25. Smooth on a little talcum powder.
26. Put nappy on first.
27. Dress him and give him his feed.

Method of 'top and tail':
1. Collect equipment:
     bowl of warm water
     cotton-wool swabs
     bin for discarded swabs
     soap
     talcum powder
     towel
     clean clothes, including nappy
     low chair and table
     nappy bucket or bin with lid
     container for soiled clothes.
2. Wash hands.
3. Spread towel on lap and undress baby to nappy.
4. Clean face with damp cotton-wool swabs, and dry.
5. Clean hands of baby with swabs.
6. Put on clean vest.
7. Remove nappy and place in bucket or bin with lid.
8. If soiled, clean bottom with cotton-wool swabs.
9. Rub soap on one hand and use this to wash nappy area thoroughly.
10. Rinse with swabs, or a flannel.
11. Dry with towel.
12. Smooth on a little talcum powder.
13. Put on clean nappy.
14. Complete dressing.

Rest – sleep

Many 'experts' claim that a young baby will sleep twenty hours a day. However, close observation of babies reveals that they vary considerably in the amount of sleep needed. A newborn baby invariably falls asleep after a feed, and should be allowed to sleep in reasonably quiet surroundings as long as he will. Many babies 'cat-nap' during the day, and when awake are content to lie watching any movement or activity around them and then fall asleep again. Crying usually indicates boredom. Therefore it is important to provide visual stimulus in the baby's surroundings to interest him when he is awake. His room should be colourful, with hanging mobiles in the air. When he is outside in his pram, put it where he can see something interesting, such as branches of a tree.

As he gets older, his periods of wakefulness become longer, and he is best put to sleep near his carer(s) during the day so that someone can talk to him when he is awake. Normal household noises should not disturb him and this is better than leaving him isolated in his room. If he has enough stimulation and contact with others during the day, he should sleep well at night. It is wise to begin a regular bedtime routine because this establishes the habit of sleep. A bath or 'top and tail' can be followed by feeding and winding, and then he can be put into his cot in his own room, with a cuddle and perhaps a lullaby. This will all suggest to him that it is time to go to sleep. He should then be left alone but someone should be within hearing distance. If his carer hovers over him to see if he will sleep, he soon begins to realise that it is easy to get attention. Many babies have a 'sleep' cry, so if he does not settle at once it is worth waiting five minutes before going to him. Of course, he should not be allowed to get too distressed and if he is still crying after five minutes, check that he is not uncomfortable. Staying with him for a while may be necessary but he should not be taken to wherever he spends his daytime hours, or he will come to want this every night.

In the early weeks the baby may wake at intervals in the night for a feed but, surprisingly quickly, will adapt to night-time sleeping as soon as he is able to take enough food during the day.

Exercise

All babies need exercise because this encourages good circulation which, in turn, improves muscle-tone, and aids development of muscles.

All movement, including crying, is exercise, and opportunity must be given for this. The baby's clothes should be loose enough to allow free movement, especially of arms and legs. Bedclothes should not be tucked in so tightly that movement is hampered.

In the past, babies were 'swaddled' most of the day and night. They were wrapped up very tightly in a shawl, or even sewn into their clothes. It was thought that this would make a baby feel more secure. Certainly, some babies will sleep better when wrapped up, but it is no coincidence that since the practice of swaddling was abandoned, babies have shown earlier motor development. When a baby is learning to move and control his body, he needs plenty of opportunity to practise. Therefore, at some time during the day, he should be placed on a rug on the floor, without his nappy, so that he can kick and move freely. In summertime this can be done outdoors. When the baby is in his bath, time should be allowed for him to kick and splash.

As the baby gets older, and stays awake for longer periods, more of his time should be spent on the floor. A play-pen can be used for short periods, but it is better to remove valuable or dangerous objects from the room and give the child freedom to explore, roll over and pull himself up on the furniture rather than imprison him in a small area.

Fresh air

We all need fresh air to provide oxygen. When air is trapped in a house it becomes stale. After it has been breathed out it contains more water vapour, more carbon-dioxide and it is much warmer. There is still a good proportion of oxygen, so the effects of poor ventilation are mainly due to increased warmth and moisture which cause an unpleasant humidity. As humidity increases, human beings become distressed and, if left in these conditions for long, can become ill and eventually die. The humidity supplies micro-organisms with ideal conditions to multiply rapidly. This is why infection can spread so easily in poorly-ventilated rooms. It is especially important for the nursery nurse to be aware of this in a nursery where several babies are together in the same room.

Babies' rooms should be aired thoroughly at least once during the day by opening windows and doors to create a strong draught. There should always be a window or ventilator open, except in very cold weather. The baby should be protected from draughts by a screen.

The baby should be taken out into the fresh air every day, suitably dressed, except in extremely cold or foggy weather. In the summer he can sleep in his pram in the garden during the day.

Sunlight is very beneficial to all human beings, but care should be taken when exposing a baby to the sun. His skin must become accustomed to sunlight gradually, to avoid sunburn, so he should be protected from very hot sunshine by a sun-shade on his pram, and a hat. Starting with five minutes exposure one can increase the length of time by five minutes every day as appropriate.

Warmth

The new baby, emerging from the constantly controlled warmth of the uterus, has little ability to maintain that temperature for himself. His temperature-regulating mechanism is very immature and will not become fully effective for many months. In addition, he has a relatively large skin area in proportion to his weight and so can rapidly lose body heat through the skin when exposed to cold air. As small babies do not move a lot, they will not generate much heat from exercise, either. It is important to realise that a baby who is cold can rapidly become colder. Unfortunately, the cold baby does not look cold and does not usually protest. In fact, he appears to be contented and has a healthy colour. It is possible for his condition to be overlooked so that he develops hypothermia, which can lead to death if undetected.

The baby should, therefore, be kept in warm surroundings, especially in the early weeks. His room should be at a temperature of 21 °C (70 °F) for the first two weeks of life, then it can be reduced to 18 °C (65 °F). A check should be kept on the temperature, especially during the night, to ensure that it does not drop below 16 °C (60 °F). The ideal source of heat is central heating, but a guarded nursery fire or fan-heater would be suitable. With constant heating the room must not be allowed to become too dry – a bowl of water placed near the heat source will prevent this.

The baby's pram should be sturdy and weatherproof, and his clothing should be loose and thin to prevent restriction of movement. Natural fibres such as wool and cotton are warmer than man-made fibres such as nylon, Courtelle, polyester and acrylic. Two thin layers are better than one thick one, because air trapped between the layers acts as insulation. The baby should be warm when his clothes are put on, or the clothes will only serve to keep him cold. The cot or pram can be pre-warmed in cold weather by a hot water bottle which is removed before the baby is put in. When bathing or exercising a baby, make sure the room is warm and after the bath dry him and dress him quickly. The clothes can be warmed before use on a radiator or in front of the fire. The baby should wear a bonnet when outdoors in cooler weather, as he can lose a lot of heat from his bare head. A sleeping-bag/dressing gown is useful at night, so that if the baby kicks off his blankets, he is still covered. He should not be put outdoors in very cold or foggy weather because breathing cold air will chill him rapidly, even if warmly clad.

To test whether a baby is warm enough, it is best to put a hand under the covers and feel his abdomen and chest which should be pleasantly warm to touch. Babies' hands and feet often feel cold, so are not a good indication of internal temperatures. If the baby is very cold, the best way to warm him up is to cuddle him, meanwhile raising the temperature in the room. Do not wrap him in more blankets, as these will only keep him cold. If he is very cold and unresponsive, then medical aid should be summoned as fast as possible.

Medical care

A baby is usually given a thorough examination after birth to ensure, as far as possible, that he is healthy and has no defects. Specific tests can be carried out for phenylketonuria, hypothyroidism, and dis-locatable hips, all of which can be corrected at this early stage (see page 209). Although it is rare to find anything wrong, it is worth examining all babies for the sake of the few who may have a defect which can probably be put right at this early stage. Even if the defect cannot be put right, it may be possible to prevent it getting worse, or to lessen the effects.

In Britain, most babies are examined at intervals throughout the first five years, to ensure that they are developing in the normal way. Usually such examinations take place at these stages: six weeks, nine months, two years and three and a half years. In some areas some of the tests are carried out by health visitors in the home, otherwise a clinical medical officer will do the tests in the Child Health Clinic. Some general practitioners have extra training so that they can test children registered with them.

Various tests can be given at different stages. For example, between six and eight months a hearing test can be carried out to ascertain whether the child has any defect of hearing. If there is such a defect, then he can be fitted with a hearing-aid, and, even if the aid does not wholly overcome the baby's deafness, it will still be immensely valuable if it lets him hear some sounds. A baby who has never heard any sounds at all will have great difficulty with language development.

Soon after birth the health visitor will call to see the mother and baby. At the first visit she will check that the mother and baby are well, and advise on the care of the baby, if the mother needs any help. Her aim is to be a friend of the family and, by giving help and advice, to make sure that the baby grows and develops into a healthy individual.

A health visitor is a state registered nurse who has had extra training and experience in child development and family welfare. Besides visiting the mothers at intervals, she also runs the local Well Baby Clinics and invites mothers to attend there with their babies. At the clinic the babies can be weighed and progress checked, while mothers can meet and compare notes. This can give reassurance to a mother and help to make friends for herself and her child.

Signs of good health:

clear firm skin	sleeping well
good colour	gaining weight slowly and steadily
bright eyes	being alert
shiny hair	being interested
firm muscles	looking contented
taking feeds well	normal development for age

Illness is rare, but there can be minor problems which may worry the inexperienced parents or nursery nurse. If there are doubts, then a health visitor or doctor should be consulted.

Hiccups. These are common in young babies and can be safely ignored.

Excessive crying. Babies vary considerably in temperament – some are placid and contented, others are active and some will cry and demand attention. If a baby is crying, go to him and pick him up and comfort him. Try to discover and correct the cause, which may be any of the following: hunger, thirst, coldness, over-heating, wet nappy, pain due to teething or colic, boredom, or it may be just that he wants his mother. This last reason may be difficult to deal with, and there are times when the only solution is to carry the baby around with you for part of the day. It is worth asking the doctor to check that the baby is well and that there is no other reason for the crying.

Colic (three-month colic). This usually occurs in the first three months of life (hence the name) and can be very distressing. A typical case is a healthy normal baby who is contented most of the time except after the 6 p.m. feed, when he appears to be in extreme pain. He screams and draws up his knees. Picking him up and cuddling him may soothe him for a short while, as will rubbing his tummy or back or giving him a drink of cool boiled water. But, whatever you do, the screaming continues on and off all the evening. Then at 10 p.m. he takes his feed and settles down and sleeps all night. There is little anyone can do in the way of treatment, apart from nursing the baby, but the doctor can prescribe medicine which *may* help. Whatever treatment is given, this evening colic will usually last for about eight weeks, so that often by three months the problem disappears. The condition is not yet fully understood, but babies do not seem to suffer any harmful effects from it.

Teething should not cause illness but it may cause a lot of discomfort which can lower a baby's resistance to infection. Teething usually begins at about six months, and this is the stage when the antibodies the baby obtained from his mother are diminishing and he has not produced enough of his own to give him protection from all infections. Therefore it is important not to assume that any illness is 'only teething', because a serious infection could possibly be overlooked until it is too late.

Signs and symptoms of teething:
a) dribbling (salivation)
b) red patches on cheeks
c) sore chin and chest from dribbling
d) child bites on anything available – his fist, mother's chin and jaw, edge of cot, etc.
e) reluctance to suck because of pain (but not sufficient to stop him eating)
f) sore bottom – this is due to loss of fluid by dribbling which leads to concentrated urine causing soreness
g) fretfulness and misery.

Treatment:
a) Give extra fluids to drink – cool boiled water.
b) Give him something to bite, e.g. hard rusk, bone ring or teething rattle.
c) Comfort him.
d) Try one of the proprietary brands of teething jelly.

Consult the doctor if the baby
a) pulls his ears
b) has diarrhoea and/or vomiting
c) becomes chesty
d) becomes very distressed.

Protection

There are two important areas of risk where a baby is especially vulnerable and will need protection:
a) *Infection* (see Chapter 8 on Germs and Disease). The newborn baby has little resistance to the germs he will meet, so he needs to be protected as far as possible until he has developed some defences.
  i)   The best protection a baby can be given is to be breast-fed, because breast milk is uncontaminated and contains antibodies which help fight infection.
  ii) The need for cleanliness has already been mentioned, especially the sterilisation of bottles.

iii) All water and milk should be boiled.

iv) If the baby has all his needs fulfilled, he should have good general health which will help him resist infection.

v) He can be immunised against specific infectious diseases, such as tuberculosis, whooping cough, diphtheria, poliomyelitis, tetanus, measles, mumps and rubella.

b) *Accidents* (see Chapter 19 on Accidents and First Aid). Accidents are one of the chief causes of death for children under five. This is because children have little sense of danger and are often in the charge of careless adults.

As a baby grows up and becomes more mobile, his natural instinct is to explore and experiment, so a safe environment must be provided to enable him to do this. Adults caring for a child must always be aware of potential dangers and should guard against them, without being too negative or frightening the child.

Security

A newborn human baby is among the most vulnerable and helpless of all animals, and to survive he must be cared for and protected. He is probably aware of this in a limited way, because he has an innate fear of falling, and if held insecurely will cry. This makes it difficult for the inexperienced parent or nursery nurse because the crying can make the adult even more nervous. The baby senses this and reacts by more crying. Therefore he needs to be handled in a firm, confident way to make him feel secure.

The establishment of a regular routine helps the parent/nursery nurse to be confident and sure, and as the baby learns to expect certain actions to follow others he begins to develop a trust that his needs will be satisfied. He learns to anticipate, and to recognise various signs. For example, the sound of water running and bath preparations tell him that it is nearly bathtime. Anticipation and regular fulfilment of his needs build up his feeling of security. This is especially true of feeding. Sucking milk gives a baby intense satisfaction because his hunger is satisfied and sucking is a comfort to him.

Having a stable, loving mother and frequent physical contact with her is very important to a child's inner security. His mother's pleasure in him will convey itself at a very early age and make him feel a worthwhile and important person in the home.

Affection

A small baby needs one person's consistent care so that he develops a deep relationship. Once this relationship is formed, he can branch out and make others and gradually widen his contacts. The quality of that first relationship is very important, because it can colour all future expectations and feelings about whether people are 'good' or 'bad'. If he is treated with love and tenderness, and all his needs are met by this person, then he will grow up with friendly feelings towards others and confidently expect that people will be kind to him.

It does not seem to make a difference to the child's well-being and development whether this first relationship is with his own mother, father or a substitute – such as a nursery nurse – provided this one person cares for him consistently for the first few months of his life.

From about two weeks, the baby recognises his 'mother' and will smile and begin to make noises when she leans over him. This brings a response from his mother and leads to a two-way communication. This is part of the process known as 'bonding', and we know from recent research that this is just as important for the mother as for the baby. It is seen also in the animal kingdom where, if the baby is separated from its mother for a period of time, the mother may completely reject it.

Among humans lack of bonding can sometimes be seen in cases of concealed parental violence (baby battering). Investigations show that the children who suffer in this way were often born prematurely and received special medical care which caused an unnatural separation from their mothers in the early weeks of life when bonding should take place.

Fortunately, most parents find it easy to love and show their love to their baby. But if there should be a feeding problem, excessive wakefulness or constant crying, then it is important to seek help and advice. If not dealt with, these problems can lead to feelings of failure and fatigue which may end in the mother rejecting her child.

The growth of love between mother and child is encouraged by close physical contact, which happens naturally as she looks after the child's physical needs. But there should be time, too, for face-to-face contact, talking and singing to the baby, and the enjoyment of playing together. It is not a question of 'spoiling', but of giving the baby the emotional necessities of life. Of course, he should be fed and allowed to sleep, but when awake he needs the company of his mother and family so that he knows where he belongs. He should not be left alone to cry for hours 'so that he will learn to amuse himself'.

Finally, lack of affection and stimulation can affect growth and development. In the past, it was noticed that children in institutions, who were looked after by a variety of people, were often small for their age and backward in many aspects of development. Some of these babies, who had never been 'mothered', later developed severe personality disorders. Now that these effects are more fully understood, most children being cared for by people other than their natural parents are placed in foster-homes where the care can be more personal. Students in nurseries will be conversant with family grouping and realise the importance of the 'mother figure'. By caring for her children over a period of time, she can create an invaluable mother/child relationship and this makes all the difference between looking after their physical needs and really 'caring' for them.

Stimulation (play)

All human beings need stimulation in order to learn about the world around them, and young babies are no exception. In the very early days of his life, a baby will appear just to sleep and feed, and not need stimulation, apart from that caused by hunger. However, even a newborn baby is awake for short periods so from the beginning ways should be found to make his environment stimulating and interesting.

Stimulation of a baby's senses should start as early as possible. By seeing, hearing, touching, tasting and smelling he experiences many objects, events and sensations. At first they make little sense, but gradually he is able to sort them out and use the information to form ideas about the world.

Sight. A baby can tell the difference between light and dark at birth and can see, but barely follow, a moving object. From about two weeks, the baby will gaze at his mother's face when she talks or attends to him. By four weeks he recognises her and smiles at her.

At birth a baby's eyes tend to work separately but, from six weeks, he is gradually able to use them efficiently together. By the time he is three months old, he can focus on an object and follow its movements quite well. So, from early days, as we have mentioned, the baby should have some visual stimulation – colours to look at, a hanging mobile, which will move gently in any current of air, and toys such as strings of beads strung across the pram. When his pram is out of doors it should be placed so that he can see something interesting, such as trees and people, when he awakes.

His carers should spend time talking to him, allowing him to gaze at their faces. Later, as he becomes more active, brightly coloured, well-designed toys should be provided for play on the floor.

Hearing sounds, and responding to them with his own noises, are the beginnings of a baby's speech.

At birth he can only hear high-pitched sounds but, by ten days, he can hear all sounds audible to the human ear and will be able to recognise his own mother's voice. From about three months he begins to turn his head, trying to see where sounds come from; he can also make all the sounds necessary for speech. By six to seven months he can locate sounds fairly accurately if they are on a level with his ears. Sounds made above his head are not usually located until about ten months of age.

To stimulate speech development, babies should be

talked to and placed where they can hear voices around them. A baby enjoys the sounds of family activity and will respond when someone talks to him, by making his own noises in reply. As he grows older, he begins to experiment and 'play' with his own voice. There is no need for absolute quiet when a baby is asleep; he can sleep undisturbed through all normal domestic noises in the same way that people living near a railway line are able to sleep with trains thundering past.

One of a baby's first playthings is a rattle, and he will react to the sound of it by first stiffening, 'quieting' and, later, by kicking and using his voice. Musical boxes and bells also stimulate a baby with their familiar, enjoyable sounds. Attractive musical sounds appeal to babies and, from early days, they can be soothed or settled to sleep by someone singing a lullaby.

Touch. A baby's skin is sensitive to touch, and very early in life he responds with pleasure to stroking and patting and the feel of bath water. Later, he enjoys being tickled and curls up in anticipation. His lips are especially sensitive,and this, combined with *taste*, makes him enjoy sucking, especially at the breast.

Sucking is necessary to a baby, not only for satisfaction and comfort, but also for finding out more about things than his senses of sight and hearing can tell him. A baby uses his sense of touch to find out more about himself by sucking his hands and, when he can manage it, his feet. As soon as he can hold an object he attempts to get it to his mouth and feel it with his lips and tongue. Touch teaches the baby the difference between a soft, woolly blanket and a smooth, cold rattle. Therefore toys with different textures should be provided for him to explore in this way.

Smell. A baby's sense of smell reinforces his visual and aural impressions. He learns to associate people, and things, with their particular odours. The smell of his mother's body becomes as familiar to him as the sight of her face or the sound of her voice.

The stimulus that adults give stirs up curiosity and enthusiasm in a baby and helps him become mentally alert. A baby should be given the chance to use all his senses. He needs freedom of movement and space to move around in, a familiar adult to talk to, and a selection of toys suitable for his age and ability.

Playthings for a baby should be chosen carefully, bearing in mind the following:

- colour – bright, primary colours attract the eye
- safety – no sharp edges or loose pieces, no dangerous wires, eyes securely attached in cuddly toys, lead-free and colour-fast paint, shatterproof
- hygiene – washable or easily cleaned
- size and weight – not too large or too heavy for a baby to handle, not too tiny or it may be swallowed
- shape – interesting and varied, suitable for a baby to hold
- texture – interesting varieties
- quantity – not too many toys should be provided at the same time, as this can be confusing.

Suggestions for play materials

0–3 months: mother's voice, own voice, mobiles and lightweight rattles (to be hung where they can be seen), strings of beads across the pram, musical box, music;

3–6 months (during this period the baby learns to grip and relax, and can hold toys): bath becomes enjoyable – kicking and splashing, bath toys, plastic cups, rattles – manufactured or home-made, bell-on-a-stick, coloured beads on a string, teething rings, teddy bear;

6–9 months (during this period the baby can sit up and may crawl): finger-plays and games – e.g. 'This little pig went to market', saucepans with lids, wooden spoons, bricks and blocks, ball, drums, cotton-reels, musical toys, more bath toys including colander, measuring jug, sponges and flannel;

9–12 months (during this period the baby becomes mobile – crawls, creeps or even walks): baskets of oddments of different textures, push-and-pull toys, push-along baby walker, strong books, small toy cars, rag doll, old handbag.

Social contacts

At first, the newborn baby needs only his mother or mother substitute. But as he grows older his interests widen to include his father, and then his brothers and sisters. Later, familiar adults such as grandparents, aunts and neighbours are greeted with smiles and gurgles. His mother remains his anchor and, during his first year, he always turns to her for reassurance and approval. He should be given opportunities to meet other people, and watch children playing – for example, in shops and supermarkets and parks, and in other people's houses.

Independence

A young baby is wholly dependent on his mother or mother-substitute, but gradually he becomes less helpless and, over the years of childhood, steadily develops the ability to take care of himself.

Part of the skill of being a parent is to let a child develop naturally as an independent being, whilst protecting him from any adverse consequences. Letting the child learn new skills when he is ready to do so, taking over when he is tired or 'just not in the mood', takes skilful observation, understanding and knowledge of a child's character. But it is of great importance, because we now know that if a child is not allowed to practise a skill when he is ready, it will take him far longer to learn.

Exploration is an important biological drive and begins very early in life, so that the baby should be allowed the freedom of the floor to kick and roll over, crawl and walk. Practice is necessary for normal physical development, and freedom to experience things first-hand is essential for emotional and intellectual development.

EXERCISES

Investigation
Find out about the child development checks and immunisation procedures that are carried out in your area. Who performs them? Make a schedule showing the ages at which these procedures take place.

Observation
Observe a baby under nine months either being bathed or breast-fed. Does he anticipate what is going to happen? What are his reactions?

In your evaluation, describe the pleasure parent and baby derived from this experience.

Project
Design/make a suitable toy for a baby under nine months. Describe how the baby reacted to it, and what you think he was learning from it.

SUGGESTIONS FOR FURTHER READING

Ronald and Cynthia Illingworth, *Babies & Young Children,* Churchill Livingstone
Mary and Richard Gordon, *A Baby in the House,* William Heinemann Ltd
Hugh Jolly, *Commonsense about Babies,* Times Newspapers Ltd
Penelope Leach, *Baby and Child Care,* Michael Joseph Ltd
James and Joyce Robertson, *A Baby in the Family,* Penguin Books Ltd
Gwen Rankin, *The First Year,* Piatkus Books
Penelope Leach, *Babyhood,* Pelican Books
Libby Purves, *How Not To Be A Perfect Mother,* Fontana

6

Food

To understand the principles of planning the feeding of babies and young children, the student must know something about the component parts of foods and how they are digested and used in the body.

Food is found in many forms and must be broken down so that the body can absorb it and then reform it into a state that it can use. For example, carbohydrate is converted into simple sugars, which can easily be absorbed and then used for energy.

We need food for various reasons:

- to form new body cells for general growth
- to repair any damaged body cells
- to provide us with energy:
  to maintain body temperature
  for all muscle movements.

DIGESTION

Food enters the body and travels through the alimentary tract (digestive system), a long hollow tube stretching from the mouth to the anus. Different parts of the tube perform different functions and may differ in shape. Food travels along the tube by peristalsis, a muscular churning action which pushes the food onward.

There are two types of digestion.

1. Mechanical. The breaking down of food by teeth and peristaltic action which grinds it into a soup-like consistency.

2. Chemical. At various stages in the alimentary tract fluids called enzymes mix with the food and cause chemical reactions which split complex food into simple forms (see page 58).

Once food is broken down it can be absorbed through the walls of the small intestine and blood vessels into the bloodstream. From there it is taken to the liver where it is re-formed into substances which the body can use and distributed by means of the bloodstream to wherever it is needed. The parts of food which cannot be digested, for example, fibre or roughage, collect in the lower part of the large intestine (rectum) and when sufficient in amount are excreted through the anus as faeces. This usually occurs every twenty-four to forty-eight hours. All the time that the residue of food remains in the large intestine water is being absorbed from it, so if there is a delay in emptying the rectum the waste products become firmer and harder and, when eventually evacuated, painful. This is known as constipation.

Digestion takes place all the time and the whole process is delicately balanced and synchronised. We feel hunger when the stomach is empty – usually about four hours after a meal. This gives us an appetite for food. When food is anticipated by the sound of preparations, the smell of cooking and the sight of a meal, saliva is produced in the mouth, ready to start the digestive process, and the stomach, too, produces its enzymes. An increased blood supply is needed by the stomach to give it the extra energy to cope with the meal. If the body is involved in other strenuous activities when digestion in the stomach is taking place, the extra blood supply is not available and indigestion may follow. For example, if a child is jigging up and down in his chair, or if he is seriously worried about his ability to eat his 'nice' dinner, any extra energy will be used up in these activities instead.

It is, therefore, best to eat at regular intervals, approximately four to six hourly. A quiet period before a meal to relax and anticipate, and a calm, unhurried atmosphere during the meal aid good digestion. Meals should be attractive and well presented, with a contrast of colour and texture, and meal times should be enjoyable, social occasions.

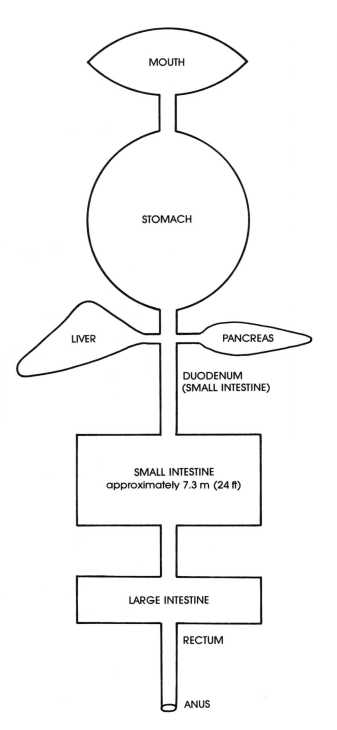

Mouth:
a) teeth – break down food;
b) tongue – rolls food into ball;
c) saliva – starts digestion of carbohydrates.

Stomach – churns food:
a) hydrochloric acid – renders food acid; kills some germs;
b) rennin – clots milk; starts digestion of milk;
c) pepsin – starts protein digestion.

Liver – bile sent to duodenum; digests fats.

Pancreas – enzymes to digest carbohydrates and fats.

Small intestine:
a) enzymes to complete digestion of starch and protein;
b) absorption of broken-down food.

Large intestine:
a) absorption of water;
b) excretion of waste products.

TYPES OF FOOD

There are many different types of food or nutrients and the student must know the classification of foods and what each type does in the body. The charts on the following pages provide a summary.

This may look a formidable list, but a study of the main sources of the nutrients will show that most people eat most of the foods mentioned. There are many fads and customs about diet, but nutritionists and dietitians generally agree that mixed diets are best. When religion forbids the eating of certain foods then alternative sources of the nutrient are usually found, so that the diet is balanced. If children are offered a wide variety of foods, they will instinctively choose a diet which is best for them, provided they have not been given an excess of sugar early in life and so developed a craving for sweetness.

It is possible to measure the *energy content* of food and this is expressed in kilojoules or the more familiar calories. We can estimate the amount of energy needed by a person, taking age, sex and occupation into account. Again, this can be expressed in kilojoules.

You will see from the charts that the main energy-giving foods are fats and carbohydrates. It is possible to use protein as an energy source as well, but this is very wasteful of an expensive resource. We know from research that a certain amount of protein is necessary, varying according to a person's age. For example, a young baby will need a high proportion of protein in his diet because he is growing rapidly and needs material for new body cells. On the other hand a person in middle age will need only enough protein for repair of wear and tear.

So diets are planned by first calculating a person's protein requirements in kilojoules, and then making up the rest of kilojoules by adding fruit and vegetables, fats and carbohydrates, making sure that enough fibre, vitamins and minerals are included.

However, if a person eats enough food to feel satisfied, and remains healthy with a static weight, then he must be having a satisfactory diet.

Name	Some main sources	Function	Effect of too little	Notes
Protein a) Animal proteins	meat fish eggs cheese milk	1. To build new body cells for growth; 2. to repair wear and tear in body cells.	1. poor growth and development; 2. poor healing powers. *Extreme* kwashiorkor – death. If early in life when brain is developing rapidly, may prevent child reaching his intellectual potential	Made up of any combination of 22 amino-acids, 8 of which are essential to humans. Excess protein is used as energy source or excreted in urine.
b) Vegetable proteins	soya bean peas beans lentils nuts			a) Contain all 8 essential amino-acids. b) Contain only some of the 8 essential amino-acids so good variety must be eaten.
Carbohydrate	foods containing sugar and cereals	To provide energy and heat.	1. lack of energy; 2. thinness; 3. feel cold.	Excess is stored as body fat.

Name	Some main sources	Function	Effect of too little	Notes
Fat	lard olive oil butter cheese nuts meat fat margarine	1. To provide energy and heat; 2. to carry fat-soluble vitamins; 3. to form padding in body; for example around kidney; 4. to make food more palatable.	1. lack of energy; 2. feel cold; 3. thinness; 4. vitamin A and D deficiency.	
Minerals Iron	liver eggs chocolate meat	Forms haemoglobin in red blood cells which carry oxygen around body.	anaemia: pallor; breathlessness; lack of energy.	
Calcium	milk cheese butter bread flour	1. To build strong bones and teeth; 2. aids clotting of blood when injured; 3. to aid normal working of muscles.	1. rickets (bones fail to harden); 2. dental caries; 3. delayed blood clotting; 4. cramp in muscles.	Works together with vitamin D and phosphorus.
Phosphorus	milk cheese fish oatmeal	1. To help build strong bones and teeth; 2. needed for the formation of body enzymes and all body tissue.		Deficiency rarely occurs alone because calcium will also be deficient.
Iodine	sea foods water supply vegetables may be added to salt	Aids working of the thyroid gland which regulates use of food in body.	*Adult* – goitre – enlarged thyroid gland. *Baby* – cretin.	
Sodium chloride (salt)	added to food kippers bacon	To maintain concentration of blood.	cramp in muscles	Excess: thirst; dehydration.
Fluoride	water supply: may be present naturally or added artificially.	To combine with calcium in teeth so making enamel more resistant to decay.	dental caries.	
Zinc	meat and dairy products breast milk infant formulae milks	Needed for growth and healing wounds. Helps activity of enzymes.	*Mild* – poor growth; poor healing. *Severe* – skin rashes; disturbances in the brain, gut and immune system.	Absorption reduced – when large amounts of dietary fibre eaten or when lead pollution or tobacco smoke present in the air.

Name	Some main sources	Function	Effect of too little	Notes
Potassium	cereals	Needed for growth.		
Copper	yeast meat eggs	Not fully understood.	brittle bones bleeding from mouth	
Vitamins A fat soluble	milk butter cheese cod liver oil margarine	1. To promote growth; 2. aid to healthy skin; 3. prevention of poor night vision.	1. retarded growth; 2. poor resistance to infection especially skin infections; 3. poor night vision. *Severe* – blindness; thickening of horny layers of skin.	
Carotene (red and yellow vegetables and fruit)	carrots tomatoes apricots mango			Humans can make vitamin A from carotene.
B (group) water soluble	yeast Marmite wheatgerm milk meat green vegetables	1. To aid healthy working of muscles and nerves; 2. to aid conversion of carbohydrate to energy and iron to haemoglobin.	1. wasting of muscles; 2. loss of appetite; 3. digestive disturbances; 4. anaemia etc.	There are at least 9 'B' vitamins.
C water soluble	oranges lemons blackcurrants green vegetables kiwi fruit	1. To act as 'cement' for bone, skin and blood; 2. to aid resistance to infection.	1. scurvy (bleeding under skin, gums); 2. poor resistance to infection.	Easily destroyed by heat.
D fat soluble	milk butter cream egg yolk margarine cod liver oil sunlight	To combine with calcium for bone and teeth formulation.	1. rickets – bones fail to harden; 2. dental decay.	Vitamin D can be made in skin by the action of sunlight on substance in skin.
Water	present in all foods	Makes up 70 per cent of body tissue. Necessary for all the workings of the body and to help eliminate waste products.	thirst; constipation; dehydration; death	

Name	Some main sources	Function	Effect of too little	Notes
Fibre	cell walls of vegetables (cellulose) apples celery bran wholemeal bread brown rice	Helps digestion by adding bulk to food which stimulates peristalsis.	constipation; diverticulitis; possibly bowel cancer.	

Nursery nurses are not expected to be experts but they do need to know how to plan a suitable diet. The following is a useful guide to the daily needs of adults and children. Starting with a basic amount of protein for the average adult, fruit and vegetables are added and then the energy requirements are made up by adding carbohydrate and fats. Obviously a manual-worker will need more energy-giving foods than a clerk but both will have the same basic protein requirements. Pregnant women, adolescent children and children under seven need extra protein because of their growth requirements. A child under seven in fact needs more protein than his father.

Daily food needs of an adult:

Protein
285 ml (½ pint) milk
1 egg
28 g (1 oz) cheese   } any 3 items of
56-84 g (2-3 oz) fish   } protein (3 of
serving of nuts, peas, beans } one kind or one
  or lentils   } each of 3)
50-100 g (2-4 oz) meat
570 ml (1 pint) water

Fruit and vegetables
orange
grapefruit   } any 3 servings
apple   } of fruit and
potato   } vegetables
swede, carrot, cabbage

Carbohydrates
Sugar and preserves – enough to make food palatable. Cereals – flour, bread, cake, etc. – variable according to energy needs and appetite.

Fats
Enough to make food palatable.

Pregnant women will need extra protein, calcium, iron and vitamins. Therefore add to normal adult diet: 570 ml (1 pint) milk, 1 egg, 1 orange, vitamin A and D tablets, iron tablets (if prescribed by a doctor).

Women who are breast-feeding need a very high calory diet, including extra fluids, protein, calcium and vitamins. Therefore add to normal adult diet: 570 ml (1 pint) milk, vitamin A and D tablets.

FEEDING CHILDREN UNDER SEVEN YEARS

The very rapid rate of growth during the first year of life means that small babies need a large amount of protein in their diet. They also need some carbohydrate and fat for energy, some calcium and all the vitamins.

Breast-feeding

All a baby's nutritional requirements can most easily be provided during the first four to six months by breast milk with the addition of vitamin A, D and C drops. From four months onwards the baby also needs iron, which can be provided by the addition of other foods such as egg yolk, liver and meat during the weaning period.

Breast milk is ideal for babies; not only does it contain almost all the nutrients they need, but the protein contains all the essential amino-acids in the correct proportion for the human body. Breast milk is therefore easily absorbed, and easily digested. There are many other advantages to breast-feeding, which can be listed as follows:

- The carbohydrate in breast milk is in the form of lactose, which is not sweet to taste, so avoids the danger of the baby developing a craving for sugar.
- The milk is unlikely to be contaminated, as it comes straight from mother to baby.
- Breast milk is at the correct temperature.
- It is economical.
- Very little preparation is required.
- Breast milk contains protective antibodies and vitamins which help protect the baby from infection.
- There is evidence to suggest that a breast-fed baby is protected from developing an allergy.
- Breast-feeding gives the ideal mother and baby contact which aids 'bonding' and therefore the baby's emotional development.
- The baby must suck vigorously in order to obtain milk and this helps good jaw development.
- Breast-feeding helps the mother's figure to return to normal by causing the uterus to contract more rapidly.
- Breast-fed babies very rarely develop obesity.
- It is impossible to over feed the baby because he will either vomit the excess or get rid of it in frequent loose stools.

The majority of mothers could breast-feed their babies if they wished. However there may be problems in the beginning and the mother will need encouragement and help to establish good breast-feeding. During the antenatal period it is important for the positive aspects of breast-feeding to be emphasised, so that the mother has an optimistic approach to the subject.

The breasts are usually examined by the midwife early in pregnancy to ensure that the nipple formation is satisfactory and so that problems such as inversion can be corrected as early as possible. Most normal babies will turn instinctively to the breast and suck and, if the mother is relaxed all she need do is guide her baby to her nipple. Problems arise if the mother becomes tense and anxious, because this will be communicated to her baby.

Occasionally the baby may be sleepy and uninterested during the first few days. Problems may then arise because the flow of milk is stimulated by vigorous sucking. Other problems which can occur include poor nipple formation, sore nipples and a temporary excess or shortage of milk. Although the baby is put to the breast soon after birth, the milk does not appear immediately. At first a fluid called colostrum is produced. This is very valuable to the baby as it contains many antibodies. About the second or third day the mother may experience discomfort as the milk 'comes in'. Expert help is usually given in maternity units and most problems can be overcome. By the time the mother leaves the care of the midwife, feeding by bottle or breast should be well established. The baby may be fed on demand or at regular intervals of three to four hours, throughout the day and night.

The feed in the middle of the night is usually discontinued by the baby himself at about four to six weeks of age when he can take enough milk during the day to last all night.

Requirements for breast-feeding
- low, comfortable chair;
- a drink for the mother;
- a tray containing bowl of water, swabs in jar with lid, container for soiled swabs, soft towel.

Method
1) The baby's nappy should be changed and he should be made comfortable.
2) The mother should wash her hands and then clean her nipples with swabs and water, drying them carefully.

3)   She should sit comfortably with baby on her knee, leaning slightly forward and guiding the baby to her breast – a pillow on her knee under the baby may help to get him in the right position.

4)   The baby will 'fix' by opening his mouth wide and taking the nipple far back into his mouth. Sucking is a 'munching' action with the lips behind the nipple.

5)   The baby's nose should be kept free to enable him to breathe.

6)   The baby can either be offered both breasts or fed on an alternate breast at each feed. Some authorities believe that the latter method is best because the baby gets the advantage of the changing composition of the milk. Fore milk is watery to quench the baby's thirst whereas the hind milk contains more fat which is more satisfying.

A baby needs about twenty minutes sucking time but this is only a guide – there is nothing rigid about the time because most babies come off the breast when they have had enough. However new mothers often feel happier if they have some guidance. A pause is needed after the first ten minutes, and when feeding is complete, in order to bring up any air (wind) swallowed with the food. To bring up baby's wind: either, support him sitting on your knee by placing one hand on his tummy then use the other hand to rub his back gently until he 'burps'; or, put the baby over your shoulder and gently rub his back.

Signs of adequate feeding

Most mothers worry about whether the baby is getting enough milk, but there are several pointers which indicate that he is satisfied:

- He will be contented.
- He will gain weight steadily at the rate of 115–225 g (4–8 oz) a week.
- His stools (faeces) will be soft, yellow and inoffensive, and may be infrequent. (This is because there is very little residue from breast milk.)

Signs of underfeeding

- Misery – the baby may cry a lot and will probably wake one to two hours after a feed.

- The baby will look anxious and worried.
- The weight gain will be small – under 56 g (2 oz) a week.
- His stools will be small and dry and may be green.
- He may become too lethargic to cry.

Test weighing

If there is any doubt about the adequacy of the feeds then the amount of each feed can be measured by test weighing. The baby is weighed just before his feed and then immediately after, without changing clothes or nappy. Subtract the first weight from the second and this will give you the amount of milk taken. To be accurate this should be recorded over twenty-four hours and averaged out.

Average requirements

For estimating a baby's food requirements, use the following formula:

2½ fl oz milk per pound body weight over 24 hours; or 150 ml milk per kilogram body weight over 24 hours.

For example:

A 4.5 kg baby needs:
   675 ml per 24 hours = 5 feeds of 135 ml (may be rounded up to 140 ml)

A 10 lb baby needs:
   25 fl oz per 24 hours = 5 feeds of 5 oz

Some babies will require up to 25 ml (1 fl oz) more in each feed to satisfy them.

Insufficient milk

If the baby is not getting enough breast milk, then the first thing to do is to reassure the mother that this often happens for a temporary period and that it is possible to increase the milk supply by various measures:

a) Feeds should be offered more frequently provided the mother's nipples are not sore.

b) A check should be made to ensure that the baby is 'fixing' properly and therefore sucking effectively.

c) Ensure that the mother is getting plenty of rest and not having too many visitors. Provide domestic help, if possible.

d) Encourage mother to eat a good diet and drink at least two pints of fluid a day – this can be milk, beer, tea, hot chocolate etc.

e) The baby can be offered extra milk (of the proprietary kind sold for bottle-feeding) at the end of each feed either by spoon or bottle. But he should continue to be put to the breast to suck as this stimulates the milk production. This is known as complementary feeding or 'topping-up' and hopefully the baby will reject it when the breast milk supply increases.

Some mothers find they can continue to breast-feed if they substitute a bottle for one feed a day. Other mothers, such as those returning to work, manage to keep up breast-feeding by feeding once or twice a day only, with the child-minder bottle-feeding at other times. It really doesn't matter what proportion of bottle milk to breast milk a baby has providing he continues to gain weight. However if he does not thrive it may be necessary to change completely to bottle-feeding. If a change from breast-feeding to bottle-feeding is decided upon, then it should be achieved gradually by substituting one bottle for one breast-feed each day until the baby is having all feeds by bottle. The mother's breast milk will then dry up naturally as the baby ceases sucking.

Artificial or bottle-feeding

Some mothers are unable to produce enough milk for their babies, especially in the case of twins; other mothers do not wish to breast-feed at all, so that a substitute has to be found. The word 'substitute' is used deliberately, because even in this modern age, we cannot make a perfect copy of breast milk.

Most artificial feeds are based on cow's milk because this is readily available. If we compare the composition of cow's milk with breast milk we notice several differences. (The percentages are approximate.)

		Breast milk %	Cow's milk %
Protein {	Casein	1	3.4
	Lactalbumin	1	0.5
Sugar		7	4.0
Fat		3.5	3.5
Mineral salts		0.2	0.7
Water		87.3	87.9

The main differences are in the protein, sugar and mineral salt content. The protein is not only increased in amount in cow's milk but there is a change in proportions. Instead of equal small amounts of casein and lactalbumin there is three times the amount of casein and the lactalbumin is reduced by half. As casein is a difficult protein to digest, this amount may cause problems to a baby.

For many years babies were fed on cow's milk modified in the following way:

Water was added to dilute the protein, the milk mixture was boiled to make the casein more digestible and sterilise the milk, and finally cane sugar was added to make the sugar content similar to that of breast milk. The mineral salt content was ignored, as it was thought that the baby could excrete any excess. When dried milk was introduced, the milk was modified in a similar way before being dried – the drying process helped to break up the casein and rendered it germ-free so that it could be kept for a much longer period. Some dried milk had some of the fat content removed and was known as 'half cream' milk, which was suitable for very small babies. Evaporated milk was also used, with similar modifications.

The next development in baby feeding was the introduction of 'humanised' milks, which were spray-dried instead of roller-dried as in the past. The result was more like breast milk, with a finer curd and therefore more easily digested. Being spray-dried, the milk powder was much easier to mix with water. These milks had vitamins and iron added as well, but the natural mineral content remained the same as straight cow's milk.

However, the majority of babies thrived on ordinary dried milks, which for many years were thought to be satisfactory substitutes for breast milk. But in the early 1970s research began to suggest that young babies' kidneys have only a limited ability to get rid of excess mineral salts. Furthermore, some have even less ability than others. If the kidneys cannot excrete excess mineral salts, the body gradually becomes overloaded and this imbalance can cause illness in susceptible babies.

To avoid these problems it was recommended in a government report in 1976 that all babies under six weeks of age should be fed on breast milk or milk with a low mineral salt content. Humanised milks were rapidly adapted so that the mineral salt content was the same as in breast milk. These milks include SMA (Gold Top), Osterfeed and Premium Cow and Gate and, in practice, most babies stay on these milks until they are fully weaned. However, a few babies seem dissatisfied with these milks because they are so rapidly digested, in which case Cow and Gate Baby Milk Plus or SMA (white cap) may be better alternatives, because they are designed to stay in the stomach longer. A baby's feed can be made by the method below. But it is always most important to follow the manufacturers' instructions.

Requirements
a) milk powder and scoop;
b) a container of sterilising fluid in which is immersed:
   i) wide-necked feeding bottle; ii) screw collar and cap; iii) 2 teats; iv) 1 plastic spatula.

For cleaning bottle after use:
c) a bottle brush;
d) detergent;
e) salt.

NB: Milk is an ideal medium for the growth of germs so cleanliness is essential to prevent infection. Dried milk should be kept in a covered container in a cool place. All equipment must be cleaned and sterilised to kill germs, and hands must be washed before making up the feed.

Preparation
1. Fill kettle and boil.
2. Read instructions on packet (for amounts see page 64).
3. Remove bottle from sterilising unit.
4. Rinse bottle and teat with boiled water.
5. Pour correct amount of boiled water into the bottle.
6. Cover with lid and screw top.
7. Cool to body temperature by holding under running cold water.
8. Measure and add correct number of scoops of powder to bottle – make sure all measures are levelled off with the spatula. The powder should not be packed down in the scoop.
9. Replace lid and screw top on bottle.
10. Shake gently until powder and water are mixed.

The milk made in this way should be at the correct temperature for the baby. Put the teat on the bottle, then check temperature by allowing a few drops of milk to fall on your wrist. It should feel pleasantly warm. If cold, the feed can be warmed up by standing the bottle in a bowl of hot water; if too hot, then cooled in a bowl of cold water. If need be, enough bottles can be made up to last twenty-four hours. They should be stored in a refrigerator and can be warmed up when required, as described above, or in a bottle 'warmer'. They should not be warmed in a microwave oven because the liquid tends to heat unevenly, so could inadvertently cause scalding. Some hospitals do not consider it necessary to warm milk and routinely give bottles at room temperature.

Immediately after the feed has been given, the bottle and other utensils should be cleaned and sterilised by the following method:

Cleaning
1. Pour away any remaining milk.
2. Rinse bottle and teat, outside and inside, under cold-water tap.
3. Wash all utensils in hot detergent solution using a bottle brush for the bottle.
4. Clean teat by turning inside-out and rubbing with salt (removes milk film).
5. Rinse all utensils again in cold water.

Sterilising
6. Immerse all utensils in a solution of one part sodium hypochlorite to eighty parts of water.
7. Make sure all equipment, including teats, is immersed in the fluid.
8. Cover and leave for at least one and a half hours or until needed.
9. The solution needs to be changed every twenty-four hours or it will lose its effectiveness.

(*NB:* Metal should not be sterilised in this way as it will rust.)

There are many brands of sterilising fluid containing sodium hypochlorite on the market and it may be obtained in liquid, crystal or tablet form. Follow the directions given on the packet for making up the correct solution. In an emergency, when a sterilised bottle is needed urgently, utensils can be sterilised by boiling. All utensils except the teat should be immersed in a saucepan of cold water, brought to the boil, and boiled for ten minutes. The teats should

be added for the last minute of boiling. A lid should be used on the saucepan and the pan should remain covered until its contents are needed.

In recent years other methods of sterilising bottles have been devised e.g. there is a steam steriliser on the market which does work very efficiently but is expensive. Despite claims in advertisements, a microwave oven is not suitable for this job because it heats fluids unevenly so may leave small areas unsterilised.

Method of giving a bottle feed
A spare sterile teat should be available in a covered container in case the one in use becomes blocked.
1. Baby's nappy should be changed and he should be made comfortable.
2. The mother/nurse should wash her hands.
3. The mother/nurse should sit comfortably and cuddle the baby as if she were breast-feeding.
4. Check temperature of milk and flow from teat.
5. Introduce the teat into the baby's mouth, holding the bottle up to ensure that the teat remains full of milk.
6. If the baby sucks the teat flat, then remove teat and allow air into bottle.
7. Halfway through feed remove bottle and 'wind' the baby as for breast-feeding and again at end of feed.

The feed should take ten to fifteen minutes and it is usually given four-hourly, as in breast-feeding.

Problems which may occur
a) The baby takes too long to feed or refuses to feed:
  i) Teat hole may be too small – enlarge by using a sterilised darning needle or try a different shaped teat.
  ii) The baby's nose may be blocked – medical aid.
  iii) The baby may be ill – medical aid.
b) The baby wakes and cries after one or two hours:
  i) The baby may be thirsty – offer boiled water.
  ii) The baby may be hungry – offer boiled water and at next feed increase milk by 25 ml (1 oz).

Vitamin supplement. All babies need extra vitamin A, D and C, usually given in the form of drops.

Water. Extra cool boiled water should be offered between feeds, especially during hot weather.

Fruit juice. If a baby is given the correct daily dosage of vitamin drops he does not need fruit juice. The proprietary brands sold for babies invariably contain sugar in one form or another so should be avoided. When checking the contents of these juices remember that dextrose, glucose, fructose, lactose, honey and sucrose are all *sugars*. If fruit juice is given it should be in the form of freshly-squeezed orange juice or pure fruit juice diluted with at least six times the amount of boiled cooled water.

Weaning

This means the gradual change over from milk to mixed diet, as in family meals. Fashions change and in the past have gone from one extreme to the other. Babies have been suddenly weaned at nine months, or gradually from two weeks onwards. However, most babies are found to be ready for extra food around three to four months and they thrive best if there is a gradual transition from milk to mixed feeding. Between three and four months the baby will be waking early for feeds and if he is given extra milk it will not satisfy him. He should not, in any case, be given more than 230 ml (8 fl oz) – a bottleful – at each feed.

It is necessary to start weaning a breast-fed baby by four months because the baby's stock of iron, obtained from his mother before birth, is being used up and breast milk does not contain enough iron to make up for this. Bottle-fed babies do have the advantage of iron being added to humanised dried milk. By about five to six months the baby is beginning to chew, whether he has teeth or not, so, at that age, he should be given food to chew on.

Methods of weaning vary, but there are several important points to remember: (see also chart opposite)

a) Start gradually by offering just one teaspoon of sieved food before one of the baby's feeds – 10 a.m., 2 p.m. or 6 p.m.

b) If he refuses, try giving some of his milk first and then the 'taste'.

c) Use a plastic spoon as this is softer to his gums.

d) Preferably give savoury foods, rather than sweet, to encourage a liking for savoury flavours.

e) Food containing iron should be introduced early, e.g. bone broth, egg yolk, chocolate, liver.

f) Once he has accepted the 'taste' at one feed time, introduce another 'taste' at another feed time, and then a third taste, so that he is having solids at 10 a.m., 2 p.m. and 6 p.m.

g) Then gradually increase and vary the solid food.

h) If baby refuses, leave for three to four days and then start again.

i) Do not introduce more than one new food at a time, so that if baby is upset, the cause will be obvious and the offending food can be avoided for a couple of weeks.

j) As soon as baby begins making chewing movements (between five and six months) whether he has teeth or not, introduce more solid food to his diet – that is, mashed instead of sieved, and hard rusks to chew.
   NB: Do not leave him alone with a rusk, as he may break off a piece and choke on it.

k) As soon as he is willing and keen, give him a spoon and let him try to feed himself. Food should be in small pieces rather than mashed, so that he can use his fingers and/or spoon easily. He should also be introduced to a cup when ready.

Stage	*6 a.m.*	*8 a.m.*	*10 a.m.*	*12 midday*	*2 p.m.*	*4 p.m.*	*6 p.m.*	*10 p.m.*
	milk		milk vitamin drops		milk		milk	milk
1 (4 months)	milk		milk vitamin drops		milk		1 teaspoon dinner milk	milk
2	milk		1 teaspoon breakfast milk vitamin drops		milk		1 teaspoon dinner milk	milk
3	milk		1 teaspoon breakfast milk vitamins		1 teaspoon dinner milk		1 tablespoon 'tea' milk	milk
4 (5 months)	milk		1 tablespoon breakfast milk vitamins		dinner + fruit juice in cup		1 tablespoon 'tea' milk	milk
5 (6-7 months)	fruit juice or water in cup	breakfast milk		dinner + fruit juice in cup		'tea' milk	milk at bedtime	
6 (9 months)	fruit juice or water	breakfast milk in cup	fruit	dinner + juice in cup		'tea' milk in cup	milk at bedtime	

Stages in weaning
Milk = milk from breast or bottle. Each stage may take from 3 days to 2 weeks.

Suitable food for weaning
Note: In the menus listed below a *choice* of suitable foods is given.

3-5½ months: All home-cooked food should be put through a 'baby-mouli' or liquidiser to make it a smooth semi-liquid mixture. No extra salt should be added, as babies need very little salt and too much can cause problems. Tins or jars of strained baby food, or packets of freeze-dried foods for weaning, are useful at this stage because of the small amounts needed. But they are expensive, and eventually the baby must get used to home cooking, so the sooner he does so the better.

Breakfast (10 a.m. feed): baby cereal – milk (no added sugar), egg yolk (lightly boiled), mashed banana, fruit purée (apple/apricot/prune), tin or jar strained baby food;
Dinner (2 p.m. feed): bone and vegetable broth, finely chopped meat from a roast joint – potato – gravy, steamed kidney, liver, white fish, braised steak, tin or jar strained 'dinner'; mixed vegetables.
Tea (6 p.m. feed): egg custard, milk pudding, cauliflower cheese, grated cheese on cereal, fruit purée or egg yolk (not the same as breakfast).

5½-8 months (from the time baby begins to chew): stop making food into purée – mash it instead.

Breakfast: as above, or: scrambled egg, Weetabix, porridge, crisp bacon, crisply fried bread, mashed sardines;

Dinner: as family: minced or chopped meat, chicken or bacon plus vegetables, steamed white fish plus vegetables, 'junior' tin or jar dinner, followed by fruit purée;

Tea: rusks, sandwiches – Marmite, egg, flesh of tomato, grated cheese, plain sponge cake, jelly, bread, jelly jam, honey, any tin or jar 'junior' supper;

8 months onwards: 'finger' food. Change to cow's milk.

Breakfast: as above; may need two courses, i.e. cereal and egg, whole boiled egg with toast fingers;

Dinner: as above, plus salad vegetables cut small;

Tea: as above, cheese on toast, wholemeal bread, tinned fish e.g. sardine in sandwiches.

Under 1 year: Avoid food which is very salty, i.e. salt bacon, kippers. Avoid highly-seasoned food such as curry. Avoid food containing pips.

Diet from one year

From about one year of age children's growth slows down and their appetite becomes less. It is important to ensure that their diet contains enough protein for growth, extra calcium and vitamin D for their bones and teeth, and A, B and C vitamins for good health. Therefore we should avoid giving too much sugary food or carbohydrate and fibre as this can destroy their appetite for the essential foods. The menus below are an example of a good selection of meals for a child of this age.

Two new forms of malnutrition in children are causing considerable problems:

1. 'Muesli-belt kids'. These children appear to be very underweight and sickly and serve to illustrate the problems when parents believe all they read about diet and apply it to their children. They are often fed on a vegetarian diet containing a large amount of high-fibre foods (hence muesli) and skimmed or semi-skimmed milk. This is an ideal diet for the overweight executive, but disastrous for a child. Children need fat because it contains the fat-soluble vitamins A and D which are essential for good growth and health. Fat also provides the energy a child needs in a fairly concentrated form. In addition high-fibre food is very filling but not nutritious, so it leaves little room for other necessary foods.

Early morning	Breakfast	Mid-morning (if wanted)	Dinner	Tea	Bedtime (if wanted)
fresh orange juice	Weetabix and milk boiled egg toast fingers milk	milk	minced beef and gravy mashed potato carrot apple water to drink	cauliflower cheese pieces of orange sponge cake milk or milky tea	milk or hot chocolate
tomato juice	porridge toast and jam milk	milk	liver and bacon casserole potato chopped cabbage fruit jelly water to drink	sandwiches wholemeal bread grated cheese Madeira cake banana milk	milk
fresh orange juice	crisply grilled bacon fried bread toast milk	milk	chicken supreme with rice pieces of orange other fruit water to drink	salad with grated cheese carrot, chopped lettuce and tomato wholemeal bread and butter	milk

2. Children fed on 'junk' food. These children are fed on a diet that consists mainly of crisps, sweets, cola-type drinks or orange squash, chips, tinned spaghetti in tomato sauce, sausages, cheaper beefburgers and fish-fingers. The biggest problem with this type of food is that it is loaded with sugar which leads to a craving for more and a reduction in appetite for meat, vegetables, fruit etc. that make up a healthy diet. Children fed on this diet are sometimes said to be hyperactive, but if you feed a child too much sugar he will have a lot of energy to use up. Excess sugar is the major cause of dental decay and of obesity. In addition a diet like this will inevitably lead to anaemia and lowered resistance to infection.

Special diets

From time to time a nursery nurse will have in her care a child on a special diet. Sometimes the child will be unable to eat certain foods because of the family's beliefs, which must be respected. In other cases the child may be suffering from a disease which can be controlled by a special diet or by avoiding certain foods. Whatever the reason, it is important for the nursery nurse to know from his mother exactly what the child can or cannot eat. *All staff at the nursery or school must be aware of this diet so that no mistakes are made.*

A vegetarian diet. The term 'vegetarian' has various meanings so it is essential to find out what is meant when the parents of a child say they are vegetarian. In some cases, the family simply does not eat meat, but others are true 'vegans' and do not eat any animal products at all.

If a child must not eat meat, then meals provide few problems because meat protein can be replaced by using eggs, cheese and milk or a mixture of vegetable proteins. But, in the case of the true vegan with his restricted diet the biggest problem is to ensure that there is enough protein for growth and sufficient iron and vitamin B12 for the maintenance of good health. Children need more of these nutrients than adults because of the large amount of growth which takes place. In non-vegetarian diets the easiest way to provide protein and iron is by including a mixture of meat and animal products in a child's meals. This is because proteins are made up from a selection of about twenty-two amino-acids, of which eight cannot be manufactured by the human body. These *eight essential* amino-acids are all found in meat, eggs, fish, milk and cheese. Iron is also present in meat and eggs, and vitamin B12 is found in all animal products.

Only human milk and eggs supply the essential amino-acids in the correct proportions for humans but, by giving a mixed diet containing meat and animal products, we can ensure a child gets sufficient protein for his needs. The protein which is present in vegetables, such as nuts, peas, beans and lentils is known as an incomplete protein because it only contains a selection of some of the essential amino-acids. This means that a child must eat a large amount and variety of vegetables to ensure that all the essential amino-acids are available. Iron is present in green vegetables, but it is in the form of iron oxide which is not readily absorbed by the human body. Fortunately iron is also present in bread, curry powder, cocoa, chocolate, baked beans and lentils. Most vegetarian diets provide adequate amounts of vitamins and minerals but true vegans who do not eat any animal products should supplement their diet with vitamin B12. This can be obtained from fermented soya products such as shoya or tempeh, spreads such as Barmene or Tastex, or fortified soya 'milk'. Children also need the regular dose of A, D and C vitamins. By co-operating with his mother, it is possible to ensure that a vegetarian child has a balanced and varied diet every day.

Some religious beliefs specifically forbid the eating of certain foods and these must be respected. Examples of these are:

Jewish diet. Observant Jews do not eat pork in any form and this includes food cooked in pork fat, pork sausages and bacon. An orthodox Jew will only buy his meat from a 'kosher' butcher because he knows that the animal has been killed and the meat prepared in the accepted way, according to the Talmudic ritual. Jews will not cook milk and meat together or eat them both at the same meal.

Hindu diet. Orthodox Hindus are strict vegetarians because they follow the doctrine of *Ahimsa,* believing it is wrong to kill any living animal for food. Some Hindus will eat animal products which do not involve killing, such as eggs, milk and butter. Non-vegetarians will not eat beef because the cow is considered a sacred animal

Muslim diet. Muslims will not eat pork or pork products and only meat that has been ritually slaughtered is *halal* (permitted by Islamic law). Any food containing animal fat or cooked in animal fat which is not *halal* is also forbidden. Fish is permitted (except fish without fins or scales) – it is seen as having died naturally when taken out of the water. Alcohol is forbidden.

Sikh diet. Sikhs will not eat any meat killed the *halal* way. Other dietary restrictions are a matter of conscience and individual religious belief but some Sikhs may be vegetarian. Some do not eat eggs because they are the source of life. Very few non-vegetarian Sikhs would eat beef. Alcohol is forbidden.

Rastafarian diet. Most Rastafarians are vegetarians and the strictly orthodox do not eat eggs or dairy foods. Pork and unscaled fish are never eaten. If the baby is not breast-fed, then he will have to be fed on a 'milk' made from soya bean. Vitamin D, iron and vitamin B12 may be insufficient, so these children and their mothers should be checked regularly to ensure they are not becoming anaemic or suffering from a vitamin deficiency.

Some children need to be on a diet for medical reasons:

A gluten-free diet. A child suffering from coeliac disease is invariably on this diet, because his bowel is unable to digest gluten, which is the protein in flour and many other cereals. Whenever he eats gluten he suffers from diarrhoea, sickness and loss of weight, so all foods containing gluten must be excluded from his diet. Cakes, bread and biscuits, etc., should be made from gluten-free flour. Manufactured foods which are gluten-free are now specially labelled with a symbol representing a crossed-out ear of wheat, so that they are easy to identify.

A diabetic diet. A child suffering from diabetes has difficulty in converting carbohydrate into energy because he does not produce enough insulin. To correct this deficiency, insulin is usually given daily by injection and the amount of carbohydrate in the diet is carefully balanced to the amount of insulin. The diet *must* be adhered to – both the timing of meals and the amount of food are important. The child must eat his meals at the time prescribed following his injection of insulin, and all food must be measured and weighed out exactly.

Diet for phenylketonuria. A child suffering from this defect is unable to make use of the amino-acid phenylalanine, which builds up in the brain, causing damage leading to mental retardation. If this condition is discovered early enough, and the child put on a diet low in phenylalanine whilst his brain is developing, then the damage is avoided. Unfortunately, most proteins contain phenylalanine, so that much of the child's food must be specially manufactured and is obtainable only on a doctor's prescription from a chemist.

Diet for galactosaemia. This is a similar condition to phenylketonuria, but in this case the affected child cannot use galactose, which is a type of sugar. Again specially manufactured foods, with a low galactose content, are necessary.

Diet for cystic fibrosis. This disease affects the chest and pancreas. Excessively sticky mucus is produced and causes problems in the lungs. Mucus also blocks the tube carrying enzymes from the pancreas, and this means that some digestion, especially that of fats, cannot take place. The child is usually given a low-fat diet and, in addition, may be prescribed pancreatin – an extract of pancreatic enzymes – to be given daily before meals.

Diet for the overweight child. A child who is overweight should be examined by a doctor who will prescribe a diet for him, usually a low carbohydrate one, so that his meals will consist mainly of protein and vegetables. He will not be allowed snacks between meals of sweets, biscuits, crisps or sweet drinks and the sugar, bread and cake content of his diet will be reduced. Chips are usually forbidden.

This can cause him a great deal of misery at first, and a child on this sort of diet needs a good deal of support and encouragement. Meals should be colourful and interesting with plenty of varied vegetables to fill up his plate. Sometimes it helps to use a smaller plate – the meal looks bigger! He can have carrots, apples and celery in between meals and this may help to console him.

Allergies

Some children are found to be allergic to certain foods. The commonest foods implicated are cow's milk, hen's eggs, fish, wheat and other cereals, pork, coffee and tea. They can also be allergic to additives.

Allergies usually cause the child to suffer from a reaction such as nettle rash, eczema, asthma, migraine, or abdominal pain and/or bleeding from the gastrointestinal tract. These symptoms will appear however the food is disguised but the allergy may be of a temporary nature, perhaps following an illness. A good example of this is the fact that many babies develop cow's milk intolerance following a severe attack of gastroenteritis but it usually clears up in about six months. Many Asian babies are unable to tolerate lactose in cow's milk and this is thought to be genetic in origin.

When a child is diagnosed as suffering from an allergy then the offending foods must be avoided at all costs. If the allergen is cow's milk then a substitute such as goat's milk or a fluid made from soya bean can be used. Eggs are more difficult to avoid because many cakes biscuits and puddings contain eggs but these must also be withheld.

Additives

In recent years people have begun to question whether the chemical additions to natural food are beneficial to human beings and to say that some may even be harmful. There is not a lot of evidence available to support this thesis.

Any attempts to avoid certain foods in a child's diet should be done with great care and under the supervision of a dietitian or a health visitor.

EXERCISES

Investigation
Visit a local supermarket. How far is cultural diversity reflected in foodstuffs available? Make a list of six products previously unknown to you. Find out about their origins and how they are used.

Observation
On your placement observe children eating their dinner. How far do their tastes and attitudes reflect what they experience at home? Look at the children's packed dinners brought from home. Do most of them bring what you consider to be a nourishing, well-balanced meal? What sort of tea/supper would they need to put right any deficiencies in their diet, and how substantial a meal should they be given?

Project
Plan meals for three days at a day nursery, catering for different diets.

SUGGESTIONS FOR FURTHER READING

Sylvia Close, *The Know-How of Breast-Feeding,* John Wright & Sons
Patty Fisher and Arnold Bender, *The Value of Food,* Oxford University Press
Elizabeth Norton, *Feeding Your Family,* Mills and Boon Ltd
Present Day Practice in Infant Feeding, HMSO
Vegetarianism and Infant feeding (leaflet), Vegetarian Society of UK Ltd.
Shirley Bond, *Eat and Be Fit,* Ladybird Books Ltd
Joan Huskisson, *Applied Nutrition and Dietetics,* Baillière Tindall
Louise Templeton, *The Right Food For Your Kids,* Century Hutchinson Publishing Ltd
Tim Lobstein, *Fast Food Facts,* Camden Press
A Guide to Asian Diets, Commission for Racial Equality (Elliot House, 10-11 Allington Street, London SW1E 5EH)

7 Care of the Child

BASIC NEEDS

- food
- cleanliness
- rest and sleep
- exercise
- fresh air and sunlight
- warmth
- good health
- protection from injury and infection
- security
- affection
- stimulation
- social contacts
- independence

The needs of a child remain the same at any age, but changes in emphasis and in the pattern of his daily routine will occur naturally as he grows from a passive baby to an active child. As he becomes more mature and more able, more will be expected of him, so that he gradually moves towards ultimate independence. The small baby's routine is based on his four-hourly feeds, but once weaning begins his mealtimes gradually change to come into line with those of the rest of the family. He can then become an active participant in family life. All his needs will overlap, but in the following pages they will be dealt with separately, before planning a routine to encompass them all.

Food

A child needs a mixed diet containing a wide variety of nutrients at regular intervals during the day. He should have one pint of full cream milk and extra vitamin A, D and C drops until he is five years old. He needs protein for growth and repair, calcium for bones and teeth, iron for his blood and some fats and carbohydrates for energy. However, he should not be given too much sugar, as this will affect his health adversely and give him a craving for more. If he is given snacks such as sweets or biscuits, or drinks such as lemonade or cola, between mealtimes, they can spoil his appetite for protein meals, cause his teeth to decay and make him grow too fat. If he should need something to chew between meals, then an apple or a carrot should be enough and if he is thirsty, water is the best thirst-quencher. Sweets are best given as a special treat after a meal.

From the time a baby is able to sit comfortably and steadily in a chair, he should be allowed to sit up at the table with the rest of the family. When he shows willingness, he should be given a spoon and allowed to try and feed himself. Help should be given, of course, and his food should be chopped into small pieces, rather than mashed, so that he can easily pick it up, either with his fingers or his spoon. He will make a mess at first, but gradually with practice becomes more proficient. Sitting with the rest of the family at the table will enable him to watch and to copy. A child learns by imitation and it is important to let him practise new skills when he is ready and willing, because that will be the right time for him to do so.

A baby of ten months will probably still be having a bottle-feed or a breast-feed last thing at night, and it is important that he continues this practice until he is ready to give it up. Not only is it a source of food but sucking brings comfort and satisfaction to a child. Most babies spontaneously give up this last feed some time between one year and eighteen months because they find other sources of comfort.

Until he is about a year old, a baby will eat almost all the food he is offered because he needs it for growth. But, from this age, his appetite will taper off for two reasons. First, he will no longer need as much for growth and secondly his interests will have widened, so that meals will not be as important to him as they once were. This reduction in appetite can cause much anguish in parents, and nurses too, if they do not realise it is a normal occurrence. A child is quick to sense anxiety and may take advantage of this and refuse to eat in order to draw more attention to himself. Provided he is offered a good balanced diet at mealtimes and is not given sweets and other snacks in between, he will eat what he needs. It is unnecessary to entice a child to eat, or to force food into him. It does a child a disservice to make him eat food he does not need, bearing in mind that one of the biggest problems of malnutrition in Britain at the present time is obesity. Fat children are not fit children and fat children often become fat adults. Once the habit of over-eating is established, it can be very difficult to break.

Small, attractive helpings should be offered at family mealtimes. Food should look inviting with a contrast of colour and texture. The child should sit with the family and no comment should be made on his eating. After a certain length of time his plate should be removed, whether the child has eaten or not. The atmosphere at mealtimes should be that of an enjoyable social get-together which is conducive to good digestion. A period of outdoor play before a meal will often stimulate an appetite, but there should be a quiet ten minutes just before a meal with a regular routine of handwashing and general preparation.

If a child has an actual dislike of a particular foodstuff, then it is best to present it in a different way, or provide a substitute without comment. For instance, milk can be given in the form of milk puddings, milk shakes or hot chocolate. If soft boiled eggs are disliked, try hard-boiling them, or a raw egg can be added when mashing potato. Some children prefer to eat vegetables raw rather than cooked and there is no reason at all why they should not have them that way. Nothing is gained by forcing a child to eat a hated food; the child usually wins anyway. He may vomit it, or store it in his cheeks like a hamster. One of the authors' children resorted to filling his pockets with mashed potato because otherwise he would have been made to eat it by his nursery school teacher.

Children can become very conservative in their tastes and mostly prefer familiar foods, so it is important in the early days, when they will accept it, to give a wide variety of different foods. If they are presented at three or four years of age with an unknown food, many children will automatically say they dislike it. Sometimes the problem can be overcome by suggesting that the child helps himself to a very small sample to taste.

As the child becomes more mature he can be encouraged to join in the conversation at the table. Later he will want to be involved in preparations, such as laying the table and cooking the meal. This will all add to his enjoyment of mealtimes.

When a child starts nursery school or begins having school meals, there may be difficulties at first, such as refusal to eat because it is all so strange to him. He may never have seen a properly set table before, or used a knife and fork. Some children are still being

Sometimes a helping hand is needed with lunch at nursery school

spoon-fed at three years of age because their mothers dislike mess; others may be fed separately from their family, and some children sit watching television while they eat and are not used to sitting at a table. Therefore it is important for a nursery nurse to ensure that a new child is made familiar with the arrangements and the routine of mealtime in the nursery. If this is done in a kindly way, the other children will follow her example and will assist the newcomer to settle down. Most children eagerly conform if they are shown the way.

Cleanliness

From about eight months of age, a baby should be on the floor most of his waking time, which means that he will need his daily bath more than before. Once a baby has achieved a sitting position, he makes great efforts to become mobile. He progresses from 'swimming' on the floor, to rolling over and over, crawling and creeping and later on standing and walking. By the end of the day his knees and elbows will have become very grimy and a bath in the evening is a good idea, as it not only cleans the child but also acts as a good prelude to bedtime.

Somewhere between six and ten months of age he will have graduated to the 'big bath' and this will give him more space in which to play. After a wash all over he should be allowed time to enjoy this and be able to splash around for pleasure. Toys which float, and those which sink, plastic cups and containers for scooping up water and sponges for squeezing all add to the fun of bathtime. After the bath it is important to ensure that the child is dried thoroughly, especially in all the creases, such as those between his toes.

A child should have his own towels, flannel, toothbrush, hairbrush and comb. They can be marked with a symbol which he can begin to recognise as his own, or in a family each child could have his own colour.

On waking in the morning the baby will need a 'top and tail', but when he has finished using nappies, washing his face and hands only will be sufficient. He should have clean underclothes and socks daily.

During the day, hands should be washed after using the lavatory or potty, and before meals. Nails should be kept clean and trimmed weekly. His hair should be brushed and combed daily and washed once a week, when a check should be made for the presence of nits and lice. His comb and brush should be washed at the same time as his hair.

Children often hate having their hair washed because they dislike water being splashed on their faces. The easiest way is probably to wash the hair while the child is having a bath.The head should be tipped back when rinsing, to avoid water on the face. A spray attachment is very useful for this. Use a baby shampoo because the solution will not sting if it should come in contact with the eyes.

Teeth cleaning, after meals and last thing at night, should begin as soon as a tooth appears. A soft toothbrush and a very small amount of fluoride toothpaste should be used.

All this starts to teach good habits, and as soon as a child is willing he should be encouraged to help with washing and dressing himself and cleaning his teeth. With practice he will gradually become more proficient, so that eventually he can take over these tasks himself.

Care of the teeth. Although the first teeth are only temporary, it is important to prevent them from decaying. There are several reasons for this:

- Care of the teeth forms a good habit which will continue throughout life.
- Decayed teeth cause pain.
- Painful teeth may prevent a child from eating properly.
- Painful teeth prevent a child chewing, which could adversely affect his jaw development.
- These first teeth act as 'spacers' for the permanent teeth; if a tooth has to be removed because of decay then the other teeth can close together, causing overcrowding when the second teeth come through.

Tooth decay (dental caries) is caused by plaque. Plaque is a jelly-like coating of carbohydrate debris which clings to the teeth. This coating forms an ideal medium for bacteria, because it provides food, warmth and moisture. Bacteria plus plaque produce acid, and it is the acid which attacks the tooth enamel. It gradually dissolves the hard enamel, eventually penetrating to the pulp or inner core of the tooth where the nerve endings are. There is no pain until the nerve endings are exposed. Once there is a hole, then bacteria can get into the pulp of the tooth and may cause an abscess. Usually the tooth has to be removed when it reaches this stage.

Prevention of dental caries can be tackled in several ways:

a) by making the enamel of the tooth harder and so more resistant to decay by giving fluoride by mouth;

b) by cutting down the amount and frequency of carbohydrate (especially sugar) consumed – don't let children chew sweets all day. If they must have sweets, then they should be given over a short period;

c) by giving food at four-hourly intervals only, so that teeth have a chance to 'recover' from an acid attack;

d) by cleaning off plaque thoroughly at least once a day – use a good toothbrush and brush all surfaces well;

e) by visiting the dentist regularly so that any early cavities can be detected and filled before they become big and painful.

Toilet training. This can begin as early as ten months but, in recent years a more relaxed attitude has been taken and parents are more prepared to wait until the child is 'ready' which is usually some time between two and two and a half years of age. If the child is at the right stage of development, then bowel control and daytime bladder control can often be achieved at this age in about two weeks. If there is no progress within that time then it is best to give up and try again a month later. The big advantage of starting toilet training later is that the child's speech and understanding is usually good enough to enable you to explain what you want him to do and so gain his co-operation.

A small child is anxious to please his parents or nursery nurse and will try to co-operate, so it is possible to capitalise on this. Praising the child for effort will help to increase his co-operation. A calm,

matter-of-fact attitude is best. Talk to him about what you want. Sit him on the pot for about five minutes after breakfast or at a time he usually has his bowels open. If he does perform, then praise him; if not, just dress him again. If he doesn't object, the child can be placed on the pot for about five minutes after every meal and this will then become part of his routine. Eventually he will get the message, but it does take time and patience. He will have some difficulty in 'letting go' at first, so that sometimes he will sit on the pot and do nothing and then when he stands up and relaxes, his bowels will open. This is not a deliberate action – he cannot help it. Gradually this problem is overcome as he becomes more mature.

Helpful hints:

a) Indications that he is 'ready':
   He may say 'I don't want a nappy'.
   He may remain dry in his nappy for an hour or more.
   He may say when he wants to have his bowels open.

b) Putting the child into pants may help because
   i)   it makes him feel grown up;
   ii) it is difficult for him to accept that it is now wrong to wet his nappy, when it was all right before;
   iii) when he does wet, he is aware of it, as there is no nappy to soak up the urine.

c) If he rebels against the pot, it is best to leave it alone for a week or two and then start again.

d) It is important to have the right size pot or lavatory for the child. He should be able to sit comfortably with his feet squarely on the floor.
   NB: If an adult-sized lavatory is used, then a small stool or box should be put in a position so that the child can rest his feet on it.

e) Some children are frightened of the lavatory and the flush and these fears should be respected. Others prefer to sit on the lavatory, possibly with a special seat to make the hole smaller. Boys may prefer to stand up to pass urine.

f) Clothes such as pants and trousers should be easily removed as the need to use the pot is often urgent.

Once control is achieved then the next step is teaching the child to cope with his own toilet needs.

Again, clothes should be easy for him to remove and he will need reminders and supervision. Regular visits to the lavatory should become part of his daily routine, especially after breakfast and before going to bed. Time must be allowed for this, so the morning and evening routines should not be rushed.

Toilet training should be straightforward, but problems can arise if too much is expected of a child too soon, or if the whole business is taken too seriously. A child cannot attain bowel and bladder control until his central nervous system has matured enough to let him control the muscles in his pelvic area. Just as there is a large variation in the age at which a baby can walk (nine months to two years) so there is also a variation of age at which a child controls his bowels and bladder. It is important for those in charge of children to be aware of these variations, so that they do not compare one child with another, or expect too much from individual children.

Even after a child has control, there may be accidents or setbacks. For instance, losing control of his bowels or bladder is one way in which a toddler can divert his mother's attention from the new baby. It can also be a way of annoying his mother, or asserting himself. It should also be remembered that if a person is frightened, he tends to pass urine more frequently and may get diarrhoea (this is a side effect to the production of adrenalin which is produced when a person is frightened, to enable him to fight or run away), so this may explain why children 'in care' are often incontinent.

Most children gain complete control of their bowels and day control of their bladder fairly easily, but night-time control of the bladder often takes much longer. In fact about twenty to twenty-five per cent of children still wet their beds at five years of age. However, by ten years of age, the figure is about 0.05 per cent. As so many children do still wet their beds at five it should not be considered abnormal. Unfortunately many people regard bed-wetting at three years of age as abnormal and can create problems by conveying to the child that this is 'dirty' and wrong. Children cannot make a distinction between what they do and what they are. So these children may begin to feel they are dirty and

unworthy of love. The tension and worry created by these feelings can increase bed-wetting. Threats used to induce the child to be dry only increase his fear.

In the authors' experience 'treatment' for bed-wetting before the age of seven years often increases the problem. If a child is still wetting the bed at the age of five he should be seen by a doctor, so that his urine can be tested in case there is a physical reason for wetting, such as a urinary infection (this is very rare). Apart from this, the best attitude to the child with this problem is one of optimism. Protect the mattress by continuing to use a plastic sheet on the bed. From the age of four years stop using a nappy at night. Make sure there is a light on at night so that he can see his way to the toilet – or give him his own torch to keep under his pillow. Train him to pass urine just before bedtime. Some people find it helpful to 'lift' the child and take him to the lavatory in the late evening. If this is done, then the child must be woken up completely, otherwise he is being trained to pass urine in his sleep. This may cause sleeping problems, and if it does the practice should be stopped.

An optimistic attitude from the whole family, praise for a dry bed and very little comment when it is wet will help a child gain control. However, if bed-wetting continues after six years of age then the doctor should be consulted again. The medical name for bed-wetting is enuresis and it is one of the common problems which concern parents and nursery nurses in the early years.

Other problems include sucking – thumbs, fingers or blankets, nail-biting or picking, masturbation, etc., and they will be discussed in Chapter 15.

Soiling

It can be distressing and irritating to find that after a child has mastered bowel control he begins soiling his pants every day. It might be that he is unable to clean himself properly after having his bowels open, so this child needs some help. More commonly this problem arises because he delays having his bowels open and consequently becomes constipated. The faeces becomes dry and hard and create a blockage around which liquid faeces tend to seep, thus soiling his pants.

The reason why a child delays having his bowels open could be one of the following:

a) He has much more interesting things to do, so he ignores the 'call'. After a while his rectum will stop signalling that it needs to be emptied.

b) His morning routine may be so rushed that he may not have the time or opportunity to try to have his bowels open.

c) He may have been constipated on a previous occasion and found it extremely painful when he did eventually pass the stool, so he tries to avoid this pain.

   NB: In some cases there may be a split in the anus caused by the passage of a very hard stool and this is extremely painful.

d) He may be rebelling against his mother trying to show her that he is in control and will have his bowels open in his own good time.

e) Extreme deprivation and other emotional reasons may result in soiling.

The best treatment for this problem is to give him a diet which contains extra fluids, and some fibre (porridge, prunes, vegetables and fruit) and to encourage the child to try and have his bowels open at the same time each day – usually after breakfast when the meal has caused peristalsis to increase. This can re-establish the habit of emptying his bowels at regular intervals.

If this does not work within two to three weeks or if the child appears to be in pain, then the family doctor should be consulted.

Another cause of soiling (and also smearing of faeces) may be threadworms in the child's intestine. These worms come out of the anus to lay their eggs around it and cause intense irritation. The child scratches in and around his anus and his fingers become contaminated with faeces which are wiped on his pants or anywhere else. Diagnosis is easy, as the worms can be seen in his faeces. They look like threads of cotton and when freshly passed will move around. Treatment is simple – a medicine prescribed by a doctor will kill the worms. The life cycle of these worms can be broken by ensuring that the child's hands and nails are scrubbed frequently to prevent his transferring the eggs to his mouth (see Chapter 9 on diseases).

Rest and sleep

As a baby grows he will need less sleep. By about a year he should be sleeping about thirteen hours a day, at least eleven of these hours being at night time. His daytime naps will gradually become shorter but he should still be given the opportunity for rest periods, one during the morning and another after his midday meal. If he does not want to sleep, then a quiet period in his cot with some toys will serve as a restful time for the child and for his parents or nursery nurse. From about two years the child will enjoy a story read to him or a quiet sitting period watching a suitable programme on television.

Children vary a lot in the amount and character of sleep needed. Some children catnap for short periods at intervals during the day, others need one to two hours of unbroken sleep at one time during the day. The child's routine should be adapted to allow for his particular needs.

A regular routine at bedtime is essential if the good sleeping habits established during babyhood are to continue. It also helps to give a child a feeling of continuity and security. The child should be warned in good time that bedtime is approaching and should be given ten minutes to finish his game. He can then be encouraged to help tidy up his toys and get undressed. A bath at bedtime should be a 'winding down' period which is soothing and conducive to sleep. If a final bedtime drink is part of the routine, then the child's teeth should be cleaned afterwards. Then he should be tucked into bed affectionately. A story should be read to him and his bedtime 'ritual' with favourite toy or 'cuddly', light on or off, curtains pulled back or not, etc., should be observed. He should then be left to sleep.

If he has had an interesting day, with his needs satisfied and adequate physical and mental stimulation, he should sleep well. A good test of whether he has had enough sleep is to note whether he wakes naturally in the morning. If he does not, and has to be woken, then he needs more sleep.

Unhappiness should be avoided at bedtime – if a child has been in trouble during the day, all should be forgiven before he goes to bed. Meals, especially the last one of the day, should be adequate and easily digested. A child's room and bed should be comfortable and welcoming. Never use bed as a punishment because it can cause sleep problems if a child comes to associate bed with misery.

Crying when put to bed.   This may be just a 'testing' time in which he tries to get his mother back, so wait at least five minutes before returning. Then comfort him, tuck him in and leave him to sleep.

Screaming when left in bed.   This is very difficult to deal with. Probably the best cure is to sit with him until he goes to sleep. Do this in a matter-of-fact way. Tell him you will stay and read a book or do your knitting and do just that. It is unwise to pick him up and take him downstairs, for he will come to expect that every night.

Try to find out the cause of his problems and remedy it. Sleep problems can be caused by:

a) a feeling of banishment from the rest of the family. This may be remedied by not rushing his bedtime preparations and by sitting with him for a while;

b) jealousy – there may be a new baby, or an older child who is allowed to stay up later. Extra attention during the day may help to overcome this;

c) insecurity – the worst kind of insecurity stems from having parents who are always in conflict with one another. The stability of the child's home is shattered each time they argue and he may be too frightened to go to bed in case one or other of his parents should leave while he is asleep. It is important for parents to avoid arguments in front of children. Small children respond more to the tones of voices raised in argument. What is only a small dispute to an adult can sound very frightening to a child, and keep him awake worrying. Similarly, other worries about events during the day can cause sleeping problems. Look over the child's routine and see if he needs more attention or more demonstrated affection;

d) fear of the dark – provide him with a light;

e) other fears – try to find out what they are and help overcome them. For example, if he is frightened of a large dark cupboard then take him in with you during the day and explore it together.

Bad dreams; screaming in the night.   This is fairly common and the child does not usually wake up. If he does, he cannot tell you what is wrong, so don't ask him. Just go to the child and cuddle and comfort him until he is calm and settled.

Falling out of his cot.   Once a toddler starts climbing and trying to get out of his cot he is likely to have a fall. The best remedy is to put him into a bed where, if he falls out, it will only be a small drop.

Waking in the night.   If a child wakes at night and comes into his parents' room, the best thing is for one parent to take him quietly and firmly back to his own bed and stay with him until he settles down to sleep again. This can be a wearisome task in the middle of the night and the temptation to take the child into his parents' bed is very great. But the alternative to taking the child back is to have him expecting to come into his parents' bed every night.

Early waking.   Place some toys at the bottom of his cot or bed so that when he wakes up there will be something for him to do.

Exercise

Exercise is essential for good growth and development. Muscles which are used become 'toned' up, which enables them to perform more tasks and to become more efficient. Active muscles need food and oxygen which is carried by the bloodstream. They also produce wastes (carbon dioxide and water) which are removed by the blood. Therefore active muscles increase and stimulate the circulation of blood. The presence of extra carbon dioxide in the blood stimulates respiration so that breathing deepens in order to expel it. Therefore, more oxygen is taken into the lungs and all the body benefits because increased oxygen supply leads to:

a) increased activity, especially in sweat glands, liver and kidneys;

b) improvement in appetite and digestion;

c) stimulation of nervous system resulting in clearer mental processes.

Children are naturally active creatures but they do need space, opportunity and stimulation for exercise. If a child is kept strapped in his pram all day he will at first make strenuous efforts to move, but after a time will give up his efforts and become passive. A baby should be placed on the floor for increasingly long periods of time, so that his natural curiosity will give him the impetus to become mobile. Furniture should be stable so that he can safely pull himself to his feet. Push-along trolleys, push-and-pull toys and balls will all help to increase his mobility. Later, as he becomes more skilful, tricycles and go-carts, a climbing frame, paddling pool and sand-pit will all provide stimulation for different activities which will aid his growth and development. The day should consist of alternating periods of quiet, restful play and active, noisy play, especially outdoors so that the child can let off steam.

Fresh air and sunlight

Activity in the fresh air has a stimulating effect on the whole body and if possible all children should play outdoors for part of every day. Good ventilation in buildings is important, because it circulates fresh air and so replenishes oxygen. Well-ventilated rooms in nurseries and schools help to reduce the spread of infection between children, because germs prefer the conditions found in unventilated rooms – warmth and humidity.

Sunlight is necessary to all life. It warms the earth and gives us light. We all feel better when the sun shines. Sunlight on the skin enables the body to produce vitamin D. It also kills some germs. However, care should be taken when exposing young children to the sun, because of the danger of burning. Sun-hats should be worn and a suntan lotion used on the skin to prevent burning. This is especially important at the seaside because a fair skin can burn very quickly when sunlight is reflected off the sea. Exposure should be for gradually increasing periods each day.

Warmth

As a child matures, his body becomes better able to control its temperature. He will still need warm surroundings for comfort, but because he is more active will be able to keep warm more easily.

Clothing. Materials used for clothing should be as follows:

- capable of being easily washed
- hard-wearing
- absorbent
- warm
- safe – flameproof.

As already discussed in the section dealing with the layette, the most suitable materials are fabrics made from natural fibres or a mixture of natural and synthetic fibres. Synthetic fibres are uncomfortable next to the skin because they do not absorb moisture.

Clothes should have the following qualities:

- They should be easy to put on and take off and fastenings should be simple, so that a child can easily learn to become independent, for his toilet needs and for dressing and undressing himself.
- They should not restrict. Restrictive clothing can be unsafe and will frustrate an active child.
- They should be safe in design. For example, there should be no loose ends, such as neck ties on anoraks which could catch on projections.
- They should be suitable for the occasion – for example, not too dressy for nursery school or the child will worry about keeping them clean.
- The child should have some choice in colour and design. When buying clothes take the child with you and select two or three suitable articles and let him choose between them.

A suitable outfit for children
a) underwear: cotton pants, cotton vest, cotton/nylon socks (summer), woollen socks (winter);
b) dungarees, trousers, skirt or dress, shirt, jumper or cardigan and anorak or other jacket (for colder weather).

In addition children need pyjamas or nightdresses and a dressing gown. In very cold weather children also need a hat and gloves. In wet weather, wellington boots are useful to keep their feet dry. A child needs at least three sets of clothing, so that one can be worn whilst one is being washed, and the other is in the drawer ready for use.

Shoes. A baby will not need shoes until he has learned to walk properly. His bare feet will give him a better grip on the floor, and shoes at this stage would only hinder him. As the bones in children's feet are not fully calcified, they are soft and can easily be deformed by shoes or socks that are too tight. In China, girl babies' feet used, at one time, to be bound tightly so that the toes were doubled back, and this meant that the feet grew that way and the forming bones set in that position. This is an extreme example of deformity, but it does serve to illustrate how a child's feet can easily be pushed out of shape. Tight all-over suits, socks, shoes, bootees and even tightly tucked-in bedclothes can damage the feet. It is not painful to the child because at this stage his bones are flexible, and the effects are not usually seen until he is much older – perhaps in middle or old age when corns, bunions, hammer toes and other allied problems give rise to pain and lack of mobility.

Children's feet grow fairly rapidly, so socks and shoes should be carefully fitted and checked every three months for size. A stretch sock should be big enough to fit the foot, not to be stretched by it. When shoes are bought, both feet should be measured for length and width and the shoes fitted by a trained fitter. Some manufacturers of children's shoes have special courses where shoe-shop assistants are trained in the correct fitting of children's shoes. It is

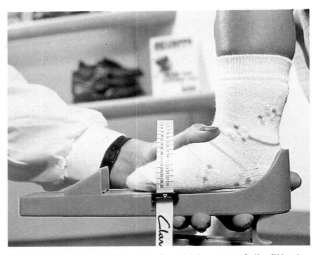

Shoes, slippers and boots should be carefully fitted

well worth seeking out a shop with trained assistants.

Slippers should also be carefully fitted. Where possible, children should be encouraged to run around without shoes and socks in the house, as the feet benefit from this freedom.

Good health

As already mentioned, children should have regular developmental assessments to ensure that they are progressing within normal limits and that there are no defects.

They are usually examined between three and four years as a pre-school check to anticipate any problems which might occur when they start school. For instance, if speech remains immature, then a mother can be shown how she can help her child overcome it, and professional help can be brought in if necessary. (See Chapter 12.)

Early visits to the dentist are important, too, so that the children will get used to him or her before any treatment is actually needed, and also to ensure that only minor future treatment will be necessary to prevent loss of teeth. Most dentists will begin regular inspections from about two and a half years of age. This is a good time to begin, because the twenty temporary teeth are usually complete by this age and a child is capable of co-operating. First visits are often just a 'ride' in the chair and a brief glimpse of the teeth but, gradually, as the surgery and dentist become more familiar, the child will allow a more thorough inspection. His parents or nursery nurse should accompany the child into the dental surgery.

Signs of good health
clear firm skin – good colour
bright eyes
firm, well-developed muscles
breathing through nose – mouth closed
eating well with good appetite
sleeping well
bowels normal
normal progress and development
weight and height within normal limits
alert and interested

contentment
ability to accept frustration of wishes

Signs of subnormal health
pallor – skin looks doughy
dull eyes
flabby muscles
mouth breathing
constantly runny nose
poor appetite
poor sleep
constipation
poor progress and development
apathy
miserable, whining disposition
dullness

If a child presents any signs of subnormal health one must check his daily routine and see if any changes can be made to improve his health. In any case, the family doctor should be consulted about the child's general health. (Signs of acute illness are dealt with in Chapter 9 on care of the sick child.)

Protection

A child over one year of age still needs some protection from infection but has developed a certain amount of immunity to his family's germs. His drinking water or cow's milk need not be boiled after he is a year old. Provided his feeding bottle and teat are cleaned thoroughly with very hot water, they no longer need to be sterilised. However, care should still be taken with handwashing, disposal of nappies, use of potty, etc. This is especially important in the day nursery and nursery school because a child takes longer to build up a resistance to the many different germs he will meet there.

The course of immunisation against whooping cough, diphtheria, tetanus and poliomyelitis is usually completed by the end of the first year, but this may vary from area to area. Usually an injection of triple vaccine (diphtheria, pertussis and tetanus) and a dose of polio vaccine by mouth is given at three months, five months and ten months of age. A new vaccine introduced in October 1988 against measles, mumps and rubella (MMR) is usually given at about fourteen months. Then the child should have a booster of triple vaccine at four and a half years of age so that he has protection when he starts school. In some areas a baby is also immunised against tuberculosis at one to two weeks of age.

Protection from accidents is especially necessary for the one to seven year old as they are a major cause of death. (See Chapter 19.)

Security

A child's security is founded on his close relationship with first his mother, then his father and, later, with all the other members of his family. He needs to be aware that he is part of a united family group. A regular and consistent routine will give structure to his life by forming a pattern so that he knows what to expect and what is expected of him. He needs a few simple rules which will maintain a simple standard of behaviour within his capability. Discipline is really a matter of control which will gradually become self-control, but until that happens we must help him, both by giving him rules to follow and showing him by example. He should be allowed to pursue his own interests provided there is reasonable consideration for others. If he is not given any rules at all and is allowed to do as he wishes, he will get the impression that nobody cares what he does.

A child likes to please his parents and this fact can be used to advantage. Praise for 'good' behaviour or efforts to help will enable a child to learn in a positive way what is acceptable. A child usually knows the meaning of the word 'No' from about nine months of age – he also responds to the tone of voice used. But 'No' should be used in moderation, or it ceases to have any meaning. A child under two and a half years is not amenable to logic, so it is better to be positive and direct his activities towards what you want than to keep using the negative. Constant criticism can destroy a child's security, but distraction from an activity you do not like is a useful alternative.

From about three years of age children love rules and regulations and will soon tell newcomers to the nursery that they are 'not allowed to do that', etc. Children enjoy belonging to an ordered society where things remain much the same, apart from certain events which are predictable – for example, birthday parties. They also like to feel that the adults in their life have similar attitudes and standards. This can be difficult in a nursery or school because standards do vary. It is very important for a nursery nurse to avoid innocently causing conflict in a child's mind by voicing criticisms or remarks which could apply to his parents. It is better to try to find out what is done at home and then resolve any differences in a tactful way. Parents should be free to visit the nursery or nursery school at any time and see for themselves how activities are carried out and how well their child is settling down. It is to be hoped that parents and nursery nurse can learn from one another for the ultimate good of the child's security and development.

A child's security also involves having his own possessions and a place to keep them – even if it is only a cardboard box. Ideally he needs a cot or a bed of his own, a cupboard and drawers for his own toys and clothes. This is especially important for the child in residential care or hospital, as keeping his own possessions and wearing his own clothes will continue to provide a link with home.

If a child during his first seven years grows up with a feeling of belonging and being a valued member of a family group, it gives him an inner security which should last all his life and which nothing is likely to destroy.

Affection

A child needs someone to love him unconditionally, despite his faults. This unconditional love is closely linked with security.

Love can, and should, be demonstrated by cuddles and hugs and other physical contact, but these are only the outward signs. To pick up a child and kiss him is an easy way to demonstrate love, and it can be done even when affection is absent. But to deal with a young child's dirty nappy cheerfully and wipe up his vomit needs a basis of real affection. The quality of care and concern brought to bear on all the duties and chores – especially the tiresome ones – of rearing a child show him just how deeply he is loved and wanted.

Parents and nursery nurses should show their affection by talking and listening to a child and praising his efforts. They should let him see the pleasure they get from his company. A child needs to be reassured that he is 'a good boy' and given approval so that he feels a valued person. The worst thing that can happen to him is to lose his parents' or nursery nurse's approval, so it is necessary to let him know, when he is naughty, that it is the deed you dislike and not him. To threaten to withdraw love is a terrible punishment and should *never* be used.

The deepest kind of love must normally come from a child's natural parents. Other people can only do their honest best. Nursery nurses must possess an affectionate nature, because a child can detect differences between impersonal concern and truly affectionate care.

Stimulation

(See Chapter 16 on play.) Much of a child's stimulation arises out of his natural curiosity which impels him to explore and discover. But curiosity needs satisfaction so that it can continue to help a child's development. Opportunity and space, as well as playthings suitable to his age and ability, must be provided to stimulate his five senses. Once he is mobile and on the floor, all kinds of things will interest him and many playthings can be improvised – saucepans and lids, wooden spoons, plastic beakers and cups and spoons, old handbags, paper bags, clothes pegs, etc. A child also needs to play with natural materials such as water, sand, clay and mud so that he can explore their qualities. In addition he also needs to be allowed to 'help' his parents in their various domestic tasks. Through such activity he learns about the world around him.

Stimulation also comes from his parents' pleasure in his efforts and achievements. They will share with him the triumph of being able to stand upright and walk and make sounds which gradually take on meaning. Talking, singing and reading to him, listening and responding to his noises, and interpreting those noises, will all help to encourage his all-round development as well as speech and language.

A child's surroundings should be bright and cheerful and his own attempts at drawing and painting should be displayed on the walls for all to see.

Social contacts

Until about two years of age a baby is very dependent upon his mother and the rest of the family and they, together with family friends and neighbours, provide all the social contacts a child needs. Between one and two years many children become shy of strangers and an enforced separation during this time (such as a hospital stay) can be harmful.

From about two years of age a child should gradually become more confident and ready for more contact with the outside world. The two-year-old child will like to play alongside other children and, towards the end of the year, the beginnings of co-operative play will be seen.

By three years of age most children are ready to join in group play, and this is the usual age for starting nursery school or play group. Provided a child has a secure background, he should settle into a group and enjoy the companionship of others, eventually being able to dispense with his mother's continual presence. Within a group he widens his outlook and learns the 'give and take' necessary in social life. From three years of age a child should be able to relate to other adults as he does to his mother and respond to a friendly approach. By the time he begins 'real' school, at five, he should be friendly, confident, able to make friends and play in harmony with others.

Independence

Gradually, a child must become less dependent on others, although his mother will remain his anchor. Until two years of age, he will want to be near her all the time. From about the age of two he begins to move away from this dependence on his mother, and this change should be encouraged. The first two years should be regarded as a preparation towards a child's independence. He must learn, gradually, the skills needed to care for himself so that he can eventually take over from his mother. Learning to feed himself, dress and undress himself, attend to his toilet needs, etc. cannot be achieved without opportunity to practise. When he shows he is ready to learn he must be encouraged to try and be praised for his efforts. Gradually from about two years of age he should take over these personal tasks so that by the time he is seven only reminders and some supervision are needed.

EXERCISES

Investigation
Visit a shoe shop and find out what facilities exist for fitting children's shoes correctly. What range of sizes and widths are kept?

Watch children coming into the shop, and note the reactions of both the children and their parents.

Observation
Watch children playing, either in the garden at your placement or in a public playground. In your evaluation, summarise what seem to be their favourite activities, and suggest reasons for this.

Project
Subject for discussion, in pairs: What do you remember most about your childhood? What sorts of things made you feel secure? Can you use these memories to help your work with children? What makes you feel secure now?

SUGGESTIONS FOR FURTHER READING

Lee Salk, *What Every Young Child Would Like His Mother to Know*, Fontana/Collins
M.L. Kelmer Pringle, *Caring for Children*, Longman Group Ltd
Dr Christopher Green, *Toddler Taming*, Century Hutchinson Publishing Ltd
Mary Sheridan, *From Birth to Five Years*, NFER – Nelson Publishing Co Ltd

8 Germs and Disease

INFECTION

People who choose to work with babies and children must always be alert to the dangers of infection which can make a child seriously ill, and even cause death. A baby is born with little defence against germs and, as they are all around us, on our skin, in our noses and throats and in the air we breathe, the child is at risk all the time. Fortunately, as children grow older and encounter many different germs, they gradually develop an ability to fight them.

We cannot keep a baby in a germ-free atmosphere, and it would not be a good idea if we could, because he would never develop any resistance to infection. But until he has developed resistance, we must protect him by minimising his exposure to disease-causing germs.

Germs are a category of micro-organism, so-called because they are so small that they can only be seen under a microscope; in fact you could fit about 80 000 on the head of a pin. They are mostly simple organisms consisting of only one cell. Many of these micro-organisms are harmless; some are even essential to maintain life on earth, but others cause various diseases in humans.

The many thousands of types of micro-organisms are divided, and subdivided, into groups. Two main groups are:

1. Non-pathogenic (harmless to humans)
These include:
a) the organisms which turn milk into cheese;
b) the organisms which convert organic matter (leaves, faeces, urine, etc.) into fertiliser.

2. Pathogenic (causing disease in humans)
There are many subdivisions but the most important ones include the following:

a) *bacteria* divided into groups according to shape:
   i) cocci (round shape); *examples:* streptococci, staphylococci;
   ii) bacilli (rod shape); *examples:* tubercle bacilli, tetanus bacilli;
   iii) vibrios (curved shape); *examples:* cholera.
b) *viruses* – these are so small that they cannot be seen under an ordinary microscope; *examples:* measles virus, influenza virus.

In addition to bacteria and viruses there are some other more complicated living organisms which can cause disease in humans. These are:
a) *protozoa* – simple one-celled animals; *example:* amoebae which cause amoebic dysentery;
b) *fungi* – *examples:* thrush, athlete's foot, ringworm;
c) *animal parasites* – *examples:* lice, intestinal worm, itch mite (scabies).

Most of the micro-organisms are able to reproduce by simply splitting into two and, when conditions are favourable, will do this every twenty minutes. Consequently, one or two germs can become millions providing that their essential needs are supplied. These are:
a) moisture
b) warmth – average human body temperature
c) food
d) time.

Some of the organisms need oxygen, but others do not. Some are tougher than others, and can survive longer in an inhospitable environment. For instance, some of the bacilli are able to form a tough outer covering and survive without food or moisture for a considerable time. This is known as a spore formation and spores can be found in dust and dirt. When conditions become favourable to spore, it will resume its old life style.

So although micro-organisms surround us, they are

more likely to be found in warm, moist places favourable to their survival. The areas on the human body providing ideal conditions for micro-organisms are warm parts where there is moisture and food (from perspiration or other body fluids). So, although we have the micro-organisms all over our skins, they are concentrated in the armpits and groin and any breaks in the skin surface. They also occur in large numbers in the body openings – mouth, throat, nose and anus and therefore will be found in used tissues, handkerchiefs, sheets and used dressings from wounds and on potties, lavatory seats and lavatories.

In the home and nursery most organisms are found in warm, moist places with poor ventilation – in the bathroom on damp, used face-flannels, sponges, toothbrushes, towels, bathmats and carpets; in the kitchen on damp tea-towels, dishcloths, floorcloths and mops, and on exposed food, utensils and crockery which has traces of left-over food. Micro-organisms also thrive in overcrowded, under-ventilated rooms, where the air breathed out is warmer and contains more water vapour.

Infection occurs when pathogenic organisms enter the body and develop and multiply, producing toxins (poisons) which cause symptoms such as raised temperature, headaches, loss of appetite and various aches and pains. An organism may also produce a specific reaction, such as a skin rash.

Some germs can cause only one particular disease. Diphtheria bacilli, for instance, only produce diphtheria in humans. Others cause different diseases according to where they are in the body. For example one type of streptococci will cause tonsillitis if lodged in the tonsils, but will cause nephritis (kidney infection) if lodged in the kidney.

Micro-organisms can enter the body in three different ways:

a) *inhalation* – breathed in through nose and throat;

b) *ingestion* – swallowed through the mouth (usually in food or drink);

c) *inoculation* – penetrating through the skin, usually through a cut or injection, or through the mucus membrane (the lining of the inner cavities of the body, e.g. mouth, vagina etc.).

A disease is said to be *infectious* when the organism causing it can easily be transmitted from one person to another, or to a live or inanimate host on which it lives until it infects another person. These are known as direct and indirect infections respectively.

A disease is said to be *contagious* when the organism causing it can only be transmitted by actual bodily contact.

Direct infection

Actual contact is not always necessary for direct infection but the person being infected must be within the range of the infecting organism.

Droplet infection. When we speak we constantly spray out mostly invisible droplets of moisture from our mouths and noses. These droplets contain any of the organisms present in a nose, mouth and throat and can be passed on to any person within the range of the droplets. If a person coughs or sneezes without covering his nose and mouth, the droplets will be propelled several metres and could be inhaled by all the occupants of the same room. Consequently a teacher with a head cold could infect all the children in the class.

Kissing. Organisms will be transferred directly from mouth to mouth, so that if one person is infected the infection will be passed on.

Sexual contact. Again a direct transfer of organisms occurs, e.g. syphilis or AIDS.

Injection.
a) If drug addicts share needles, infected blood from one member of the group will infect the others.
b) If a nurse accidentally stabs herself with a needle previously used on an infected person, she will be infected. Diseases which may be passed on this way include AIDS and hepititus B.

Touch. Touching infected skin will result in a transfer of organisms, but is unlikely to cause illness unless your skin is broken, as intact skin acts as a barrier.

Indirect infection

Objects which carry infective organisms must supply some of their needs as well, or the organisms would not be able to survive for long. So, although cups, plates, pens, books and so on are often blamed for the spread of infection, they are not such a likely cause as hands, which are warm and moist with sweat. The exceptions to this are bacteria that form spores and survive for long periods without food, moisture and warmth. However, the commonest diseases caused by spore-forming organisms are tuberculosis, tetanus and diphtheria and we can be protected from these by immunisation.

The commonest causes of indirect spread of infection are as follows:

Hands. Hands can become contaminated with pathogenic organisms, especially by airborne droplets from urine and faeces around the lavatory area. People can infect themselves by licking their fingers or eating food with contaminated hands. They can also infect other people if they prepare food and drink for them.

Flies. The common house-fly prefers to feed on excreta and garbage, which are ideal breeding sites for infective organisms. Flies carry these germs in their bodies and stomachs and distribute them wherever they land. As flies feed by regurgitating some of their stomach contents on to food before sucking it up, it is easy to see how the organisms can be transferred to exposed foodstuffs prepared for human consumption. Typhoid fever and food poisoning are two examples of diseases spread this way.

Mice, rats and cockroaches. These can all carry pathogenic organisms on their bodies and contaminate food.

Food and water. Both can be contaminated at source and so infect the people who eat or drink them.

People can also inhale infected water. An example of this was an outbreak of Legionnaires' disease which was traced to a building containing an infected air-conditioning tank. Droplets from the tank were sprayed into the atmosphere around the building to be inhaled by passers-by.

Certain types of dust. Those which contain animal dung and street rubbish may contain pathogenic organisms which can contaminate uncovered food.

Carriers. Some people are carriers of pathogenic organisms, although they are not ill at all. They may have suffered in the past from the disease but are now fit. The organisms may be carried in large numbers in the nose and throat or bowel. The commonest organisms carried in this way are the streptococci in the throat and the food poisoning germ in the bowel.

Such people can be a menace if they are not careful of personal hygiene, especially if their work is the care of young children or the preparation of food for others. They can infect large numbers of people before being detected.

Example 1: A nursery nurse is a carrier of haemolytic streptococci, so these organisms live in her throat. Every time she coughs without covering her nose and mouth she will spray streptococci over any children within range. If she uses her hand to cover her mouth and subsequently handles food the children can be infected by eating it. Infected children may develop tonsillitis or a kidney infection. Example 2: a chef in a restaurant carries salmonella in his bowel. Every time he has his bowels open his hands will become contaminated with the germ. If he subsequently prepares food for others without first washing his hands thoroughly the salmonella can be transferred to the food so that the consumer then develops food poisoning.

These types of carriers can be identified by taking a throat swab or a sample of faeces for tests in a laboratory. These tests are often carried out when an outbreak of disease occurs in one locality. Tests may also be carried out on prospective employees if they are to work in an area where being a carrier would be hazardous to others, e.g. in a food-processing factory, or in a maternity hospital.

Another type of carrier is a person who is incubating a disease, but is not yet feeling any symptoms or showing any signs of the infection. This period is the most infectious time when the organism can easily be passed on unknowingly and this can cause problems in the control of the spread of disease, especially those which have a long incubation period.

Fortunately we do have certain natural defences against pathogenic organisms and sufficient knowledge to protect ourselves and those most vulnerable to infection.

Natural defences

1. Good general health. This will help a person fight infection.

2. Natural specific protections – examples of these are:
a) Acid produced by the stomach will destroy some organisms.
b) Tears contain an antiseptic which prevents organisms multiplying.
c) An intact skin acts as a barrier to most organisms.

3. The white blood cells. These will devour pathogenic organisms. When infection begins, the white blood cells increase and, travelling via the lymphatic system, go to the site of the invasion and fight the organisms either on the site or in the nearest lymphatic glands.

4. Immunity. Antibodies present in the bloodstream are able to neutralise specific pathogenic organisms. There are several types of immunity:

Natural immunity
Antibodies are passed on from mother to child before birth and after birth in breast milk. This will protect a baby to a certain extent, until he is able to produce his own antibodies.

Actively acquired immunity
a) If a person has an attack of an infectious disease, the presence of the organism and its toxins stimulates the body to produce antibodies to neutralise them. Afterwards the body retains the ability to produce these antibodies should the organism be met again.
b) A similar reaction will occur if the person is given a modified (weakened) organism or its toxins. The disease itself does not appear but the stimulus is sufficient to induce the body to produce antibodies. This is known as vaccination or immunisation.

Passively acquired immunity
Antibodies can be given to a child who has been in contact with a serious infectious disease. Serum (liquid part of blood) is taken from a person who is convalescent from the disease as it will contain antibodies. This protection does not last long, but protects the child long enough for him to make his own antibodies.

Other defences

We can also protect against infection in several other ways:

- by building up resistance
- by reducing the number of pathogenic organisms
- by preventing the spread of the organisms.

Build up resistance
a) Ensure that people are as fit as possible by supplying their physical and mental needs.
b) Ensure that the skin is not damaged and thus prevent organisms entering the body in this way:
  i)   Avoid cuts, grazes and burns.
  ii) Use hand cream to prevent 'chapping'.
  iii) Good nutrition aids good skin.
c) Breast-feed babies so that they receive the maximum amount of antibodies from their mothers. Also breast-fed babies usually have good general health so can resist infection.
d) Protect babies from specific infections with immunisation. Diseases which can be prevented by immunisation include measles, mumps, diphtheria, poliomyelitis, whooping cough, tetanus, rubella and tuberculosis. A doctor will advise on when immunisation should take place.

Although there are slight risks attached to immunisation procedures, they are statistically very small compared with the risk of catching these diseases and developing complications leading to permanent disability or death.

Reduce the number of pathogenic organisms. There are several methods of doing this:

a) Kill the organisms. It is impossible to kill all pathogenic organisms because any effective method would kill *all living organisms* indiscriminately. However, sometimes one has to kill organisms. Those which cause gastroenteritis, for example, may be present in a baby's feeding bottle, and they can be destroyed by sterilisation. Pathogenic organisms can be killed by several methods:
   i)   application of a chemical solution such as sodium hypochlorite solution
   ii) exposure to heat by boiling, cooking and pressure cooking
   iii) exposure to radiation.

b) Prevent reproduction of the organisms. This can be achieved by depriving the organism of one or more of its conditions for survival. For example:
   i)   moisture – therefore we should dry articles; hang up towels and face flannels to dry
   ii) warmth – most pathogenic organisms need the same temperature as human beings, so we can either raise or reduce the temperature to prevent reproduction (as in pasteurisation of milk or the refrigeration or freezing of food)
   iii) food – we should wash skin to remove perspiration
   iv) time – we should eat meals as soon as they are ready.

c) Dilute the organisms. Good ventilation ensures circulation of air which dilutes the organisms. Washing the skin with soap dilutes the number of organisms on our skin.

Prevent the spread of pathogenic organisms by:
• good personal hygiene
• good hygiene in the home and nursery
• public health measures.

Good personal hygiene
This is essential for anyone caring for children, because not only does it help to prevent the spread of infection but it teaches the child good habits. Children learn by imitation, and much of the teaching of good hygiene they absorb unconsciously. It is far easier to be clean if one has been trained since childhood, as it becomes automatic.

Good personal hygiene should include the following:
a) a daily all-over wash or bath
b) handwashing and nail-scrubbing: before meals, before preparing food, before touching baby, after using a lavatory, after changing a nappy, after touching a pet, after using a handkerchief
c) use of handcream to prevent cracks in the skin
d) regular nail-trimming and filing
e) cleaning of teeth after meals and before going to bed
f) daily brushing and combing of hair and weekly washing; it should be trimmed regularly
g) covering of nose and mouth when coughing or sneezing
h) careful disposal of tissues and handkerchiefs – used handkerchiefs and tissues should be put in a covered container (a paper bag will do) until they can be dealt with – handkerchiefs must be washed and boiled; tissues should be burned or flushed down the lavatory

i) frequent changing and washing of clothing – underclothes and tights should be washed daily, and other clothing as necessary

j) isolation of sick adults and children – if an adult in contact with children develops a cold, sore throat, diarrhoea or a skin infection, she should report sick and remain isolated from children until she is better.

In addition, adults should avoid promiscuity because the more partners a person has, the greater the risk of becoming infected and they should protect against infection in sexual contacts by using a condom.

Hygiene in the home and nursery
Home: General cleanliness and neatness in the home are necessary, to reduce the numbers of pathogenic organisms present and to help prevent accidents. It is better to rely on a good standard of cleanliness and good ventilation to prevent the spread of infection, rather than lavish use of disinfectant, which tends to give a false sense of security. In any case, if a disinfectant is powerful enough to kill all germs, it will also destroy our body cells, so is a very dangerous thing to have in the house. Most domestic disinfectants sold in the shops are really antiseptics, which means that in the correct solution they prevent germs multiplying. This can also be achieved by reducing the temperature or depriving the germs of food or moisture.

There should be a daily routine of tidying and cleaning. Floors should be cleaned regularly and furniture and ledges dusted with a clean, damp duster. Carpets, rugs and upholstery should be cleaned regularly with a vacuum cleaner to remove dust. Rooms should be well ventilated so that they get a change of air. Beds and bedding should be aired daily by turning the bedclothes back and opening the windows wide for about twenty minutes. Sheets, pillowcases and towels need to be changed weekly. In addition to these daily chores, regular washing and cleaning of walls, paintwork and windows is needed. The kitchen and the bathroom need extra care because both can provide ideal conditions in which germs can multiply.

Kitchen: Modern fittings and surfaces have made kitchens much easier to clean. All working surfaces and the floor should be washed daily with hot, soapy water and scrubbed once a week. However, repeated scrubbing may in some cases be rather drastic and not necessary for modern laminates and composition flooring, and here manufacturers' instructions should be followed. Cupboards should be kept tidy. The food cupboard or store-room should be well-ventilated. This cupboard and the refrigerator should be cleaned weekly. Perishable foods should be kept in a refrigerator. Cooked food should never be left exposed because of the danger of contamination, especially from flies. Flies can be kept out by fitting fly-screens over the windows and a plastic strip curtain over the doorway. If they do find their way into the kitchen, they can be killed by the careful use of fly-spray. However, if the kitchen is kept clean and all food is covered, they will not be tempted in. Food scraps, dirty plates, milk bottles and open rubbish bins all invite the presence of flies. So food scraps should be disposed of quickly, and the rubbish-bin should have a lid on at all times and should be emptied at least once a day. A waste-disposal unit under the sink is very useful and hygienic because it minces up all organic rubbish, which is then flushed down the drain.

Washing-up should be done immediately after meals, and the sink and draining board wiped down after use. Sink cleaning with a suitable proprietary cleaner should be carried out after washing-up the utensils from the main meal of the day. Mops, dishcloths and floorcloths should be well rinsed after use and hung out to dry. Once a week they should be sterilised by soaking in household bleach or boiling in water.

Washing-up is best carried out by the following method, using a double sink:
a) Remove food scraps.
b) Rinse all food debris by holding the plates under a running water tap and using a mop or brush.
c) Use very hot water and detergent to wash crockery and utensils – start with the cleanest glasses and crockery, leaving the dirtiest items and saucepans until last.
d) Rinse in very hot water in the second sink.
e) Place in a rack and allow to dry – if the rinsing water was hot enough, this will only take a few minutes.

Hand washing facilities should always be available in the kitchen so that hands can be washed before preparing food.

Bathroom: All members of the family should have their own flannel, towel, toothbrush, etc. There should be enough hooks, racks and rails for these items to be hung up to dry after use. Family members should be trained to rinse the washbasin and clean the bath after use and to hang up towels and flannels and the bath mat to dry. If this procedure is followed, then the bath and basin will only need a thorough cleaning once a week, using an appropriate cleanser.

The lavatory should be checked daily, the seat should be kept dry, and bleach or some other cleanser put down last thing at night. Once a week the seat and lavatory basin should be scrubbed with hot soapy water and rinsed and dried. The lavatory brush should be hung up to dry after use. The floor of the bathroom and lavatory should be washed weekly. Ventilation is important, so windows should be left open when practicable.

The nursery or nursery school: As in the home, a regular routine of tidying and cleaning must be carried out daily. In addition, extra care must be taken to prevent the spread of infection from child to child. Children can fairly easily build up a resistance to the germs present in their own homes, but take far longer to do so for the many and varied germs of all the other children. The younger the child, the longer it will take for him to build up such a resistance. It follows that in the day nursery where there are very young children a high standard of cleanliness is absolutely necessary. Many children are admitted to day nursery because of poor social conditions, which means they are often in a poor state of health because they live in substandard housing and eat an inadequate diet. Consequently they have even less resistance to infection. Another reason why infection can spread rapidly and easily in a nursery is that children have habits which encourage the spread of germs. For example, they pick their noses, lick their fingers and cough over other people unless they are watched every moment of the day.

Nurseries and schools usually have their own routines to ensure cleanliness and these will vary. Student nursery nurses will learn in their practical situations how to clean and care for the nursery as well as for the children. Although actual practices vary, the principles remain the same – cleanliness and good ventilation both help to reduce the number of pathogenic organisms.

In the children's rooms floors are usually cleaned daily by cleaners, but nursery nurses often carry out the damp dusting and general tidying necessary. Waste paper bins and bins containing used tissues must be emptied daily. Tables will need to be wiped down before and after use. All rooms should be thoroughly aired by opening all the windows for a while before the children arrive in the morning and again at mealtimes. A window should be left open during the day.

In the bathroom every child should have his own flannel, towel, toothbrush, brush and comb. These are usually marked with a symbol for each child so that he can recognise his own. There should be provision to hang these articles up separately so that they dry between uses. They should be washed weekly in hot, soapy water, and rinsed and dried in the open air.

Each child who needs one should have his own potty, which should be emptied and washed thoroughly in hot, soapy water after use.

Lavatories should be kept dry. Once a day the seats, lavatory pans and surrounds should be scrubbed with hot, soapy water and rinsed and dried. Household bleach can be left in the lavatory-pan overnight and flushed away in the morning before the children arrive. Children should be supervised at all times in the lavatory and bathroom so that puddles and spills can be wiped up immediately they occur. The children should be taught to pull the flush and to wash their hands after using the lavatory. The handbasins should be rinsed after use and cleaned once a day with a cleaning powder.

Nappies – any excreta can be brushed off into a lavatory pan or sluice (this task is made easy by the use of disposable nappy liners). The nappy should then be rinsed thoroughly in cold water, wrung out and placed in a covered container. Methods of washing nappies depend on the facilities available. They can be soaked in a nappy cleaning solution (according to directions on the packet) or they can be washed in hot, soapy water and boiled. Whatever method is used, they must be rinsed thoroughly in plenty of water and dried in the open air if possible.

Used disposable nappies should be put into a covered container preferably lined with a plastic bag, so that when the bin is emptied the nappies will not have to be handled. They should be disposed of hygienically – the safest way is to incinerate them.

In the nursery kitchen, as in the home, all surfaces must be kept clean and flies and other pests must be kept out. Washing-up is often carried out in a washing-up machine which, because of the heat produced, will sterilise crockery and utensils. If there are babies under one year of age in a nursery, there should be a separate milk kitchen where feeds can be prepared and feeding equipment cleaned and sterilised. All babies should have their own feeding utensils marked with their name and kept separate from one another. The room should be cleaned daily – all surfaces should be washed and dried.

Cots for babies and beds for the older children should each be marked with the child's name and kept separate, not only from the point of view of hygiene but also so that the child has a place of his own. Bedding should be changed frequently and the cot or bed should be cleaned thoroughly after a child leaves the nursery, before using it for another child.

Any child suffering from a cold, sore throat, diarrhoea, vomiting or a skin infection should be isolated from other children until he has recovered. Similarly, any nurse suffering in this way should stay away from work until cured.

Public health measures. It was not until the early 1800s that it was recognised that the public authorities could take various sanitary measures which would help to prevent the spread of infection and improve health standards. The first Public

Health Act was passed in 1848 and was followed by another in 1878 which laid the foundations for modern public health. These are based on the environmental needs of any community which are:

a) a supply of pure water
b) the prevention of water and air pollution
c) the provision of adequate drainage
d) the removal and treatment of sewerage and refuse
e) a supply of clean, wholesome food
f) healthy dwelling houses
g) the regulation of disease by notification and prevention of the spread of infectious diseases
h) the provision for burial of the dead
i) the registration of births and deaths.

The Public Health Acts are administered by Environmental Health Officers who work in the Public Health Departments of the Local Health Authority.

EXERCISES

Investigation
During your practical placement find out what measures are taken to prevent the spread of infection.

Observation
With your tutor's assistance, obtain some dishes containing agar and try to grow your own organisms from your hands, using:

a) clean hands
b) hands contaminated with dough
c) unwashed hands of someone who has visited the lavatory.

Observe the results under a microscope.

Project
Find out about the work of the Environmental Health Inspector. What would he or she be looking for in the nursery kitchen?

SUGGESTIONS FOR FURTHER READING

A.B. Christie, _Infectious Diseases,_ Faber and Faber Ltd

9 Common Infectious Diseases and the Sick Child

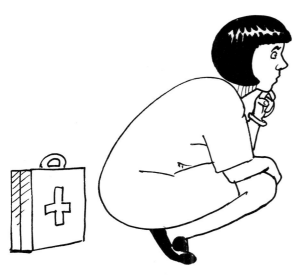

Infectious diseases which affect young children are becoming much less common since the advent of mass immunisation campaigns and public health measures to prevent the spread of infection. We are able to protect children from many diseases by means of immunisation. Unfortunately, as a generation grows up with no experience of these serious and damaging diseases, the number of children being immunised drops. This leads to another epidemic.

There are risks attached to being immunised, just as there are to any medical procedure, but many people fail to realise that the risk of an adverse reaction from immunisation is far lower than the risk of damage from the actual disease. In the past, thousands of children died from complications following diseases such as measles, whooping cough and diphtheria.

Most infectious diseases follow a similar pattern, although the organisms causing the disease and their manifestations are different. First the organism enters the body. Then follows a period of incubation during which the organism multiplies rapidly. This is when the child will be most infectious, but there will be no outward signs of the disease, although the child may be miserable and 'off colour' towards the end of this stage. The next stage is when the disease manifests itself and causes the child to become obviously ill. His temperature will be raised, causing him to shiver and be generally miserable with aches and pains, and a rash or some other specific sign will appear. After a period of illness, the signs and symptoms will subside and the child will either recover or will become more ill with complications.

Although nursery nurses are not expected to diagnose a child's illness, they should be aware of the signs and symptoms and the progress of the common infectious diseases. It is important for them to know when medical aid is needed and to know what to expect if a child in their care has been in contact with an infection. In all cases of suspected infectious disease a doctor should be called and his or her instructions should be followed if the child is subsequently nursed at home. The following charts summarise the causes, symptoms and treatment of the commonest infectious diseases.

Infectious diseases

Disease	Cause	Spread	Incubation period	Signs and symptoms	Rash or specific sign	Treatment	Complications
Chicken pox	virus	direct contact droplets	7–14 days	slight fever, irritating rash	*1st day:* red spots with white raised centre on trunk and limbs, mostly very irritating	rest, fluids, lactocalamine or solution of bicarb. of soda on spots	impetigo
Diphtheria	bacteria	direct contact	1–6 days	sore throat, slight temperature, prostration, pallor	grey membrane in throat	rest, fluids, diphtheria anti-toxin, antibiotics, diphtheria toxoid	paralysis of muscles, throat obstruction, heart involvement
Dysentery	1) bacilli 2) amoeba	indirect: flies, infected food	1–7 days	vomiting, diarrhoea – blood and mucus in stool, abdominal pain	no rash	fluids and medical aid	dehydration death
Food poisoning	may be bacteria or virus	indirect: infected food or drink	½ hour – 36 hours	vomiting, diarrhoea, abdominal pain	no rash	fluids only 24 hours, doctor if no better	dehydration death in vulnerable children
Gastro-enteritis	may be bacteria or virus	direct contact; indirect – infected food and drink	Bacterial: 7–14 days Viral: ½ hour – 36 hours	vomiting, diarrhoea, dehydration	no rash	fluids – water or Dioralyte, urgent medical aid	weight loss, dehydration, debility, death
Infective hepatitis ('jaundice')	virus	direct contact: especially droplet; indirect contact: food or water	23–35 days	gradual onset of headache, loss of appetite, nausea, urine dark, faeces pale putty colour	*5th–7th day* yellow skin, itching, also yellow conjunctiva	fluids with glucose, fat-free diet; isolation	liver damage, meningitis

Disease	Cause	Spread	Incubation period	Signs and symptoms	Rash or specific sign	Treatment	Complications
Measles	virus	direct contact; especially droplets	10–15 days	misery, high temperature, heavy cold with discharging nose and eyes, later harsh cough, conjunctivitis	2nd day: Koplik's spots; white spots inside cheek 4th day: dusky red, patchy rash; starts behind ears and along hair-line, spreads to face, trunk and limbs	rest, fluids, sponging to reduce temperature, dark room if photophobia	eye infection, chest infection, middle ear infection, encephalitis
Meningitis Inflammation of meninges (the covering of the brain)	bacteria or virus	droplet infection	2–10 days	severe headache, neck stiffness, fever, vomiting, drowsiness or confusion, dislike of bright lights	sometimes tiny red/ purple spots or bruises	hospital, antibiotics	deafness, brain damage, death
Mumps	virus	direct contact droplets	7–28 days	fever, headache, swelling of jaw in front of ears, difficulty opening mouth	no rash	rest, bland fluids through straw	orchitis (inflamation of testicles), meningitis encephalitis (rare)
Pertussis (whooping cough)	bacteria	direct contact droplets	10–14 days	heavy cold with fever followed by cough	spasmodic cough with characteristic whoop and vomiting	rest, supporting during bouts of coughing, feed after bout of coughing	bronchitis, broncho-pneumonia, haemorrhage, due to strain of coughing, prolapse of rectum, mouth ulcers, debility, encephalitis
Poliomyelitis	virus	direct contact: especially droplets indirect contact: food or water	5–14 days	sudden onset of headache, stiffness of neck and back followed by paralysis	no rash	rest, medical supervision	permanent paralysis

Disease	Cause	Spread	Incubation period	Signs and symptoms	Rash or specific sign	Treatment	Complications
Rubella (German measles)	virus	direct contact droplets	14–21 days	slight cold, sore throat, slight fever, enlarged glands behind ears, pains in small joints	*1st day:* rash-like sweat rash, bright pink; starts at roots of hair; may last 2–24 hours	rest if necessary (mild disease)	none unless patient pregnant woman; virus can seriously affect foetus in first 12 weeks of pregnancy
Scarlet fever	bacteria	direct contact: droplets; indirect contact	2–5 days	sudden onset of fever, sore throat, vomiting, 'strawberry' tongue, flushed cheeks, pallor around mouth	*1st or 2nd day:* bright red rash with raised pinpoint spots behind ears, spreading to trunk, arms and legs; skin peels after 7 days	rest, fluids, observation for complications, antibiotics	middle ear infection, kidney infection, heart involvement
Tonsillitis	bacteria	direct infection droplets		very sore throat, white patches (pus) on tonsils, swollen glands in neck, aches and pains in back and limbs	no rash	rest, fluids, medical aid – antibiotics	middle ear infection nephritis (kidney infection)
Typhoid and paratyphoid fever	bacteria	direct contact; indirect contact: especially food and drink	12–14 days	headache, malaise, diarrhoea/ constipation, fever	*7th day:* red papules on abdomen	rest, hospital (medical aid)	intestinal haemorrhage, intestinal perforation

Further charts on children's ailments

The following charts set out a further list of ailments, including skin diseases, which may occur in the early years of childhood, with notes on symptoms and when to seek a doctor's advice. Some of these ailments are contagious, and are therefore transmitted by close physical contact. In a day nursery or nursery school it is usual to exclude the child until he is said by a doctor to be free from infection. In the home, isolation is not necessary, provided treatment is being given and the normal rules of hygiene are adhered to.

Ailment	Cause	Contagious or not	Signs and symptoms	Treatment
Skin conditions Cradle-cap (scurf on head)	(a) inefficient washing of hair, especially rinsing (b) too much washing of hair	no	(a) brown greasy patches or (b) flaky white patches on scalp	once a week: apply liquid paraffin or olive oil overnight; wash thoroughly next day; prevent by washing hair once a week only – rinse very well
Eczema	not always known, may be allergy	no	red angry rash, especially at backs of knees and in front of elbows; may be dry and scaly or moist; very irritating	doctor – special creams; stop child scratching; avoid use of wool in clothing; oily additive to bath water
Impetigo	bacteria	yes	yellow, oozing sores with scab on top; itching; usually around nose and mouth	doctor – usually antibiotic cream
Intertrigo (sores in creases, e.g. neck)	insufficient drying after bath	no	sore red areas in neck creases or under arms or groin	zinc and castor oil cream; prevent by drying child thoroughly after bath

Ailment	Cause	Contagious or not	Signs and symptoms	Treatment
Nappy rash	variety of causes: 1) faulty washing of nappies 2) dirty nappy left on too long 3) diarrhoea 4) insufficient fluids, leading to concentrated urine 5) infection, such as thrush 6) allergy to nappy liner/cream/softener in nappy, etc. 7) eczema	no	red area over buttocks and groin; may be scaly; may be blisters or raw patches	find cause and eliminate 1) wash nappies – boil or use sanitising powder; rinse very well; dry in fresh air 2) change nappy frequently 3) treatment for diarrhoea (doctor) 4) give extra boiled water to drink 5) treatment for thrush (doctor) 6) change nappy liner brand; stop using creams/lotions or washing softener in nappy. Expose buttocks to air – leave off nappy as much as possible; Proprietary cream (medical advice)
Nettle rash	allergy to food or drugs, etc.	no	pink raised weals or blotches; may be swelling; itching	find allergen and avoid it; calamine lotion; doctor if associated with sneezing, raised temperature or runny nose
Ringworm	fungus	yes (may be caught from family pet)	circular red, raised area with white scaly centre; itching; if on scalp – hair breaks off	doctor – usually antibiotic cream
Scabies	'itch' mite; female mite burrows under skin and lays 20–30 eggs; eggs hatch out in 3–4 weeks and repeat cycle	yes	burrows visible as red raised spots especially between fingers; intense irritation; sleeplessness	doctor – Lorexane or benzyl benzoate lotion; all family members should be treated as instructed; sheets, pillowcases, blankets, clothing should all be washed thoroughly before re-use after treatment
Sweat rash	heat too many clothes	no	pinpoint red spots; fretful baby	cool bath, calamine lotion; less clothing;

Ailment	Cause	Contagious or not	Signs and symptoms	Treatment
Verruca	possibly virus	probably	wart on sole of foot – looks like a black speck – hurts when pressed	if painful doctor or chiropodist for removal (if left will eventually disappear)
Eye conditions Blepharitis	not known	no	crusts (like scurf) on eyelashes; may be redness	bathe with cool boiled water and sterile swabs 5 times a day; doctor if no improvement
Conjunctivitis ('pink eye')	virus or bacteria	yes	itching and pain in eyes; red inflamed eyes; may be discharge	doctor; isolation; separate towel, flannel, etc.
Stye (abscess on root of eyelash)	bacteria (poor health predisposes)	no	painful swelling at root of eyelash; pus collects (as boil)	doctor
Other conditions Asthma	allergy – often to house dust, or animals, not fully understood	no	shortness of breath, wheezing, attacks vary in intensity	doctor for acute attack; sit child up, reassure; use drugs prescribed by doctor (may be in form of medicine or inhalant)
Colic ('3 months colic')	air (wind) in bowels baby takes in air when feeding	no	screaming baby draws up legs in obvious pain often 6 p.m. to 10 p.m.	warm boiled water to drink; massage 'tummy'; comfort him; put baby on his abdomen to sleep; 'gripe' water may help; usually improves after 3 months of age; doctor, if severe
Constipation	various poor diet – lack of fluid; lack of fibre; lack of vitamin B faulty habit training poor muscle tone emotional blackmail	no	hard stool painful evacuation headache listlessness abdominal pain	give extra fluids, extra fibre, extra vitamin B; encourage more exercise; encourage daily attempt to have bowels open

Ailment	Cause	Contagious or not	Signs and symptoms	Treatment
Croup	virus infecting the vocal cords causing them to swell and reduce air flow into the lungs.	no	hollow barking cough, difficulty in getting his breath	sit child up, reassure; create a humid atmosphere (boil a kettle in room or take child into bathroom and turn on hot tap); get medical aid. NB do not leave child alone in heated room
Diarrhoea	various infection diet	yes no	loose, frequent stools abdominal pain	doctor within 24 hours if under 1 year old, 2 days for older child; boiled water or 'Dioralyte' only to drink for 24 hours.
Head lice	*Pediculi capitti*	yes	head scratching; presence of nits (eggs) – white specks which are stuck to hair; presence of lice – small insects which move along hair	Prioderm lotion – follow directions; 'Derbac' comb – a metal comb used on hair to remove nits; all family should be treated; prevent by frequent brushing and combing of hair
Hernia	weakness in muscle wall	no	1) umbilical: bulge around umbilicus 2) inguinal: bulge in groin 3) hiatus: constant vomiting	1) doctor – may correct itself – usually left until baby 1 year, then possibly surgery 2) doctor – usually surgery necessary 3) doctor; sit child up, especially after meals
Hypothermia	extreme cold	no	quiet 'good' baby; unnaturally 'healthy' colour; body feels icy; later: unconsciousness	doctor; meanwhile: remove covers, raise temperature in room, cuddle baby; (try to prevent – warm room)

Ailment	Cause	Contagious or not	Signs and symptoms	Treatment
Infantile convulsions	high temperature	no	pale bluish colour; eyes turn up; twitching of muscles; unconsciousness; may stop breathing	doctor; meanwhile: cool bath or sponge down to bring temperature down; (try to prevent – see pages 105–6)
Sickle cell crisis	child with sickle cell anaemia experiences a worsening of pain or infection or anaemia	no	suddenly becomes unwell, may have – severe pain – neck stiffness – headache – drowsiness	urgent hospital treatment as soon as possible
Threadworms	threadworms 1) egg swallowed 2) develop into worms in intestine 3) worms come outside anus at night to lay eggs 4) this causes itching 5) child scratches – eggs are deposited under nails 6) child licks fingers or sucks thumb – swallow eggs	yes	presence of threadworms in stool (white cotton-like pieces); sore anus; itchy bottom; sleeplessness; lack of appetite	doctor; Pripsen – all children in family should be treated; hygienic measures to prevent infestation: prevent scratching – tight pyjamas; nails cut short; scrub hands and nails before eating
Thrush	fungus, via unsterile dummy or bottle teat, or unwashed hands	yes	white patches inside mouth; sore mouth; diarrhoea, vomiting may be present sore bottom	doctor strict hygiene measures to prevent spread via dirty hands
Vomiting	various may be infection may be feed wrong may be defect, e.g. pyloric stenosis may be regurgitation	yes no no	evacuation of stomach contents	doctor within 24 hours if under 1 year old; doctor if continuous in older child; boiled water or 'Dioralyte' only to drink for 24 hours.

CARING FOR SICK CHILDREN AT HOME

Many parents and nursery nurses are hesitant to call a doctor to a sick child because they fear it may prove to be something trivial which does not warrant a doctor's attention. However, it is better to be safe than sorry and as a child's condition can change from hour to hour he can become seriously ill very rapidly. If you are in doubt, telephone the child's doctor and ask advice, rather than wait until late at night and have to call him or her out. The following list of conditions indicate an urgent need for a doctor's advice:

1. severe pain
2. suspected ear infection – pulling ears, banging head, etc.
3. vomiting – for twenty-four hours if a baby under one year
4. diarrhoea – for twenty-four hours if a baby under one year
5. abnormal urine
6. hoarseness or noisy breathing
7. loss of interest in what is going on around him by baby under one year
8. rash which causes irritation or is accompanied by illness
9. convulsions or fits
10. raised temperature:
    – a temperature of 38.3 °C (101 °F) or higher
    – a temperature above 37.3 °C (100 °F) over a period of four hours.

Every nursery nurse should be able to take a child's temperature and read a thermometer. The normal temperature range for a child is 36.1 °C to 37.2 °C (97 ° to 99 °F) and temperatures are usually slightly higher in the evening. Young children do not have an efficient temperature regulating mechanism, so their temperatures rise easily when they are excited or playing. Therefore a raised temperature must not be used as the only indication of illness.

To take a temperature. Always shake mercury column down to below 35 °C (95 °F). For children under fourteen years of age temperatures should be taken in the axilla (armpit) or groin.

1. Explain to the child what you are doing and show him the thermometer.
2. Sit child on your lap.
3. Dry axilla (or groin) with a towel.
4. Place thermometer between two folds of skin.
5. Hold limb and keep thermometer in position for *three minutes*.
6. Remove thermometer, put child in cot.
7. Read thermometer and record temperature.

Temperatures may also be taken in the rectum but only by a trained and experienced person. When quoting a temperature to a doctor, always say where temperature was obtained, as there is a slight difference in reading.

Care of thermometer
Wash well in luke-warm water after use. Shake mercury column down to below 35 °C (95 °F).

Casual use: Dry and replace in case.

Daily use: Place in a small jar of antiseptic solution. Cotton wool in base of jar will prevent damage. The thermometer will not need to be washed again before use.

A useful, quick way of finding out if a child has a high temperature is by using a plastic 'Fever tape' which you hold onto the child's forehead for a few seconds. This is not as accurate as a thermometer, but can serve as a useful guide without disturbing the sick child too much.

To check the pulse. It is useful to be able to count a child's pulse rate as well as take his temperature, because the pulse can give information regarding the rate and force with which the heart is beating. It may be felt on the thumb side of the wrist where an artery passes over a bone. The first three fingers should be placed over the artery and the rate counted for a full minute. A child's pulse is usually about 120 beats a minute.

Routine for the sick child. When a child is ill he tends to regress and act as though younger than his true age. He may become very frightened so he needs a familar person to care for him and to stay close to him. It is a good idea to keep as much as possible to his normal routine, whilst making adjustments for his illness, because this makes him feel secure. He still has the same needs for cleanliness, rest and food, etc. but the provision of these needs will have to be adapted to his condition.

The sick room should be warm, cheerful and uncluttered. It will need to be well-ventilated and easily cleaned without causing too much disturbance to the child. If possible there should be a water supply and washing facilities in the same room. A potty should be available for the child so that he doesn't have to be taken to the lavatory. The mattress should be protected by a plastic sheet because even if he has achieved bladder control, he may regress during his illness. Whilst he is very ill a child will want to stay in bed, but once he is on the mend he should be allowed to get up and dress. He can lie on the top of the bed or a settee for rest periods. When he is in bed let him lie in the most comfortable position for him. For example, if he has a cough he will want to be propped in a sitting position. This can be done with pillows for the child over a year, but if it is a young baby then the head of his cot can be raised by propping the legs securely on blocks. In this case make sure the baby is lying on his side.

A child will still need his daily bath, but, if necessary, this can be in the form of an all-over wash in bed. His hair should be brushed and combed daily and his teeth should be cleaned after every meal to keep his mouth fresh. He will need to be encouraged to use the potty before and after meals, and his hands should be washed after the toilet and before he eats. His bed should be made night and morning, and sheets and pillowcases changed frequently.

A sick child will not feel like eating, so meals must be light and appetising and in small helpings. Suitable foods include egg custard, steamed fish, chicken, milk pudding and ice cream. If he does not wish to eat, offer plenty of fluids and make sure that he drinks them.

If you have to carry out any nursing procedures explain what you are going to do first, and then proceed. Medicines are best measured into a small

glass or cup rather than a spoon, and the child can be offered a sweet afterwards. Tablets can be crushed and mixed with jam. Do not put medicines in a baby's bottle or a child's food because unless all the milk or food is eaten the correct dose will not be taken. Medicine must be taken and most children will accept the fact if you are firm and honest with them.

Hygiene during sickness. A sick child becomes very vulnerable to any infection because his resistance is lowered by his illness. Therefore the nurse should be scrupulous in her personal hygiene to protect him from further illness (see page 90).

Prevention of infection. If a child is suffering from an infectious disease it may be necessary to isolate him from people who have not already had the disease. Some doctors believe that, as the most infectious time is during the incubation period, it could be too late to prevent infection spreading when the disease becomes obvious. However, the dangers of infection remain until the main signs and symptoms, such as a rash, have subsided; so if you do not want other children to be infected they should be kept away from the sufferer until this period is over. A child attending day nursery or nursery school will usually be excluded until his doctor says he is clear of infection.

Very high temperature and dehydration. These are two of the most dangerous conditions for a child and they often occur together, causing serious problems needing hospital treatment. As a child is unable to regulate his temperature as finely as an adult, it can rise rapidly, causing a convulsion or fit. This can be very frightening to the child and to the adult in charge and may even lead to brain damage. The best treatment is prevention. Even without a thermometer it is possible to tell that a child's temperature is rising. He looks limp and miserable. He shivers because the air feels cold to his hot skin and when you touch him his body feels very hot. The easiest way to bring down a child's temperature is to put him in a bath of tepid water for about ten to fifteen minutes. This can be repeated at intervals. In bed he should be lightly clad and be covered with only a sheet. Resist the temptation to wrap him up because he is shivering – this will only make his temperature go higher. If a bath is not practicable, then strip off his clothes, place a towel under him and sponge him down with very tepid water. Pat him dry with another towel. Like the bath, this can be repeated whilst waiting for the doctor to arrive.

Dehydration occurs with fever or if the illness causes a loss of fluid, such as vomiting, diarrhoea or a head cold. The mouth and tongue become dry and parched and cracks appear on the lips. The child's urine is sparse and very concentrated, which gives it a dark colour. Dehydration means that the body fluids are not balanced and as this balance is necessary for health the child can become very ill. The treatment is prevention, by giving a sick child frequent drinks of water or any other fluid. If it is a baby under a year, then the fluid should be cool, boiled water and if he is too weak to suck from a bottle, then he must be spoon-fed at frequent intervals. The older child can have a variety of fluids – freshly squeezed orange juice or ice lolly, tomato juice, lemon barley water, glucose drink, clear soup, beef broth, or beef extract. These must be offered at frequent intervals because he will not ask for them or help himself. A straw (especially a 'bendy' one) may be useful to persuade him to drink, or a special glass or a doll's cup and saucer.

Convalescence. Fortunately, because a child's condition can change so rapidly, he usually recovers very quickly. He will need a period of convalescence so that he can recover his strength and adjust back to normal life again. He will also need a nourishing diet high in protein to repair his damaged body cells and he should not be allowed to get over-tired.

Amusing a sick or convalescent child means planning ahead and being organised. As the child will regress, activities suitable for a younger-aged child should be provided, remembering that a child has a very short attention span. If he is confined to bed, a large tray or bed table is useful for his games. He can have a variety of materials and toys and most of the activities carried on in nurseries can be adapted to play in bed. If he must rest, reading stories, letting him listen to records and singing to him will all help him to relax. (See Chapter 16 on play.)

HOSPITAL

When a child has to be admitted to hospital, if at all possible time should be given to prepare him for this, so that he knows what to expect. Explain as simply and truthfully as you can what will happen to him and emphasise that he will be coming home again. Most hospitals have arrangements for mothers (or nannies) to stay with their child all day and in some cases sleep in. It is very important for the child to have his mother (or mother substitute) with him to maintain his emotional security. Before admission, find out the policy of the hospital concerned so that you can be realistic. Many hospitals send out a booklet explaining procedures. You can also obtain information from The National Association for the Welfare of Children in Hospital (NAWCH) which publishes several helpful leaflets for parents and books for young children. Of course, if the hospital admission is an emergency, there will be little time for preparation, but despite the haste and probable panic, try to make some truthful explanation, such as, 'The doctor in hospital will try to make your pain better.'

When packing, make sure you take the child's favourite toy as a link with home. If he usually has a piece of blanket to suck, or a 'cuddly', or a dummy, let him take it with him. Tell the staff his nickname and any special word he may use for the potty, etc.

If the child is to have an operation then explain to him in simple language what will happen. Children are much better than adults at accepting the truth and can cope with pain provided they are not scared of the unknown.

When you have to leave the child be calm, tell him when you will be back, say goodbye and go quickly – don't try to slip away unnoticed because this will make him lose faith in you. It may help to leave your scarf or glove for him 'to look after', as this will reassure him you will be back.

Children's wards are mostly informal, homely places with specially trained staff who are aware of children's needs. Parents are usually welcomed and help with much of the nursing care. The children are allowed to be up and dressed in their own clothes as soon as they are fit enough. Play is encouraged by 'the play lady' who is probably a trained nursery nurse. School-aged children attend the hospital school during school hours. The majority of children enjoy their time in hospital and settle well. Occasionally there are problems when the child comes home. He may regress in behaviour and be difficult for a while. So long as sympathy and understanding are given, he will soon regain his sense of security.

EXERCISES

Investigation
Find out what is meant by the term 'notifiable disease'. Which diseases does it apply to?

Observation
Observe a parent caring for his/her sick child, either at home or in hospital. In your evaluation, suggest how the parent copes with the emotional strain.

Project
This exercise can be done in pairs.

Choose one of the common infectious diseases and research it in depth, including how to care for the child affected by it. Present your findings to the rest of the group.

SUGGESTIONS FOR FURTHER READING

Gerard Vaughan, *A Pictorial Guide to Common Childhood Illness,* Arcade Publishing Magazine Ltd

Eva Noble, *Play and the Sick Child*, Faber & Faber Ltd

James Robertson, ed., *Hospitals and Children*, Victor Gollancz Ltd

Dr Patricia Gilbert, *Common Childhood Illnesses*, Sheldon Press

R Illingworth, *Common Ailments in Babies*, British Medical Association

Barbara Weller, *Helping Sick Children Play*, Baillière Tindall

10 Growth and Physical Development

Whilst growth is an increase in a child's size, development is an increase in his ability. In practice, it is difficult to separate the two. The process of growth and all the different aspects of development interact with and are dependent on one another. For example, a baby will not start responding to his mother until he is capable of identifying her as a distinct person. However, for the purposes of study, it is necessary to separate these aspects but, at the same time, to note how the interactions take place. All babies follow the same pattern but, as they are all individuals with different environments and experiences, there are bound to be variations within this pattern, especially in the timing of the various stages. It is useful to know this pattern and its variation because it gives us a means of measuring progress.

For many years babies and children have been regularly weighed and measured and these results compared with a table of average weights and heights for various ages. But although this was a useful pointer to normal development, it was by no means a thorough guide.

The concept of developmental tests in conjunction with measuring was much slower to materialise. Hundreds of children were examined to determine the average ages for the various stages of development. Tests were devised to make use of this research. Now it is common for children to be examined at intervals from birth onwards for developmental assessment – that is to make sure that the child is growing and developing at an average rate. This has led to an earlier diagnosis of 'backwardness' or 'failure to progress' and enabled help to be given much earlier. A good example of this is the story of Michael. Michael was nine months old when brought for his first check-up, his very young mother not having thought it necessary before this time. He was found to be about three months behind in his development. His mother described him as a 'good' baby who never gave any trouble. Investigations revealed no physical reason for delay in development, but on talking to his mother it became obvious that Michael lacked stimulation. His mother expected him to lie in his cot all day. She seldom spoke to him because she herself was desperately unhappy and depressed. An attempt was made to explain to her Michael's need for attention and she was referred to her own doctor for treatment of her depression. Because there was very little improvement in the situation, Michael was admitted to a day nursery where he rapidly responded to the stimulating environment. Fortunately his mother formed a good relationship with his nursery nurse and began to take pride in Michael's achievements. At two years of age Michael was well within the normal range of development. But if the deprivation had continued, he could have remained backward all his life. Michael was fortunate, firstly because his mother eventually took him to the clinic for a check and secondly because there was a nursery place available to him.

On the whole the results of developmental testing have been disappointing apart from the detection of impairment of hearing and sight.

These developmental defects can be recognised by specific tests and can often be helped easily. For example, if a child is found to have poor hearing, he can be fitted with a hearing aid from about six months of age. This means that he may hear normal speech and therefore have a chance to learn to speak normally.

Other defects are not so obvious and so can go undetected. Many tests are subjective and need skilled interpretation. Some parents, especially those in the lower socio-economic groups, do not attend clinics for checks as they do not understand why it is necessary. In areas where health visitors check children's development at home there are still parents who regard this as an intrusion and do not co-operate. In addition, facilities which would help children to catch up, such as nursery provision or help for the mother at home, do not exist in some areas – it is pointless to identify children in need and then be unable to help them. This is a great pity because the earlier a defect or delay can be detected, the sooner help can be given and the possibility of minimising the damage is much greater. Some authorities have tried to pick out children who are 'at risk' and concentrate on testing and providing help for this group only, but this is difficult to do accurately and it could mean that many children needing attention are missed. In an effort to encourage parents to understand the value of regular checks and the need to find problems as early as possible, many authorities have introduced a child health record book to contain all the relevant details of the child's examinations and treatment,

such as immunisations, and this is held by the parents. Parents are encouraged to add any relevant information and to produce the book when attending clinics or hospitals.

It is essential for nursery nurses to know how a child grows and develops. They are often the closest person to a child and, by their knowledge and observation, they could be the first to notice that a child is not progressing as well as he should. So, as well as learning in theory what to expect at various ages, student nursery nurses should also develop their powers of observation by watching children wherever they go. There are always babies and children in shops, buses and parks, etc. as well as in the nursery or school. An interesting and useful exercise is to watch children playing and try to estimate their ages. This helps you to know what is normal, and is essential if you are to be able to detect what is abnormal. Your written observations, which are part of the NNEB course, are meant to help you develop these powers of observation.

GROWTH OF CHILDREN

If you compare a newborn baby with an adult, you will see that not only is the baby obviously a lot smaller, but he is a different shape as well, because his proportions are all very different. His head appears to be very large compared with his body; in fact it is just over half the size of an adult head. Although the baby's body is small, it is his arms and legs that are extremely short. Therefore it is obvious that most of his growth must take place in the long bones of his legs and arms. Indeed, by four months of age his limbs will already be beginning to lengthen and his proportions will have changed.

Compare the sizes of the mother's head and limbs with those of the baby on her lap

Long bones form early in foetal life as cartilage, a thick, rubbery substance which bends easily. During later pregnancy and childhood, calcium, phosphorus and vitamin D are gradually deposited on to the cartilage to form hard bone. The process is known as ossification and it continues until all growth ceases, which is usually some time between twenty and twenty-four years of age. Most of the ossification takes place during foetal life and early childhood – hence the need to ensure a good supply of calcium, phosphorus and vitamin D in the diet during the first five years of life.

The ossification of the long bones starts at both the extreme ends and the centre of the cartilage, and the patches gradually spread towards each other, eventually leaving a 'neck' of cartilage at each end which enables growth to continue (see diagram).

By studying X-rays of children's long bones, it is possible to estimate a child's age by the degree of ossification. This is known as the 'bone age'. It is a useful guide for estimating future growth. For example, if a teenager is very small, X-rays may reveal that there is still a fair amount of cartilage present so that the child can be reassured that he will continue to grow. But once the long bones of the legs and arms are fully ossified, then no more growth can take place. In most people this occurs at about twenty-one years of age.

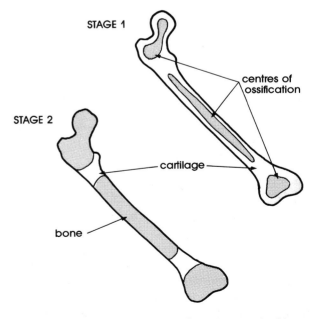

Development of bone

Teeth develop in a similar way. Here the process of ossification is called calcification, and the outer surface of the teeth (the enamel) becomes much harder than bone. The first 'teeth buds' form in the gums by about four months of pregnancy and the buds of the second, or permanent, teeth form just before birth. The buds are small pieces of cartilage and, by birth, the process of calcification of the first teeth has begun. Some babies are born with one or two teeth, but more commonly they begin to erupt between six and ten months of age when they are fully calcified. The second teeth will have already begun calcifying and they will begin to erupt from about five years of age.

The first teeth are usually complete by about two and a half years of age. There are twenty in all and they consist of eight incisors which are chisel-shaped for biting and are in the front of the mouth, four canines and eight molars which are flatter in shape to enable chewing and mastication to take place. They usually erupt in a definite order:

a) two lower central incisors
b) two upper central incisors
c) two upper lateral incisors
d) two lower lateral incisors
e) four first molars
f) four canines
g) four second molars.

They are known as deciduous teeth because, like the leaves of deciduous trees, they are shed. Around five years of age the roots of the first teeth are gradually absorbed by the body so that they become loose because of lack of anchorage. At the same time the second teeth are pushing upwards. Eventually, one by one, the first teeth fall out and the new ones erupt. In most children these processes occur at the same time, but sometimes a child will have a gap for a while before the new tooth appears. There are thirty-two permanent teeth, consisting of four incisors, two canines, four premolars and six molars in each jaw, and they gradually erupt during the next ten years or so, during which time the jaw must grow forward to accommodate the thirty-two larger teeth which will replace the twenty small 'baby' teeth. This growth of the jaw is a gradual process from about six months of age but there is a spurt of growth between five and

seven years of age and this accounts for the change from a 'baby face' to one with more adult characteristics.

Since the teeth calcify early in life, it follows that calcium, phosphorus and vitamin D are extremely important in the diet for the first five years of life. If fluoride is also given by mouth in the first five years, it will combine with calcium and phosphorus to make the enamel surface of the tooth harder and more resistant to attack from bacteria which leads to decay. Applications of fluoride after the teeth have erupted are not so effective because the fluoride must be absorbed through the surface of the teeth, which limits the amount available. However, this treatment will help to reduce the rate of decay.

Although most growth continues at a steady rate throughout the body, there are exceptions, the most striking being the brain, the skull and the reproductive organs.

Brain and skull. The growth and development of the brain, spinal cord, eyes and ears are very rapid until about two years of age, when sixty per cent of their development is complete. By the time the child is seven years of age, they are almost adult size. The skull also grows rapidly to accommodate the enlarging brain. At birth it is 33–35 cm (13–14 in) in circumference, while at one year of age it is approximately 45 cm (18 in) and by seven years it is about 50 cm (20 in). The average circumference of an adult head is 55.8 cm (22 in).

The skull is made up of flat plates of bone which join together to form a box-like structure. There are two gaps (called fontanelles) created by the spaces at the joints of the skull bones.

The fontanelles are covered with membrane which protects the brain. They gradually close as the bones of the skull grow together. The posterior (back) fontanelle is usually closed by six to seven weeks, the anterior (front) one by about eighteen months. If the fontanelles are slow in closing it is an indication of poor bone growth, possibly owing to lack of calcium and vitamin D.

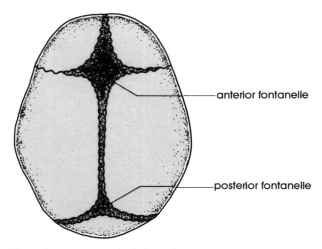

Top of a young baby's head

Sexual organs. In contrast to the rapid early growth and development of the brain and skull, the sexual organs grow very slowly until about the age of ten, and then, with the onset of puberty, there is a period of rapid growth and development, which begins earlier in girls than boys.

Weight. Weighing and measuring a child at regular intervals is a useful guide to his state of health, especially during the first year of life. If a baby is gaining weight steadily then we know that he must be getting enough food and making use of it for growth. If, in addition, he is happy, lively and active we can be sure that all is well. On the other hand, if a small baby does not gain any weight for two to three weeks it is an indication that something is wrong. It may simply be that he is not getting enough food or it could be that because of vomiting or some other reason he is unable to absorb the food. (If too much weight is gained, then it is an indication for the child's diet to be regulated to prevent obesity.)

However, weighing and measuring need to be carried out over a period of time at regular intervals so that the pattern of growth can be seen. The average newborn baby weighs about 3.400 kg (7 lb 8 oz) but his weight could be anything between 2.50 and 6 kg (5½ lb–14 lb), so when studying a baby's weight gain it is necessary to know his birth weight. Variations in the lengths of babies are not so big, the average length being 50 cm (20½ in) within a range of 45.5 cm–55.8 cm (18–22 in). Boys are usually slightly heavier than girls, although boys and girls tend to grow at much the same rate in the first seven to ten years.

Many clinics use percentile charts (see opposite) to record the measurements of children in their first five years because they are a very useful guide to a child's well-being. They show the average weight and height (the fiftieth percentile) and the variations within the normal range of growth. A summary of the individual child's progress can be easily compared to the average rate of growth. They are often used in cases such as suspected abuse to demonstrate the child's state of health.

The figures below show that a baby grows very rapidly indeed during the first year of life. After this, growth slows down to a steady rate. This fact is important because it demonstrates how unreasonable it is to expect the one to five year old to eat as enormously as he did in his first year. He does not need such large meals because his growth has slowed down.

Age	Height (cm)	Weight (kg)	Height (in)	Weight (lb)
Birth	52	3.400	20½	7½
5 months	63.5	6.800 Double birth weight	25	15
1 year	71	10.200 Treble birth weight	28	22½
1½ years	76	11.700	30	26
2 years	83.5	13.600 Four times birth weight	33	30
3 years	94	16.000	37	34
4 years	101.5	18.000	40	39
5 years	106.5	20.400 Six times birth weight	42	45
6 years	111.5	22.000	44	48
7 years	119.5	23.800 Seven times birth weight	47	52

Girls

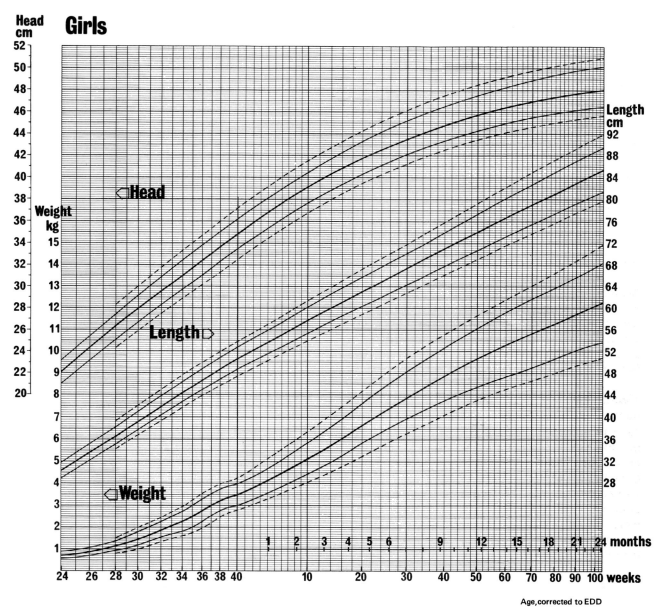

Head cm
52 — 50 — 48 — 46 — 44 — 42 — 40 — 38 — 36 — 34 — 32 — 30 — 28 — 26 — 24 — 22 — 20

Weight kg
15 — 14 — 13 — 12 — 11 — 10 — 9 — 8 — 7 — 6 — 5 — 4 — 3 — 2 — 1

Head

Length

Weight

Length cm
92 — 88 — 84 — 80 — 76 — 72 — 68 — 64 — 60 — 56 — 52 — 48 — 44 — 40 — 36 — 32 — 28

1 2 3 4 5 6 9 12 15 18 21 24 **months**

24 26 28 30 32 34 36 38 40 10 20 30 40 50 60 70 80 90 100 **weeks**

Age, corrected to EDD

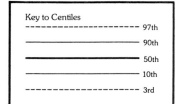

Key to Centiles

– – – – – – – – – 97th

———————— 90th

———————— 50th

———————— 10th

– – – – – – – – – 3rd

Growth and development chart for girls from preterm (twenty-fourth week of pregnancy) to two years old, showing the normal range of growth in length, weight and head circumference

Chart prepared by Drs D Gairdner and J Pearson; first published in Archives of Disease in Childhood *(1971); Ref GPG3; © Castlemead Publications*

The child's eventual height will depend mostly on hereditary factors, bearing in mind that most children are slightly taller than their parents. A useful prediction of a child's eventual height is obtained by doubling his height at two years of age.

Factors which affect growth adversely are as follows:
1. poor diet, especially lack of protein
2. poor general health, often associated with poor diet
3. serious illness
4. lack of exercise
5. lack of sufficient rest and sleep
6. lack of affection, security and stimulation
7. lack of growth hormone which is produced by the pituitary gland (very rare).

1. It is no accident that the teenagers of today are larger than their grandparents. Increasing knowledge of diet, and the lessening of dire poverty, have meant that most children today have the right foods for growth and good health. Before the Second World War it was possible to guess the social class of a person by his height and his health. People from the upper classes always had adequate food so their children tended to grow tall and strong. They also appeared to be, on average, brighter and more attractive. This has led to the belief that a poor protein diet in the first two years of life (when the brain is growing and developing rapidly) will prevent a person reaching his full intellectual potential. Such a theory is difficult to prove because poor diet is often linked with so many other socio-economic problems in a child's life.

2. and 3. If a child has a series of minor illnesses or one serious illness, growth is often held back for a while, although most children catch up rapidly when they are fit again.

4. Lack of exercise will lead to poor muscle 'tone' which slows down growth.

5. Lack of rest and sleep tends to slow down growth.

6. Evidence suggests that emotional problems in a child caused by lack of affection, security and stimulation can result in a slowing down of growth.

THE DEVELOPMENT OF CHILDREN

The process of development is continuous from conception to maturity. So the first observable signs are when the baby begins to kick in his mother's womb.

Although a human being is an animal, there are some differences that make us superior in some respects to all other animals. These differences can be summarised as follows:

1. the ability to stand upright and walk, thus leaving the hands free for food gathering, defence and other activities

2. the ability to use the index-finger in opposition to the thumb. This enables humans to perform fine movements and to use implements

3. the ability to use a spoken language and to think abstractly – this allows humans to communicate and reason

4. the complexity of human emotions and social relationships.

The study of a child's development, therefore, is observations of these aspects.

The human baby is one of the most helpless of creatures at birth, yet, by the time he is a year old, he has a rudimentary mastery of many of the skills necessary for his future life. By his first birthday he is mobile, in some way or other – either by rolling over, 'swimming' on the floor or by crawling, creeping or even walking. He has an understanding of speech and will be communicating his needs by pointing and/or using his voice. His manipulative powers are developing, so that he can pick up objects, examine them and discard them if not wanted.

Physical and motor development

The newborn baby has very little control of his body but he does have reflex movements which are essential to his survival. A reflex movement is an automatic response to certain stimulus – there is no conscious control. A good example of a reflex movement is seen when a person treads on an upturned drawing pin. The foot is removed very rapidly without the need to think 'I must move my foot'.

The baby's reflexes include the following:

'Rooting' reflex – when his cheek is touched he will turn his head and 'search' with his mouth for the nipple.

'I can walk'

Sucking reflex – when a nipple or teat or any other object enters his mouth he will suck strongly.

Palmar and plantar reflexes – when an object is placed in the palm of the hand, the fingers will grip the object firmly. Similarly, if an object is placed on the sole of the foot, the toes will curl around it. This reflex was essential when the baby had to cling to his mother's hair. It is a throw-back to our prehistoric ancestry.

'Startle' reflex – in response to any sudden movement or noise, the baby will visibly 'jump' and spread his arms and legs wide whilst screaming.

Stepping reflex – if you hold a newborn baby upright on a flat surface, he will make stepping movements with his feet.

In addition to these reflex movements, the newborn baby communicates by crying; he can wave his arms and legs and turn his head from side to side. When placed on his tummy, he can lift his head from the floor momentarily, but when he is held upright his head will fall back unless it is supported.

Gradually the reflexes vanish and are taken over by conscious controlled movements. His crying becomes more concentrated and more a demand for services.

Motor development. Motor development and control of movement follows a set pattern, the earliest development being the control of the eyes and lips. From then on development follows two principles:

1. The control of the head and back is followed by the gradual control of the rest of the body from the head downwards.

2. The control of the larger muscles and big movements must come before control of the smaller muscles and finer movements.

In addition there are various periods in a baby's life during which he is 'ready' to master a certain skill, such as sitting up or walking, because his body has become capable of doing so. And if the right stimulus is given at this time then he will achieve this skill easily. On the other hand, if stimulus is lacking then his development will be impaired. This means that a child cannot be 'taught' a motor skill until his muscles are capable of performing it. Therefore it is essential to supply the correct stimulus at the right moment for him and most mothers will do this instinctively.

Motor development follows a pattern, although the age at which a child reaches each stage varies quite considerably. Some stages of this development may be apparent for only a day or two, others may last for many weeks.

A baby starts to 'learn' to walk even before he is born. By kicking and other movements in the uterus, he is exercising his muscles and helping in their development. After birth the first stage towards becoming upright is the raising of his head, followed by the lifting of his head and shoulders. He must gain control of his back, trunk and arm muscles, so that he can sit up, before he gains control of the leg muscles so that he can walk. This is why it is important to give a baby plenty of opportunity to move from early days. Equally important is to let him walk in his own time and not try to force this development by putting him in a baby walker contraption.

A chart to show the progression towards walking and dexterity is printed below.

Factors that will help him are:

* good diet and good health

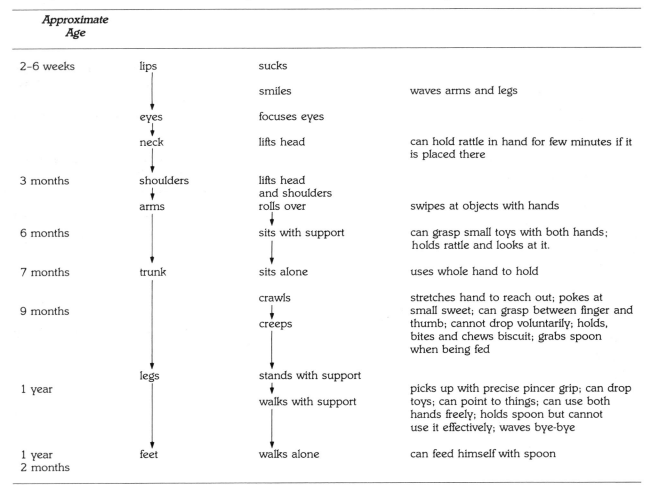

Approximate Age			
2–6 weeks	lips	sucks	
		smiles	waves arms and legs
	eyes	focuses eyes	
	neck	lifts head	can hold rattle in hand for few minutes if it is placed there
3 months	shoulders	lifts head and shoulders	
	arms	rolls over	swipes at objects with hands
6 months		sits with support	can grasp small toys with both hands; holds rattle and looks at it.
7 months	trunk	sits alone	uses whole hand to hold
9 months		crawls	stretches hand to reach out; pokes at small sweet; can grasp between finger and thumb; cannot drop voluntarily; holds, bites and chews biscuit; grabs spoon when being fed
		creeps	
	legs	stands with support	
1 year		walks with support	picks up with precise pincer grip; can drop toys; can point to things; can use both hands freely; holds spoon but cannot use it effectively; waves bye-bye
1 year 2 months	feet	walks alone	can feed himself with spoon

- opportunity to exercise – because this increases muscle tone which helps development
- plenty of freedom to move around and explore from early days
- bare feet – avoiding any restrictions of shoes; better grip on floor
- stimulation – fun and encouragement from parents/nursery nurse
- push and pull-along toys.

Walking may be accomplished at any time between about seven months and two years and still be within the normal range. Some children seem to make determined efforts to get on their feet early, whereas others learn to crawl very efficiently and do not try very hard to walk at all until they are a year old or more. From mastery of walking, the child progresses to running, climbing, and walking up and down stairs. From about three years of age he can throw and kick a ball with some degree of accuracy and ride a tricycle. By the time he is approaching seven years old he will be able to run on his toes and will be active and skilful in sliding, climbing, swinging and hopping. He will also be able to dance to music.

The hands become more and more efficient, especially for finer movements, so that the child learns to use them purposefully. By eighteen months he should be able to feed himself with a cup and spoon, although he may still need help to finish his dinner. At two years he can unwrap a small sweet and pick up pins and needles. By two and a half he can pull down his own pants at the toilet, although he cannot always get them up, and can eat skilfully with spoon and may use a fork.

By the time he is approaching seven years of age he can use a knife and fork, print accurately and draw recognisable pictures.

At the same time as all this progress is being made, the child's speech is also developing rapidly, so that by two years of age he can indicate his needs and should be able to put two words together. By this time too, he also understands a good deal more than he can say, and by the age of seven he will be able to communicate well in sentences.

EXERCISES

Observation
Draw a block graph of the heights of the children at your placement. Obtain the relevant percentile charts and work out how many are below the fiftieth percentile, and how many are above it.

Investigation
Following on from the observation exercise above, see if you can find out, *tactfully*, why some children are below average height.

Project
Plan a health education project for school-age children on teeth. State your aims. The project should incorporate the different types of teeth, why we care for them and how, and include contact with dentists.

SUGGESTIONS FOR FURTHER READING

Arnold Gesell, *How a Baby Grows*, Hamish Hamilton Ltd
Arnold Gesell, *The First Five Years*, Methuen & Co., Ltd
Mary D. Sheridan, *The Developmental Progression in Young Children*, HMSO
Mary D. Sheridan, *Spontaneous Play in Early Childhood*, NFER-Nelson Publishing Co Ltd
Mary D. Sheridan, *Children's Developmental Progress*, NFER-Nelson Publishing Co Ltd
The First Years of Life, (Open University in association with The Health Education Council), Ward Lock Ltd

11 Cognitive Development

What is actually going on inside the human head, when a person thinks, learns, remembers, understands, solves problems? We can see the results of these processes. We know a good deal about the composition of the brain, and its function as the headquarters of a most complicated communications network. But knowing exactly *how* it works, to produce rational human beings, distinct from all other primates, is still beyond the best efforts of scientists, psychologists, philosophers, neuro-surgeons, and neurophysiologists.

Some people have compared the function of the brain to a computer, solving problems from given data. Other people have described it as a massive telephone exchange, receiving and connecting incoming calls, and transmitting appropriate outgoing messages. Others have likened it to the flight deck of an aeroplane. But none of these analogies are complete. They do not take account of biological or environmental factors, or further dimensions such as conscience, experience and intention, which all influence human behaviour.

What we do know is that mind, behaviour and personality depend on the effective interaction of brain and body.

oblongata, which takes care of automatic functions like the pumping of the heart and breathing. The cerebellum controls the voluntary actions of the muscles. The cerebrum is the seat of consciousness, memory, reason – affecting learning and personality.

The brain is almost fully supplied with nerve cells (neurons) as early as eighteen foetal weeks. Its growth will be virtually complete by age seven. Both nerve cells and interlinking dendrites will continue to develop rapidly up to two years of age. Different parts will develop at different rates. For example, we have already seen that a child gains control over the upper parts of his body before the lower. This is because those centres in the brain which govern the hands, arms and upper body develop first. The skin and sense organs, well developed at birth, are richly supplied with nerve cells which respond to touch, pain etc., and these convert information received into nerve impulses which are sent to the brain. Information requiring action can come from inside the body as well as outside, hunger pangs for example.

Almost every action we take supplies feedback to the brain. The process of learning is the individual making sense of all this feedback, thus making sense of the world, and bringing it under his control.

THE HUMAN BRAIN AND NERVOUS SYSTEM

The brain weighs about 1.3 kg and consists of a pinkish-grey mass protected by the skull. It is cushioned against bumps and blows by shock-absorbing fluid, and is wrapped in three membranes. Its outer surface resembles a walnut without its shell.

There are three main message centres: the medulla

THE BABY LEARNS

An observer might think the newborn baby is a stranger to the world, and yet he has already been a part of it for nine months. He has heard his mother's voice from within; he has also reacted to loud noises and shocks.

The new baby can see, hear, suck and cry. His actions are reflex actions, which bypass the brain (see page 115). All other skills and responses have to be learned, and the way he learns is first through the thousands of sense impressions (perceptions) his nerve cells receive and transmit to the brain. Although newborn babies are awake for only short periods of time, they very quickly show adaptive responses to the information flooding in. They will turn their head towards the source of a noise made near by. They can get rid of an irritant on one leg by rubbing it with the other leg. They will look intently at their mother or main carer, and can distinguish this person from others.

At a young age they will not only turn their head to a noise, but look keenly for the source of the noise, thus showing that they are making mental connections. Watching their own hands and feet is giving them feedback about body movement, which will help in later coordination.

Babies seem to have inbuilt aids to learning. While awake, they:

- are ceaselessly active (watch a slowed down film of a young baby)
- can attend to items that interest them (watch a baby looking at a fluttering mobile)
- show curiosity to attend to further items of interest
- appear to enjoy mastering new skills such as hand clapping
- want to repeat such new-found skills again and again
- imitate sounds and actions demonstrated to them – babies who later prove to have extrovert personalities will imitate much more than introverts
- display the power of motivation in learning, for example, anticipating the bestowing of attention, love, and/or food, when mother or carer appears.

The baby is already interacting with the environment, and the stimulus of this develops and matures his vision and other senses.

Until about a year old, babies are highly distractible: a tantalizingly hidden toy will be forgotten if he finds something more interesting during the search. A toy

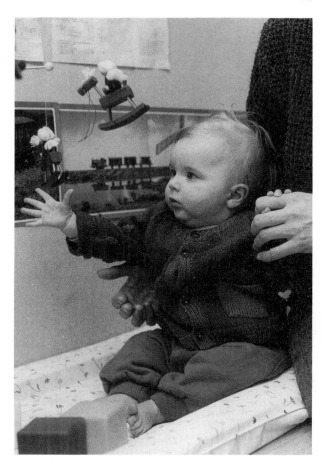

Mobiles offer visual stimulation from an early age

thrown out of a pram is not sought or wanted. But soon after this stage, internal memories and expectations begin to control his behaviour. He will have grasped the concept of object permanence i.e. he understands that objects and people still exist even if he cannot see them. He begins to see a consistency and pattern in the way things behave, and this knowledge becomes a series of concepts (ideas) which will continue to expand and strengthen as he grows up. This process is known as concept formation or conceptualisation.

Before the age of two, he will be able to make mental deductions, show purpose and intention in his actions, and have a little understanding of space and time, cause and effect.

THE PRE-SCHOOL CHILD LEARNS

Nearly 50 per cent of the child's mental capability will be developed between birth and age four, which makes this period a critically important and impressionable time.

As he continues to explore his world, and interact with his carers, the child's growing range of adaptive responses can be seen as intelligence.

Memories,
a) of sensory information received
b) short term (fleeting impressions)
c) long term (of things that happened some time before),
all feed the child's adaptive responses. Memories of experiences are stored and organised, and those that have meaning for his current situation are selected and used to influence his responses. For example, if he remembers strawberry ice-cream as being good to eat, he will probably tackle with gusto a new type of pudding that resembles it, even though this may be shortlived!

Things are easier to remember if they make sense. Look at the following diagram. Each square contains the same number and shapes of curving marks. However, you will probably react to and therefore remember, only one of them – the one associated with meaning.

Children learn by:

- observing
- doing
- mental association.

New skills demand that the individual makes links not only between past experiences and the present situation, but also between senses and muscles. Can you remember when you first tried to roll out pastry? You were probably somewhere between three and five years old and begged a piece of pastry from your mother having watched her making pies or tarts. You probably grasped the rolling pin fiercely, with tense elbows and hands, and clenched jaw. You thumped it onto the pastry and rolled for all you were worth. But somehow, bumps and ridges still remained. You ground the cutter onto the pastry, and, using both hands, leaned on it with all your might. When you came to pick pieces up, they stuck to the worktop, or broke. As you continued to work on it, the pastry became harder (and probably greyer), and increasingly difficult to work. You were very slow, and your mother's patience was sorely tried as she oversaw your persistent efforts. On subsequent occasions, partly through trial and error, and partly through adults' suggestions, you gradually built up more know-how. Your arms, hands and jaws relaxed; your touch was lighter; your movements became more deft, co-ordinated and quick. You built up a steady rhythm of roll, cut, lift, place. Over the years, helped by further practice and tuition at school, you have probably used this basic skill to make all kinds of pastry-based recipes.

Pastry rolling is a physical skill. But these same stages of:
a) fumbling, uncoordinated first attempts
b) repeated attempts, gaining proficiency by trial and error
c) building up co-ordination, speed, and rhythm
d) creative elaboration
apply equally to any new skill children (and adults) tackle.

We can also see the importance of incentive; in the case of the pastry making, the incentive was wanting to feel grown-up and create a tasty end product. Praise and recognition also has an important part to play: 'Who'd like some of this delicious quiche that David's made?'

LANGUAGE

We need words in order to learn. Indeed, the whole process of thought and learning is unimaginable, without language.

Language provides order, labels, and gives constant meaning to the world around us. Even purely visual information, such as a road sign, will need to be explained in words to a child, in the first place.

Language also enables us to learn about less direct and tangible things other than our immediate surroundings. We learn about attitudes, hopes, fears, detailed facts and instructions. We can learn about people who are far away from us or who have been dead for years, through words recorded in books or on tape.

PIAGET'S THEORIES ON CHILDREN'S COGNITIVE DEVELOPMENT

In the 1960s, Jean Piaget, a Swiss psychologist, changed people's understanding of how children think and learn by extensive experimentation and investigation into the way children performed certain tasks, solved problems, and understood various concepts. His findings led him to the following conclusions.

There are four stages through which children pass in the development of their mental capacities.

Stage 1. Sensori-motor stage, from birth to age two.

The child perceives and learns directly from his five senses and own actions. In fact, he does not so much *think* as *do*.

Stage 2. Pre-operational stage, approximately age two to seven.

The child looks at the world from an egocentric standpoint, and operates essentially in a 'here and now' dimension. He assumes all natural objects are alike and have feelings because he does. He cannot project into the points of view of other people. He is easily taken in by appearances. He finds it difficult to associate two different attributes with the same thing/person (e.g. how can a doctor be a Dad as well?). He shows us in his drawings, language, dreams and play that he deals with symbolic representation. He conceptualises, but in an over-generalised way. For example, if his mother is at home all day, he assumes *all* mothers stay at home.

He has very crude ideas of right and wrong, and the degree of guilt is based on the size of misdemeanour (e.g. *number* of plates broken), rather than whether the act was intentional or accidental.

He sees adults as being in control of the universe, and may blame them angrily for unavoidable disappointments. He attributes his own tastes to everyone, as can be seen sometimes in his choice of presents. He steps easily from the world of reality to fantasy, and back again. He has hazy ideas about ownership.

Stage 3. Concrete operations, approximately age seven to twelve.

The child can think logically about things he has experienced, and can mentally manipulate them through symbols e.g. arithmetic. He understands that some actions are reversible, and he is less deceived by appearances: for instance, if a cup of orange juice is poured from a short wide beaker into a tall thin one, he understands that the quantity of juice remains the same.

Stage 4. Formal operations, approximately age twelve to adulthood.

He can reason logically about abstract matters, even when he has never directly experienced them, e.g. mathematical and scientific problems.

Piagetian thought on children's need for rich first-hand experience in manipulating materials has substantially influenced ideas on education in the last thirty years. This can clearly be seen in the play/work environment at nursery schools and primary schools. The children are seen as active learners, discovering and conceptualising for themselves.

The starting point for most themes and projects is the child himself. For example, a project on all the different people in the world might begin with the children looking in the mirror to study their faces, skin colour etc.

But in more recent times, other educators such as Margaret Donaldson have queried other aspects of Piaget's work. For example we now know young children are capable of 'de-centring', or seeing a task or subject from the point of view of someone other than themselves, if they are given the information and explanations in appropriate language.

Children are also known to be fairly accurate 'guessers', using everyday knowledge and common sense, which is not the same as adults' logical thought, but often effective nonetheless.

Piaget is now also thought to have under-appreciated the part played in learning by social interaction, and the importance of input by good teachers.

CONDITIONS FOR SUCCESSFUL LEARNING

Learning requires effort. The individual must link what is confronting him with what he has learned before.

If the task seems useful and interesting, the effort seems less. This fact has strong implications for the way we present, structure and oversee new skills/tasks for children to master.

Look back to your childhood and recall a subject, topic or skill which you enjoyed learning, were successful at, and still remember clearly. How many of the following statements were true?

1. The subject/skill seemed highly relevant and useful to you at that stage in your life.
2. It was presented in a lively and appealing way.
3. It involved firsthand experience.
4. It was within your ability, but not really easy.
5. The teacher was a person you liked/respected, and who clearly enjoyed his/her subject.
6. You were given regular feedback on your performance, and encouraged to evaluate your own progress.
7. The praise you received acted as a further spur to attainment.
8. The new skill/topic clearly led to other, more advanced activity.

If you have learned a new skill recently, such as driving a car, or operating a computer, you will probably agree that many of the above factors apply equally to that, as they do to most effective learning.

Furthermore, we should remember that physical, environmental, social and emotional factors also have a strong influence on successful learning. A child must be feeling neither ravenously hungry, nor uncomfortably full. He must feel wide awake. He needs to feel relatively relaxed, secure, confident enough to make mistakes, accepted and at ease with peers and adults alike.

Some obstacles to effective learning are:

- a stuffy, dark, cold or overheated environment
- fatigue
- discomfort
- tension or conflict
- fear of making mistakes/appearing a fool/getting into trouble
- a hostile attitude to authority
- discrimination
- non-involvement with other children
- a discouraging or dismissive atmosphere
- lack of trust in an adult.

EXERCISES

Investigation

If you have anatomical models at your college, look at the position and composition of the human brain, identifying the parts mentioned in this chapter.

Also study diagrams, X-ray pictures and videos of the baby in the uterus. Notice the proportion of head to body throughout the period of development.

Observation

Teach a child of eighteen months to two years where his eyes, nose, mouth etc. are. (Ensure that this is something new for the child and ask his carers not to coach him.) Record his stages of learning.

A few days later, see if he remembers anything you taught him.

In your evaluation, suggest what helped him to learn this new knowledge.

Project

Talk to the children at your placement about their early memories. ('What is the first thing in your life that you can remember, when you were very young?')

If appropriate, talk with their parents about this, checking the age of the children at the time of the incident.

Draw up a table with columns for: name of child, incident described, approximate age at the time, age as told by parent, reason you think this incident was clearly remembered (e.g. fear experienced when 'lost' at seaside). Add your own, and your friends' earliest memories.

Write a summary of your findings, also covering the children's reactions to being asked about their memories.

SUGGESTIONS FOR FURTHER READING

Beve Hornsby, *Before Alpha*, Souvenir Press

Richard Lansdown, *Child Development Made Simple*, Heinemann Professional Publishing

Vorna Hildebrand, *Introduction to Early Childhood Education*, Macmillan Publishers Ltd

David Fontana, *The Education of the Young Child* Open Books Publishing Ltd

Margaret Donaldson, *Children's Minds*, Fontana Books

Sara Meadows, *Understanding Child Development*, Hutchinson Education Ltd.

J. Bruner, M. Cole, B. Lloyd (ed.), *The Perceptual World of the Child*, Fontana Books

M.A. Spencer Pulaski, *Your Baby's Mind and How It Grows*, Cassell

B. Tizard and M. Hughes, *Young Children Learning*, Fontana Books

Martin Woodhead, *Preschool Education in Western Europe*, Longman Group Ltd

Kathy Sylva and Ingrid Lunt, *Child Development*, Basil Blackwell Ltd

Jennie Linden and Gillian Pugh (ed.), *Developing a Curriculum for the Early Years*, National Children's Bureau

John Oates (ed.), *Early Cognitive Development*, Open University

Arnold Gesell, *The First Five Years of Life*, Methuen Educational Ltd

12 Language and Communication

The question 'Does he talk yet?' is often asked with more eagerness than might be shown on the question of whether a child can crawl or walk. This is probably because language is the key to the child's personality, developing thought processes and intelligence. It is mainly through language that the child will interact with his early carers, and, increasingly, with the wider world.

The father who said 'I'll be more interested in him when he can talk', was making the same wrong assumption as the questioner above: that is, that talking (language) is something which happens suddenly, almost like a tooth erupting overnight, and in a state of completeness. The parent or carer who is asked the 'Does he talk yet?' question will seldom be able to give a straight 'yes' or 'no'. Talking, like all other aspects of children's development, is something which happens gradually and involves much foundation work.

There are three aspects of language development:

- receptive speech (what a child understands, which is always more than he can say)
- expressive speech (words he produces himself)
- articulation (his actual pronunciation of words).

THE FIRST YEAR – PRE-LINGUISTIC STAGE

The newborn baby has a daunting task ahead – to master all the complexities of a communication system in a few years. The English language consists of over one million words, and contains many irregularities in its grammatical structure.

The baby's first breath is a cry. This in itself is a signal that he has been born active and healthy, with a fully functioning pair of lungs and vocal cords.

This *urgent* cry comes out as a nasal 'a' sound and usually denotes the need for:

- food
- relief from pain (possibly colic)
- relief from discomfort (soiled, cold nappy)
- relief from boredom and/or loneliness.

The baby's face will probably be contorted, with eyes screwed up and lips stretched wide. The baby's carer will interpret the cries and attend to his needs, so immediately a basic form of dialogue is established.

From about six weeks, the baby will produce 'comfort sounds', something like a wet 'goo-goo'. These often occur after a feed, when the baby is full and happy. There is often saliva still present in the mouth. The baby may even be reliving the pleasurable sucking sensation. As young as he is, he will respond to the carer and, at about four months, his throaty chuckles and laughs will greatly enliven their interaction. Mothers instinctively hold their babies at the right distance for maximum eye contact. The baby will look intently at the mother or carer's face as she talks, will try to copy her lip movements, and 'blow raspberries' in an attempt to join in a conversation. Such 'practice' is of great importance.

The earliest definite sounds the baby produces are vowels, and come out quite unintentionally, as a result of experimenting with sounds he can make. The head and neck are growing, and vocal organs taking up their mature positions. The tongue can move more, and the lips are strengthened by much sucking and feeding. Strings of odd sounds are articulated. This is known as babbling. Sometimes it will consist of one repeated phrase like 'abababababababa'. Sometimes it will vary greatly in pitch, and take on a musical quality, or resemble the ups and downs of an adult conversation. Early consonants will be: h, d, b, m, g, w, j. Double consonants such as 'sp' or 'st' will not be mastered for a long time. The opportunity to chew and eat lumpy foods when the baby is ready to do so, from about five or six months, also has a part to play in developing the mechanisms of speech.

These early, unintentional utterances are made by babies the world over, including deaf and severely subnormal babies, in whom it does not develop naturally into speech. The purpose and pleasure derived from it must therefore be predominantly active and physical – like wiggling your toes – rather than satisfaction from the sounds produced.

During this stage, the baby's 'received language' is all-important. It starts from birth onwards, as his carers talk to him and for his benefit. Without necessarily indulging in baby talk of the 'bow wow' variety, his carers will speak more slowly than they do to each other, they will use an exaggerated range of pitch with much rising intonation, simplify their statements, and repeat significant ones. 'There's a lovely smile for Mummy, isn't it? Yes, it's a lovely smile, a *lovely* smile . . . ', and so on, all of which is designed to set up interaction with the baby, and gradually he becomes an increasingly active participant. This sort of communication is known as 'motherese'.

The repetition of certain familiar and key words, accompanied by appropriate actions, for instance the word 'dinner' with the sight of food being heated or mashed, appetising smells, the sound of a fork against a plate, all set up paths of understanding from the 'trigger' word. Other trigger words might be 'bath', 'bye-bye', etc.

Although he is still not talking, he is progressing all the time in making sense of his world. He is learning to distinguish familiar from unfamiliar voices, attend to rhythm and intonation, recognise tones of approval ('Oh *good* boy, you've eaten all your dinner') or warning ('No – HOT!'), as he crawls near the fireplace, or playfulness ('Let's have a little *tickle* then'). In interaction with his carers, he sometimes puts his hand over, or in, their mouths, thus finding out about vibration, and how lips move as words form.

An early conversation

Non-verbal communication

Babies certainly do not have to wait until they can talk in order to express their tastes, wants and reactions. Besides the obvious signals of crying when hungry or in pain, they:

- squeal from pleasure or excitement
- smile, laugh and crow, when played with, or when a loved adult appears
- 'bump' up and down where they sit, in impatience, or anticipation of action
- reject and wriggle with stiff arms, legs, body when picked up by strangers, or to curtail play
- grimace and spit out food they dislike (often new foods offered in weaning)
- kick and splash with pleasure in the bath
- hold out arms to be picked up
- point to objects they want to investigate (from about nine months).

Many of these actions will be accompanied by whimpers, screeches, grunts, whinges or vocal protests. Body language will continue to be a subtle but powerful way of communicating throughout life, but it is never more telling than in early childhood.

Nursery nurse students are often required in examination questions to describe how babies learn to communicate. In their eagerness to cover which words might be uttered at which ages, they all too often neglect the whole business of received language, non-verbal communication, and the dialogue with carers that goes on virtually from birth.

As with all good construction work, a solid foundation, though less apparent than the wall which comes later, is absolutely vital, and must never be neglected.

THE SECOND YEAR

While remembering that all children are individuals, the *sequence* of development in this chapter is approximately the same, even though it may happen at different times. Within the same family, at sixteen months, Richard was speaking in short but clear phrases and sentences, Christopher had just uttered his first word, and Alison was holding long conversations with adults.

By about one year old, most babies have experimented sufficiently with their early sounds to produce something like 'dada', and, probably by coincidence, to say it at what seems to be an appropriate moment. We all know what happens next. The word is siezed upon, meaning is attached to it, and the baby is rewarded by repetition, tones of pleasure, hugs and kisses. Anyone would enjoy such attention, and the baby quickly learns to repeat the sound at will, in the correct context. Obviously the sounds he makes will vary according to the language that surrounds him. In English, 'dada' usually precedes a word for mother; probably because the 'd' sound is easier to pronounce and not because of role significance. To the amusement and sometimes embarrassment of his mother, baby will often refer to any passing man as 'dada'!

Approximately six words will grow in similar fashion. These may be the child's versions of mother, baby (to refer to himself), the family pet, grandparent, teddy, and so on.

Just as the carers believe that their child is about to string words together – a thrilling prospect, particularly with a first baby – there is very often a pause in progress, as the child gains mastery over walking. After all, to gain access to that special toy placed out of reach, or to stumble after a disappearing cat is a far more exciting possibility than mouthing words. Occasionally first-time parents worry about this apparent lack of progress, but it is only temporary. The child cannot learn two major new things at once, and anyway, useful mental consolidation is taking place. Mobility will also give the child much more to talk *about*. Often, this stage points up the difference between males and females. The boys are more likely to concentrate on movement and girls on speech.

When the build-up of words proceeds, it will be mainly nouns, or labels for things in the child's world which is essentially 'here and now'. Many will be associated with pleasure for him, e.g. dinner, drink, orange, push-chair, buggie, bricks, potty. Even though his version of orange may be 'onging', for instance, and may be unintelligible to strangers, if the same version is used for referring to the same thing, it is definitely *a word*.

The child's ability to copy an adult's tone of voice, sense of rhythm and melody in speech is developing. He picks up key phrases like 'more', 'get down', 'all gone' – the latter being said in a sing-song way. He may apply one of these phrases to a number of different situations. It may be a made-up word; Richard used to say 'bee-gaa' to mean that something in his environment was stuck, inaccessible, broken, or irretrievable. Aided by tone of voice, including a questioning tone, one word can mean many things. For instance, when a child says 'moke' while sitting in his chair in the kitchen, it may mean, 'Please may I have a drink of milk?', or it may mean, 'I can see a bottle of milk when you open the fridge door like that', or it may mean (uttered sadly), 'I have tipped my milk onto the floor'. These one word, but meaningful utterances are called 'holophrases'.

The negative will be mastered before the positive, and used very effectively to give the infant power and choice: 'No bed' and so on.

Some location phrases, to describe the position of things, such as 'on top' may also be learned, while the list of labels will carry on growing.

Often a young child will repeatedly ask, 'Whatdat – Whatdat?' in order to add to his knowledge of the world. He does not necessarily listen to each answer. Or he will ask the name of a certain thing a dozen times. This shows his fascination with language, and his desire to stay in communication with an adult.

During the second year, the infant will grasp the concept of object permanence, that is, he can mentally visualise the existence and appearance of an object when it is not in sight. If, therefore, you ask a child of approximately fourteen months 'Where's teddy?', he will look round for it. This shows that he has *internalised* that word.

By about eighteen months, many children utter at least fifty words. Many go through a phase of reduplication, that is repeating a syllable instead of uttering the next correct one. For example, 'bottle' will be 'bo-bo'. Many children also go through a phase of echolalia, when they repeat the last word of adult's sentences:

Parent: Shall we go into the garden?
John: Garden.

During the second year, the infant will begin to put nouns with verbs, thus forming rudimentary sentences, for example: 'Dadda gone', 'Pussy eat' etc. And before long, it will be: 'Dadda gone work', 'Pussy eat dinner'.

Now the carers will get excited, because this is really the threshold of talking. This stage is generally known as telegraphese, because no little linking words appear, only the essential gist of the message. The carers should, at this stage, expand the child's utterances, so that his received language is being stimulated all the time, feeding his expressed language.

Ben: Ganny gone.
Parent: Yes, Granny's gone home now to get Grandad's tea. I expect she'll tell him all about our walk to the park today.
Ben: (Pause for thought) Feed duck.
Parent: Yes, we fed the ducks, didn't we? Do you remember the big brown one?
Ben: Geedie
Parent: Yes, wasn't he greedy? He kept gobbling up all the food we'd taken.
Ben: Shoo! Shoo!
Parent: That's what we said to him, wasn't it? Shoo, go away you greedy duck. Leave some for the others.

The parent here is 'stretching' the child, or, to use another phrase, is setting up a sort of scaffold within which the child can develop a set of thoughts. The child's perseverance pays off; the response he engenders makes for fun, a kind of power, and causes other interesting things to happen. This sort of fond dialogue comes naturally to most carers of young children, and gives great pleasure. The unfortunate children whose comments and questions are met by, 'Shut up. Eat your crisps and watch TV,' already begin to lag behind in their linguistic and cognitive ability.

THE THIRD YEAR

The progress made during this period is often referred to as an explosion of language. Not only does the vocabulary grow dramatically, but sentences lengthen and confidence develops. The child is now able to recall, which helps him to retain new words, and also gives him more to talk about. He will be able to converse with another child. You will no doubt have noticed that toddlers younger than this communicate with each other mainly by snatching, grabbing, pushing and repeatedly exclaiming, 'no', 'me', 'mine'.

By the age of three, most children have mastered:

- the present continuous tense, 'I am jumping'
- prepositions such as 'in', 'on'
- plurals: 'bricks'
- possessives: 'Mummy's coat'
- 'a' and 'the'

- regular past tenses, 'I jump*ed*'
- superlatives: 'best'
- comparatives: 'bigger than'
- some adverbs: 'quickly'.

The way children of this age characteristically cope with past tenses of irregular verbs is both interesting and endearing to adult ears. They add 'ed' because that is what they have learned to do with other verbs, e.g. jump and jumped. Thus they have abstracted and applied a rule of grammar, regardless of the fact that they have never heard an adult say 'I runned', for example. This can be called a creative error and is a sign of advancement. It also demonstrates that language acquisition is not a simple process of imitation but involves the child in actively building his own grammar.

Most children of this age will know some colours and parts of the body. They will also begin to get to grips with the confusing business of pronouns. Before the age of three, this is beyond them. Natalie, aged two, when tired on a walk, would put up her arms and say, 'Daddy carry you'. Pronouns are, in fact, the most frequently used words in our language, so early mastery is important.

By the age of three, the child's vocabulary may exceed 800 words. Syntax (word order) is still strange sometimes.

THE FOURTH YEAR

This stage sees further expansion in all aspects of language. More questions will arise, 'what?' will still be used, but will be joined by 'when?' and 'where?' Constructions become more complex. 'And' is the most frequently used link word when relating an event:

'We went to Nannie's, and we went in a field, and we saw some cows, and they didn't like our dog, and they nearly chased us', and so on. Soon, 'because', 'but', 'or' and 'if' will appear, enabling the child to use clauses correctly in order to explain, give reasons, acknowledge cause and effect. 'Don't give Niamh any peas, 'cause they make her sick.'

The three-year-old can manage consonant 'clusters', for example 'br' in 'bread' and 'str' in 'strong'.

The three-year-old can also use different styles of conversation as appropriate. For example, he will adopt a polite raconteur's tone when relating an incident to an adult, speak patronisingly to a baby or copy an adult's social phrases on the telephone.

THE FIFTH YEAR

Between the ages of four and five is the classic period when a child plays with, and enjoys, language. By now, he is fairly articulate, and his syntax, pronunciation, and noun/verb agreement are nearly perfect. He loves jokes, riddles, tongue-twisters, nonsense language and telling tall stories. He responds well to poetry, rhymes and word games. He may stumble over himself in his eagerness to relate a long tale.

This is *the* age for endless questions and these are now of the 'why?' and 'how?' type, seeking reasons and explanations, or sometimes information that is difficult for the adult to simplify appropriately. Often the adult just doesn't know the answer. Alison, aged four, was asking, 'Who made the clouds?', 'Where does God live?'. Sometimes the child does not want a real answer. 'Why do I have to go to bed now?', is clearly not seeking a reasoned discourse on the benefits of adequate sleep for young children; it is a protest and/or delaying tactic. Where information is sought, carers owe it to lively-minded four-year-olds to supply it, even if it is about a potentially embarrassing or sensitive subject like birth or death. Such subjects usually seem to come up in a crowded bus! Fobbing the child off, or stating irritably, 'Because I say so' is not going to encourage the spirit of enquiry which will foster cognitive and academic development in these impressionable years.

Four-year-olds often give a running commentary on what they are doing, which is like thinking aloud.
Ben: I'm painting Daddy's garage. His car's inside. It's a blue Volvo. I'm going to have a Volvo when I'm bigger, only it'll be a red one. This is our house. Now it's all raining . . . Schwww . . . Schw . . .

They are probably unaware that they are doing it.

Four-year-olds are more skilled at turn-taking in conversation, and are less likely to interrupt. They have developed ways of getting into conversations with adults and other children, and can slip easily into role play.

Some pronunciations will still be imperfect (mis-articulations), for example 'th' may come out like 'v', as in 'wiv' or 'brover'. But essentially, by the time the child reaches the age of five, he has effectively mastered his mother tongue, and probably has a vocabulary of about 2000 words.

When he goes to school, he will meet various new styles of language: the one employed by the teacher, and the children's own playground language, including rhymes, chants, slang, catcalls, swear words etc.

The years between ages five and seven will be spent consolidating his language skills. Some errors may persist, such as 'Him and me went to the park' and 'No, I never'. The passive tense is not clearly understood or used, for example 'The food was eaten by the cat'.

Effective powers of communication based on using words as symbols are critical to the use of other forms of symbolisation, such as in reading, writing and mathematics, on which the child will now be embarking.

THE USES OF LANGUAGE

As adults, we know that it is very largely through the tool of language that we organise and arrange our lives. Through language we come to understand more and more of the world about us. With it we initiate and sustain relationships. We select and manage events and people to our advantage (as in pay negotiations), convenience (as in domestic arrangements) and pleasure (as in social invitations). Language allows us to discuss and resolve problems, effect compromises, and gives us the key to the delights of literature and intellectual challenge. We therefore use language in a variety of ways – ways so different that the style of the language itself changes enormously. Compare, for instance, the language employed by barristers in a court of law, with that used by teenagers chatting on the telephone. Yet all are using their mother tongue, and using it appropriately to the particular need. Without the power to talk and make ourselves understood, we should probably be ineffectual, passive, ignorant, friendless, exploited, boring and bored individuals. We might even be pugnacious, because clashes of will must be resolved somehow.

It is interesting to watch the young child develop his use of language, so that eventually for him, too, it becomes this invaluable tool.

If we listen to any short snatches, or longer sustained conversations at nursery, we are soon aware that from the third year onwards all children seem to use language for:

- protecting their own rights and property ('Get off! I had it first!') and ensuring their own comfort and pleasure ('I like this swing. I'm going to stay here all day.')
- initiating and maintaining relationships with other children and adults ('Will you be my friend?')
- reporting on present experience ('I'm painting a big, big lorry.')
- directing their own and others' actions ('You're the baby and I'm the mummy.')
- asserting their own superiority ('My one's better than yours.').

The following, more adult, uses of language, however, are noticeable only in children who are cared for by adults who actively encourage the child to communicate:

- reporting on past experiences ('When I went to Longleat ')
- co-operating with others towards agreed ends ('I know! Let's be spacemen!')
- anticipating and predicting the future ('It might fall down if we do it like that.')
- comparing possible alternatives ('Glue's better than sticky tape.')
- seeing cause and effect, and connections between events ('Now it's raining, so we can't go outside.')

- explaining how and why things happen ('He pressed it too hard – that's why the wheel fell off.')
- attending to abstract problems (for instance, of a character in a book) and suggesting possible solutions ('*I* would have chopped the dragon's head off!')
- referring to symbolic uses of materials in imaginative games (while placing grass on small plastic plates: 'This is our supper. It's spaghetti. Umm, lovely!')
- justifying behaviour ('Anyway, *he* pushed *me* first!')
- reflecting upon his own and other people's feelings ('When our Gran died, my mum cried all day, she was so sad.').

It is not difficult to see how these latter uses of language give the child a much more powerful grasp of events, and much greater depth as a thinking, self-regulating individual, bound up as they are with thought, learning, understanding, reason, choices, emotion, and empathy with others.

How, then, can the nursery nurse help to enrich children's language skills?

THE ROLE OF THE ADULT

Carers of young children need to be aware of the stage their charges have reached in their communication skills, and do all in their power, in a low-key, relaxed way to enhance and further the child's skills and understanding.

The following are some suggested approaches.

Pre-linguistic stage

- Sustain eye contact while talking to the baby.
- Include a soft toy or similar in the 'conversation' to arrest and share the baby's attention.
- Pause in 'conversation', to give ideas of 'spaces' in which the next speaker speaks.
- Encourage all forms of communication, bubble blowing, gurgling, etc., sometimes imitating the baby's efforts.
- Make funny faces and smile.

- Synchronise your head movements with the baby's.
- Play games with tongue and lips, making funny noises.
- Give a running commentary while tending to the baby.
- Give the baby the chance to pay complete attention, without constant background noise of a radio or TV.
- Play games such as 'I'm coming , I'm coming' etc.
- Play face-to-face knee games such as 'Ride-a-cock-horse'.
- Play 'peek-a-boo' and 'Bo' games; hide play-things behind cushion and say 'Where's it gone?'
- Play back and forth games with ball, toy vehicles etc. (to build idea of turn-taking).
- Play physical games such as 'rowing boats' with appropriate actions.
- Make sound effects for toys and familiar objects, for example 'brrrmmm, brrrmmm' and 'miaow'.
- Make onomatopoeic noises as appropriate, e.g. 'splashsh' at bath-time.
- Sing to child.
- Make allowances for the presence of strangers inhibiting his responses.
- From about six or seven months, the child should be given food of different textures, rather than all mashed up, to exercise the muscles of his mouth and jaw.
- From about one year of age, he should be weaned away from both dummy and bottle, for the same reason.

Pre-school period

Many of the above approaches will continue during the next few years, as the child grows in his language acquisition.

Carers can now also:

- Listen to him properly, looking at him and remaining on the same level as the child; give appropriate responses.
- Start at the point the child is at.
- Give every encouragement, making comments genuine and meaningful.

- Pick up topics of current interest and share the child's enthusiasms.

- Avoid finishing sentences for the child, dominating the conversation yourself, or allowing older siblings to speak for him.

- Answer questions truthfully, simply, and without adding unnecessary detail.

- Avoid correcting him in an obvious way. (Carers can usually find a more subtle way of letting him hear the correct version, as long as it does not sound contrived.)

- Provide a varied and stimulating world, with plenty of happenings, places, people, and things to talk about.

- Observe and encourage play which promotes language, for example a toy telephone, puppets.

- Read and tell stories to child, also use rhymes, finger plays, poetry.

- Offer a good language model yourself, in constructions used, enriching vocabulary introduced, and tones adopted.

- Seize on every opportunity for discussion, for example a thunderstorm or a workman in the house.

- Question the child, at the appropriate level. Three and four-year-olds respond well to open-ended questions such as, 'I wonder what you would do if . . . ' etc. Such questions require a properly thought out and formulated sentence by way of reply, rather than a one-word answer.

- Use the media with discrimination; focus children's attention on words and content. Do not use the TV as a child-minder.

- Encourage social interaction at family and group meal times.

- Use mime, song, rhythm, rhyme, and other forms of expression. All of these help children to retain, understand and enjoy language.

- Notice any difficulties or delay, without letting your anxiety be apparent.

- Tape-record your conversations with the child, to monitor your own conversational skills, or lack of them.

DIFFICULTIES AND DELAY

Poor speech and poor language may be two very different things, although they are sometimes found together.

If it is purely a problem of articulation, probably stemming from defects in the speech mechanisms, the child will require expert professional help and the skills of the speech therapist. Unfortunately, these specialists are too few in number to work with individual children in a very concentrated way. But, having identified difficulties, they can usually help parents and carers to continue a programme of exercises and approaches.

A failure to develop expressive language, however, is a complex yet relatively common problem. The reasons will probably involve social, emotional, physical and psychological factors. When seeking reasons, it is often possible to eliminate or identify certain physical factors, which is the first stage in obtaining help.

Most children have a hearing test at seven months, conducted by a health visitor, who is trained in the technique. All children, whatever their age, who give rise to concern about their ability to talk, should have a hearing test carried out by a specialist, whether or not they have previously had one.

Here are some conditions which may be responsible for the child's difficulties:

- Malformation of palate or teeth
- Cerebral palsy (e.g. an athetoid child could have disarthric (slurred) speech, see page 204)
- Learning difficulties
- Periods of hearing loss due to past or present catarrhal conditions affecting the ears, otitis media, or enlarged adenoids (this may affect as many as 20 per cent of children)
- Permanent hearing loss
- Background lacking in stimulation (the child may have been kept in his pram or cot for hours on end). Alternatively, the child's early carers may not have realised the importance of talking to a baby, or they may have been suffering from depression

- Lack of parental affection, and/or unsatisfactory substitute care e.g. an unregistered child-minder looking after a lot of children whom she wants to keep quiet
- History of unhappiness or instability in home background
- Shyness
- Mixed language home, or home/nursery situation
- Over-indulgent home where all the child's needs are met by others, thus rendering his own efforts unnecessary. (This could apply to the last child in a big family)
- Twins
- Deaf parents who have poor expressive language
- Temporarily unsettled state (caused by starting nursery, moving house, or birth of a sibling).

How the adult can help

- Remain informed about the causes of communication problems, and ongoing programmes being offered by professionals. Half an hour a week with a professional specialist, will have little effect on its own.
- Concentrate on building a relationship of trust, and relaxed and friendly interaction with the child.
- Avoid drawing attention to the individual in group situations, or putting him in the limelight which might be embarrassing.
- Occasionally insist on speech, if the child is reluctant or 'lazy' about making himself understood. (However, the adult should be sensitive about not adding to a child's frustrations.)
- Introduce word games, tongue-twisters, rhymes and so on, which will make particular pronunciations fun.
- Remember blowing, sucking and licking activities can be helpful in exercising muscles used in speech. (Bubble blowing, candle blowing, transporting a ping pong ball by sucking a wide straw.)
- Use movement, painting, and other forms of expression, to release tension and encourage communication.
- Introduce stories and rhymes with repeated phrases, for example some of the Dr Seuss books, to encourage unselfconscious participation.

- Speak clearly and slowly, keeping eye contact wherever possible.
- Encourage all attempts at verbalisation, with praise and active approval.
- Work from the child's own interests, and build on these e.g. favourite toys and activities.

CHILDREN FOR WHOM ENGLISH IS THEIR SECOND LANGUAGE

A recent survey showed that there are over 140 languages being spoken in Inner London alone.

To grow up truly bilingual is an asset, but a child needs to be fluent in at least one language in order to conceptualise. Carers who speak only English must respect the fact that the child has expertise in something of which they are ignorant. It can be difficult for a child who has not mixed with English-speaking people to come into a nursery and 'pick up' the language spoken there.

In many multicultural nurseries and first schools, parents are encouraged to work with groups of children in their own home/community language. Stories, rhymes, games, cookery and so on, in Gujerati, for example, offer children the opportunity to consolidate their fluency in that language; it offers legitimacy to the language spoken by their family, and a respite for the child from any possible strain due to struggling with a foreign language. It widens the cultural horizons of the other children, and also forms an ideal way to encourage parent participation.

In helping children to become confident and competent in English, we should remember the following points:

- Aim to build up a friendly, relaxed relationship of trust with the child and his parents.
- Remember that it takes many children about a year of listening to a language before speaking it.
- Learn, from the beginning, how to pronounce the child's name, his family's name, and how to greet them.
- Use eye contact, body language, mime and gesture to help explain what you mean.

- Keep sentences short and simple. Give clear directions one at a time.
- Relate early sentences to the child and his immediate environment, e.g. 'Parveen's coat'.
- Use repetition and reinforcement of new words e.g. later the same day by looking at and identifying pictures of coats in books.
- Introduce safe, non-threatening ways to encourage attempts at communication: the form does not matter, (e.g. games, use of a cassette player, music, action songs.)
- Use pictures, toys and games to teach new vocabulary. Photographs of the children themselves are a good lead-in, and can be made into a class book – 'Our Day at School', for example.
- Identify specific difficulties of construction such as present continuous tense of verbs and double consonants, and improvise games to give practice in these. Wrapping paper and card can be useful here, for example, a game of seeking a hidden object/character, under flaps of paper, to reinforce the present continuous construction along these lines: 'Where is the dog? Is he climbing up the tree? Is he sitting in his basket? Is he chewing his bone?' etc.
- Use dual language books and books which offer repetitive language.
- Build yourself a vocabulary of important phrases in the child's own language to facilitate understanding, e.g. 'I need to use the toilet'.
- Use special withdrawal sessions, and group times, to reinforce language in a light-hearted way.
- Avoid confusion. Be consistent. Watch the language used in finger plays etc – are those things you are holding up fingers, or 'five fat sausages'?
- Use praise and positive reinforcement for all the child's efforts and successes in expressing himself.
- Recognise that this child can feel very isolated by his limited knowledge of English. Other children tend to ignore totally attempts at communication in another language.
- Wherever possible, try to make activities both stimulating and interesting, for both adult and child.

BOOKS, STORIES AND POETRY

These deserve separate consideration since they play such a dynamic part in children's acquisition and enjoyment of language.

The amount of early exposure to these forms of communication experienced by children in our care will vary greatly. Those children whose parents turn naturally to the printed word – be it novels, manuals, newspapers, magazines, dictionaries – for information and enjoyment, are greatly advantaged in their receptiveness to an education system which, despite all modern technology, still relies heavily on books and the ability to read.

The world of literature offers enlightenment, escape, reassurance, companionship, insight into people and relationships, beauty, humour, inspiration, and a window onto worlds – real and imagined – that we would otherwise never know.

Choosing books for children

About 3000 new books for children are published every year. It is therefore impossible to keep abreast of everything on the market. However, it *is* possible to:

- obtain the most recent *Children's Books of the Year* (published by the National Book League)
- obtain booklists and catalogues from publishers
- read book reviews in magazines (*Nursery World* and *Child Education* are helpful here)
- talk to colleagues in other establishments
- talk to children's librarians
- visit exhibitions of children's books, such as the National Book League's touring exhibition
- visit large book shops with good selections of children's books.

Factors governing choice. Taste in books is a very personal and subjective matter. When choosing a book adults will consider:

- the appearance, impact and 'feel' (cover, type face, print size, secure binding, layout, proportion of text to illustrations, quality of illustrations)

- the plot or theme (suitability to age group; well-shaped; convincing; satisfactory ending)
- characterisation (target audience will identify with them; credible; avoiding race, class or sex stereotyping)
- the attitudes or messages conveyed (should be positive, honest, give children something to think about; be conveyed by humour, suspense, relief or pathos)
- the language used (should be pitched at the level of the target audience, but also to 'stretch' them slightly, through lively, descriptive, unfamiliar or humorous modes of expression)
- price, in relation to all other considerations, and likely durability (books have effectively come down in price in recent years, thanks to advances in production technology, and popular demand)
- author(s) (might be well-known, new, a favourite from adult's own childhood or recommended by a friend).

The adult doing the choosing *must* like the book him/herself in order to convey enthusiasm when reading aloud. Children enjoy being involved in choosing new books, from shops and libraries. Often they will present you with their choice of nursery books, comics, backs of cereal packets that they treasure or have found stimulating. The adult must then clearly set value on these offerings, however unsuitable we may privately consider them, or however impossible they are to 'read to the whole class' (as in the case of strip cartoons). It may have been given by a beloved relative, and, in any case, we should welcome the child's enjoyment of the printed word, in whatever form.

Books for children from birth to seven years

Desired characteristics in books cannot be limited by age suitability. Appeal will vary greatly among individual chidren. A 'baby book' may continue to be a great favourite and friend well into childhood, while a bright or imaginative three-year-old may derive pleasure from a book intended for children aged six and above.

Specific authors and titles have deliberately not been named here. Some enjoy long-lasting popularity; others are quickly forgotten or become dated. The follow-up work at the end of this chapter will alert you to some of the excellent books which, happily, are available today. Constantly extending and updating your knowledge of books will enhance the contribution you are able to make to any establishment, big or small, in which you work.

Six months to one year. As soon as a child can sit, supported, on a lap, and can perceive shapes and colours on a page, he can enjoy a book. Earliest books need to be tough, wipeable, light and easy to handle on a lap, with rounded corners. They should feature familiar objects (to the infant), pictured with clear outlines and bright colours, uncluttered by background detail or shadows. Because it means something to him, each picture – of a mug, buggy, or teddy bear – is a talking point. By about a year old, he will be pointing and verbalising about the pictures, encouraged by the adult.

Adult: 'Car, yes a car. It's like our car, isn't it? How does our car go? It goes brrm, brmm, doesn't it?'

In this way, the child learns to identify picture symbols with real objects, and associate these with the correct words. He is finding out about functions and contexts. He associates books with contact with those he loves, and with pleasure. Print is superfluous at this stage.

It is also possible to buy plastic books which change colours to use in the bath to supplement early conventional books.

During the second year the child will come to spend a little longer with a book. Now that he is independently mobile and upright, his knowledge of his surroundings has become wide enough for the subject matter of the book to be slightly less domestic.

By about age two he will now be able to follow a simple unfolding story of events he knows about – *Thomas's Day*, or *Sarah's Birthday*. These will probably not consist of a plot as such, but there will be a little action, and maybe a sort of climax, for instance when Sarah blows out the candles on her cake. Such a book may have a few words with each picture, but the adult will still expand the content and meaning – such as 'shall we blow out the candles?' and so on.

A slightly more advanced version of this kind of book might be *Shopping with Dad*, or *Leon goes to the zoo*. Now there is more action; it takes place outside the home, but it is still very much based on a character and events with which the child can identify. Happenings should be of a fairly serene and positive kind; age two to three is no age to confront the child with the prospect of Leon getting shut in the zoo and having to spend a night there, or, worse still, Leon getting eaten by tigers! Pictures will continue to play an important part in this book; they will be bold, clear, colourful, and free from sentimentality.

At about age three the child should now be ready for a simple plot, and the central character may be an animal, or animated vehicle (train, truck etc.). Children of this age happily accept the idea of such a talking, thinking, feeling hero; this is because they do not yet differentiate between reality and fantasy (this convention is called anthropomorphism). On the whole, children of this age are less happy with pure fantasy, such as goblins, witches, or creatures from other planets, because they do not *know* that such creatures will not visit them in the night, so themes of this kind may cause night terrors. However, now that television programmes form such a large part of young children's everyday lives, adults are sometimes surprised at how readily even very young children accept fantastic happenings. Perhaps, to see fantastic characters moving and speaking in the living room, is less alarming than bringing them to life in your own imagination.

Events and characters should reinforce the child's sense of security and his place in the world. Tales of rejecting stepmothers, for example, should be avoided, bearing in mind how many children live with a stepmother or stepfather.

The three-year-old loves stories that invite participation in a repeated phrase, and an element of predictability, since his imagination and memory are both developing. There can be more print per page, but illustrations should still reflect ongoing action; the child can then 'read' the story on his own, or to his friends, without the adult.

Between ages three and five books can now begin to broaden the child's horizons. The setting of a tale may now be on a boat, or on a farm, for instance. Among the wide range of books we should offer are books about all sorts of families and backgrounds to which children from all social classes and ethnic groups can relate. This applies to *all* children, and may be specially valuable in rural, ethnically uniform, or socially narrow areas.

There will be more than one central character now, and these characters will be more three-dimensional, thus feeding the child's greater capacity for awareness of self and others. The characters may do 'naughty' things, or undergo some disquieting experience, but all will be well in the end.

At this stage, 'situation books' (bibliotherapy) can play a valuable part in helping children realise they are not alone in an emotionally charged situation. By hearing about another child going through similar experiences to their own, they can be helped to come to terms with their situation. Traditionally, situations treated in this way have been: the new baby, going into hospital, starting school and moving house. Nowadays, children's writers address even more sensitive situations such as death and divorce. (For slightly older children, topics such as child abuse, unemployment and alcoholism are dealt with.)

Humorous books come into their own now that the child has a good grasp of what is, and is not, likely to happen in the real world. Children enjoy slapstick, topsy-turvy situations, or a disagreeable character getting his/her 'comeuppance'. Accumulation of one kind and another is popular, offering more chances to anticipate and participate. A familiar theme is how 'small and defenceless wins the day over large and powerful'. It is not difficult to appreciate how gratifying and appealing such a theme must be to small children functioning in an adult-directed world.

After the age of about five or six the child is beginning to distinguish between fact and fantasy. He is also beginning to reach out more, in thought and imagination, to the world of long ago and far away. This, then, is the age at which we can introduce the rich inheritance we possess of fables, fairy stories, legends and traditional tales. Besides representing many cultures, these stories also show how universal are human beings' beliefs and concerns: worries about strength, poverty, exploitation, death, dependency relationships between parents and children. Such stories also embody many age-old values which we still try to uphold today, and which can speak directly to children: goodness brings its rightful reward; appearances can be deceiving; crime does not pay; perseverance brings results; money does not necessarily bring happiness; life is full of 'alarums and excursions', but things usually work out all right in the end. Set down like this, they read like a string of truisms but children often respond well to such themes, when they are wrapped up in colourful characters and flamboyant settings. Stories in which a clear moral predominates are not generally appreciated today. Lessons for life can come through naturally in the characters and events themselves. Traditional tales also possess a pleasing symmetry, and well-balanced elements of predictability and surprise. There is usually a climax, and a happy ending.

Because older children are more able to project, they are more interested in people who lived in the past, may live in the future, or live on the other side of the world. This is a very receptive time for children to learn about differing cultures and life styles, and it is most important that books available should reflect this aspect of society.

Plots in fiction, for this age range, can be more complex and contain numerous characters, including 'baddies'. They like 'scariness', especially when everything is satisfactorily explained away, or resolved in the end. Some books, old and new, exploit this thrill or grotesque angle to a marked degree. Adults often speak wryly of how eagerly their charges respond to such tales. 'The more blood-thirsty it gets, the better they like it.' It should be remembered of course, that most groups of robust, seemingly well-adjusted six-year-olds, contain at least one highly imaginative child who may afterwards be tormented by night terrors. Stories should *always*

be read through and accepted or rejected beforehand by the adult, with a specific audience in mind.

Children of this age still enjoy being read to, even though many will be quite competent readers themselves. They cannot attain the speed, nor therefore the anticipated expression in the voice that comes easily to adults. What is more, adults' willing participation in story-time reinforces the child's enthusiasm for books, and continues to be a shared and intimate joy, for which no amount of cassettes, played by himself, to himself, is a substitute.

Many infant schools today supplement a formal reading scheme by surrounding the child with 'real' books of all kinds, at all levels, and, with the co-operation of parents, aim to teach reading skills through the child's own choices and interests. 'Shared' reading (with parents) as it is called, has been found to contribute substantially to children's progress.

Reading and telling stories

Both approaches have their merits: reading introduces directly the charms of a book, complete with illustrations. Telling enables the adult to enter into a dramatic situation with his/her listeners, using facial expressions, gestures and voices; effective eye contact can also be maintained. Both approaches need preparation.

Timing. About five minutes is long enough for very young children, ten minutes for the under-fives. Over-fives can concentrate for a quarter of an hour or so.

Seating. Children should be grouped, not squashed, together for intimacy. All must be able to see and hear clearly. Potential disrupters should be separated and placed strategically at the outset.

Creating the right mood. It is foolish to start a story without everyone's attention, hoping the children will be won over gradually by your performance. Children who have been denied outdoor play for some time, or who have just come indoors after very boisterious play, will need to be 'settled' before you can begin. A listening game, or some quiet finger plays, or familiar rhymes will sometimes do the trick. The adult needs to keep her voice hushed, indicating pleasurable anticipation. This is always much more effective than yelling for silence! If there is a particular reason for this story, it can be the lead-in, when all the children are quiet: 'I wonder if anyone knows what day it is tomorrow? Yes, Karlene, Pancake Day. Now I've got a story to tell you today about a pancake. But it isn't the sort you can eat. It's a very different sort of . . . but let's begin the story and find out for ourselves.'

Weaving a spell.   Read or speak clearly, neither gabbling nor dragging it out. Use pauses effectively, especially where there is a new or difficult idea for children to absorb. Quicken or slow down your pace as desired, depending on whether a part of the story is exciting, sad or 'winding down'. Vary volume, again according to plot or characters; whispers can effectively convey suspense, or secrecy. Use a variety of voices for the different characters. (This is impossible unless you prepare it well.) Invite participation where appropriate, but don't let this get out of hand. Any listeners who fidget can be brought back to the story by a ploy, such as bringing the child's name into the story: 'The engine was the same lovely red as your pullover, Craig'.

Try to weave in interruptions and comments.
Adult: 'So Leroy and his Mum and Dad all set off for the Zoo.'
Ben: 'I've been to the zoo.'
Adult: (quickly, before all the rest join in): 'When the story's over I'm going to ask everyone who's been to the zoo to tell us about it.'

Visual aids.   These can be helpful in providing a focus for children's visual attention when telling a story. They should be introduced at a suitable time, and presented in such a way that all the children can handle or touch, but not squabble over, during the story. Some adults like to use puppets or felt characters placed on a felt-covered board to illustrate

a story. The focus then switches from the teller to the puppet.

At the end of the story pause a second or two. Your audience have to 'come back' from the world you have created and into the real world again. They may ask you to 'read it again', which is their way of saying how much they have enjoyed it. Take your cue from the children about how much or how little they want to discuss it. Do not put them through a comprehension test on what it was about. Let any discussion be of an open-ended kind: 'I wonder what you would have done if you had found a dragon sitting on the end of your bed?' This will prolong the mood and the interest, and call for much more complex answers than a one word 'yes' or 'no', 'blue' or 'red'. Asking all the children to draw a picture of it, or (certainly with nursery children) getting them to act it out, are not to be recommended. If your story has been a success, it has been an immensely enriching experience in its own right, and will live on in the children's imagination, where it took root.

Poetry and rhyme

Poetry is generally no longer regarded as something 'cissy', contrived or removed from everyday life. At its best – and there is a great deal of good modern children's poetry about – it reflects all aspects of life itself, from the trivial or funny to the most powerful experiences.

It offers:

- a new, intimate and personal form of communication
- the beauty of language and ideas
- a means of keeping alive many people's cultural heritage
- new and enriching vocabulary
- projection into the roles and feelings of others
- reassurance about emotionally charged situations
- reinforcement of knowledge about the environment e.g. the seasons, colours, animals, counting and number
- humour (limericks, nonsense rhymes, absurd situations)
- escape into a world of fantasy

- practice in listening skills and concentration
- practice in articulation and voice control
- rhyme, that aids memorising and predictability
- rhythm, that harnesses the child's inborn response to rhythm
- practice in manipulation of fingers and hands
- body awareness
- links with story, music and drama.

The adult should choose and introduce poems he or she likes and link them to other topics of current interest. A new one should be preceded by a couple of old favourites, and then introduced in the same sort of way as a story (see pages 137–8). A poem should be said once, then repeated after a pause, before moving on to something else. Repeated recitation at later dates will gradually work it into the repertoire of old favourites. Children quickly pick up short poems, especially ones with a strong beat and rhyming patterns. Actions, too, aid memorising. For proof of this, try reciting Rose Fyleman's 'Mice' a couple of times, with appropriate actions. 'Teaching'

a poem, line by line, is not advisable; it spoils the flow, and inhibits a spontaneous response.

Poems can be written out effectively, in large, clear print, to form part of a display, e.g. about water, a colour, balloons. Because they know it by heart, children will stand in front of it and 'read' it – a useful pre-reading exercise.

Ways of encouraging children to develop an interest in books

- Begin with children under a year old. Make 'book' times intimate times of shared, relaxed enjoyment.
- Provide children at home with a variety of books and a proper place to store them.
- Be interested in books, and share your interest with children. Let children see adults turning readily to books for pleasure and for information, e.g. cookery.

The use of a listening centre is one way to enjoy a story

- In group settings, arrange and keep an attractive book corner. Involve children in helping to change displays and keeping it tidy.
- Offer a varied collection of books: picture books, story books, situation books, books about people and children from different cultural backgrounds.
- Tell and read stories frequently to groups and individuals. Make story-times lively, inviting children's participation in a variety of ways.
- Cultivate and enhance storytelling skills, such as the use of visual aids etc.
- Use books in connection with visits, visitors, play, conversations, the garden, music, weather, seasonal/topical happenings, displays.
- Make an 'occasion' of introducing a new book.
- Encourage children to join the library in infancy. Take children on frequent library visits, and to storytelling sessions. Support competitions, campaigns, book-making projects, exhibitions and so on, held at, or by, local libraries.
- Support library and borrowing facilities at school. Encourage older children and parents to assist as 'librarians'.
- Support book fairs and book clubs held at school.
- Visit local travelling exhibitions of children's books.
- Use books and themes, as a focus of interest for meetings with parents. Sometimes children's authors can be persuaded to visit schools and talk about their work.
- Make class or group books about cookery activities, pets, visits or topical events.
- Welcome books brought in from home. Show you attach value to them.
- Encourage children to bring to adults' attention any books that are damaged or torn. Involve children with repairs where possible.
- Try to keep abreast of new titles, authors, and trends. Be ready to suggest these to parents if asked, or when the school is ordering new books.
- Encourage the use of cassettes and listening centres in connection with stories.

EXERCISES

Language and communication

Investigation
1) Ask your family how, and at what ages, you expressed yourself in some of the ways outlined in this chapter e.g. effective methods of non-verbal communication, first single words, first sentences.

2) At your placement, study the listening skills employed by adults working with a group of small children. List skills such as 'got down to same level as child', 'maintained eye contact' etc.

Observation
Observe the same child's ability to communicate at three different ages (suggested ages are: birth to six months, six to twelve months, twelve to eighteen months).

Notice:
a) early vocalisation and jargon
b) use of gesture, facial expression, tone of voice
c) clearly articulated words
d) length of sentences
e) word order (syntax)
f) new and interesting vocabulary
g) confidence and spontaneity when talking to adults or other children.

Record on tape a conversation between children of infant age. Analyse how the participants were using language.

Books and stories

Investigation
1) After thorough browsing in local children's book shops make a list of your 'top thirty' favourites. State first your main criteria for selection. (They may differ from those on pages 133–4.)

2) Next time you are at placement, notice which book or books are constantly being chosen and enjoyed by individual children. Can you identify reasons for popularity? Your placement supervisor may be able to help here.

3) Accompany a small group of children to a local library. How do the children react to the library surroundings? Take note of any special promotions/activities happening there. Children may like to talk about it afterwards. How do you think they benefitted?

4) Find out if there are any TV programmes currently featuring children's books. Watch and evaluate.

Observation

1) Position yourself outside the book corner with a notebook, so that you cannot be seen but can hear readers' comments. Note down what several children say as they look at books. In your evaluation suggest how each child was benefitting.

2) Observe a teacher's story session. Watch the expressions on children's faces as they listen. Notice moments of rapt attention, fidgetting, sadness, tension, fright. Note down what events in the story produced these reactions. In your evaluation state what skills and ploys the teacher used to make it an absorbing session.

Project

1) Make an anthology of your favourite children's poetry. Preface it with an introduction stating what you believe poetry has to offer young children, and how you set about making your choice. Sectionalise it, and illustrate some of the poems. (This can be an on-going project, lasting perhaps a year or more, and will be a valuable resource for you in the future.)

2) Make up a ten-minute story for a stated age group of children. After preparation, record your delivery of it on a cassette recorder. Play it back and criticise your performance and the story itself. Was the story the right length? Was it gripping? Were the characters believable? Could children empathise with them? Was the language you used simple, but slightly 'stretching'? Was your delivery a) too fast, b) too slow, c) over-expressive, d) under-expressive?

Try your story (live) on a group of children, trying to improve on your weak points. Evaluate this session.

SUGGESTIONS FOR FURTHER READING

Jerome Bruner, *Child's Talk*, Oxford University Press

Peter and Jill de Villiers, *Early Language*, Fontana Books

V.J. Cook, *Young Children and Language*, Edward Arnold Ltd

Catherine Garvey, *Children's Talk*, Fontana Books

David Crystal, *Listen to your Child*, Penguin Books Ltd

Gwen Gawith, *Reading Alive*, A C Black

Gwen Gawith, *Library Alive*, A C Black

Hilary Minns, *Read It To Me Now*, Virago Press Ltd

Gordon Wells, *Language, Learning and Education*, NFER Nelson

13 Social and Emotional Development

The newborn baby is an entirely self-centred creature. His emotions are few but extreme – rage or satisfaction – and in so far as he perceives other people at all, it is only in their degree of usefulness in administering to his needs.

Over the next seven years these two extreme emotions are refined and diversified and he becomes better able to handle and control them. His social development leads him to interact in an acceptable way with other people, and in the end to take his place in society on his own or as a member of a group.

The whole process is slow and gradual. There will sometimes appear to be reverses or periods of no progress, but these are perfectly normal; no aspect of learning or development proceeds at a uniform, uninterrupted rate. It must be borne in mind what a great deal of discovering the child has to do, both about himself and the world he finds himself in; moreover it all happens during a period of tremendous physical growth.

To set down ages and stages in this, as in any other aspect of young children's lives, is artificial. Likewise, generalisations can be foolish, even dangerous.

What we have to do is to build up a picture of what, for many children, is *often the sequence of development*. For the purpose of clarity, we have divided the sequence into age bands.

INFANCY

The newborn baby is entirely dependent on the person who looks after him – usually mother – for all his needs, food and comfort. Rage or contentment are clearly visible – and audible – and are mainly associated with feeding and excretion. Therefore he lives in a very sensuous and self-centred world.

By bringing pleasure and relief the mother or nurse becomes familiar and from early days the child realises, through his senses, the pleasure she takes in caring for him, her loving and sure handling of him and her voice. As soon as his eyes focus, he will see her eyes and her face and their relationship forms. With a normal, happy mother and baby these happenings bring about *bonding*. Midwives and obstetricians believe that this process is given a positive start by the baby's being placed into his mother's arms as soon after birth as possible. Some even place the naked baby on his mother's abdomen. The baby is also put to the breast as soon as possible.

If bonding, or emotional attachment of mother to baby and baby to mother, does not take place in the early weeks (and there could be many reasons for this), all sorts of other things can go wrong. From the experience of this first relationship the child builds all his other relationships. From his mother's demonstrated love for him he begins to feel secure about himself. This knowledge is sometimes called self-image, or self-concept, and is not to be confused with conceit or inflated ideas of one's importance. If a child feels at ease with himself and secure in others' love for him, he is able to face life confidently and cope with challenges and limitations both within and outside himself.

This bonding process, then, becomes more established during the child's first months of life. By about four weeks the baby can recognise his mother as a separate person from himself, and will smile and respond to her. Play, encouraged by parents, makes him smile, kick and respond happily. By the age of three months, just the appearance of his mother often produces a joyful response. About this age he begins to chuckle, and at four months or so he laughs out loud.

The baby is thus already responding socially. His

perception ensures that moving, changing sights, such as people, attract and hold his attention more than inanimate objects. From about three months, other familiar adults will elicit a special response, and soon after, the baby will welcome the attention of strangers, although still keeping his own special reactions for parents, brothers, sisters and familiar adults, such as grandparents. This distinguishing between familiar and strange adults shows us that his awareness of the world is widening.

By about seven months, the baby has a clear attachment to one person, and shows lack of interest, or wariness, towards others.

Between about six and nine months he will make determined efforts to communicate by smiles, babbling and gestures. His ability to laugh at funny situations will play an important part in his later social life, as laughter is a useful safety valve. The baby of this age enjoys games with less familiar adults, and even deliberately tries to start them by dropping objects repeatedly out of his pram. His understanding of speech, especially the word 'No' and tone of voice, influence his behaviour. Again, we see that his social development proceeds from his close family outwards.

His range of discernible emotions is widening too. Because he has developed trust of his parents, he can withstand a certain amount of delay, restraint, withdrawal of satisfaction, frustration. Weaning, which he will experience before he is one, is built on this trust, leading to compliance with his carer's expectations. Pleasure in giving pleasure to his trusted carer also aids the process. He may, at other times, display defiance, or jealousy, as for instance when father is taking too much of mother's attention away from him.

The mother's temperament and quality of care will be influential factors in his early social and emotional responses. But even at this tender age babies differ widely one from the other for no apparent reason. Some are friendly, happy and amenable from the first; others are fretful, demanding and unresponsive. It is undoubtedly true that certain personality characteristics are laid down at or, more accurately, before birth, some inherited

from several generations back. These varying characteristics bring out varying responses from early carers: a fretful baby will cause a tense and impatient mother to become quickly exasperated, which will probably make the fretfulness worse. Thus it can be seen that the quality and style of the child/parent relationship is a two-way thing.

Characteristics in the parents' contribution which are thought to be of crucial importance throughout the infancy years are: warmth, consistency, responsivity, and discipline that is based on reason and explanation where appropriate.

ONE TO TWO

The importance of the baby's relationships with his first carers continues into his second year, and will colour other relationships. Security, affection and trust are essential in his emotional background, and will provide the safe harbour from which he will increasingly sally forth to meet the world.

As he becomes more and more mobile, he will spend a great deal of time exploring his surroundings, but he still very much needs a parent's presence around all the time to return to if puzzled or frightened.

Research in the past thirty years has alerted people who care for children to the important role of the mother in these early years. Not so long ago it was believed that the lack of such a background of consistent, loving handling by the same mother, or even the experience of an interruption in this relationship (such as in the case of a spell in hospital), could cause the child to grow up scarred for life. It is now believed, however, that such damage may not be irreversible, and that skilled, sensitive handling of separation by all concerned can do much to minimise emotional damage. But it is thought, nevertheless, that handling by too many different people who are caring for the child can result in little bond formation, whereas too few contacts with strangers can lead to later narrowness of outlook or shyness.

The relevance of this research to our discussion here

is that ideally the under-two-year-old should be cared for by one or two consistent loving parents or carers, but also be exposed to contacts with friends of the family.

During his second year, the child's sense of his personal identity begins to develop. Because of this, and aided by his growing acquisition of language, he begins to be interested in other children. He will not be able to play with them in any real sense, of course, but if put together with another child about his age, he will reach out, stare, touch, circle, possibly hand out temporarily a plaything, which will then quickly become the focus of a tug-of-war. There will probably be squeals and tears, and little talking, apart from frequent claims of 'mine'. Such early battles, trying as they are to adults, are unavoidable and healthy because they are situations from which the child will learn. In such clashes, the child is asserting himself and his rights in the only way he is able. As adults, we control or hide such feelings, mutter darkly to ourselves or tell a friend later what we would *like* to have done. But a child of this age is much more direct. He simply lashes out as the occasion demands. He *understands* adult restraints, although they may have little effect. However, he is quite easily distracted, which means that his aggression may soon die down.

It has been found that, limited though interaction is at this stage, companionship from the second year on has a stimulating effect on development generally.

Often during this period the child goes through a phase of refusing to conform in some way to the routines of his day; he may refuse to eat, sit at table, use the potty, or go to sleep at bedtime. This worries many mothers who previously took pride in their child's compliance. Because his growth rate has slowed down, his physical needs are changing. The comparatively new exercise and satisfaction of asserting his individual will, aided by growing language ability and the power of the negative, all combine to make this refusal a normal part of growing up. Usually, the less fuss that is made, the sooner will the phase pass. If, however, his refusals are allowed to become the centre of pitched battles between himself and a fraught, tense mother, their once-happy relationship may be temporarily affected.

This relationship becomes more complex during his second year. Although the child loves mother and wants to please her, sometimes he hates her for thwarting him. Then he feels guilt and a torment of doubt about her continuing love for him. He cannot release this build-up of emotion as adults do, by words. (We call this mixed-up state of love and hate ambivalent feelings; they are present in most intense relationships – for example marriage. To accept this fact is to go a long way towards understanding a great deal of human behaviour.)

The child of this age can also be possessive of his mother or first carer. He may accept the fact that she has household tasks, but hates her to read a book, for instance, go by herself to the bathroom, or maybe make a fuss of another child. This is when he will appear demanding or draw attention to himself. From experience with male carers he will learn about special male characteristics and qualities, which lays the foundations for understanding of male roles.

By the end of the second year he is no longer a baby. He is a confident young child who works hard at establishing and demonstrating his independence. However, he can easily return to baby dependence when frustrated or ill. There is a possibility that we may expect too much of him because he can appear so competent.

TWO TO THREE

These various trends continue into his third year. Particularly noticeable are the eagerness and unpredictability of his exploring, and his self-assertiveness. His own possessions mean a great deal to him; their positions at bedtime or around the home are an integral part of his security. His emotional base is still very much the home, and any weaning away from it should be gentle and gradual. He may be willing to stay an occasional night with grandparents or a favourite aunt.

As he becomes more and more aware of all the

possible choices in his world, he may feel some confusion, and also change his mind and direction suddenly and frequently. He does not like adult interference in his schemes, and sometimes does not welcome friendly advances by adults. Sometimes he goes through a very shy or clinging phase, which can be a great trial to parents.

This is the classic age of temper tantrums – the natural consequence of his self-assertiveness, exploratory impulses, lack of expressive speech, inability to get inside the feelings of other people, or understand cause and effect. His rage and distress, when aroused, can be formidable. The over-whelming nature of them can be frightening to him.

Because his outlook on life is inevitably so self-centred and limited in understanding, he may think he is to blame for unhappy incidents such as his mother's temporary absence. Because he does not distinguish between reality and fantasy, he may have occasional nightmares or irrational fears.

With other children, he will still play side by side and although there will be more conversation, there will still be many clashes of will, snatching and grabbing. Given the choice, he will often choose to play alone.

Through his developing mental perception, he is observing and absorbing more and more about what is acceptable behaviour, and he learns this almost entirely from those within the family circle. Because he wants to feel accepted and loved, he will gradually learn to conform to these ideas, and so by the end of the third year he will be complying with many adult expectations.

Towards the end of this period one can also see tendencies which will be important in his adult personality – characteristics like leadership or submissiveness, gregariousness or detachment, dependence or independence.

THREE TO FOUR

By this age the child starts to look at the world in a less self-centred way, and this stage sees the beginning of social relationships with his contemporaries.

Friendships from now on will occupy a good deal of the child's life. From them, he will experience all the unpleasant aspects of close relationships – resentment, jealousy, insecurity – as well as the pleasant ones – fun, companionship, loyalty, support – just as adults do. Adults are, however, more sophisticated in the way they manage their reactions to evolving friendships. Loss of friends can bring great pain, which is probably underestimated by adults. Through friendships, the child will learn how to survive among equals without parents to act as a go-between. He will learn to cope with conflict. He will learn more about himself, as he makes mental comparisons. He will learn to compromise and act diplomatically. Friendships will satisfy a basic need to feel 'togetherness' and exclusivity with another human being. Peer friendships are vital in childhood, especially for only children, supplying as they do quite different characteristics from those found in parent/child relationships.

Cross-age friendships can be beneficial to children's development, but are not so common in our age-graded society of small nuclear families.

The three-year-old is interested in the actions and reactions of other children, and this forms the basis of real play. He will make friendly overtures to other children and want to sustain periods of play with them. He can, literally, give and take in a limited fashion, and can wait a short while, but, of course, he is still mainly concerned with getting his own way. However, he begins to learn that to acquire and keep companions, he sometimes has to compromise over this. He has greater emotional control, and also more 'know-how' about life and its limitations. Although there will still be clashes with other children, clashes with adults will be fewer.

Adults sometimes worry about over-dependence of one child on another, or of one child 'terrorising' others, but such features of early friendships usually work themselves out naturally.

Jealousy, rivalry and bickering among brothers and sisters (siblings) are commonplace during this period, if not before. This can be another trial to parents and carers who are often surrounded by apparent discord for hours each day, and it sometimes goes on for years. There is good and bad about every child's position in the family, and all, in a sense, are rivals for their parents' love. Within such a close-knit group in restricted premises there is bound to be friction. Through it, however, the siblings build their relationships from which they derive much happiness and security. Loyalty between family members in the face of criticism or threats from outside is also built up by such interaction. It is interesting to note how often childhood warring between two siblings grows into close enduring friendship and love in later life.

By this age the child can work out, through play, many of his aggressive feelings and distressing experiences. He likes rough and tumble play with an adult. Exasperating though it can be, especially just before bedtime, it is a normal and healthy testing out of his own strength, and outlet for exuberant spirits. He likes also to order his parents about in a playful way.

Adult patterns for acceptable social behaviour and harmony in the home are very important now. He needs practical, consistent demonstrations of affection, care, truthfulness and patience. The limits set on his behaviour in the home and the way these are put into practice should help him to conform, feel safe and be liked. He should be building up a good image of himself, but he cannot do this if overstepping the boundaries is linked with guilt. He will understand most logical explanations for limits, but will need constant reminders of abiding by them. Simple courtesies are learned from parents and mean little at first, but gradually the child will come to see them as signs of thoughtfulness to others.

During this stage the child may show curiosity about sex; children will explore one another's bodies and perhaps indulge in mutual genital manipulation; no emotions except sensuous pleasure are involved, and guilt is often only introduced by a worried parent.

Also during this stage, the child may invent an imaginary friend. This is an interesting, and often long-remembered development. It fulfils not so much a need for companionship as for someone on whom the child can project the other side of his personality. For instance, the 'friend' (one small boy's was 'Dob' who always had to be spoken to in a very gruff voice) may do all kinds of dreadful things, when the real child is feeling particularly good and conforming, while at other times the 'friend' may be a paragon of all the virtues. Thus the child is helped to handle his ambivalent feelings. Parents can play along with this fantasy without fear of rearing a neurotic, but, of course, it should not be carried to ridiculous extremes. When the child is emotionally ready to abandon the 'friend', he will.

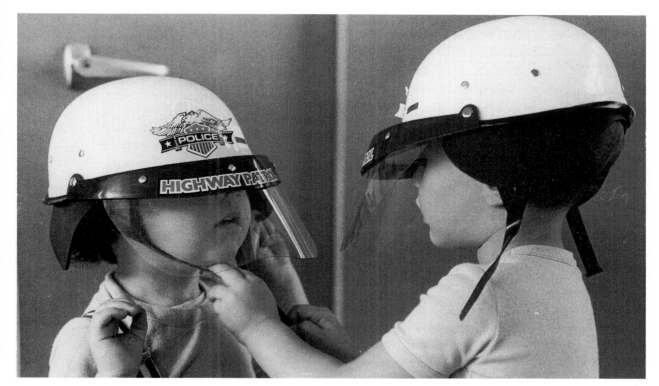

With a little help from my friend

FOUR TO FIVE

The imaginary friend will probably survive into his fifth year, but the four-year-old's own real life personality is by now well established. Through the examples around him, and his greater life experience, he has standards by which to judge his own behaviour and that of others. He will begin to rely on his own judgements.

He will alternate between dependence and independence, but will on the whole be self-confident and often boisterous. He is fairly amenable to reasonable adult demands, and fairly good at controlling his feelings. He can show patience if there is delay.

Four-year-olds are often happy to play together for long periods in groups. The groups frequently break up and form again, or there may be one pair of close friends within or outside it. Four-year-olds like to know that adults are dependably in the background, and while not liking an adult to interfere, they will turn to them for advice, approval or material help.

Nevertheless, they are essentially acting as individuals within the group. The first signs of genuine concern for others usually appear during this stage. A child will inform an adult about one of his group who is in trouble. On the other hand, four-year-olds are quick to condemn or reject a child they do not like. Young children are most likely to behave selflessly (provided they are not doing it to buy their way into favour) if their early carers have helped them to empathise with others through explanation.

Imaginative and imitative play flourishes, reflecting the child's observation of real life as well as the fulfilment of his desires. His heightened imaginative powers are evident, too, in his boasting about his family and possessions and the telling of tall stories. He constantly demands our praise and recognition:

'Watch how fast I can run!' and so on. He is asserting his own ability, and this 'showing off as it is sometimes called, is a natural step to building skills and self-confidence.

Sometimes adults, particularly parents, are concerned at an apparent change which comes about in the child's behaviour between four and five. Boys may swear, shout, defy adults, show off ostentatiously. Girls may giggle secretively or become pert or insolent. Both may dawdle or talk among themselves to avoid complying with adult requests. There may be several explanations for this. The adults may not be acknowledging the child's need for greater independence as he is becoming more grown up. The child may be ready for more stimulation than home, playgroup or nursery can supply. The child may also be apprehensive about moving to 'big school' soon.

FIVE TO SIX

This is the stage when the school years begin and it is a widening experience away from the family which will bring the child both happiness and unhappiness. He will welcome the new social contacts, but he will expect to be liked and valued by all, and if this does not happen, can feel hurt. Girls usually take to their new role more happily than boys; being eager to please the teacher, and being more mature as a rule, girls tend to get off to a good early start with literacy and numeracy skills. Boys often find the break from their mother more upsetting than girls. (Why this may be so could form the basis of an interesting discussion.)

Five-year-olds find apparent failure of any kind difficult to accept. They regard their contemporaries largely as rivals rather than friends, and as yet there is little real interest in team enterprises. Quarrelling and teasing can arise out of aggression, but some aggressive behaviour is inevitable as the child comes to terms with the outside and more grown-up world. Five-year-olds sometimes revel in destructive acts, through which they test out their own power and strength.

Five-year-olds will play in groups, but the groups are quite fluid. They are often happiest playing in pairs; if there are three, invariably one will be left out and hurt feelings will result, particularly among small girls who, by this age, are choosing 'best friends', who themselves change frequently. Separate boy and girl groups begin to form for play at about this age, with separate interests. Girls usually like nurturant play (in the home corner, with dolls, 'good pupil' contact with teacher) in the company of a few close friends. Boys often prefer physical games and contact with a larger group, some of whom they may not even like. This could be said to be a better preparation for adult life.

It is interesting to note that, despite the best efforts of adults to eliminate sex/role stereotyping in play, many children still self-segregate. However, nursery nurses can play an important part in discouraging sex stereotyping.

With skilful adult help, a group of children may stay together, perhaps for several days, and work for a common purpose. There will be many quarrels along the way; one child will appear content with a minor role, then suddenly demand a major one. Group leaders can be clearly identified by now. The children's developing sense of humour, growing out of a knowledge of what is real and what is ridiculous, will help to promote a happy atmosphere within a group of five-year-olds.

The five-year-old is still very much an individual, however. He can make deliberate independent decisions and put them into effect. In this sense, he has taken a big step towards becoming a self-directing person. He is still building up his own image of himself, and because he wants it to be a good one, he constantly asks questions and seeks praise about himself, his past, his abilities, etc. He cannot accept self-blame, although irrationally still feels guilty at things for which he is not to blame, thus revealing his muddled ideas on reality and fantasy. Despite his apparent move towards independence, he still needs his parents' support and companionship a great deal, especially in times of stress. He likes the familiarity of routine in the home.

SIX TO SEVEN

By six, most children have become adjusted to the greater demands of school. Belonging to a group, and being accepted by their peers, means a great deal to them. They dread being rejected, and it is rare to find six-year-olds playing alone. Groups have grown bigger, and sometimes they become very over-excited, and play, including much 'horse-play', becomes uncontrolled. Sometimes a scapegoat is created. Six-year-olds often make up their own rules for group play as they go along. They can take part in organised games – for instance, party games, which involve competitiveness – but the games must allow each child to have his chance to shine. There is a good deal of rivalry and jostling for positions of influence in their social setting, and sometimes the strain brought about by this results in silly behaviour at home.

Changes of mood are very common in six-year-olds. They may be in turn dogmatic and impulsive. Some children of this age present entirely different personalities at home and at school. To all appearances, the teacher tends to have more influence than the parents, therefore the degree of co-operation with each varies, and can cause irritation at home. Fluctuating feelings make choices difficult, and sometimes six-year-olds let their parents down in a social setting.

They are highly imaginative, and although they enjoy fear and titillation of manageable proportions in stories, they may be a prey to imagined terrors, such as burglars breaking into their home. Nightmares accompany such fears.

They are very proud of their possessions, and only reluctantly allow others to play with or use them. They begin to be critical of their own achievements.

Although not generally outwardly affectionate, they do appreciate scope for happy activities and things of their own, as provided by adults. They can also usually be trusted not to hurt younger brothers and sisters if left in charge for a short period.

This stage probably sees the height of individualism.

Sometimes adults assume a greater degree of maturity within the six-year-old than is really there, particularly if the child is well developed physically.

AGE SEVEN

The set of friends, though transitory, of which the six-year-old was aspiring to become an accepted member, now merges into a gang or club. With groups of children, sometimes there is one shared predominating interest, maybe football or skipping. In other settings, it may be Cub Scouts, Brownies, cowboys and Indians, space travellers, or secret societies with dens. Having friends with interests in common who like and respect you brings satisfaction and builds self-confidence at this stage. 'Best friends' are still important. The groups will invent and pay lip-service to rules, but individuals still find it difficult to apply the rules to themselves, and one child may quickly walk off in a huff if tackled by others, and be stubborn about admitting it if he is wrong.

Seven-year-olds can also be very sensitive to teasing and being made to look silly in front of their peers. They will tell tales about each other because they like to feel righteous. This shows that they have adopted adult standards of what is acceptable behaviour. Brothers and sisters of this age will complain to parents of unfair treatment when they feel adults have deviated from these standards.

By age seven, aggressiveness has become largely verbal rather than physical; it can be personal, hostile, and deeply hurtful, for example between former 'best' girl friends.

In their activities at home and at school we can see other typical seven-year-old characteristics – a striving towards perfection, through self-criticism which now becomes very marked. Children of this age can be very persistent in working towards their goal, and get angry at interference or interruption, especially by younger siblings. This has been called 'the eraser age', meaning that the seven-year-old is forever rubbing out things he has written and drawn because 'I'm no good,' or 'It's rubbish,' – both common enough cries during this phase. At other times, however, the seven-year-old will be full of exuberance and enthusiasm for life. Moods change from exuberance to depression; brooding and preoccupied behaviour are very common.

About this age the child begins to feel genuine appreciation of others' efforts. Team games and competitive sports can now be enjoyed, although feelings may run high at times.

Sometimes a seven-year-old will fall in love for the first time. This is an interesting development, because it represents a move away from individuality and a recognition of the need for companionship.

MORAL DEVELOPMENT

Growing up into a self-regulating being involves humans in formulating standards of personal conduct which they believe to be right, necessary, and applicable to the whole of everyday life, the avoidance, of lying, stealing, or knowingly hurting other people, for example. Such standards are called ethics or morals.

Opinions differ on whether this can rightly be considered a separate aspect of children's development, or whether it is an integral part of the child's socio-emotional development, and a direct reflection of his parents' value systems.

Abstract notions of right and wrong are not easily grasped by children under eight. Accepted morality does not fit easily with egocentricity. Situational factors, such as the intensity of a temptation, the likelihood of getting 'found out', the esteem of their group, are very powerful. Personal interest and advantage are still paramount.

Although for many people there no longer exists the dominant moral influence of religious beliefs, parents and society still consider it important that children be brought up both to know and follow certain rules of behaviour. The rules will vary according to the culture and traditions of their society.

Much will be absorbed and copied quite unconsciously by the child from a very early age. As the existence of rules of behaviour impinges on him, he will gradually modify his own behaviour to match them. This process we often call the development of 'conscience'. It frequently involves restraining his natural impulses to self-gratification. Later, the child will learn to make judgements about moral behaviour, and eventually to see the 'rules' as a positive framework for guidance in living, rather than a series of negative curbs. He will develop a sense of justice and sensitivity to others.

Some traditional values in our society are honesty, courage, industriousness, compassion to weak and defenceless people and animals, enterprise, ambition and perseverance.

Adults who help the child gain control over his conduct through explanations are more likely to be successful than those who coax, bribe or threaten.

EXERCISES

Investigation
Talk to your supervisor(s) at placement about:
a) any special friendships they have known between pairs of children under the age of seven
b) whether they agree that many children 'self segregate' by sex for play and friendship purposes after the age of about five
c) whether they believe there is a place for any form of competitiveness for children before age seven.

Observation
Arrange a visit to a mother and toddler group. Record the approaches of children to one another. You may like to do this in the form of a check-list, for example:

Crawled/walked intentionally to another child
Put out hand to touch child

Attempted to touch/take other child's toy
Vocalised
Other forms of interaction
Length of interaction
Intervention by adult

In your evaluation, try to identify who is benefitting from this experience and in what ways.

Project
Make a collection of infant-age children's stated feelings about a given subject, e.g. friends, babies, Monday mornings, being ill, bedtime etc. The children could illustrate their contributions to make this into an attractive book.

SUGGESTIONS FOR FURTHER READING

Zick Rubin, *Children's Friendships*, Open Books Publishing Ltd

Vivien Todd and Helen Hefferman, *The Years Before School*, Macmillan New York

Joseph Church, *Understanding Your Child from Birth to Three*, Fontana Books

Rudolf Dreikers and Vicki Soltz, *Happy Children*, Fontana Books

Geoffrey Brown, *Child Development*, Open Books Publishing Ltd

Catherine Lee, *The Growth and Development of Children (4th Edition)*, Longman

Jeanie Laishley, *Working With Young Children*, Hodder & Stoughton

14   The School-Age Child

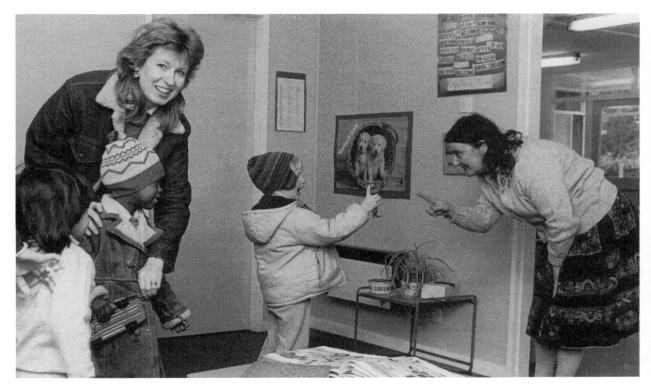

There is a statutory requirement in Britain for all children, from the age of five years, to attend primary school. Many education authorities permit children to enter school at the start of the academic year during which they will be five; thus, many children have only just attained their fourth birthday when they take this big step.

If children have attended a nursery class or playgroup, the break from home, which used to be described as the most traumatic happening in the child's life since his birth, is far less painful. Perhaps best of all is where a child transfers from a nursery class in an infant school to the reception class. He will already know the building and the headteacher – he may have been taken to the hall for PE, or a special festival. Teachers are able to confer and monitor the

child's development concerning when they believe is the best time for him to transfer.

Some children at four are little more than chubby toddlers; in this case, a term's delay will be beneficial. Other children are ready for the social and intellectual challenge of the 'big school'.

Most parents want their child to get an early start with his education, but they can usually see when he is not ready for full-time attendance. They should then liaise with the headteacher about the next step – probably to reconsider the position in a few months' time, or to consider part-time attendance. Most headteachers are essentially flexible in their approach, and will accommodate the parents' wishes whenever possible.

PREPARING THE CHILD FOR SCHOOL

Much can be done at home to achieve a state of readiness for school. Parents/early carers can:

- buy or borrow children's books dealing with the subject
- link up with another child due to begin school at the same time
- encourage the child to spend time away from parents and home – if it is not possible to attend a playgroup, reciprocal play session arrangements with friends are a good second best
- drop references to school into conversations, stressing the positive aspects, such as all the exciting things he will be doing
- ensure that the child goes past the outside of the school on trips to the shops etc.
- encourage independence skills, such as putting on and taking off shoes, cardigans and pullovers, managing on his own in the toilet, asking for the toilet in a comprehensible way, washing his hands
- encourage recognition of colours, shapes and symbols
- familiarise the child with books of all kinds
- offer painting, drawing, crayoning, chalking, puzzle books, sorting and matching games
- encourage the child to tidy up play materials when he has finished playing with them
- avoid using school as a threat in fraught moments ('Just you wait till you get to school, my lad, they'll soon sort you out' etc.)
- involve the child in the buying of a school bag or other symbol of his forthcoming life
- take the child to a summer fête, jumble sale, coffee morning, or other social event at the school which may be open to the public
- co-operate with school staff in preliminary visit arrangements
- send the child in serviceable clothes which he can undo quickly and easily when needing the toilet (dungarees, boiler suits etc., look attractive but can be difficult for the child). Ensure they are marked with his name or a symbol he can recognise
- if he is to take a packed lunch, make sure he can unwrap it
- make sure he is used to sitting up at a table to eat
- tell the class teacher if he is not able to cope alone with toilet or dressing procedures, or if he has any difficulties, dietary requirements or foibles that could cause problems, e.g. a paranoic fear of dogs
- ensure that he is in good health.

Starting school can be a difficult time for many children, especially if they have not had the advantage of a period in nursery school. Therefore it is very important that the child should be in good health in order to cope with any problems and to benefit fully from normal education. To this end most health authorities offer a pre-school medical check in order to find any defects or health problems. The medical check includes sight and hearing tests, an assessment of speech and comprehension, and a physical examination. Height and weight are recorded as this is a good indication of the general state of health. The previous medical records and health visiting records are usually studied and parent/s are given the opportunity to discuss any health concern. This examination is usually carried out between three and four years of age, in order to allow time for treatment to be started before the child begins school, where necessary. It also allows time for educational authorities to be informed of any potential problems. Most of these would be fairly minor, such as poor co-ordination, as it is unlikely that a child with a major handicapping problem would not be known to the medical officer and health visitor as a result of the normal course of health surveillance of the pre-school child.

Providing no problems come to light at this examination and the child makes normal progress at school, subsequently school medical checks would only be carried out (in most areas) if the parent/s or teacher expressed concern about any aspect of the child's health. To ensure that a child does not slip through this net, a questionnaire is sent to parents at intervals, asking about their child's health. Following the return of these, the school medical officer, school nurse and teacher get together to discuss each child and decide whether they need to be examined – the main criterion being whether there is any concern about his ability to learn and benefit from his education. This is called a 'paper' medical. Parents are informed and invited to be present if a real medical examination is decided upon.

In addition to the discussion each child is seen at intervals by a school nurse when a health survey is carried out. Hygiene is checked, height and weight are recorded, and sight and hearing are tested. Hair is also inspected for the presence of nits and lice. In many schools this inspection is used for health education on a one to one basis, e.g. advice about diet to the overweight, etc.

THE FIRST DAY

Children are usually admitted four or five at a time over the first few weeks of term, rather than all at once on the first day. Therefore, a new entrant will ordinarily receive a good deal of individual attention, and sensitive handling.

Taking a favourite bit of blanket or teddy from home, (a 'comforter'), is perfectly permissible, and it will be well looked after. The parent will usually be invited to stay in the room for a while, or as long as the child needs him/her. Usually, the wealth of enticing activities available soon helps the child to become absorbed, and accept the fact that 'Mum is going now, and will be back later to collect you'. It is never wise for the parent to 'slip out' unseen while the child is preoccupied. For the child to discover soon afterwards that he has apparently been abandoned must be very alarming and can cause unnecessary upset.

Unless a long journey is involved, parents should not expect the child to stay for lunch straight away. Part-time attendance is less exhausting for everyone than tediously repeated journeys to and from school. It is most important that parents collecting the child should be at the school promptly; the sight of other parents, and not your own, can be very disquieting.

EARLY DIFFICULTIES

With sensitive preparation, and gradual integration, most children nowadays settle quite quickly and easily into their new daytime environment. This is more true of girls than boys; boys at this age are often less confident, socially assured and independent of parents than girls.

Some aspects of school life which can cause upsets are:

- separation from parent(s)
- large buildings, high ceiling, long corridors, distance of classroom from main door (escape route!) – it is useful for adults to remember how limited the child's known world has been up to this point, and also to bear in mind that the average four-year-old's eye level is little more than a metre from the ground
- noise of large numbers of children; resonance in rooms with high ceilings
- having to share the attention of one or two adults with numerous other children
- having to share toys and play materials
- adults' expectations of the child, especially as part of a group (e.g. sitting still together in the book corner for a story)
- the playground – rough, noisy play can appear threatening; there may be bullies around
- milk time – plain, cold milk may be unfamiliar, as may be drinking through a straw
- meal times – unfamiliar foods; being expected to 'try' new ones (parents/carers at home may have pandered to his favourite foods)
- adapting to toilet and hand-washing procedure; also strange toilet and flush, banging doors etc.
- dressing and undressing – not only might this be tedious and time consuming, but in his undressed state (for PE), the child feels extra vulnerable
- fatigue – all those new experiences, requiring newly-learned responses can be exhausting

- being prone to infection because of:
  a) lowered resistance due to fatigue
  b) lack of resistance to the germs of other children, especially if this is the first introduction to groups
  c) lowered resistance due to the fact that starting school coincides with the growth spurt between the ages of five and seven
- the first weekend – children's memories are very short, and by Sunday night they may have conveniently forgotten the reality of school.

HELPING THE CHILD TO SETTLE

Staff at school will:

- accept the child at the stage he has reached, in all respects
- let him discover and master new experiences/ skills at his own individual rate
- refrain from making undue demands too early
- make every allowance for aspects he finds difficult
- encourage attachment to one adult, and build this into a close relationship
- encourage friendship with one other child who is slightly less new
- familiarise the child gradually with the school environment
- observe, and keep a close and protective eye all through the day, especially at playtimes and other vulnerable times. (A reception class may have playtime apart from the rest of the school for a while.)
- gradually encourage the growth of group-belonging feelings
- offer reassurance and help whenever this is needed
- talk to parents about any worries, or answer any questions.

Parents and carers at home can:

- carry out delivery and collection of their child with a cheerful, positive approach (some parents show far more apprehension than the child)

- help the child to feel 'the same as' others in his class, in terms of clothes, lunch box etc.
- show interest in school happenings, but refrain from quizzing the child too much. The standard answer to 'What did you do today?' is often 'Nothing', as the tired child switches off and his brain subconsciously assimilates all that has happened
- display with pride pictures or other offerings brought home
- invite newly-made friends in to play or to have tea
- co-operate with school approaches, asking school staff if anything is puzzling or worrying them
- help the child over the hurdle of returning to school after weekends and holidays, by giving him something of interest to take to school
- respect the child's need for privacy, solitude, or exuberant mood-switch in evenings and at weekends
- be on the alert for any clues about sources of unhappiness and try to get to the bottom of it. Children often misunderstand things said about forthcoming events, for example; they have no framework of reference through which to anticipate it, and sometimes work themselves up into an unnecessary 'state'
- help build up his resistance to infection by ensuring that he eats a good diet and has sufficient rest. Institute a regular bedtime on weekdays, a winding down period such as a bath, a hot, milky drink, teeth cleaning and a story, then sleep
- ensure that the child is up early enough in the morning to allow time for him to prepare for school and eat breakfast. (If he has difficulty in eating at this time, a mug of hot chocolate makes a good substitute.)
- to safeguard his physical well-being and reduce risk of absenteeism at this time, it is also wise to check the child's hair weekly for infestation with nits and lice
- ensure he attends the dentist at regular intervals.

THE DEVELOPMENT OF COGNITIVE SKILLS

Parents are eager for their child to acquire competency in reading, writing and arithmetic, seeing them as essential skills for coping with everyday life, succeeding in the educational system with its attendant examinations, and eventually in obtaining employment. Infant school staff are required to follow a centrally standardised National Curriculum, of which the core subjects are English, Science and Mathematics, and the others are History and Geography, Art, Physical Education and Music. Children work towards prescribed attainment targets.

Much valuable foundation work will have been done at nursery school or playgroup, to prepare the child for the more formal approach to learning. Parents and early carers can do even more, from earliest days, to give children first hand experience of our system of ordering, labelling and organising the world for consistent meaning and our own convenience.

Reading

We have already seen how children whose parents turn naturally to books for information and pleasure, whose homes contain much printed material, and who read regularly to their children, are greatly advantaged in their attitude to reading. Such parents are giving their child practice in extracting meaning from the printed word, and making connections between written symbols and meaning.

Reading ability is often seen as the most important aspect of education. Not only is it a tool with which to gather information throughout the child's school and later life, it is also used as a significant measure of adequate intelligence.

At its simplest level, reading consists of decoding visual information into verbal form. It involves many skills:

- perception: seeing shapes and patterns of words; spotting small differences, for example between 'b' and 'd', 'saw' and 'was'

- knowledge and awareness of language, to make informed guesses
- remembering, associating and recognising letters and clusters of letters seen elsewhere
- ability to pay attention and concentrate.

At pre-school stage, the child will retell a story previously read to him, while going through the book on his own. He often knows some letters of the alphabet. He probably recognises his own name and some words such as road signs and words seen frequently on TV. In the early stages of learning to read, it is mainly a matter of visual word recognition, greatly aided by context 'clues'. A child may be able to 'read' a word on an everyday object, such as a toy box, but will not recognise it in another context. This stage is sometimes known as 'glance and guess'. The next stage is to see resemblances between known and new words.

As the child becomes more competent in this, teachers offer a phonic approach, that is helping the child to 'sound out' letters and words that are puzzling him. It has to be remembered, however, that the English language is full of inconsistencies. Being helped to sound out consonant clusters, such as 'th', for example, is of more general use than being able to sound out 't', 'h', 'e' separately, which does not produce the desired result, 'the'.

Reception, and later class environments surround the child with the printed word, at appropriate levels. Sentences will be set in context, for example, 'Only four people allowed in the home corner', 'We are watching our tadpoles grow', and so on. Statements will appeal to the children's interests and sense of achievement: 'This is Emma's bungalow. What sort of house do you live in?', 'Our book of favourite television programmes', and so on.

There will be a plentiful supply of books of all kinds. Most teachers aim to give instructions and practice in reading to each child every day, where numbers and ancillary help allow. But many schools have now adapted the former practice of putting the child 'through' a reading scheme, with supplementary books for additional practice. Children are given much more choice, within a graded and coded (known to the teacher) range of books. Children are encouraged to take books home and read with parents.

Without motivation, learning to read is tedious and up-hill work for many children. Therefore, today's teachers try to present reading as a means to a highly desirable end, a key to all sorts of delights – knowing how to operate the computer, researching North American Indians before making a model tepee, and so on.

The skill of reading continues to develop in speed and accuracy throughout the child's primary school life. Boys are sometimes slower to get going than girls, this being linked to their relative linguistic attainment, but the difference is evened out before the age of eleven.

Writing

Writing can be thought of as a special sort of drawing which represents language. Early carers who give the child much opportunity to scribble on paper and handle all sorts of art media suitable to his age and stage are providing him with a headstart. If the adults are in the habit of making shopping lists themselves, taking telephone messages, writing letters, and encourage the child to 'draw a picture for Grandma to say thank you for your lovely present', they are doing more to familiarise the child with the act of writing, and letting him see it as an accepted part of everyday life.

Writing involves the use of fine muscle movements – of fingers, wrists, arms, shoulders, head and eye. It means producing patterns that are varied yet co-ordinated. Constant visual monitoring will be required, and skill in imitating. Considerable control is called for. Each letter must be formed in a certain way from point of starting, proceed in a certain direction, be of uniform size with the other letters, and conform to a set spacing system. Much practice will be needed before fluency is achieved.

At pre-school and early school stage, the child will be encouraged to do such activities as 'join the dots' to make pictures and later letters and words, to trace pictures, then already formed letters and words, to 'go over' the teacher's letters, and later to copy underneath. Use of templates and stencils also helps letter formation and control of a pencil, as does pattern making of many kinds, including within parallel horizontal lines. Writing letters and words with brightly coloured chalk on a large blackboard at child height on a wall is found to be helpful in promoting arm and hand movements, which can then be 'fined down'.

Again, to maintain motivation, teachers try to work through children's own interests and spontaneous ideas. Putting his own name on a painting will make a child feel proud. 'News books', diaries, and accounts of many kinds reflect the egocentricity of the child, and accord value to his home and personal life. As he becomes more fluent, the ability to put on paper his own stories and flights of imaginative fancy brings satisfaction. Project work, following the child's genuine interests, channels writing into lively forms.

In the early stages, correction is done in such a way as not to discourage the child from further efforts. A joyous, spontaneous outpouring of family news, or an original story should not be returned to the child like a battlefield, covered with red ink.

Numeracy skills and mathematical thinking

Competency in this field is needed more than ever before in the high tech world in which we live. Calculators and computers have not absolved us from the need to do our own mental computing. In order to obtain accurate answers to problems we feed into such appliances, we must understand exactly what we are doing.

Mathematics is a world of abstractions and symbols, invented by humans to help us to order and record structures, and the relationships between objects in our surroundings.

Through a variety of concrete experiences, children abstract particular ideas, for example, that wooden bricks are heavier than plastic ones. These ideas, or concepts, develop only as a result of the children's active experience. Concepts are acquired; they cannot be directly taught. Mathematical language

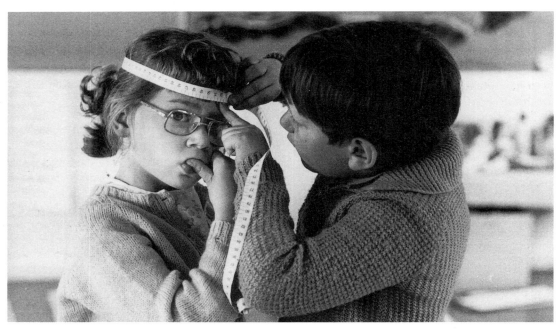

accompanies children's active experience, helping them to clarify, organise and store their discoveries.

Once again, early carers can do a great deal to familiarise the child with mathematical thinking and language as applied to everyday life. Examples are: 'Put it in the middle', 'How many more forks do we need?', 'Who is the taller of you two?', 'These shoes are getting too small for you', 'How many candles did Gary have on his cake?', 'Let's see who is the fastest', 'The river is very deep today.' Fun activities like counting the stairs together as they ascend, or finger and toe rhymes, all add to the child's earliest experiences of the meaning and language of mathematics.

Infant school will build on this basic understanding and continue to provide him with concrete, relevant experiences, and the skills to record his findings and computations in simple form.

Some well-meaning adults teach their child to count at a very early age, in 'rote' fashion. This is of very little use, divorced from meaning and without any real objects to count. In school, his true understanding of 'three', 'five', and so on, will be reinforced at every opportunity – by giving out the milk cartons, seeing how many children are staying to dinner, by number rhymes and singing games. When counting is mastered, he is ready for simple computing. Adding can be seen as 'counting on' or 'counting all', subtracting as 'separating from'.

Through handling, arranging and rearranging such objects as plastic cubes, conkers and beads, he will find out about constancy of number. He will learn some 'ordinals' (first, second, third).

Seriation – putting things in order of size or other attribute – is another useful mathematical exercise, as are sorting, pairing, matching, classifying.

An awareness of spatial relationships must precede all forms of measuring, whether it is of area, length, mass or speed. Again, the teacher will relate this experience to the child himself and his life. Height charts, hand prints to compare sizes, projects on babies and the growth of bean sprouts are all familiar sights in the infant classroom.

Children are encouraged to record their findings in a lively and often visual way, maybe through block graphs, or making 'sets' with hoops.

Play with basic materials such as water and sand, domestic play, shop play and construction play are all rich in mathematical opportunities. (See Chapter 16.) Much of this play can be structured by the teacher to set the child tasks, reinforce understanding and give him practice in recording: 'Buy three cakes and two apples at the shop. How much have you spent altogether?' 'Make a robot with four arms. How many pieces have you used? How many pieces are left over?'

The concept of the passing of time, and the way this is recorded, is quite difficult for children to grasp. The teacher, therefore, will present this in a tangible way. Activities may involve egg-timers, 'pingers', old clocks, looking at old photographs, cookery, growing bulbs, cardboard and toy clocks, daily weather charts and simplified calendars such as Advent calendars.

Methods of recording will become more formal and conventional as the child proceeds through infant school. By the time he enters the junior school, he should be ready for more mental computing and problem solving, based on his rich life experience.

CHILDREN'S PARTIES

With the making of school friends come invitations to tea and the holding of parties. These often assume great importance in children's eyes.

There are some good books which deal solely with the subject of parties. However, included here are a few general guidelines for the organisers of such parties – this is often a nanny's job.

Planning

- Discuss plans with children's parents, and have a clear idea of what is going to happen and how much money can be spent, before you let the child think he has complete freedom of choice. (See also Chapter 20, pages 242–3.)
- Create the illusion of choice if you can, e.g. 'Which six friends would you like . . .?'
- Avoid potentially hurtful situations such as handing out invitations to pre-selected children at the school gate. It is worth posting or delivering invitations.
- Official invitations can set a theme, create excitement, reassure parents that it is 'for real', and make timing clear. Novel invitations can be written on balloons, sticker badges or on animal shapes.
- Be clear and firm about which rooms in the house can and cannot be used. The main party room(s) can sometimes be decorated to help create a theme, e.g. the teddy bears' picnic, or Treasure Island.
- Remember that parties held in the garden reduce mess, but that *you* are responsible for children's safety, wherever they are.
- Plates, beakers, serviettes and table-cloths can be disposable. This reduces work and worry.

Games

- Alternate rowdy games such as balloon race, wheelbarrow race, with quieter ones such as 'Simon says.'
- Have plenty of games prepared: although they may *seem* to prefer just 'mucking about' or running wild in the garden, most children actually enjoy being organised in a fun way. They feel safer, knowing that the adult is in control, and a well-balanced repertoire of games can eliminate much over-excitement, potential accidents and tears.
- Keep games at the right level for the guests, that is, not too scary or sophisticated for younger or nervous children.
- Have a quiet game to precede and follow the tea/meal.
- Try to hold *all* children's interest during games, e.g. 'Pass the parcel' with a small present inside *each* layer of wrapping (have a waste-paper basket handy for rubbish).
- Keep games short.
- Do not single out 'winners' and 'losers'. If there are to be presents or prizes, ensure that *each* guest takes one home.
- Many traditional games can be slightly adapted to fit a theme, e.g. 'Statues' all have to be animals, or 'Stick the nose on the teddy bear'.

Parties held in the garden reduce mess . . .

- The use of face paints and fabric paints can add to imaginative possibilities in games, competitions, fancy dress and theme parties, at very little cost.
- Be aware of individual children's fears, e.g. some children are terrified of bursting balloons, or being blindfolded.

Food

- If there is a theme, food can complement this, e.g. sausages and beans for a cowboy party, bridge roll 'boats' with cheese 'sails' for a Treasure Island party, jacket potatoes and beefburgers or vegeburgers for a bonfire night party.
- Remember that few children today like a lot of sweet stuff such as jellies and fruitcake. Healthy eating can extend to parties as well, if it is presented attractively. Many children enjoy crunchy savouries and nibbles. Portions of everything should be bite-sized: these will not

look daunting to shy or wary children and they can always accept more portions.
- Remember that children will not want to linger long over a meal, even if they are devouring huge quantities. They may like to come back later if they are allowed.
- Be alert to a specially overwhelmed child, or one who is not able to eat some of the foods on offer.
- Cake can be a centre piece, again designed to fit a theme, and the chorusing of the traditional song and ceremony of blowing out the candles can be the signal that tea is over. It is quite easy to find recipe books which give pictures and instructions for making a variety of novelty cakes, such as a gingerbread house, or a train, or a rocket launcher. They are usually simple to make by assembling ingredients like swiss rolls, and covering them with butter-icing and confectionery of different kinds. They are satisfying to produce, and give children great joy, a feeling of 'specialness', and a vivid memory of the occasion.

EXERCISES

Investigation

Talk to your supervisors at infant school placement about current methods used in the teaching of literacy and numeracy skills.

If there is a system of keeping folders of individual children's work to show progress over a period of time, ask whether someone can talk you through one or two. Find out, if you can, what stage the children will progress to next in the development of these skills in the near future.

Observation

Record the words and actions of a group of infant school children working together on a project which involves literacy or numeracy skills.

In your evaluation, suggest what benefits these children were deriving from this method of working.

Project

1) Compile a leaflet to be distributed to parents of prospective infant school children giving them:
   a) brief information about this (fictitious) school and the way it functions
   b) ideas on how best to prepare their child for starting school.

2) Draw up an action plan for a child's fifth birthday party, giving details of numbers, venue, timing, theme (if applicable), food, and games.

SUGGESTIONS FOR FURTHER READING

Denison Deasey, *Education Under Six*, Croom Helm Ltd

Alice Yardly, *Structure in Early Learning*, Evans Brothers Ltd

Sheldon White and Barbara N. White, *Childhood – Pathways of Discovery*, Harper and Row Ltd

Margaret Basham, *Getting Ready for School*, Longman Group Ltd

Dorothy Clark, *Your Child at School*, Surrey County Council Publication

Joyce Nicholson, *Children's Party and Games Book*, Paperfronts

E. Andrew Pollard, *School Age Children and their Primary Schools*, Falmer Press

Betty Root, *40 Reading Games to Make and Play*, Macmillan Publishers Ltd

David Fontana (Ed.), *The Education of the Young Child*, Basil Blackwell Ltd

Jane Asher, *Children's Parties*, Pelham Books

Derek Haylock, *Understanding Early Years Mathematics*, Paul Chapman

Pamela Liebeck, *How Children Learn Mathematics*, Penguin

Alan Ward, *1000 Ideas for Primary Science*, Hodder & Stoughton

Max de Bovo, *Bright Ideas for the Early Years: Science Activities*, Scholastic Publications Ltd

Ruth Merttens and Jeff Vass, *Bringing School Home*, Hodder & Stoughton

Ann Kinmont, *The Dimensions of Writing*, David Fulton Publishers

Judith Makoff and Linda Duncan, *Display for All Seasons*, Belair Publishing Ltd

15 Difficulties in the Early Years

Behaviour which gives rise to adult concern is common in children under five. Sometimes this stems from a new phase of growth the child has entered – the discovery of being able to exercise power over adults by refusal to comply, for example. At other times it stems from an inner lack of unity within the developing personality, or it is the result of adults' expectations conflicting with the egocentric stage the child is passing through.

'It's just a passing phase – he'll grow out of it', has become a cliché, yet it encompasses a good deal of wisdom. Ignoring, as far as possible, the small child's trying behaviour, while reinforcing his acceptable behaviour with approval and attention, within a warm environment where the child is cared about unconditionally, usually has the desired effect.

It is counterproductive to label one facet of a child's behaviour 'a problem', still worse to label him a 'problem child'. Even if this is no more than the adult's thought process, it must inevitably colour attitudes towards, and expectations of, that child, and we know how most children live up to others' expectations of them. 'Naughty' is another word still used a good deal with children. It has a slightly wicked connotation and is associated with receiving attention, which some children find attractive. It is also a non-specific word used to cover many different kinds of behaviour, and focuses on the child himself, rather than the behaviour being addressed.

This is not to say, however, that small children are never trying, or in need of restraint. They can make great demands on our patience and self control. It is inevitable that this should be so. They are far from ready to cope with all the demands that life makes on them. Their feelings are intense and rapidly changeable. They want instant gratification of those feelings. They lack, on the whole, the ability to control them if met with frustration or denial. They also lack the ability to foresee the consequences of their actions. They have not learned adult strategies for manipulating people and events, in an acceptable manner, to get their own way, nor the social skills to hide negative and unlovable feelings. They are surrounded by big, powerful adults who can dictate events, while they, the children, have to allow events to happen to them.

However, if disturbed behaviour is very frequent, persistent, continues well after age five, or quite suddenly brings about a dramatic personality change in the child, these are reasons to take it more seriously.

Sometimes a child gets locked into a pattern of behaviour which neither he nor his early carers seem able to break out of. He will present problems of discipline, teaching and communication, and may eventually require special placement, unless he can be helped at an early stage.

There are no magic formulas or easy answers to any of these difficulties, nor can any one theory be applied in a wholesale manner. What follows are some general guidelines, the two cornerstones of which are the development of personal adequacy in the child, and the development of teamwork therapy. Students need not feel overawed by this last term; it simply means everybody who is concerned for the child's well-being working together. There are plenty of illustrations of this happening in the stories of the children which follow.

The reader is reminded that no two children react to the same approach in exactly the same way. Neither does the same highly commendable approach work well for everyone. In addition we must all be true to our own personalities; effective management techniques rely on this.

Let us look at the case of one small child who is giving cause for concern to his carers.

Mark has been admitted at just four years old to his local infant school. Very little is known about him or his background. Staff see only his day-to-day conduct. He appears isolated and does not seem to want friends. He communicates very little, indulges in much attention-seeking and clinging behaviour, and is uncooperative with adults.

It may help to draw up a diagram of the 'web' of influences surrounding Mark and happenings in his life so far.

MARK

Medical history

Problems at birth?
Developmental delay?
Accident?
Illness?
Trauma?
Hospitalisation?
Any hearing loss?
Speech problems?

Previous care/group experience

Grandparent?
Playgroup?
Child-minder?
Nanny?
Day nursery?
Nursery school?
Social integration in other group(s)?

Contact with other professionals

Child and family guidance?
Speech therapist?
Educational psychologist?
Clinics?
Health visitor?
Social worker?
Any programmes being carried out?

Family background

Parents: very young, older, one or two?
Siblings: how many? Any step-siblings?
Position in family: oldest, youngest, middle of three, one of two, born after a long gap?
Emotional climate: stable, tranquil, tense, troubled, uncertain, erratic?
Style of discipline: authoritarian, easy-going, inconsistent, implemented by one parent?
Manner of communication: free, encouraging, relaxed, restricted, critical?
Awareness of difficulties: concerned, defensive, blinkered, unaware, uninformed?

Changes in environment

New house?
New district?
New school?
Changed constitution of family?
New sibling?
Bereavement?
Any of these changes may have caused feelings of threat, pressure, confusion, sadness or jealousy.

Creating an action plan

Any plans to help Mark function more normally and happily must begin with finding answers to some of these questions. This will require forging a good relationship with parents, possibly 'stage managing' an initial home visit if parents do not bring him to school. If it appears that there are serious problems at home, you will not be able substantially to change these, but you should be able to help him feel more comfortable about them.

Staff at school will need to identify their chief concerns. Here, close observation can bring surprises. Sometimes a child who is thought of as 'always quarrelling' is found, through accurate record keeping, to engage in perhaps two or three quarrels a week.

Sometimes it helps for a staff team, with parents if possible, to draw up a list of specific behaviour they want to decrease, e.g. throwing food on the floor, and those they want to increase, e.g. concentrating on one toy at a time.

Then an action, or management plan can be drawn up. In all cases, this should include a medical inspection by the medical officer, when parents will be invited to attend, and his previous child health and health-visiting records can be available. This will give valuable insight into the child's background and any difficulties he may have experienced in the past. His hearing and sight can be checked at this time, and his general health and development monitored.

His socialisation programme might include linking him with one other child, and one adult; giving him small responsibilities; verbalising about his behaviour – 'That was kind of you to share your crisps with Jason', and so on. Many adults favour a system of rewards such as 'smiley' stickers, or privileges of some kind, to reinforce desired behaviour.

His daily progress will need to be recorded. A time limit, possibly a month, should be set after which a first review meeting will be held, at which, parents will be present of course. If the plan does not seem to be working, other strategies need to be tried. Other specialists may need to be drawn in, possibly an educational psychologist, or the services of a Family Therapy Centre.

The aim is to help Mark achieve a sense of self worth, to exercise control over his actions, to handle negative emotions, to integrate with his peers. Then his need to attack or deny his environment will fade. A child with a strong sense of self worth will be more able to withstand frustration, and more eager to embrace all the exciting and stimulating experiences that school, and life, have to offer. Once we realise this, we can see the foolishness and insensitivity of humiliating and punitive measures; anything that stresses how 'bad' a child is, is likely to cause further damage.

SOME COMMON DIFFICULTIES

Between toddler stage and approximately age seven, the following forms of behaviour are commonly seen from time to time.

- Tantrums
- Destructive and aggressive behaviour and bullying
- Negative/defiant behaviour
- Extreme shyness/withdrawal
- Lack of concentration
- Fears and anxieties
- Jealousy
- Lying and stealing
- School refusal
- Friendlessness
- Sucking, nail-biting, rocking, masturbating.

As we look at some approaches which are thought to be helpful, we shall also briefly describe some real children who have experienced these difficulties and what has been done to overcome them.

Temper tantrums. The classic age for temper tantrums is commonly between two and three. The child by now is fully mobile, is increasingly able to explore his environment and gratify his curiosity and his desires. Yet, while wanting to assert his developing personality and his will, he is conscious of apparently being frustrated at every turn. 'No' is all too familiar to him, as is having exciting-looking objects removed from his grasp or path. Physically, he attempts more than he is able to accomplish, in manoeuvring objects and so on. Although he can understand much more than he is able to express, he as yet cannot understand explanations about, for instance, why he may not help himself from the tempting sweet display in the supermarket – all within easy grabbing reach. His reaction on not getting his own way is often to throw himself on the floor, perhaps with arms and legs flailing, and scream until he is red in the face, by which time both he and his carer are the centre of a part-sympathetic, part-critical crowd of onlookers. This, in itself, often complicates things, as does the problem of a trolley full of shopping to be dealt with somehow at the same time!

Children older than three also often revert to these tactics in very 'fraught' moments, or if they have found in the past that they can get their own way by such means.

Although it is much easier to say rather than do, the important thing is for the adult to keep calm and maintain an atmosphere of firm, patient affection. Do not give in to the child 'for the sake of a quiet life', but do not, either, turn the tantrum into a pitched battle between you; screaming back at him will do no good at all. The child is temporarily out of control and you must help him to regain that control. He will probably need to be removed bodily from the scene, away from staring or frightened children, or anyone who is likely to get physically hurt. Restraining the child, in a firm hold, from damaging property or himself will gradually have a calming effect on him, and will make him physically aware of your strength and resolve. If the tantrum lasts any time, he should not be left alone, so stay with him while these frightening, overpowering feelings last. When he has calmed down, quiet, comforting talk, and a gentle face wash will all help him feel better. You will probably need to involve him in a non-demanding activity or task you are doing, so that he recovers his composure gradually, before rejoining the group. Do not refer to the episode again, and certainly do not adopt the attitude, 'Jackie doesn't love you when you

A stormy moment, calling for a calm approach by carers

do that'. The alarming experience he has gone through will be all the worse if you threaten to withdraw your friendly feelings towards him. The calmness with which you handle the situation also reassures the whole group, who feel they will be given the same help any time they need it.

Stacey, at three and a half, had been used to her mother giving in to her every whim, but only at the end of individual battles. It took the birth of her sister, and Grandma coming to stay in mother's absence, for Stacey to experience the influence of a firm adult, who was kind but consistent, and laid down clear guidelines for conduct. 'When we've finished the shopping', Grandma would explain before they set out, 'you can choose a packet of sweets to eat after lunch.' A week of this handling, much tempered with affection and approval, was sufficient to help both Stacey and her mother to break out of the confrontation-and-surrender pattern they had built up.

Prevention is always better than cure, and an observant adult can often foresee possible trigger points. Fortunately the two-year-old is easily distracted by having an attractive alternative offered. Remove obvious and unnecessary frustrations from his environment, for example treasured ornaments that he mustn't touch. We all have to endure frustration in our lives, but the young child's life abounds in it, so you need not fear you are smoothing his path too much.

Destructive, aggressive behaviour and bullying. We all have aggressive feelings and impulses. How far and in what ways we channel that aggression depends very much on the society we live in and our early environmental influences. Films featuring aggression are shown every day on television. If a child has seen a pattern of arguments involving physical or verbal abuse among those closest to him, this behaviour will probably be reflected in his own actions. His anger and aggressiveness may have been reinforced at home by bringing him attention, especially if he receives little attention for other sorts of behaviour.

As civilised adults, we curb our destructive impulses – for instance, to strangle the neighbour's cat. We respect other people's property rights; we can foresee the consequences. Small children have not acquired these adult attributes. What is more, some children need to destroy before they can create.

Boredom can lead to aggressive behaviour. It is not surprising that there are so many fights between children in some primary school playgrounds where there is so little of interest to do. We should ensure that small children's surroundings and their routines are sufficiently stimulating. A variety of play materials, the arrangement of the room, visits and visitors, the introduction of new games, can all help to maintain interest. Older children, at nursery, school or playgroup who have already experienced all that the establishment has to offer, need extra stimuli.

Children with abundant physical energy, and often strength, need constant outlets if these are not going to be used for disruptive ends. An exciting garden, well equipped, and the opportunity to use it in an unhampered way, will use up a good deal of energy. Wet weather poses a problem for such children, and then they will require alternative vigorous activities such as movement and music-making and building with blocks. Play material which gives outlets for banging, cutting, pinching, tearing, destroying legitimately (such as woodwork, clay and dough, papier mâché, sand and painting), all channel destructive impulses, although needing careful supervision, especially where a potentially aggressive child is using tools or scissors. A home-made cardboard or wooden target figure on a pivot, to be aimed at with bean bags or something similar, is a popular toy for outside play. Play and tasks involving water can have a soothing effect on an aggressive child.

Sometimes an aggressive child is literally 'hitting back' at life which has been less than kind to him, and is making his mark and seeking attention. To let him see what a nuisance he is, or worse, how much he is disliked by one and all, will only satisfy his perverse impulse. The chances are that he will then go on making life more and more uncomfortable for everyone, living up to his bad reputation.

Praise him whenever possible to boost his self esteem, and ensure small successes. Assign him small responsibilities; perhaps a disruptive child can take messages, help lay the tables, although, of course, it must never appear that you are rewarding him for being difficult, or paying him too much attention. Experienced staff recommend what they call 'catching' such a child first thing in the morning, by involving him straightaway in an interesting, demanding activity.

Aggressive behaviour, although it will occur frequently in minor ways, cannot be tolerated incessantly or in severe forms. The child must realise that he is inflicting harm and hurt, and that you care enough about all the children to protect them from this. Hitting back, or corporal punishment, of course, can never be condoned by an adult. We are sometimes aware that a child may be punished in this way at home, and our approach must seem weak and ineffectual in comparison. Sending a child out of the classroom to the Headteacher's office can be counter-productive. It tends to highlight the fact that the classroom staff could not cope with this behaviour and, for an attention-seeking child, this brings rewards. It is better if the teacher can be relieved of the demands of the rest of the class in order to deal effectively with this individual.

Learning to settle differences, or manipulate a situation through words rather than actions, is a very important part of the socialising process which all nurseries must work towards. Give reasons why a certain kind of aggressive conduct cannot be tolerated, and make it clear that you are condemning the deed, not the child. Although it often does not appear so, he badly wants to retain your liking for him. Reprimand him quietly but firmly, away from other children. Shouting or emotional reactions on your part will only incite him to further unsocial behaviour; the presence of his friends around will encourage him to make the most of this attention. Where practicable, let him experience the consequences of his actions, not as a punishment but rather as an unemotional matter of cause and effect. If he has deliberately 'flooded' the bathroom, supervise him calmly while *he* mops it up. He may think this fun at first, but the novelty will soon wear off, and he will probably think twice before doing it another time.

The emergence of both a bully and a victim figure must be quickly observed and steps taken, otherwise real harm could be done to both children, and trouble will arise in nursery/home relationships.

Supervision outside the classroom must be very close, but the opportunity to participate in all the exciting activities often minimises bullying, and offers outlets for aggression. The victim should be given opportunities to succeed and win praise in all sorts of activities, so that his self-confidence is boosted. The aggressor should be kept busy with all the various activities already suggested. Acts of kindness, sharing, etc., however small, should be noted and praised. Sometimes an aggressor will be helped by involvement with the nursery pet, but close supervision will be necessary. Incidents of bullying must be stopped and condemned, but soul-searching sessions of 'Why did you do it?', 'How would you like it if . . .?' or 'You're to wait here till you've said sorry' and so on are ineffectual. The egocentric child cannot sufficiently think himself into another person's feelings; moreover the incident is past and forgotten as far as he is concerned. If there ever was a reason for his action (which is not always the case) he has probably forgotten it by now, or at any rate will not be able to put

it into words. 'Sorry', if it is forced reluctantly out of a child, means little. What is worse, if he utterly refuses to say it, you have placed yourself in a position from which you will have to climb down – never a desirable course for an adult in charge.

Simon, at seven, was a real nuisance to peers, teachers, and parents who were ambitious for him and perhaps expected him to achieve more at school than he was capable of. In an attempt to make him see the error of his disruptive ways, his parents visited his school to discuss with his teacher their intention of withdrawing from him the privilege of going swimming, both with the school and with them. His teacher was aghast. 'That is the one thing he really works hard at, and excels in', she explained. 'We must find ways of building on that ability, not rob him of his one chance to shine and win praise.' They began to work together on ways of channelling all that physical energy into acceptable activities such as Cub Scouts, diving lessons and so on.

Negative/defiant behaviour. The child who exhibits this type of behaviour may be used to getting things all his own way at home, and be protesting about the demands made of him at school/nursery. He may be going through a self-assertive phase and feel he can make his mark by gestures of noncooperation.

Adults may be best advised to ignore his negativism over little matters, and not to regard these as a threat to their authority. They should practise a positive approach in voice and manner when requesting children to do something. 'Now we're *all* going into the garden to hear a story.' Imply in your voice that you confidently expect everyone to participate in this exciting prospect.

Ian, at six, used to object to many routine parts of the day, for example, putting on his coat to play outside in winter, or getting undressed for movement or PE. His teacher would not wheedle or coax him, but would just say to all the children, 'We must put on our coats today, it's so cold.' Ian would stay inside the classroom, sullen faced, apparently ignored, but, of course, being discreetly observed by the teacher outside. Having watched his friends laughing and playing outside, Ian would appear within a few minutes, plus coat. The teacher would refrain from any reaction, and would hide her private amusement.

Avoid making unreasonable demands on him, or blowing up a refusal into a confrontation between you and the child. The following methods will help. Giving him a choice of two definite alternatives often distracts him from the fact that he doesn't really want to do either. Try to find something he is interested in and encourage him to join in. Praise his efforts in group activities; if he wants to remain one of a group, he will have to learn to conform.

Extreme shyness/withdrawal. These two manifestations appear similar, but may be fundamentally different. A child may be severely withdrawn because of distressing circumstances or events in his early life; he has literally retreated, mentally and emotionally, from the possibility of further hurt and disappointment over relationships. Such a child may also withdraw physically, perhaps constantly to the book corner, home corner, or in small dens he finds or builds for himself. This is a very difficult child to help, and all approaches must be made exceedingly sensitively, gently and gradually. Forcing him to join in things, or badgering him with questions, will only make matters worse. Try to notice anything that seems to arouse his interest and this may lead into communicating with him and drawing him more out of himself and eventually into the group, but it will certainly not happen overnight. If withdrawal seems total, or persistent over a period of time, this child may need expert help, or it may be that he is not yet ready for full-time attendance at school/nursery.

Shyness is present in many of us, and to a certain extent can be hereditary. It may be a result of the child's not having mixed much with other children in the early years. It will be more helpful to this child to experience playing with other children on his home ground before being plunged into a larger group away from home. He should never be forced to join in something, or have attention drawn to his shyness, with, for example, apologies made for it. His mother may need to stay with him over a number of days or longer before he is able to be left happily at the nursery school. Direct close physical contact with strangers will paralyse him with shyness, so at first, contact needs to be indirect – a sideways, gradual drawing of him into activities, slowly merging into a warm, gentle relationship with adults and others. Praise will boost his self-confidence.

Ho-man, at five, was responding slowly to these gentle tactics, when a puppet theatre visited the school. He was much taken with all the action, colour and humour. The next day, the teacher and nursery nurse listened with enthusiasm to the children's pleas for their own puppet theatre. To everyone's surprise, as the project got underway, Ho-man was the keenest of all, in a quiet way. When it came to putting on plays he became a different person, 'speaking through' his funny dragon character, revelling in the attention and laughs, while he himself was still tucked out of sight. The beginnings of a new self-confidence for Ho-man stemmed from this project.

Lack of concentration. A child who flits from one group or activity to another, can be a disruptive influence in the nursery/school, and a trial to adults. Such a child may come from a flat, or other home which lacks suitable play space. He may be new to the nursery, or come from a home lacking in play materials. Such children are frequently referred to as 'hyperactive' by their parents.

Sometimes adults make the mistake of giving *only* vigorous noisy play activities to a child of this kind, thinking it will channel the restless energy. It can therefore become a way of life for the child. Darren, at five, had been exposed to this kind of approach. His home was noticeably lacking in quiet, constructive activities, and there was also a tacit understanding in the family that boys are *expected* to be tearaways most of the time. Parents would alternately scold, despair, and smile ruefully, especially at the fact that he had been 'expelled' from playgroup. These mixed messages did nothing to help his behaviour. At school, the usual vigorous activities were available to him, but staff also worked with him on a programme of seated activities. His concentration, starting at a very low ebb, was gradually increased a minute at a time, as he eventually completed jigsaws he became interested in, and made simple construction kit models from diagrams. A chair with arms, pushed up to the table, and a friendly adult arm put round his back, both helped create an atmosphere of calm, gentle restraint. At meal-times, he would be seated next to 'his' adult, and at storytimes too, when he would often be asked to hold up the book to show illustrations to others.

Fears and anxieties. A child who is under pressure at home, perhaps by over-ambitious parents, or threatened domestic relationships, may appear generally anxious and 'nervy', afraid to accept the smallest new challenge. We can help by providing a happy and stable atmosphere at the nursery where he receives much praise, encouragement and affection.

Specific fears are very common, especially around three years of age. A fearful response to danger, real or apparent, and appropriate evasive action is part of our physical self-preservation mechanism, and is therefore a normal phenomenon. In dealing with young children's fears we should also remember the scale of the adult world as it appears to them. An Alsatian dog must appear as a large horse does to us, a swimming pool as an endless expanse of water. Then, too, with our greater knowledge of the world we can rationalise and reassure ourselves that certain fears are groundless; we *know* that the dark corridor does not contain hobgoblins; nor is a clockwork spider really alive and threatening us. Young children are still finding out about such things.

Sometimes we actually *create* children's fears, for instance by squealing about a slow worm (legless lizard), looking frightened in a thunderstorm or, as parents, giving children the impression, through open quarrelling, that mother or father is about to leave them.

To understand the reasons for and the intensity of children's fears is to go some way towards helping because then, clearly, we will not ridicule, tease, or force the child to 'face his fear'. A *gradual* facing and coming to terms with feared objects or situations will be necessary eventually, and often children set the pace themselves.

Looking after the nursery's pet gerbil helped Anna, aged three, to come to terms with her fear of animals.

Joanne, aged four, was terrified of the sea, it was discovered on a seaside holiday. Her nanny abandoned any attempt to persuade her into it, but encouraged her to explore a small rock pool. This was near where the family were sitting, it was limited in size, relatively warm, and she could see clearly the tiny shells, weeds and creatures at the sides and bottom. After a few days of this, she was prepared to watch while her older sister went in the sea. Later she progressed to playing, kicking at the small waves at the edge, and later still to paddle.

Jealousy. Jealousy can arise at many times in a young child's life. Probably the classic occasion is when the child has to accept the arrival of a brother or sister. We have tried to offer help over this in Chapter 4. Introduction of new step-parents and siblings into children's lives can also cause jealousy.

Leon, at five, was asked to accept a number of changes in his life at the same time: his parents had divorced, and Leon and his mother had moved in with a man he was expected to relate to as a new

father figure. At the new infant school he started to attend, the adults noticed signs of his emotional turmoil and tension. Talks with his mother revealed that she had not discussed or explained the situation to Leon, nor encouraged him to talk about the way he felt. In her new-found life and love, she had been thoughtless. She was helped to realise that Leon was grieving for his absent father, and that he saw her behaviour as essentially disloyal. He was also jealous of the attention she was giving her new partner, following a period of some unhappiness when she had clung to Leon. A more sensitive and mature approach helped Leon. The new partner was not forced onto him at home. The two adults refrained from excessive displays of affection for each other. A pet kitten was bought for Leon which brought him much love and comfort. Access to Leon's father was negotiated. Meanwhile adults at school tolerated with understanding his clinging behaviour and occasional antisocial outbursts.

But other circumstances, too, can produce feelings of jealousy. A child with few possessions of his own can be very envious of peers with more. A child less gifted, or less obviously loved than his brothers or sisters may feel extremely jealous of them. Children without fathers can envy those with them.

Jealousy is often linked with lack of self-confidence and inner security. Therefore the adults caring for such a child need to bolster his confidence in himself. He needs a great deal of affection and opportunities to succeed and excel in all kinds of activities. If his jealousy is expressed in aggression, suitable play material can do much to channel these impulses into acceptable forms. A large rag doll can be thrown about and punished, clay can be pounded, and nails hammered energetically. Playing with dolls can awaken ideas of tender care. Books and stories about fictional children with similar feelings can help the child to see, in an indirect way, that his situation is not unique. This alleviates the guilt which may be complicating his jealous feelings.

Tactful approaches can be made to parents about the child's abilities and likeable characteristics, if it is the case that the jealousy stems from favouritism in the family.

'Lying' and 'stealing'.   These words are in inverted commas, because the use of such words presupposes that young children can distinguish between truth and fantasy, yours and mine. We know from their enjoyment of stories and books which constantly step in and out of the real world (for example, engines that talk and have definite personalities) that they cannot make such distinctions. Therefore, why should they not make up their own 'tall stories' about, for instance, seeing a dragon on the way to the nursery? Adults should never react sharply to this as telling lies, but enter into the spirit of the story, while letting the child see by their facial expression that it is a shared joke. This will help the child to know that it is only a joke, without deflating him.

If tall stories and boasting persist well into the infant stage, it may be a sign that the child is not getting enough opportunity to succeed and win praise and admiration in other fields. Children also lie when they are afraid of the consequences of telling the truth, so that it may be a sign that we, or his parents, are being over-strict, or expecting too much of him. We have to help him understand, in a quite unemotional way, that it is important for us to feel able to believe him; otherwise we shall not know when he is telling the truth. Lying can also denote an escape from an undesirable world. Sometimes boasting about heroic acts and so on can represent what the child *would do* if the need arose, or what he would like to do. We should remember that there are many different kinds of truth, as well as untruths.

In the case of 'stealing', we should remember that moral principles of right and wrong are not really grasped until children are about seven or eight. We should also remind ourselves that the little child lives entirely in a here-and-now world, and that his feelings and impulses can be quite overwhelming. If he sees an apple in a friend's coat pocket, and is feeling a bit hungry, he wants it there and then, and that is all there is to it. This applies even more to children who have little in the way of treats and personal possessions at home. Children who are experiencing emotional upsets, lack of affection or loneliness in their personal lives may help themselves to tempting items as a form of compensation, much in the same way that we turn to the biscuit tin, refrigerator or chocolate box when we are feeling let down or miserable.

Parents are often unduly horrified and upset by the fact that their child is taking things. Emotive words like 'pilfering' and 'thieving' spring to mind, with an apparent future of juvenile delinquency. What the neighbours know or think about it also affects parents. It is important that if the child is taking things which do not belong to him, certainly for the five-to-seven-year-old, his parents and school staff should consider whether it may be a distress signal.

Matthew, at six, was constantly taking other children's possessions and money, whenever he got the opportunity. He would vehemently deny doing so, of course, when accused by affronted classmates. Contact with his parents, who knew of his behaviour, revealed that, in order to make him appreciate the value of money, they insisted that he earn fixed sums for performing set tasks – so much for the washing-up, cleaning the car etc. They were amazed when it was suggested to them that regular pocket money given unconditionally might bring about a change. 'Extra' pocket money might then be earned on top of that. They were delighted when the new policy worked, and found that Matthew was much better able to get to grips with the beginnings of budgeting, now that he had a reliable amount to start with, and the incentive to earn more.

Thomas, at five, repeatedly brought home school pencils, rubbers, crayons, paper and other writing materials. He lived in a household where both parents were writers, and where all five family members shared and used whatever materials were to hand. All that was needed in Thomas's case was a clear explanation that school property was for school use only, and not intended to be more widely shared.

Jane, at seven, also began taking other people's possessions, during a period when her father was absent abroad. The middle one of three girls, she had been compensating for this perhaps unenviable position by encouraging the 'Daddy's favourite' syndrome. When he was no longer around, she was desolate. In Jane's case, a visit to an educational psychologist afforded helpful explanations to her mother. Thereafter, on father's weekend visits home, he made a special point of spending extra time with her. He gave her his old wallet to 'look after', (she kept it under her pillow), and put her in charge of the family's pet rabbit, who was generally acknowledged to be father's responsibility.

If we know we have in our care a child who has a tendency to 'steal', we should take sensible precautions not to leave tempting items in his path. Avoid asking the children to bring money to school whenever possible. Certainly never leave money around the room, or in an adult's desk. Snacks and special birthday presents, toys, etc. can be admired and then put on a high shelf for safe-keeping. If we find items belonging to other people, we should return them to the owner, explaining casually to the child. We should never search children (parents could accuse us of physical assault if they chose), or turn the search for a missing item into a witchhunt, with a demand for confessions, and so forth.

Sometimes, an item known to be missing will mysteriously and suddenly reappear when children are encouraged to hunt for it. The understanding and co-operation of parents can be utilised in returning missing school items, although staff should obviously avoid singling out particular parents in this.

As realists, we have to face the fact that regrettably there is a whole so-called grey area between the two extremes of honesty and dishonesty. How many people declare every penny of their earnings to the tax man, or return to a shop with excess change? How many of us exaggerate anecdotes slightly to make a better or funnier story? Then there is evidence in some homes of items like tins of paint which have 'fallen off the back of a lorry', teaspoons, towels and ashtrays marked with the name of public houses, hotels and transport companies in various parts of the world. This is to state facts, though not to condone.

Children are not deceived. They practise what we practise rather than what we preach.

School refusal. Most of us remember what it was like to experience Monday morning tummy ache –

perhaps we still feel that way occasionally! The adjustment from weekend relaxation at home to structured organisation away from home and family, can demand a good deal from the child. His mind will focus on particular things he is not too keen on – school dinners, maybe – which can become a big hurdle in his imagination. If school reluctance/refusal is happening most days, we need to look more closely into it.

The parents of John, aged six, had recently reversed their roles: the mother started work, while the father was temporarily unemployed. It was about this time that the mere prospect of school would find John crying and doubling up with pain. His harrassed mother would tell him briskly that there was nothing wrong with him as she hurried off to work, leaving his father to deal with it. The father was worried enough to take John to the doctor. Discussion helped them all to see that the pain was real enough, but it was brought on by anxiety. John felt unsettled by the change in the family situation: it was quite different from that of his friends, and had upset his former certainties. Deep down, he was worried that this was the first step towards his mother going away altogether. School took him away from the home he felt so unsure about, and so he had come to hate and resent it. Patient explanation to John about the family's present circumstances went some way to help. Mother was able to readjust her working hours slightly to enable her to pick him up from school each afternoon. The parents also found it helped to get up slightly earlier each morning, and have a calm, unhurried breakfast together before dropping John off at school. If he was complaining, he would be told 'You can come home if it gets really bad.' Building up understanding and assurance, and sharing the situation with his teacher, helped to renew stability, and got him through this bad patch.

Friendlessness. Some children stand out as being without friends. Sometimes it is easy to see why they appear different from other children. It is similar to what happens in nature, when wild birds attack a strange budgerigar who has escaped and strayed into their territory, for example. Sometimes children lack friends because they are spiteful. Sometimes they appear to make it clear that they are not bothered about friendships.

Children can be very cruel to outsiders. We owe it to all concerned to try and change this situation, if the child's later adjustment to society in general is not to be impaired.

Nadia, at seven, was an unusual child who did not seem to relate to either sex. She was large, ungainly, somewhat uncoordinated, self-conscious and intense. She seemed not to share any of her classmates' interests in sports, animals, dolls, gangs, clubs or adventure stories. In the playground, while others played and joked joyously, she was to be seen on her own, watching half-heartedly and often getting cold.

Through a children's TV programme, the class became interested in Roman Britain. This was something Nadia could relate to. History was her secret passion, and she revelled in the information and illustrations the class assembled. When it was decided that they would write and perform a play on the subject, her joy knew no bounds. Her parents supplied her with all kinds of 'props', sheets for togas, jewellery, armour etc. which resulted in her becoming suddenly very popular with the other children. The amused teacher monitored the situation, but it needed little intervention from her. The children moved on from ingratiating themselves with her to suit their own ends, to respecting her superior knowledge and being willing to try out her ideas. The gulf between them was never again so wide.

Sucking, nail-biting, rocking, masturbating. A baby has a natural instinct for sucking and it is essential for his survival. Besides being a means of getting food, sucking, or touching things with his lips, is a means of finding out the shape and texture of an article. It is also very comforting. As soon as a baby is able, he will put his hand or foot into his mouth to suck. Despite what people say, sucking does not cause a misshapen jaw or overcrowded teeth. From about six months, many babies will suck a thumb or two fingers as they go off to sleep and as this is a very comforting, soothing habit babies continue to do this, sometimes until they are three, four or even five years of age. Some children will, at the same time as sucking, stroke or pick at a small blanket or 'cuddly'. Others will just carry a blanket around with them.

If a baby admitted to the day nursery is used to sucking a dummy, or if a toddler still needs bottles, then care and judgement should be used to wean them gradually away from their comforters. The best method is to try to give them enough stimulation and care so that they no longer need the comfort of these things to suck.

Nail-biting, another comfort habit, can sometimes be checked by giving an older infant a nailfile and helping him to smooth his nails so that there are no jagged edges to bite. Also, oil around the nail will help to prevent jagged pieces of cuticle forming.

Rocking may be performed as a kind of masturbation, or it may simply be a rhythmic form of self comfort.

Of all these habits, masturbation (stroking and rubbing the genital organs) is the one which upsets adults most. But all babies find their genital organs and handle them in the same way as they find their hands and feet. The fact that masturbation is pleasant and comforting encourages the child to continue.

If these babyish habits continue well into the second and third years, one must ask why the child is needing so much comfort. Does he need more stimulation or more demonstrated love? Is he happy? Are all his needs being satisfied? More seriously, is he being abused?

If there does not appear to be much wrong, it is best to leave him alone. As he gets older he will find other interests and satisfactions and should gradually drop the habit. If it disturbs you, then try distracting the child by giving him something different to do, or perhaps doing some activity with him. Naturally, if it becomes very persistent, outside help should be sought.

EXERCISES

Investigation
Ask your supervisor at placement to tell you about a child, past or present, who has experienced definite problems with behaviour. If possible, draw up an action plan about what is/was being done to help this child. Is/was it successful?

NB: Be careful not to make this child aware that he is the focus of your attention, and remember that anything you may learn about him must be treated with the greatest confidentiality.

Observation
Record the words/actions of a child you know who is either solitary, or inclined to aggression. Try to follow him (unobtrusively) with your eyes and ears, throughout the course of one day. Can you come to any conclusions?

Project
Working in pairs, imagine you are the parents of a child who is presenting behaviour problems. Write a letter to an 'Agony Aunt' for advice.

Now join up with another pair, listen to each other, in turn, and try to offer helpful comments and suggestions.

SUGGESTIONS FOR FURTHER READING

Martin Herbert, *Problems of Childhood*, Pan Books Ltd
John Gabriel, *Children Growing Up*, Hodder and Stoughton Ltd
Westmacott and Cameron, *Behaviour Can Change*, Macmillan Publishers Ltd
Lesley Webb, *Children with Special Needs in the Infant School*, Fontana Books
James Dobson, *Dare to Discipline*, Kingsway Publications
Virginia Axline, *Dibs: In Search of Self*, Pelican Books
Martin Herbert, *Working with Children and their Families*, British Psychological Society and Routledge & Kegan Paul Ltd
Michèle Hegard and Vic Blickem, *Befriending*, The Oleander Press

16   **Play and Development**

The meaning and significance of children's play has been the focus of study by philosophers and educationists for more than two centuries. Play has been thought to represent:

- an overspilling of excess energy
- a way of learning essential adult skills – in the same way that kittens chase leaves while cats will chase and kill birds and mice
- a reflection of the evolutionary stages through which man has passed – look, for example, at the passion for 'gangs' and 'dens' which boys and girls show at about the age of seven and eight.

It was probably the German, Friedrich Froebel (1782–1852) who first focused attention on the importance of the early nurturing years, and who developed the concept of a kindergarten (rearing place for children). He saw humans as essentially active and creative. He introduced the idea of graduated toys ('gifts') which provided early exercise in geometric, artistic and mathematical skills.

Friedrich Froebel

A century later, Maria Montessori, (1870–1952), Italy's first woman doctor, developed structured, self-correcting play materials for children, designed to further pre-mathematical understanding, left to right eye movement, and sensory training. Working with children from the slums, she believed in the adult providing the apparatus, demonstrating it, and then standing back. She also believed in periods of critical sensitivity, when children are at a stage of optimum learning of certain concepts/skills.

The Freudian theories of therapy (healing) through play, and the ways in which children come to terms with sexuality, have also influenced thinking about play.

Educators in this century have tried to build on the earlier understanding of children's play, in many cases through concentrated observational studies. Thinking about how free or structured children's play ought to be, based on such studies, has fluctuated over the years.

Barbara Tizzard, working in the 1970s, tried to assess how effectively young children learn through play. She found the level of pre-school play in a variety of different settings to be disappointing: it was frequently pleasurable enough, but too often simple, repetitive, unstructured, uninventive, un-involving and brief.

In recent years many pre-school and infant groups have instigated the American Highscope programme in an attempt to avoid this situation. This approach to structuring and evaluating play recognises the importance of children learning 'key concepts' through play. Children have a large measure of choice in planning and performing their play activities. Later, after clearing away after themselves, they describe their play to a group, with the adult drawing out the child's powers of expression, encouraging recall, building in enriching language, encouraging listening skills in the audience, and giving a sense of purpose and value to the whole procedure. The adult's role is to set the scene, instigate key experiences and act as an enabler.

Exponents of Highscope claim many long-term benefits to children who have experienced this system. Few people would quarrel with the notion that to plan and take responsibility for one's life, from an early age, must be a good habit to get into.

Nor would many people disagree with the importance of the adult role in interacting with children at play. The skill lies in doing this in a way which is not overtly directive or repressive, but which extends and channels the natural exuberance and inventiveness of children, and elevates play not just into a way of learning, but also a way of life, and a delightful one at that.

THE STAGES OF PLAY

With all new play materials, children pass through certain stages in their approach; first, they explore the material with their senses – and whole bodies, where possible. Then they experiment with it to find out its possibilities, potential and limitations. Later they imitate what they have seen other children do with it, or adults do with a similar substance. Ultimately, they play with it according to their own creative and original ideas.

Of course, the stages have little connection with the age of the child. A three-year-old, through frequent opportunity, may have passed through to the creative stage with sand play, whereas a five or six-year-old presented with clay for the first time will begin with the exploratory approach. Opportunity and discreet encouragement are key factors in children's working through the stages.

There are also definite stages through which children pass with regard to the social aspect of play. The very young child, or the child who has had little experience of mixing, will play first – with whatever materials – in a solitary way.

Later, he will act as a spectator to others' play, which will lead to parallel play, where he and another child play side by side with similar material, but still essentially as separate individuals. Then the child will begin to associate himself with the other child in a momentary or tentative way. Lastly he will involve himself fully in co-operative play with a group; he will give and take, share, take turns, submit and lead as the occasion demands.

TYPES OF PLAY

It is impossible here to do more than outline essentials about the various types of play we offer small children. There is a good deal of overlap between the different types, which makes categorisation somewhat artificial. The tables on pp. 180–92 are intended as starting points for further reading and discussion. They may also be used as a basis for *re*-examination of what play opportunities we provide, how we do it, and – most important – why.

Although nursery space and resources are assumed, and in some cases are essential, in what follows, a good deal is easily adaptable or improvisable by enterprising playgroup leaders and carers at home in more restricted premises, and on a far slimmer budget.

Music and movement. Musical experience is one of the activities arranged by adults, and though it cannot be called 'play', it greatly enriches the life of babies and young children. They are surrounded by it for much of the time on television and radio, but we can make it far more than 'audio-wallpaper' for them. We can transform music into another avenue of expression.

Enjoyment and participation by children and adults should be the keywords in all we do. Music for young children should not be regarded as either a spectator or performer art; rather it is an action art.

The adult does not need instrumental skills or a good singing voice. If he/she looks to his/her own creativity and tries hard to overcome any lack of self-confidence, success will follow. Intelligent use of a record player and tape recorder, for example, will also more than compensate for lack of skill in piano playing.

Music has been said to be a blend of mathematics and magic, and both strands have a part to play in the musical experience we offer young children.

Four main aspects of musical experience
a) *Cultivating auditory discrimination through attentive listening*. Here are just a few ideas: children close eyes and listen for sound they can identify: adult sings a well-known song, but changes one word for children to spot; children have to guess the contents of sealed yogurt pots (peas? rice? money?); collecting sounds, using tape recorder (for example, all morning sounds: kettle boiling, Dad shaving, milkman delivering, etc.); matching sounds (in the environment and using tapes); making sound patterns, alerting children to intensity and pitch. Full use should be made of children's natural response to rhythm. Remember, our bodies function to rhythm – heartbeat, etc. Simple time-beat can lead to definite rhythm. A climax will also be satisfying to end phrases of rhythmic beat.

b) *Developing vocal skills*: activities here can include 'mouth' music, humming, singing individually, singing together (which entails discipline of stopping and starting, etc.). Remember, however poor you think your voice is or however embarrassed you are to perform in front of another adult, the children will be impressed and will not laugh at you. When introducing a new song, first sing a couple of familiar ones, then sing the new one through twice or three times (if short). Do not separate or teach it line by line. If you like it and are putting it over well, the children will soon be joining in.

c) *Developing instrumental skills*: activities here might include making instruments (for example, from shells, coconuts) and household junk (painted and filled squeezy-bottle shakers, date-box and sandpaper scrapers, etc.), experimenting with these, using them as sound effects in stories and songs, playing *some* together with melodic

music; being aware of commercial instruments and the most suitable buys for the nursery (big cymbals and xylophone?); encouraging children to join in songs, etc. with single notes of tuned instruments as appropriate; providing a music workshop, or trolley, offering a chance to experiment with making sounds (what makes the longest/shortest/quietest sound?). Two children can play different instruments, with one echoing the other. Let children see and hear live instrument-alists, for example, a parent who plays guitar; maybe get close enough to feel vibrations.

d) *Adding to our repertoire of songs and music, and improving techniques*: there are many books of lively songs suitable for young children on the market today. Funny songs, rousing songs, gentle lullabies all have a place. We should make use of children's familiarity with TV jingles. Compose your own songs and musical phrases to accompany everyday actions like dressing, going upstairs, clearing bricks away, etc. because this can be fun. 'Children's' records can be evaluated, but tend to be limiting; we should make use of adult music – traditional, classical, modern, popular – which creates a mood, or is character-ised by a strong beat. Songs and music should be drawn from all cultures. Parents should be invited to come and share their knowledge and enthusiasms for different styles of music.

Movement
Joy in music will lead quite naturally into movement and dance. Small children are rarely inactive, and reponse to beat and rhythm will be expressed in activity. Some children, in fact, are unable to stay still when music with a strong or 'catchy' beat is being played. We should welcome such a response and encourage spontaneous expression.

There is a wealth of music available on tape and record which can be used appropriately as a basis for movement. Saint Saen's 'Carnival of the Animals' and Prokofiev's 'Peter and the Wolf' are two well-known examples, but such pieces as Debussy's 'Snowflakes are Dancing' and much Afro-Caribbean music also create moods and offer an invitation to respond.

Of course, music is not essential for children to enjoy movement. With a skilled adult to guide them, young children can move imaginatively, stimulated by experience such as having watched snails move, or a piece of machinery in action. Exciting work can be done using a variety of materials which inspire and facilitate different styles of reaction and movement, both by individuals, and groups working co-operatively. Such materials might include large pieces of netting, elastic, silk, ribbons and streamers.

Children must have adequate space in which to move, and a prearranged signal – not a shout – will be needed to attract their attention for each fresh activity. Uniformity in how children move is not the goal; we should encourage individual experimentation and expression.

Creative movement brings the emotions into play – sadness, solemnity, joy. It helps children to gain control over their bodies, and develops body-awareness, which we now know to be of vital importance for many reasons. Co-ordination and control bring poise, grace and economy of movement. An uninhibited, joyful approach at this stage will lead naturally into creative dance and drama later on.

Movement has been found to be specially beneficial to children of all ages with special needs. It offers them release, and new possibilities for expressing themselves.

Groups of parents and small children 'moving' together can also be very rewarding. The experience strengthens the idea of physical contact being explored in a loving but controlled way. Many day nurseries, family centres and playgroups have developed this activity successfully.

Investigation Children are born explorers. They explore through their five senses and through their bodies. Much of their exploring will be of play materials that we provide for them, but much will also be of objects they meet in their daily life. Some objects will be living, some inanimate. Some they will find on their own – in the nursery garden, on their way home, at Grandma's. Others we will deliberately bring into the nursery for them to look at, handle, manipulate, ask questions about.

Perhaps these processes can be better described as *investigation* rather than play. Such investigation performs the following functions:

- It satisfies and also feeds a child's curiosity and spirit of enquiry.
- It encourages powers of reasoning, memory, classification, association, problem-solving.
- It promotes language development through discussion, and through 'how', 'when' and 'why' questions and answers.
- It encourages use of reference books.
- It sharpens observation skills.
- It fosters ideas of caring, reliable tending, personal responsibility (e.g. for pets, plants).
- It teaches patience (e.g. waiting for bulbs to appear).
- It extends the child's knowledge and under-standing of the world around him, including dangers (poisonous berries, etc.).
- It teaches respect for forms of life other than human.
- It builds a foundation for later formal scientific experimentation; in the same way, later recording, ordering and measuring of findings (mathematics) will also stem from this. Life in an increasingly complex technological society makes these aspects of education more and more important.
- It fosters a sense of wonder, and appreciation of patterns and order in the world around the child, and awareness of life cycles – birth and death.

If we are to care effectually for the environment of the present and the future, and find ways of making life on earth better for *all* humanity, then surely we need to give young children plenty of opportunity to begin developing these skills and attitudes as early as possible.

Starting points for investigation. We have to decide how much of the animate and inanimate world we can bring into the nursery and school, or take the children to visit. Here are some ideas:

- keep pets (but do inform yourself fully before-hand on care and possible difficulties, health hazards, etc.), also wormery, aquarium

- gardening activities (quick-maturing vegetables which can later be made into sandwiches or soups are especially good)
- keep plants and flower arrangements
- grow spring flowering bulbs indoors
- take children on frequent walks, particularly to see trees, wild flowers, ducks, animals, etc., fostering ideas on conservation
- use natural materials in displays (e.g. leaves, bark, shells)
- use natural materials in activities (e.g. collage, leaf prints)
- make a bottle garden
- make a bird table and observe activities on it, providing winter foodstuffs for birds, 'Christmas pudding' etc.
- draw children's attention to changing weather, clouds, seasons, temperature
- keep seeds and watch them germinate indoors
- follow up interest aroused by discovery of beetle, snail, etc., in garden
- keep a 'discovery' table with changing assortment of such items as bells, clocks, taps, washers, pumps, syringes, egg-timer, springs, pendulums, cogs, levers, pulleys, mirrors, magnets, keys and locks, shells, birdseed, salt, dried seaweed
- organise walks to watch work of all sorts being carried out, for example, cranes at the docks, concrete mixer in the road
- draw children's attention to different means of transport, in books, pictures and real life; different sources of power (light, heat, water) and different types of construction (bridge, flats, tower, etc.)
- encourage inventiveness in many different forms; junk modelling and work with construction sets are a favourite means of expressing this
- growth is an aspect that can be studied in many ways: a good starting point for finding out about human growth is for adults and children to bring to school photographs of themselves as babies. With the co-operation of a parent, this can be followed up by showing baby clothes and comparing sizes, demonstration bathing of a baby etc.

- play games which foster concepts of conservation, e.g. pond games, tree webbing. Older children may be able to make a board game like 'Help a toad to cross the road'
- visit different habitats (woodlands, meadows), with a specific aim in mind e.g. making a colour palette, doing bark rubbings
- do simple experiments on the properties of air and water e.g. testing waterproof materials, absorbency of different materials
- look at soil e.g. different types of animals in soil, making bricks with different types of soil.

The wider world.   Children will find out more about the environment outside their home, nursery and school on various outings throughout the year (see pages 240–2). But we can also bring into the school or nursery people from the world of work, service and entertainment to give children further information, understanding and insight. Such visitors might include a fire officer, police officer, farmer, road safety officer, dentist, music instrumentalist or puppeteers. Badges of office, tools of the trade, vehicles, and other visual aids that children can see and touch are particularly well received. However, a great deal can also be conveyed by talking and answering questions. The first-hand freshness and authenticity of the communicator make his words far more effective than any book, and such contact with new adults, in a familiar setting, builds confidence.

Adults who interact with children in this way are truly educators. Sometimes it is a specific message they want to convey: 'Never go with strangers', 'Stop, look and listen', and so on. Sometimes it is a more subtle matter of influencing attitudes: in some areas, for example, police officers may be perceived as enemies rather than as people whose role it is to help and protect the community.

VIGOROUS PHYSICAL PLAY, OFTEN OUTDOORS

Value	Provision	Role of Adult	Progression
Emotional benefits: Enjoyment Freedom from tensions and restrictions Opportunities for challenge and adventure, element of risk Builds self-confidence *Physical benefits:* Stimulates: appetite, digestion, circulation, respiration, sound sleep, mental alertness, skin health Promotes: muscle tone, bodily co-ordination, balance, control, body awareness Builds resistance to infection Develops physical skills such as: running, stopping and starting, hopping, aiming, climbing, swinging, steering, carrying, throwing and catching *Social benefits:* Fosters social adjustment: through levelling of abilities in new setting, sharing, turn-taking, collaborating *Cognitive benefits:* Builds concepts of: height, weight, width, speed, distance, spatial relationships, position Stimulates curiosity, powers of observation, aesthetic awareness and sense of wonder (e.g. changing seasons, reflections in a puddle) Affords knowledge and language about natural world, e.g. insects Feeds the imagination and leads to imaginative play	A well and imaginatively-planned garden with paved area and grass, different levels, paths, trees, digging and growing areas, possibilities for dens and privacy, storage for equipment, easy access to and from nursery Large but manoeuvrable apparatus, such as: climbing frame (with impact-absorbing surface underneath it), see-saw, rocker, rope ladder, trestle units and plank, hollow cubes, packing-case boxes, tyres, barrels, space hopper Some large fixed apparatus: swing (with shock absorbing seat), scramble net Small apparatus such as: hoops, skipping ropes, balls, bats Wheeled vehicles such as: trucks, carts, scooters, tricycles, wheel-barrows	Exercise constant watchfulness over safety matters (of children and equipment). Undertake arrangement and rearrangement of apparatus, and encourage children to do this. Encourage children, without directing or urging them to perform actions beyond their capabilities. Introduce new ideas. Make the most of language opportunities (with children, not other adults). Introduce idea of fair play, and 'police' for bullying, dangerous quarrels, or large numbers on apparatus. Train children in tidying away. Initiate ring games or singing games, if children are cold, bored or clinging. Sharpen your own and children's powers of observation. Keep informed of new equipment available, and critically evaluate it. Keep a watchful eye on gates, entrances to school, and 'disappearing' children.	*Mastery of new skills:* Tentative exploratory approach Simple repetition Individual interpretation and creative elaboration, e.g. skipping Increase in co-ordination, control, agility, economy of movement Growth in confidence and acceptance of challenge, e.g. balance walking, holding adult's hand; balance walking with adult alongside, sometimes touching fingertips; balance walking unaided Heightened awareness of life outdoors, insects and small creatures, the fascination of growing things *Children:* observe with interest, ask questions and comment, use reference books, carry interest indoors The following developments apply to this, and all other types of play. The child passes through a) solitary b) spectator c) parallel d) co-operative stages of play. Attention span lengthens Increasing use of language and interaction

Value	Provision	Role of Adult	Progression

PLAY WITH BASIC MATERIALS

a) Water

Value	Provision	Role of Adult	Progression
Emotional benefits: Enjoyment Fascination of primitive element Release of tension Soothing effect Endless scope – there is no right or wrong way *Physical benefits:* Sensory experience Encourages manipulative skills, e.g. pouring accurately *Social benefits:* Can be played with in solitary parallel or co-operative way *Cognitive benefits:* Promotes concentration Leads into imaginative play, e.g. underwater exploration, sharks, seaside Leads to mathematical and scientific discoveries and concept-building concerning: volume, capacity, gradation, comparisons, proportions, floating and sinking, absorbency, changes to substances when wet/dry, conservation of quantity, evaporation, syphoning, condensation, dissolving; properties of water such as cleansing, life-sustaining, metal corrosion Equipment can be categorised Familiarises child with standard units of measurement	Play with paddling pool, water painting with bucket and decorator's brush, hoses, sprinklers, (all outside) Equipment for washing dolls and dolls' clothes Suitable large container, preferably peninsula play sink, plumbed in, at child height Equipment to use with it: tubing, squeezy bottles, graded jugs and beakers, cups with holes at bottom or side, sponges, loofah, spoons and ladles, household articles such as colander, plastic dishes, lids, cotton reels, rubber ball and golf ball, table-tennis ball, bubble blowing equipment Also, shallow trays of water with stones, wood, seaweed, boats, rubber dinosaurs and play people, paper, bark Out-of-doors, two trays or containers can be linked, one deeper, or on a different level Large buckets, linked with funnels and tubing Protection for floor, if necessary Protection for children Table, or sectioned container nearby to hold categorised equipment Tepid water, sometimes made bubbly, sometimes coloured with vegetable colouring or crepe paper	Site and plan water play for safety, comfort, accessibility of tap and sink. Supervise protection of child, looking out for wet sleeves, socks, etc. Vary, perhaps limit, equipment provided each day. Observe children closely for discoveries, ask meaningful questions and give extending suggestions. Be inventive, encouraging children to try experiments, e.g. using dropper with dye in water container. Make the most of language opportunities. Intervene if play becomes too boisterous. *Constantly* watch small children in paddling pool. (Drowning is very quick and very quiet, and can happen in a few centimetres of water). Involve children in clearing away.	Early experiences in the home: bath time, paddling pool, household and garden tasks Organised water play at nursery Simple pouring, filling, emptying, squirting, experimenting with properties of water. Child makes incidental discoveries, develops these possibilities, carries out simple tasks, e.g. 'Can you make a raft?' Structured water activities at infant school Child carries out tasks based on capacity, conservation of quantity, etc. Verbalises concepts learned Works from workcards and can record results If given suitable opportunities, will progress from splashing in pool, through 'doggy paddle' with armbands, to swimming on his own

Value	Provision	Role of Adult	Progression
Gives rich opportunities for language building, e.g. descriptive, mathematical, naming items of equipment	Opportunities to join in cleaning tasks with water (washing play-room furniture and equipment, washing-up after cookery) and life-sustaining functions (watering plants, changing pets' water) Mop to be kept handy		

b) Sand

Value	Provision	Role of Adult	Progression
Emotional benefits: Enjoyment Pleasurable association with seaside Outlet for aggression Opportunity to destroy legitimately Endless scope – there is no right or wrong way	Varieties of sand – silver, from builders' merchants Large indoor sandpit, if possible (outside sandpits are now usually thought to be too vulnerable to fouling by animals, and it is impossible to get lightweight covers that are both weather-proof and vandal proof) Paddling pools used for sand	Supervise children for safe and non-wasteful play. Top up and replace sand. Allow free flow from sand play to other forms of play (imaginative). Make the most of language opportunities. Introduce new ideas. Involve children in sweeping up and caring for equipment.	*Stages of sand play:* Exploratory play for texture, e.g. dry sand trickling through fingers, damp sand being squeezed, patting Experimental play for properties of wet and dry sand, sieving, pattern-making, digging, moulding Creative play
Physical benefits: Sensory experience Offers vigorous activity Encourages manipulative skills, e.g. accurate turning out of castle	Shallow trays for different sorts of sand: damp, dry, silver Equipment for all containers: spades (not metal), buckets, cups, cartons, rakes, funnels, colander,	Observe stages children are at. Vary ways in which sand is offered, e.g. sometimes very wet (slurry). This can lead to fascinating discoveries about	Development of manual dexterity, wrist strength and control to enable sand castles to be successfully turned out Elaboration of sand castles
Social benefits: Can be played with in a solitary, parallel or co-operative way Beach play often leads to new friendships Beach play attracts adults' participation	sieve, flour sifter, plastic tubing, scoops, ladles, ice-cream scoop, water wheel, toy vehicles, play people, rubber animals, shells Protection for floor if needed Protection for children's hair may be advisable especially for tightly-plaited hairstyles – sand can be	properties of both sand and water, and the way they react together.	Makes 'gardens', 'building sites', 'road layouts' Use of sand as weighing material in early mathematics Use of tray of shallow dry sand for tracing letters and numbers (useful for children with learning difficulties)
Cognitive benefits: Provides opportunities for language, link with imaginative play, avenue for creativity Offers scientific discoveries concerning: properties of wet and dry sand, weight, capacity quantity, grains, moulding, continuous flow, imprinting, pressure	damaging to hair Dustpan and brush to be kept handy		Using sand in sand pictures, with glued paper

c) Malleable materials (such as dough, clay etc.)

Value	Provision	Role of Adult	Progression
Emotional benefits: Enjoyment Endless scope; there is no right or wrong way Legitimate 'mucky' play Outlet for aggression (e.g. prodding, poking, cutting, banging) Therapeutic effect of handling plastic material Novelty of clay (too messy for most homes) Link with home in case of dough and plasticene Opportunity to indulge children's interest in bodily products, play with which is forbidden	Protection for children Tables and chairs of suitable height to permit thumping and rolling with pressure Sufficient amounts of red and white clay (best bought in ready-to-use state from local pottery) Plain and different coloured dough, 'cooked' dough, scented dough (with cooking essences), plasticene Proprietary brands of self-hardening 'clay', if desired	Site tables appropriately, near tap and sink. Keep bowl of soapy water and cloth nearby for immediate 'wipes'. Supervise for undue mess (e.g. door handles, clothes, hair). Keep clay in plastic containers with lid, cover balls of clay with wrung-out old towel. Check on condition of clay. Keep in cool place. Mix dough to preferred recipe (often three parts flour to one part salt, with enough water to make pliable consistency, oil colouring and scent are optional). Remember cooked dough is silkier and lasts longer. Involve children in making dough. Experiment with different sorts of flour. Wholemeal is interesting and cornflour spectacular! Keep dough in airtight plastic bag. Check plasticene for grittiness, or unpleasant, boring colour. Vary materials offered. Dough can be offered with or without cutters, patty tins, rolling pin, plastic knife. Clay should be offered, at first without any other equipment. Make the most of language opportunities. Refrain from making models for children to copy (with possible exception of top infants). Show that you value the process far more than the end product. With older children's models, carefully dry, and encourage firing (if facilities permit) or painting, varnishing and displaying.	Exploratory play for feel of substances Experimental play for properties e.g. elasticity of dough, retained imprint of clay Accidental creativity – 'Look I've made a snake!' Intentional creativity: child comes to substance with preconceived ideas of recognisable object to be made Elaboration of creative play: child wants to keep, dry, paint, varnish, take home, use, clay items
Physical benefits: Sensory, particularly tactile, experience Promotes manipulative skills Strengthens hand and finger muscles			
Social benefits: Can be played with in solitary, parallel or co-operative way Requires social training in clearing up afterwards Dough play is linked to social/domestic skills			
Cognitive benefits: Provides opportunities for language Offers scientific discoveries about properties of materials, e.g. elasticity, contrast of wet and dry, part played by water			

Value	Provision	Role of Adult	Progression

d) Wood

Emotional benefits:
Enjoyment
Outlet for tension and aggression, satisfaction of making a legitimate noise, sense of power, sense of achievement

Physical benefits:
Offers vigorous activity
Promotes manipulative skills, e.g. eye/hand co-ordination, banging in a nail
Offers tactile experience

Social benefits:
Solitary activity can lead to group interest
Opportunity to learn adult skills

Cognitive benefits:
Provides opportunities for language and avenue of creativity, perhaps leading to adult interest
Encourages perseverance and concentration
Offers mathematical and scientific discoveries related to: length, breadth, angles, stress, pressure, properties and texture of different woods

Provision:
Suitably sized, rigid woodwork bench
Scaled-down real tools (toy tools break and can cause accidents and frustration) such as: hammers, tenon saw, screwdriver, awl, vice, spanner
Suitable, easily checkable storage for tools
Assortment of variously shaped and sized soft wood pieces
Balsa wood, cardboard 'corner' pieces, sandpaper, string, glue, pieces of fabric (leather, suede, fur), tin lids, other odds and ends to provide scope and fire imagination
Assorted nails and screws in transparent containers with lids
Categorised storage for all materials used (a jumble of everything mixed up in one large container will not inspire meaningful play)

Role of Adult:
Plan and site bench appropriately, so that it gives minimum disturbance to others.
Teach correct handling of tools.
Supervise closely and constantly for safety.
Keep numbers small; no spectators or distractions should be allowed to disturb children's concentration or lead to accidents.
Interact and offer help and suggestions where appropriate, without 'taking over' play.
Make the most of language opportunities.
Observe and respond to stage each child is at.
Offer more advanced children opportunity to paint, display, talk about and use models.
Value the process more than the product.

Progression:
Exploratory play for feel of wood, power of tools
Children may spend a long time just randomly banging nails into wood, or even into bench
Experimental play for properties of wood, own abilities
Accidental creativity: shape of wood pieces suggests ideas, e.g. aeroplane
Intentional creativity: child comes to wood with preconceived ideas; selects appropriate pieces, nails, tools; uses tools; wants to finish his creation, paint it, talk about it

CONSTRUCTION PLAY

a) Junk materials

Emotional benefits:
Enjoyment
Sense of achievement

Physical benefits:
Offers tactile experience
Encourages fine manipulative skills

Social benefits:
Encourages social play

Provision:
Sufficient time and space
Large cardboard boxes, sheets of corrugated cardboard, spools from paper bales, sugar paper, newspapers, brown paper
Household junk: cereal packets, egg boxes (not polystyrene variety), lolly sticks, margarine tubs, yogurt pots, bottle tops, odds and ends of fabric, pipe

Role of Adult:
Initiate and maintain a satisfactory system for collecting and storing junk. Check stores of junk for spoiled or unsuitable items.
Oversee use of scissors, staples, glue, etc.
Discuss work with children, introducing extending ideas and new vocabulary.

Progression:
Exploratory play with shapes, objects, textures
Child haphazardly assembles pieces and may or may not fix them together
Inaccurate gluing, tearing, cutting
Experimental play for possibilities of materials
Accidental creativity – a cereal box and lolly sticks resemble a robot

Value	Provision	Role of Adult	Progression
Involves parents and children in provision Easily leads into group interest e.g. train, shop, zoo *Cognitive benefits:* Feeds imagination Offers first-hand experiences in three-dimensional material and spatial relationships (next to, underneath, on top of, etc.) Promotes resourcefulness and ideas of conservation and recycling Offers rich language opportunities Offers mathematical and scientific experience/discoveries about shape, angles, strength, comparisons (of suitability of methods of sticking) Encourages inventiveness, problem solving, originality, recall, decision making, concentration	cleaners, string, elastic bands Variety of adhesives: glue, cellulose paste, PVA, Sellotape, glue sticks, stapler (supervised use) Scissors (sharp but with rounded ends) Paint Easily checkable storage system, with categorisation, for all materials on offer: can be 'unit' made up of cardboard boxes on their sides or stacking plastic cake tins; labelled receptacles look more efficient and enable children to select materials and parents to contribute easily. Purposeful selection by children from labelled storage system is fundamental to Highscope.	Offer help as required. Use reference books as appropriate, e.g. to find out, with a child, what a space rocket looks like). Arrange attractive displays. Involve children in care and storage of materials.	Intentional creativity – child selects appropriate items to carry out preconceived ideas; assembles, cuts, places, glues precisely; solving problems as they arise, wants to dry, paint, display, label, take home May be able to follow simple directions from books, TV programmes, to make specific items

b) Blocks

Value	Provision	Role of Adult	Progression
Emotional benefits: Enjoyment Link with home (bricks are popular home toys) Outlet for aggression, satisfaction of making loud noise, chance to destroy as well as create Soothing, non-threatening feel of woods and plastics Feeling of power: child can make life-size models (walls, houses, etc) Sense of achievement *Physical benefits:* Tactile experience Promotes eye/hand co-ordination, balance, control, precision Develops muscle tone by stretching, lifting, carrying	Adequate time and space A corner, or at least a wall, against which to build Noise-deadening carpet, if preferred A variety of sets of wooden blocks; some manufactured in geometric proportions (e.g. two short = one long), some made from off-cuts in different types of wood; some small and painted; some large and containing hollow wedges, hidey-holes, long planks etc. A variety of plastic bricks; large interlocking, solid, hollow, made of foam Accessibility of other play materials such as blankets for 'roofs', toy vehicles, dolls, steering	Site play where children will not be disturbed or disturb others, and where stray items are least likely to cause accidents. Discuss children's constructions with them, feeding in new vocabulary, and suggesting other ideas to extend play, as appropriate. Allow for privacy and quiet concentration, if desired. Give adequate time warnings about putting away. Sometimes constructions can be kept up for continuation of play at another time, or to discuss with whole group. Check materials for splintering, or missing pieces. Involve children in clearing away,	Exploratory play: baby bangs, throws, scatters, builds tower of two blocks inaccurately placed Easy constructional play, child lines up bricks on floor, moves them as cars, fills and empties trucks and boxes, builds towers of up to about seven blocks, enjoys crashing these down Later constructional play: builds towers, walls, dens, houses Complex constructional play: child carries out preconceived ideas, e.g. airport, multi-storey car park, space station, uses vehicles, play people and accessories Enters realms of fantasy play

Value	Provision	Role of Adult	Progression
Social benefits: Can be played with in solitary, parallel or co-operative way Often leads into group play of imaginative kind *Cognitive benefits:* Feeds imagination Offers opportunities for language Offers mathematical and scientific discoveries/concept building about height, weight, proportion, spanning, symmetry, gradients, round things rolling, alignment, space-filling (especially in putting away), matching, categorising	wheel Adequate and systemised storage facilities: open shelving, wooden boxes or trucks, duffle bags in strong materials	making it a pleasant part of the whole experience, encouraging use of systems, matching items to pictures, symbols, labels etc.	

c) Construction sets

Value	Provision	Role of Adult	Progression
Most of the points made for junk materials and blocks apply equally here. Additional values include: Convenience: available and experienced in the home; possibility of building up from starter set; suitability to limited space, sick child in bed, etc. *Physical benefits:* Develops wide range of fine manipulative skills, screwing, fixing *Cognitive benefits:* Encourages problem-solving by trial and error Encourages inventive thinking, and understanding of engineering principles Encourages child to follow diagrammatic models, involving close observation, selection, logical thinking Involves matching, grouping, sorting, comparing, counting	Readers will be familiar with the wide and ever-increasing range of sets on the market. Group provision should reflect this range in size, scope and characteristics of sets. Some are designed for individual play, some for group play. Containers should be assessed for durability. Good and clearly systemised storage should be provided. Where only limited purchases are possible, one set should have enough pieces for several children to play at one time.	Oversee selection and putting away of sets, checking for missing pieces. Interact with children, asking questions, extending play, offering suggestions: 'How does your windmill work?' Encourage children to show and talk about models with other children.	Small child randomly fixes a few pieces Child makes simple models based on own observations of vehicles, people and explores possibilities Child comes to set with pre-conceived ideas, or wants to follow diagram Exercises patience, closely follows diagram, selects pieces, discards unsuccessful attempts, tries again Child appreciates a challenge: 'Make a lorry that can carry something' Older children can follow work cards giving such instructions

Value	Provision	Role of Adult	Progression

CREATIVE AND IMAGINATIVE PLAY

a) Painting and visual arts

Emotional benefits:
Enjoyment
Novelty for many nursery children
Sense of achievement
End-product admired by adults
Offers release of emotions: unhappy experiences can be 'painted out', happy experiences can be relived and shared

Physical benefits:
Offers experience in handling brushes, crayons, pencils, etc. leading eventually to mastery and control

Social benefits:
Can be enjoyed in solitary, parallel or co-operative way

Cognitive benefits:
Feeds imagination
Offers language opportunities (during and after painting)
Develops creativity
Develops aesthetic awareness of colour, shape, pattern, composition
Offers experience in depicting and interpreting meaningful symbols on paper (foundation for later reading and writing)
Promotes individual tastes and preferences
Encourages perception of shape, area, spatial relationships
Offers discoveries about textures, consistencies, mixing colours

---

Provision

Easels, tables
Brightly coloured paints of creamy consistency, mainly primary colours
Different width brushes
Paper of varying textures, shapes, sizes, colours (including textured paper like wallpaper samples)
Occasional opportunities to paint on windows, wall boards, pegged up transparent plastic sheets
Non-spill paint pots
Containers for mixing paints
Items for printing – leaves, string, pastry cutters, screwed up blobs of paper, sponges
Protection for floor, if needed
Aprons on hooks
Means of drying individual paintings
Space to display work
Large chalk boards, chalks, felt tip pens, oil pastels, charcoal, crayons

---

Role of Adult

Site facilities in good light, with easy access to water and sink.
Involve children in mixing of paint, offering chance to experiment.
Maintain appeal of equipment (easels, brushes and clear colours).
Interact with child during or after painting, if he wants to. Do not disturb, nor cross-question, nor seek representations/likenesses.
Occasionally introduce different techniques using paint in a semi-directed way, e.g. marble rolling, scattering dry paint on wet paper, butterfly painting, patch painting, painting with fruit or vegetables.
Write children's names on backs of painting; dry them and allow them to be taken home.
Mount frequent displays of *all* children's work, remembering to enhance it but not to chop it about, or make the mount more important than their work. Add captions in neat, uniform, lower-case alphabet lettering nearby, using children's own suggested phrases as far as possible.
Observe for developing stages.

Progression

Approach to paint:
Tentative at first, touches, tastes, paints hand.
Holds brush like dagger in stiff arm; blobs, scrubs, overloads brush; applies marks, lines, patches of colour, paints blocks of colour
Discovers pattern, repeated patterns, symmetry
Supple wrist and greater control facilitate deliberate and more delicate brush strokes

Symbolic representation
a) Human figure-random scribble; oval emerges, becomes big head (cephalopod) with features;
legs sprout from head; legs blocked in to form body: arms, ears, fingers, 'tent' dress with details, hair styles, head gear
b) House-square with random placement of doors and windows, later more accurate placement, and chimney; smoke etc; 'strip' earth and sky, sun with radials, path, flowers, stairs, figures inside or outside
House with wheels becomes vehicle
Age six to seven is 'golden age' of children's art-child is unaware of difficulties of scale, proportion, perspective and is uncritical; fills page with flat and pleasing compositions

Value	Provision	Role of Adult	Progression
			Age seven and above becomes critical, loses some spontaneity, strives after accuracy and detail

b) Collage (using a variety of materials)

Value	Provision	Role of Adult	Progression
All the values listed for painting apply equally here. Additional values include: *Physical benefits:* Tactile experience Promotes fine manipulative skills, e.g. placing, using scissors *Social benefits:* Lends itself readily to group projects/activities, current themes *Cognitive benefits:* Promotes resourcefulness Invites judgements, comparisons, personal choices.	Supply of scrap materials: fabrics, including shiny, metallic, transparent, ethnic prints and materials, wool, string, cotton wool, sequins Paper of all kinds: tissue, wall paper, crepe paper, colour magazines and catalogues natural materials: bark, shells, twigs, hay and straw, seaweed, pebbles, sand, wood-shavings, leaves Pasta and pulses of all shapes and colours (e.g. pasta shells, red lentils, mungo beans, split peas) (NB Some adults object to the use of foodstuffs in play when millions of the world's children are starving. This point of view must be talked through and respected. It may apply equally to play with dough.) Bottle tops, tin foil, wrapping material from chocolate boxes, egg boxes (not polystyrene), pipe cleaners, straws Scissors Strong glue Backing card, or strong paper Categorised and attractive system for collection and storage (e.g. by colour) Paste brushes and spreaders Protection for children Protection for table	Similar to that for painting. Additional aspects: Initiate themes for group collage work. Organise execution of large pieces (on floor). Sustain ideas and encourage children to make suggestions which you help to carry out. NB 1) A word of warning: in order to achieve quick results and cover bare walls, many adults draw outlines of, e.g. nursery rhymes and ask children to fill in designated areas with scraps of appropriate colour. This is a particularly mindless and boring occupation – if you don't believe this, try it! All displays should be child-centred and start from the child's efforts. Children can draw round one another to achieve a large figure. Let *them* suggest colours to be used. Large expanses of sky or fields can be done by sponge painting or finger painting. NB 2) Remember a three-dimensional effect always has more impact than a flat one, e.g. a bonfire night display will be greatly enlivened by painted cardboard tube 'rockets' and real twigs and straw for the fire.	Similar to that for junk modelling Child becomes increasingly selective of colours, textures and suitability

Value	Provision	Role of Adult	Progression
c) Dramatic Play			
Emotional benefits: Enjoyment Enables child to play out fears, confusions, unhappy experiences, or relive happy experiences Offers wish fulfilment and escape from drab lives Outlet for tensions and aggressions	Adequate time and space Dressing-up clothes, props, masks, artifacts – for both sexes, reflecting cultural diversity, shalwar kemise, sari etc. Jewellery: bangles, beads (from broken necklaces can be rethreaded on shirring elastic) Combs, scarves, embroidered slippers, fans	Provide a relaxed and encouraging atmosphere. Allow privacy if children require it. Allow play to spread outdoors, and to link with other play, e.g. people going shopping may travel on bus made from blocks. Follow up spontaneous enthusiasms with equipment, visits, use of reference books.	Simple 'pretend' games from approximately fifteen months onwards, child substitutes e.g. soft toy for pillow Imitative play on everyday themes: shopping, tea parties, bed-time routine Simple role play with props e.g. fire officer's helmet Re-enactment of observed incidents
Physical benefits: Offers vigorous exercise Promotes fine motor skills Heightens sensory awareness	Variety of puppets (sock, glove, finger, stick), and an improvised puppet theatre – shop counter or home-corner window	Interact where invited, or appropriate, without directing. Stimulate play through questions, props, suggestions if it flags.	Imaginary playmate Sequences of actions, more detailed role play
Social benefits: Invites children to project into other roles and personalities Builds self-confidence Encourages co-operation and interaction Allows children to experiment with powerful roles, in protected setting	Storage for clothes where they will be visible and not crumpled Categorised system of storage for props	Ensure equal opportunities for all, and avoid sex stereotyping. Keep clothes in good state of cleanliness and repair. Invite contributions to dressing-up clothes, adapting where necessary.	TV heroes and heroines. Play imitative of older siblings Play moves away from domestic and familiar themes into realms of fantasy and escapism e.g. hunting for buried treasure, space-walking on the moon
Cognitive benefits: Stimulates language (imitative, adult, wider, specialised vocabulary, e.g. about hospital, space travel) Gains new knowledge about imagined situation Provides insight for adults, about thoughts, feelings, backgrounds of children		Change selections of clothes made available e.g. one week for shalwar kemise, sari and so on, another week for witches and wizards, kings and queens etc. Intervene when necessary for noise level or safety. Give adequate time warnings.	
d) Domestic play			
All the values listed for dramatic play apply equally here Additional values include:	Home corner, preferably large enough for sleeping and living areas, to reflect cultural diversity and modern technology	Similar to that for dramatic play. Encourage home corner to be converted into whatever children desire, or is currently appropriate, e.g. if one child is about to go into hospital, a ward can be created; if there is current interest	Similar to that for dramatic play Play sequences lengthen, become more diverse, complex and sophisticated Play 'spreads' in all directions Play can be highly verbal and full of humour
Emotional benefits: Link with home (specially valuable for new or insecure child).	Equipment: bed and bedding, rug or carpet, table and chairs, cooker (split level, micro-wave) washing-		

Value	Provision	Role of Adult	Progression
Social benefits: Offers wider knowledge of functioning of other people's homes. Promotes social skills, e.g. hospitality, group eating etc. *Cognitive benefits:* Offers mathematical experiences such as one-to-one correspondence, pairs, matching, sorting, comparative sizes (for example, laying the table)	machine, TV Cutlery and crockery: tawa (chappati pan), wok, chopsticks Sink and drainers Cleaning equipment Telephones Pictures, clock (pictures can be children's own, framed) 'Pretend' food (can be made from slow-baked dough items painted, or papier mâché, or bought plastic items). Food can reflect cultural diversity: samosas, chillies, guavas, etc. Ornaments, wind chimes, wall hangings	in food, it can be a café or fast food take-away. *Domestic activity* around the classroom can also include the children taking part in spring cleaning, looking after nursery pets and plants etc. They should be given clear and helpful supervision by adult.	

e) Doll play

Value	Provision	Role of Adult	Progression
Emotional benefits: Enjoyment Offers ideas on caring, tenderness Outlet for tension and aggression (e.g. if there is new baby at home) Outlet for curiosity about the human body, process of reproduction *Physical benefits:* Offers exercise in dressing skills, transferable to child himself Offers tactile experience of materials *Social benefits:* Offers experience in projecting into feelings of others Invites identification with parents' role *Cognitive benefits:* Offers knowledge on baby care Offers language opportunities	Variety of dolls: different sizes, skin colours, ethnic type, both sexes, baby dolls, rag dolls, soft toys Size-graded dolls with matching clothes Variety of clothes to reflect cultural diversity, for indoors and outdoors, day and night, different occasions, baby wear Bath, soap, talc, bottle, nappies etc. Dolls' beds, bedding, pram, buggy, chairs Equipment for washing dolls' clothes Storage for dolls' clothes Open dolls' houses, with furniture and families of dolls reflecting cultural diversity Road layout, farm, railway station, Noah's ark for animals and dolls	Similar to above. Additional aspects: Interact with children, and make the most of all opportunities to demonstrate and talk about mathematical processes, caring role etc. Encourage children to make dolls and dolls' clothes out of materials, card, paper, etc. Encourage children to wash dolls and dolls' clothes. Observe any indications of upset, puzzlement, confusion as reflected in doll play. Encourage children sometimes to bring in own dolls of topical interest e.g. teddy bears for picnic, or dolls in traditional costume. Involve children in clearing away and tidying storage.	*Six months to one year* Grasps, sucks, drops soft toy *One to three years* Pushes or drags around doll in bath or bed; carries it by arm, leg, head; may undress it, wrap it in blanket; gives it a name Plays imitative games Talks to doll, puts it to bed; attempts to dress it; may handle roughly, punish doll *Three to five years* Doll often becomes constant and necessary companion, especially at bedtime, occasions of insecurity (hospital visit) Doll now treated more like human being Sequences of play become more varied (clinic, bathing, feeding) Doll's house play is popular

Value	Provision	Role of Adult	Progression
Offers mathematical experiences/concept building on e.g. size, gradation, counting, pairs, matching, reversibility, one-to-one correspondence, sequencing, categorisation, ordering			*Five to seven years* Teenage dolls become popular 'Combat' male dolls have impact All accessories required Children enjoy making dolls and clothes Child becomes more like 'puppeteer' with dolls, inventing and playing out sequences of activity in which s/he does not play a direct role

COOKERY (An adult-directed activity)

Value	Practical organisation	Role of Adult	Progression
Emotional benefits: Enjoyment Link with home Emotional release (in beating, kneading, cutting, mixing) Satisfaction and pride in end product *Physical benefits:* Sensory experience (feel, smell, taste) Offers experience leading to control over implements, and mastery of new skills *Social benefits:* Involves working with a group towards joint goal, turn-taking, consulting with adults, sharing end products, contributing towards special occasions (sweets for Diwali, biscuits for coffee-morning etc.) Involves learning about home safety and hygiene Offers wider awareness of patterns of eating	Link cookery/food activities to an occasion, story, topical interest e.g. 'Food all over the world', Diwali, Harvest Festival, 'The Ginger-bread Man'. Involve children in discussion, prior to activity. Take them shopping for ingredients, involve them in preparation of activity, collecting implements etc. Organise time, place, use of cooker etc. beforehand. Prepare illustrated recipe card, or find place in book. Keep a record of which children take part (approximately four). Pre-heat oven if necessary. Make sure children go to toilet, wash hands, tie back long hair, put on aprons. Give clear instructions, one at a time, and demonstrate what you mean (e.g. creaming margarine).	The adult will stage-manage and oversee progression in: language used and understood, skills acquired, concepts learned, knowledge broadened, level of concentration required	

Value	Practical organisation	Progression
and traditional dishes reflecting cultural diversity e.g. chappatis, uses of Afro-Caribbean fruits and vegetables) *Cognitive benefits:* Offers rich language opportunities, with much adult interaction Heightens children's awareness of nutritional principles (emphasis should be on savoury dishes and wholefoods) Affords links with reading and writing: labels on goods, use of recipe cards (left-to-right eye movement) seeing adults consult books, recording which children made what and when Offers many different scientific and mathematical experiences: shopping, standard units of measurement, passing of time, weighing, balancing, volume and capacity, counting, dividing, fractions, one-to-one correspondence, classification, estimates, effects of heat on substances, introduction of air bubbles, absorption, changes in texture, pressure, sequencing	Keep every child occupied all the time, as far as possible, and let every child have a turn at each process. Supervise, give advice and suggestions, and invite comments throughout. Make the most of language opportunities: names of implements new to children, descriptions of mixtures, mathematical concepts (half full, not enough, two each, etc.) Involve all children in clearing up. Give out, or sell, goods fairly. Encourage 'cooks' to describe activity to larger group. NB 1) Food activities do not need the use of a cooker. Novelty sandwiches, bridge rolls, making of sweets or icing of biscuits, can be valuable and enjoyable. 2) Quick-maturing vegetables can be grown by children and made into soups or sandwiches.	

EXERCISES

Investigation

Draw a plan of your nursery/school placement room showing the layout for different kinds of play.

At fifteen-minute intervals, for the morning or afternoon, keep a tally chart of how many children are involved with each activity. Draw a graph of your results. Can you come to any conclusions about, for example, boys' and girls' choices, influence of time of day, influence of interacting adult, novelty factors?

Observation

1. Record the actions of a group of children taking part in a movement session, focusing especially on, say, three children. In your evaluation, suggest what techniques the adult/presenter used to fire the children's imagination and hold their concentration.

2. Be an observer when a parent or nursery nurse takes a small group of children for cookery or a food activity. Record the children's words and actions. In your evaluation, try to identify the 'values' (see chart on pages 191–2) you consider the children were gaining from this activity.

Project

Find out more about the early exponents of play for children, mentioned in this chapter. Have any significant ones been omitted? If so, what was their contribution, and how can this be traced in what we see today?

SUGGESTIONS FOR FURTHER READING

J. and E. Newson, *Toys and Playthings*, Pelican Books
David Evans, *Sharing Sounds*, Longman Group Ltd
Dr. Miriam Stoppard, *My First Food Book*, Dorling Kindersley Ltd
E. Matherson, *Play With A Purpose For The Under Sevens*, Penguin Books
Janet Morris and Linda Mort, *Bright Ideas for the Early Years: Learning Through Play*, Scholastic Publications Ltd.
Jill Bennett and Arline Millar, *Bright Ideas for the Early Years: Festivals*, Scholastic Publications Ltd
Rhona Whiteford and Jim Fitzsimmons, *Bright Ideas for the Early Years: Music and Movement*, Scholastic Publications Ltd
Pauline Tambling, *Performing Arts in the Primary School*, Blackwell Education

17 Children with Special Needs

The conditions we are going to look at in this chapter are:

- prematurity
- handicap
- giftedness.

Each of these conditions gives rise to special needs, whether dietary, medical or educational, in addition to the standard needs of any baby or child (see page 46).

PREMATURITY

By international agreement in 1937 the definition of prematurity was given as a baby weighing less than 2.5 kg (5 lb 8 oz). However, in 1961 the World Health Organization recommended that the term prematurity should be replaced by 'low birth-weight'. Gradually this terminology has been accepted by British hospitals but members of the general public still refer to these babies as premature.

Low birth-weight infants are usually either:
a) Pre-term – born before thirty-seven completed weeks of pregnancy
b) Light-for-dates or dysmature – weight below the expected weight for his gestational age. These babies are often referred to as suffering from IUGR (inter-uterine growth retardation).

Of course, some babies are both pre-term and light-for-dates.

The causes of low birth-weight are not always known, as there are many contributory factors. The dysmature baby has suffered a reduction in his food and oxygen supply during pregnancy which may be due to failure or malfunction of the placenta. This could be caused by toxaemia of pregnancy or by a rapidly ageing placenta. Heavy smoking by the mother can also be a contributory cause. Another reason for dysmaturity could be a multiple pregnancy, where one baby takes most of the food at the expense of another baby. Sometimes the baby has a congenital malformation or a chromosomal abnormality.

The pre-term baby is more common in the lower socio-economic group and this may result from many factors, including poor general health in the mother, especially when this stems from poor nutrition. Lack of regular antenatal care aggravates the problem. Again, multiple births are often premature. Further, if there is any abnormality in the baby, he may be premature.

The proportion of premature babies who are subsequently found to be handicapped is higher than in full-term babies, despite the expert care they receive in special care units. So the best treatment is the prevention of prematurity and, of course, this is one of the main aims of good antenatal care. First, it is necessary to ensure that the mother is as healthy as possible, by making sure that she has a good diet and by giving her advice about her general health. Secondly, it is necessary to examine mothers at intervals (so that if there are any signs of developing toxaemia it can be treated immediately) and to check that the baby is growing at the normal rate. If a mother does start to have her baby too early, then if at all possible the labour should be stopped.

The appearance of a premature baby will depend on its size, but the very tiny babies are extremely thin, because they have very little fat under the skin. They are wrinkled and have a worried look on their faces, like wizened old men. The limbs of such a baby are thin but the abdomen is large and the head appears to be very large in proportion to the body. Fontanelles are large and easily palpable. There may be fine hairs on the body, and fingernails are very soft.

The dysmature baby's problems are mainly the need to 'catch up' with the normal baby by feeding and putting on weight. If the baby is over about 2.35 kg (3 lb) in weight, in most cases his systems are mature enough to support him, although he may have problems initially with breathing. However he will need skilled nursing care in his early days and he is usually admitted to the special care baby unit. Care is the same for all low weight babies.

The pre-term infant has problems, because he has missed the last few weeks in the uterus and the more weeks he has missed, the smaller he will be and the greater his problems. Towards the end of pregnancy a lot of development takes place to equip the baby for the outside world:

1. The respiratory centre in the brain matures.

2. The baby learns and practises the art of sucking and swallowing.

3. The heat-regulating mechanism centre in the brain begins to mature.

4. Fat is laid down under the baby's skin.

5. Calcium is being deposited in the bones.

6. Iron is being stored in the liver.

7. Antibodies against infection are being passed over from mother to baby.

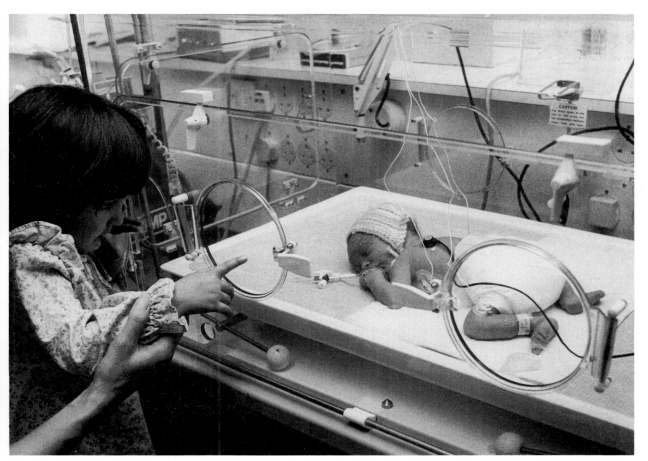

This little girl's new sister is protected from infection in the carefully controlled environment inside the incubator

So his problems can be as follows:

1. poor respiration (breathing) due to immature respiratory system;
2. inability to suck and swallow;
3. inability to regulate his temperature;
4. inability to keep warm;
5. soft bones owing to lack of calcium – this may lead to damage to the brain at birth as it lacks the protection of a hard skull;
6. anaemia owing to lack of iron;
7. poor defences against infection.

The majority of these babies are placed in an incubator and cared for in a special care unit for premature and sick babies. The incubator is a transparent box-like structure with 'portholes' so that the baby can be attended to without being taken out of it. Inside an incubator, the environment can be controlled and made to resemble the conditions in the uterus. Very warm, humid air with the correct amount of oxygen is supplied. The warmth enables the baby to be nursed with very light clothing, which will not restrict his breathing. He is protected from droplet and airborne infection by being in the incubator, and strict hygiene measures are taken by doctors and nurses to minimise the spread of infection via their hands. He can be fed by means of a tube into his stomach, or fluids can be given into the veins. Iron, vitamins and possibly calcium can be given via the tube or by injection. Handling the baby is kept to a minimum to avoid trauma.

Babies weighing 1.5 kg or of twenty-six weeks or more gestation stand a very good chance of survival with modern methods of special care. The baby with the highest mortality rate is the one who is both light-for-dates and pre-term. It is also very rare for a baby of less than twenty-four weeks gestation to survive because his lungs are not mature enough to allow him to breathe unaided.

Because of the inevitable early separation, premature babies and their mothers often lack the feeling of belonging to each other (bonding) and this may lead to emotional problems. Efforts are being made to counteract this by giving the mother access to the special care unit so that she can sit beside her baby and put her hands in the incubator to touch him.

Premature babies are now sent home much earlier than was once the case, so that the mother will have closer contact. In the past the baby was not allowed home until he weighed 3.17 kg (7 lb) which could take months. Now, in many areas, there are specially trained health visitors called Premature Baby Visitors who can supervise the mother and baby by visiting daily. Because of this service, it is possible to send the baby home once he is out of immediate danger.

General care of low birth-weight infants will be similar to that of the normal newborn baby, but extra special care must be taken over all aspects.

- *Warmth*: the room must be kept to 21°C (70°F) and some humidity may need to be supplied by putting bowls of water near the heat source.
- *Lightweight clothing* which will not restrict breathing or irritate the baby's delicate skin should be used.
- *Cleanliness and prevention of infection*: no visitors; one person should care for the baby; care must be taken with hand washing and a gown used when attending to the baby.
- *Care with feeding*: the baby is usually fed three-hourly with small feeds because he can become very tired from the effort of sucking. Some babies may need a special bottle so that the milk can be squirted into the mouth, e.g. a Belcroy feeder.
- *Iron and vitamin supplements* are continued for the first year.

All low birth-weight infants are carefully monitored during their first two years to assess their developmental progress. The pre-term baby will normally 'catch up' by about two years of age. The light-for-dates baby who has suffered severe malnutrition in the last three months of pregnancy is likely to remain small and may possibly have some degree of brain damage. It is important to diagnose this as early as possible, so that the best help may be given.

CHILDREN WITH HANDICAPS

The definition of a handicapped child is one whose development is impaired by disease or injury. One in every twenty children born will have some abnormality or defect, but many of these will be minor ones, such as a birthmark, webbed fingers or toes or an extra finger. Others will be of a more serious nature such as cleft palate or spina bifida. The known causes of handicaps can be classified as follows:

- an inherited defect – e.g. haemophilia
- injury to the foetus – deafness caused by rubella in early pregnancy
- injury at birth – e.g. failure to breathe immediately after birth starves the brain of oxygen, causes brain damage – cerebral palsy
- disease after birth – e.g. jaundice in new baby can cause brain damage – cerebral palsy
- injury after birth – e.g. head injury causing brain damage – mental deficiency
- severe deprivation – e.g. child never stimulated – mental backwardness.

A congenital disease is one which originates before birth, so it may be either inherited or a result of injury in the uterus. Some handicapping conditions are predictable during pregnancy (see page 33), so some affected babies will be aborted. Better antenatal and postnatal care could prevent some conditions, such as cerebral palsy. However, many handicapped children come from the lower socio-economic groups, which suggests that an improvement in living standards, especially housing and nutrition, could reduce the numbers more than any specific care.

Although all babies are examined by a midwife and a doctor at birth and during the first two weeks of life, many of these handicaps are not obvious and are therefore not detected at this time. Some defects can be found by using special tests. For example, all babies have a blood test for phenylketonuria, a rare inherited disease which, if not treated within the first two weeks of life by putting the baby on a special diet, leads to mental handicap. Another test commonly carried out on newborn babies is that which detects congenital dislocation of the hips. This is a condition which, if treated early enough, can usually be completely cured.

The majority of handicaps only become obvious as the baby grows and often developmental assessments during the first five years of life reveal that the baby is not progressing as he should. In other cases the parents of the child suspect there is something wrong and take him to their doctor. In many areas there are diagnostic units where the child can be examined by various consultants, and investigations alleviate some of the associated problems. Otherwise the child may be referred to a paediatrician at a local hospital.

Brief descriptions of some of the more common handicaps are given in the charts on pages 202–10.

The effect on the family

Discovering that their child has a handicap is a terrible shock to most parents. Despite the fact that a mother's first question after her baby is born is often 'Is he all right?', mothers and fathers expect their babies to be normal and fortunately this is usually the case. If the defect is obvious at birth, then the parents should be told immediately, so that acceptance and adjustment will occur as early as possible. They will need to be told again after the initial shock is over, to enable them to ask questions and so that plans can be made as early as possible about the baby's future. Similarly, should a handicap be detected later in a child's life, his parents should be told as soon as possible.

Reaction to the fact that a child is handicapped can range from a rejection of the child to a complete refusal to believe that there is anything wrong at all. Fortunately, most parents do eventually accept their child as he is and do their best to help him. But nearly all parents ask themselves 'Why should this happen to me?' and there may be a tendency for one parent to blame the other, especially if the disease is hereditary. The arrival of a handicapped child can cause much marital stress, and the ability to cope will depend on the maturity of the parents and the strength of their marriage. Another factor in the acceptance of the handicap is the child's position in the family. If the parents already have a normal child, then it is often easier to accept a handicapped child.

It is difficult to understand how a mother can reject her own child, unless we are aware that we are animals and it is usual for animals to reject the abnormal. If, for instance, a mother cat has a litter containing a deformed kitten, she will ignore it and concentrate on the healthy kittens. In fact she will allow the kitten to die.

Sometimes the child is not rejected, but the handicap is. The parents ignore the handicap altogether and expect the child to behave like a normal one and to achieve the same standards. This can place a tremendous strain on the child.

Over-protection is another parental reaction to a handicapped child and can bring problems both for the child and for his brothers and sisters. They will resent the attention given to the child.

Brothers and sisters may be embarrassed about a handicapped child and will not bring friends home. Family friends and relatives often keep away, because they do not know how to deal with the situation; consequently the family may become isolated. Conflicting medical opinions as to the degree of handicap and frequent visits to hospital with long waiting periods can be physically and emotionally exhausting. Many families lack the financial and emotional resources to cope.

The care of the child places a burden on all the family; the mother in many cases is unable to work because of the demands of this child. Holidays are difficult, because the child may need special facilities. The child may be incontinent, which causes endless washing and cleaning. Babysitters are difficult to get. In such circumstances even everyday chores such as shopping for food may become an insoluble problem because of the necessity of caring for the child.

The majority of parents eventually come to terms with their child's handicap and many handicapped children have special qualities which contribute to family life. It should be remembered that this is a child (first) with a handicap (second) because his physical, mental and emotional needs are exactly the same as those of a normal child. Handicapped children and their families benefit if they are able to attend a day nursery, nursery school or playgroup and mix with normal children. Under the guidance of trained staff, with space to play and a variety of play materials, their experience can be widened and confidence can be gained.

Education

It is the responsibility of the local education authority to be aware of children in their area who may have special educational needs, and to provide any specialised help the child may require when he starts school. In the past, handicapped children were placed in one of several categories e.g. blind, deaf etc., and would usually attend a special school provided for that category. Parents had little choice in the matter even though the principle that no child should be sent to a special school if he could be educated in a normal one was laid down as long ago as 1954.

However, following the Warnock Report, the Education Act of 1983 laid down specific procedures to enable decisions to be made about a child's education on an individual basis. The main differences from the old procedures are as follows:
1. Statutory categories of handicap are abolished so that no child has a single label of handicap.
2. The local education authority has a statutory obligation to make special educational provision for any child judged to be in need.
3. A positive written statement of the type of special provision required by the individual child must be made as early as possible.

The aim is for these points to be part of a much wider scheme designed to ensure that the individual needs of all children who might require special educational provision at any time in their school career are appropriately assessed and met, and that their parents are involved as fully as possible. This has changed the emphasis from classifying children by their disability, to considering each child's ability to learn and finding the best way to help him individually. It has also blurred the dividing line between children with a medically recognisable handicap, and those with minor learning difficulties. The system involves reports from a multi-professional team including an educational psychologist, a medical officer or doctor, the child's parents, members of the nursery or school staff etc., which are incorporated into the form of a statement of the child's needs and how they can best be provided for.

Often it is obvious at a very early age that a child will need help, but in other cases the existence of a handicap will be discovered at a child's pre-school medical. Occasionally there will be no indication until the child has been attending school for a while and perhaps run into difficulties.

All kinds of factors affect children's ability to learn effectively. They must be well and comfortable, physically. They must feel secure, confident and relaxed. They need to trust adults and be at ease both with adults and their peer group. But some children are disadvantaged in their learning tasks for specific and serious reasons.

a) Some have limited inherited intellectual endowment.

b) Some are brain-damaged, during or after birth, due to factors such as oxygen depletion before or during birth, low protein diet, or exposure to lead pollution in early childhood. This may affect the development of perceiving, moving, talking. They may be easily distracted and hyperactive (not to be confused with a normal lively child).

c) Some develop inadequately functioning sensory organs (for example, hearing, sight) which, to some extent, will cut them off from stimulation in their environment and the normal feedback. This tends to be self-reinforcing.

d) Some children are not stimulated by adults; early learning opportunities, and critical learning times are missed.

All these children will exhibit restricted cognitive (learning) development.

Factors such as physical handicap, communication problems and disturbed or bizarre behaviour will also naturally affect children's learning ability. In the last case, it is often unclear whether the behaviour is a cause or result of children failing to make progress; attention-seeking behaviour is a common alternative means of self-assertion. Many children will exhibit more than one of the characteristics listed above.

Most of them are only mildly handicapped and are catered for in normal facilities. A good day nursery, which offers nurture, individual attention and stimulation by adults and other children, can do much to compensate a child with reduced intellectual capacity. The ratio of such children to 'normal' children should not be high, otherwise this measure will be self-defeating.

Nursery schools are particularly well equipped to help such children and prevent real retardation. Much attention is paid to the development of perceptual, motor and language skills and also emotional maturity. There must, however, be sufficient adjustment to the need, speed, interest and capacity of each child.

Modern infant schools, too, with their emphasis on active experience, group work, non-streaming and individual attention, can offer compensatory and preventative help. Such children will, though, take longer and need more help, and carefully graded steps, in order to develop concepts, see relationships, understand explanations and instructions, and be able to apply specific concepts learned to general situations.

Obviously, it is very important for all professionals dealing with children to be observant and to ensure that every child with a potential problem is referred to the appropriate agency as early as possible. Teachers are to be given additional training to enable them to anticipate and detect children likely to need help. Parents who express concern about their child must be taken seriously – they know their child better than anyone else.

This is where the nursery nurse's observation skills and knowledge of normal child development could be invaluable. Any professional dealing with children can refer a child to an educational psychologist, although if a nursery nurse is working in a nursery or school she would be expected to report her suspicions to the head of the unit.

If the need for specialised help is proven then the child is made the subject of 'a statement' which describes the child's needs and the provision to be made. Throughout the child's school life this statement is reviewed annually. Parents contribute to the statement and are given a copy so that, if they disagree, they can appeal against the decision. The statement is usually prepared by the educational psychologist whose job covers the following areas:

- Helping children who have learning and behaviour difficulties.
- Advising their families and schools.
- Making educational assessments.
- Investigating, with others, whether or not a child needs special educational help and recommending what form of help is needed.

If at all possible the child should first attend a local nursery school/class followed by the local neighbourhood school. Special help may be provided by, for instance, an assistant such as a nursery nurse to assist with physical needs, or by withdrawal for specialised lessons for part of the school day. Sometimes the educational psychologist will design a programme for a child which the teacher can follow. Specialists, such as a speech therapist can visit the child at school and carry out treatment.

If the problem is primarily one of behaviour, the child and his family may need regular sessions at the Child and Family Guidance Clinic, where a programme of behaviour modifications and therapy will be carried out.

Local authorities are expected to be imaginative about the ways in which individual children can be helped to get the maximum benefit from their education.

Of course, there will always be some children, such as the severely mentally handicapped, who are likely to need special schools, because of the degree of physical care needed. Many are incontinent, and need to be fed. The Warnock Report divided them into three groups:

1. Those with severe and complex difficulties who need special facilities or teaching expertise which would be too difficult or too costly to provide in a normal school.
2. Those with severe emotional problems who would cause disruption in a normal school.
3. Those with, perhaps, multiple disabilities who, despite help, do not flourish in a normal school.

In addition, there are those children who may need to go to a specialised residential school because their parents are unable to cope with them at home.

What are the advantages of a child attending a normal school?

- Most parents prefer it.
- The child can go to the same school as his siblings.
- Normal schools are larger and therefore offer a wider spread of subjects.
- The child will benefit from mixing with non-handicapped children:
  - provides more challenge and competition
  - his friends will be local to his home (in the past children attending special schools came from a wide area, so friendships were difficult to pursue out of school).
- Hopefully, this will lead to a better understanding of disabled people's needs, and acceptance in the community.

Unfortunately, in some areas of Britain, the integration of the handicapped into normal schools is taking a long time to accomplish. The main reason for this is financial – so many schools need to be adapted for children with mobility problems, teachers need to be given the necessary extra training, and helpers have to be recruited and trained to enable these children to take part fully in school life. However, most authorities have made some progress and already the process of statementing is having great impact upon people's attitudes to the needs of children.

Help available

Parents of handicapped children need a good deal of support to enable them to care for their child. Family doctors, health visitors and local authority social workers can all provide that support and can also put the family in touch with other agencies which may offer specific help. The following list shows the sort of help which may be available. It does, however, vary from area to area.

1. Education.   The local education authority provides the following services:
a) assessment by an educational psychologist
b) education from age three, suitable for the child's age and ability
c) transport to and from nursery or school
d) a place at a residential school, if necessary
e) child guidance.

2. Health.   The health authority may provide any of the following:
a) a health visitor to give advice
b) free wheelchairs, crutches, glasses, hearing aids and other appliances
c) free disposable nappies and incontinence pads from the age of two.

3. Social Services Department.   This department may provide any of the following:
a) a social worker
b) aids, such as a telephone, hoist, ramps and lifts, bath aids, either free of charge or at a reduced cost
c) a home help
d) respite care, so that parents can have a holiday.

4. Housing.   The local housing authority has the power to help as follows:
a) if a family is living in council housing, alterations may be made to make it more suitable
b) they may provide a specially adapted house
c) they may give grants to owner-occupiers to enable them to alter the house.

5. Money.   Financial help is available in the form of allowances from the Department of Social Security.
a) Attendance allowance. This is a weekly sum of money for adults and children over the age of two who are severely handicapped, either physically or mentally, and need to be looked after for six months or more. There is a rate for day attention and a higher rate for those who need constant attention day and night.
b) Invalid care allowance. This is a weekly allowance for a person of working age unable to work because he or she is needed at home to care for a disabled relative.
c) Mobility allowance. If a child aged five years or over is unable, or virtually unable, to walk, then a monthly sum of money is paid to enable him to be taken out.

6. Car tax.   Recipients of the mobility allowance are excused car tax for their vehicles (in the case of a child, the parent or guardian's vehicle which is used to take him out).

7. Car badge scheme.   Parents of a physically handicapped child can obtain an orange badge for their car which entitles them to free parking.

8. The family fund (Joseph Rowntree Memorial Trust). This is a trust fund set up to help disabled children and their families. The aim is to fill in the gaps of statutory care, so help depends on individual needs, e.g., provision of a washing machine for parents of an incontinent child.

9. Voluntary organisations:
a) Many parents of children with specific handicaps have formed their own societies for mutual help and support and collect funds for research into their children's disease. One example is The Muscular Dystrophy Association.
b) The local Red Cross Society, Women's Royal Voluntary Service and others will often give specific help to handicapped children and their families, for example holidays.

10. Genetic Counselling Centre.   This is a special centre where advice on hereditary diseases is available to parents and relatives.

Condition	Possible causes	Diagnosis	Treatment	Outlook
Hearing defects a) Deafness	hereditary; rubella in pregnancy; brain damage caused by a) lack of oxygen at birth; b) jaundice after birth; meningitis; repeated ear infections; congenital syphilis; head injury; exposure to high noise levels	usually detected early in life when a baby: does not respond to noises; looks startled when someone stands over him (did not hear him coming); stops making his own noises (no pleasure if he cannot hear); fails routine hearing test at 7 months; does not develop speech	early diagnosis; hearing aid for any residual hearing; speech therapy – always talk face to face; home tutor to show mother how to help; special tuition at school; child learns to lip read and to use sign language	cannot be cured; ability to speak normally depends on: a) amount of residual hearing b) how early the diagnosis is made c) child's intelligence d) level and value of tuition
b) Partial hearing 1) may be unable to hear high pitched sounds such as 's'; may be unable to hear low tones;	1) as above	failure of routine test at 7 months; poor speech	early diagnosis; hearing aid; speech therapy	1) cannot be cured but child can overcome problem with specialised help
2) may be intermittent deafness	2) catarrhal and sinus problems, including enlarged adenoids, 'glue' ear	test should be repeated at intervals, especially if speech problems	may need drainage of middle ear, and/or removal of adenoids; insertion of grommets	2) may be completely cured
Speech defects a) Disorder of articulation (dysarthria) b) Disorder of fluency c) Delayed language d) Delay of phonology (sound system)	hearing loss; associated with other handicaps e.g. cerebral palsy; cleft palate; weakness of muscles of lips, tongue, jaw; lack of stimulation;emotional deprivation; cognitive/intellectual delay; stress	a) history of feeding problems; drooling; tongue thrust; slow speech development b) stammer c) and d) garbled speech, difficult for others to understand; temper tantrums in frustration	correct any hearing loss as soon as possible with hearing aid; speech therapy; relaxation; music therapy; bubble blowing; rarely – drugs for relaxation	with early expert help most children can overcome these problems

Condition	Possible causes	Diagnosis	Treatment	Outlook
Cleft palate and/or Cleft lip opening dividing upper palate and lip into two or three sections	failure in facial development in third month of pregnancy; cause not known	if lip *and* palate: obvious at birth palate only: should be detected at examination immediately after birth; feeding problems	plastic surgery – lip repaired in first 6 weeks; palate at about 18 months; meanwhile removable dental plate is made to cover gap in palate during feeding; may need to be spoon-fed because of difficulty with sucking; teeth may be irregular – orthodontist; speech may be affected – speech therapy	usually surgery effects a complete cure
Visual defects a) *Blindness* vision 3/60 or less, so may have some sight but not enough to learn by sighted methods	hereditary; rubella in pregnancy; congenital syphilis; optic nerve tumour; cataract; glaucoma	usually detected very early when a baby shows: no early eye-to-eye contact; slowness to smile; no response to visual stimulation; *delayed development*	early diagnosis; stimulation of other senses and education to make use of them, e.g., hearing touch smell	cannot be cured
b) *Partially sighted* vision 6/18 or less when corrected by spectacles; may be nystagmus (rapid involuntary movements of eyeball)	hereditary; rubella in pregnancy; infection; refractive errors due to shape of eye; astigmatism; albinism	'clumsy' child; 'rolling ball' test available at 9 months, but not very accurate; vision test at 2 years or 3½ years; may be squint	correction with unbreakable spectacles or contact lenses to best possible sight; large-print books; stimulation of other senses	cannot be cured; vision can be improved with use of spectacles
c) *Strabismus (Squint)*	hereditary; astigmatism (irregular-shaped eye); rarely – brain damage	may be very obvious from 3 months; 'cover' test; one or both eyes turn in or out	early diagnosis to prevent deterioration of sight; orthoptics – eye exercises; black patch on good eye to make 'lazy' eye work; spectacles; surgery	variable; many can be completely corrected if diagnosed early.

Condition	Possible causes	Diagnosis	Treatment	Outlook
Autism (a disorder of cognition and language development) child lacks awareness or understanding of others; appears to retreat from normal relationships; may be highly intelligent Ratio: boys 4:1 girls	not yet understood; 25 per cent associated with brain damage; 50 per cent of sufferers have other handicaps from physical illness or injury	early feeding difficulties e.g. poor sucking, difficulty in chewing; no speech; seem unable to interpret gestures, facial expressions, and sounds of speech; socially immature; withdrawn; temper tantrums; sleeplessness	early diagnosis; speech therapy; special schooling tailored to child's ability; development of one-to-one relationship; music; tranquillising drugs	if detected early then good possibility of normal development
Dyslexia (word blindness) a specific learning difficulty; inability to translate sounds into letter symbols	may be inherited; associated with lack of cerebral dominance	may be any degree from mild spelling difficulty to complete illiteracy; problems with learning to read	early diagnosis; remedial lessons from a specially trained teacher	if detected early, good possibility of normal development
Cerebral palsy disorder of movement and posture; can be any degree from clumsiness to complete paralysis	hereditary (rare); rubella in early pregnancy; brain damage at birth due to: a) lack of oxygen b) bleeding into brain c) prematurity; brain damage after birth due to: a) jaundice b) injury c) convulsion d) meningitis e) poisoning f) brain tumour	may be obvious at birth; birth history; development delay Three types: a) spastic – unable to relax muscles b) athetoid – frequent involuntary movements which mask and interfere with intentional movements c) ataxic – poor balance and difficulty in eye/hand co-ordination (clumsy)	complete assessment as early as possible; may have other problems such as deafness or epilepsy; may have very low or very high intelligence physiotherapy; hydrotherapy; speech therapy; drugs to relax muscles; crutches, leg irons, wheelchairs, etc.; conductive education	no cure for underlying problem but it is possible to teach the child to overcome some problems by establishing control over affected motor systems

Condition	Possible causes	Diagnosis	Treatment	Outlook
Spina Bifida (split spine) vertebrae fail to unite and protect developing spinal cord; this prevents proper development of nerves in area a) Spina bifida occulta b) Meningocele c) Myelomeningocele	was thought to be hereditary; recent research has indicated poor maternal diet prior to conception, especially in lack of folic acid and vitamin B	obvious at birth protruding spinal cord causes lesion on back; mostly in lumbar region; varying degree of paralysis of lower part of body, depending on site and type of lesion a) dimple or tuft of hair on back b) sac contains meninges only (covering to spinal cord) c) sac contains spinal cord and nerves	a) minimal problems b) and c) require surgery to repair opening in back and protect spinal cord from infection; physiotherapy	b) and c) without surgery child will die from infection; result of surgery depends on degree of abnormality present, varies from weakness in legs to complete paralysis of body below lesion; incontinence – bowel and bladder
Hydrocephalus (Water on the brain) cerebro-spinal fluid collects in the brain instead of circulating around the body	often associated with Spina bifida; brain tumour; meningitis; may be congenital, of unknown cause	enlarging head; baby – fontanelles remain open and sutures may open to accommodate increasing size; older child – headaches due to increasing pressure on the brain	following early diagnosis, introduction of a tube containing a valve to allow fluid to drain into the bloodstream (shunt)	early stages can be controlled, late diagnosis – brain damage due to increasing pressure
Microcephalus	not known	abnormally small head; fontanelles close early; child becomes increasingly mentally and physically retarded	physiotherapy; training in social skills	no cure; increasing mental and physical disability as pressure increases on growing brain; early death
Talipes	partly genetic; partly due to malposition when in uterus	Equinovarus – inward curve to feet and legs Calcaneo-Valgus – outward turning feet and legs	physiotherapy; manipulation; may be strapped or put into plaster cast; may need surgery; special boots	treatment usually successful in correcting deformity

Condition	Possible causes	Diagnosis	Treatment	Outlook
Brittle bone disease	inborn abnormality in the structure of bones thought to be a combination of at least seven distinct disorders.	easily fractured bones; may be born with a fracture; flattened head; bluish whites of eyes	child put into a 'space suit' to protect him and reduce the number of fractures	poor outlook – increasing deformity due to frequent fractures; poor growth; no cure
The muscular dystrophies a progressive degeneration of the muscles; several types, classified by their mode of inheritance Examples are:	hereditary; precise cause not known but thought to be due to an inability to manufacture a certain muscle protein			recent research very hopeful of a cure in the near future
a) Duchenne	defective gene on X chromosome; sex-linked hereditary, i.e. passed on by a normal 'carrier' mother to 50 per cent of her sons, boys only are affected	baby may have slow motor development; from about 3 years, increasing difficulty in walking; frequent falls, walks on toes; blood tests; muscle biopsy; electro-myogram	aim to keep child walking as long as possible; stimulation of muscles; vigorous physiotherapy; surgery to lengthen Achilles tendon; leg-irons or crutches may be used; wheelchair from about 10 years	child's condition deteriorates slowly; the less he uses his muscles, the more they weaken; process starts with leg muscles then, when child chairbound, other muscles deteriorate; heart and respiratory muscles are affected last, causing death in early adulthood
b) Becker type c) Facio-scapulo	hereditary, may affect either sex	increasing muscular weakness but much less severe than 'Duchenne', and onset may be delayed until adulthood	physiotherapy	as above, but disease develops more slowly and may affect different muscles initially; genetic counselling for family
Spinal muscular atrophy	not known	muscle weakness due to loss of nerve cells	physiotherapy	no cure; wheelchair bound

Condition	Possible causes	Diagnosis	Treatment	Outlook
Haemophilia failure of the blood to clot following an injury; rare in girls	hereditary; mostly sex-linked; defective production of any one of thirteen factors required to enable blood to clot	excessive bleeding following injury; baby: excessive bruising; child: bleeding into joints as child becomes more mobile, leading to eventual deformity; bleeding from any organ, e.g. kidney; blood tests	replacement of missing factor at 3-4 weekly intervals; transfusion of blood or of missing factor as soon as injury occurs	cannot be cured but child can live a reasonably normal life provided missing factor is replaced at regular intervals; any operative procedure remains hazardous; genetic counselling for family
Sickle cell anaemia Sickle cell thalassaemia Haemoglobin SC disease	hereditary; both parents carry a sickle cell trait	blood test; sickle cell crises – sudden worsening of either: pain in back, chest, jaw or limbs; anaemia; infection or inflammation	maintenance of good general health; avoidance of situations likely to precipitate crises, e.g. dehydration, anaesthetics, acidosis; avoidance of infection	no cure; genetic counselling for family
Heart defects faulty development of heart during foetal life; or failure of ductus to close at birth	rubella in early pregnancy; drugs in early pregnancy; mostly unknown	if severe, diagnosed at birth: 'blue' baby breathing problems; less severe: usually found at 6-week developmental check when heart sounds are abnormal; slow weight gain; chest infections; failure to thrive	surgery to correct deformity; may be a temporary relief operation at birth, with main surgery postponed until child is older; may need drugs	outlook much improved in past 10 years or so; children who survive birth and surgery usually live a normal life
Diabetes	possibly hereditary; pancreas unable to produce enough insulin	poor growth; excessive thirst; frequent urination; coma; urine test reveals sugar present	insulin by injection; diet (see page 72)	no cure so far; outlook good providing child stays on diet and insulin which will have to be adjusted as he grows

Condition	Possible causes	Diagnosis	Treatment	Outlook
Epilepsy abnormal electrical discharge from the brain, causing fits	hereditary; brain damage due to injury; brain tumour; sometimes associated with low mental ability; in most cases unknown	1) psychomotor attacks; twitching, lip-smacking; appears conscious but unable to speak or respond 2) Petit Mal – occasional momentary fits; child looks blank and loses concentration. 3) Grand Mal – convulsive fits with loss of consciousness and bladder control	investigations for any underlying cause; anti-convulsive drugs to control fits	if brain tumour – may be possible to remove it, otherwise no cure; control of fits usually possible so that child can live a normal life
Cystic fibrosis mucus glands secrete abnormally sticky mucus which clogs digestive and respiratory systems; sweat glands secrete very salty sweat	hereditary; both parents carry the gene; actual cause not known	newborn may have blocked intestine; poor weight gain and slow growth due to poor absorption of food; repeated chest infections; wheeziness; stools offensive –contain unabsorbed fat; sweat test	antibiotics for infections; physiotherapy to keep chest clear; pancreatic enzyme given with meals (because this enzyme cannot get to intestine as tubes are blocked with mucus)	recent research hopeful but so far no cure; 20 per cent of children die in first year; otherwise gradual deterioration to death in early twenties; genetic counselling
Coeliac disease inability to absorb gluten because of missing enzyme, leading to: 1) inflammation of intestinal cells which produce mucus 2) interference with absorption of fats	hereditary; unable to make a necessary enzyme	failure to thrive; retarded growth; poor appetite; pot belly; stools – pale, large and offensive (contain excessive fat)	gluten-free diet; (gluten present in flour and many common foodstuffs)	normal outlook, provided child stays on diet

Condition	Possible causes	Diagnosis	Treatment	Outlook
Phenylketonuria	hereditary; inability to use phenalynin (a protein) leads to build-up in brain, causing damage	at birth – routine Guthrie blood test is abnormal	diet reducing amount of phenalynin	provided child remains on diet whilst brain is developing he will grow into normal adult; if not, child will become mentally retarded
Hypothyroidism	defective thyroid function in foetal life	blood test (this is often done automatically in the first week of life so this condition is preventable); failure to thrive; stunted growth; increasing mental and physical deterioration	thyroid extract is administered for life	provided child continues on medication, he can lead a normal life
Asthma wheezing and breathlessness; varies from mild to very severe	probably an inherited allergy – a sensitivity which may manifest as asthma, eczema or hay fever	attacks of 'wheezing' which gradually become more incapacitating	physiotherapy; drugs; 'Spinhaler'; hospital for acute attacks	variable sometimes disappears spontaneously as child grows up, but can be life-long and cause increasing incapacity; barrel chest
Children with below average intelligence who have difficulty in coping with normal life a) those with moderate learning difficulties	mostly unknown; may be: hereditary; deprivation; brain damage due to: a) lack of oxygen at birth b) jaundice c) meningitis d) injury – accidental, child abuse; e) conditions such as Down's syndrome (see page 210)	may not be detected until child reaches school age; slow physical and mental development; poor speech; poor powers of concentration; poor progress at school	recognition and assessment as early as possible; child treated according to mental age; small classes with individual attention to enable child to work at his own pace; stimulation to all senses; conductive education	no cure; training may enable child to cope with normal life – this depends on level and value of tuition

Condition	Possible causes	Diagnosis	Treatment	Outlook
b) children with severe learning difficulties	as above	usually obvious at birth; excessive delay in all aspects of development; may have other defects; poor control of bowel and bladder (often life-long incontinence); susceptible to chest infections	as above, plus extra training in social skills, care and protection	no cure; will need life-long care and protection
Down's syndrome (Mongolism)	hereditary (extra chromosome)	diagnosed at birth; typical appearance – broad, flat face, slant eyes; retarded development; may have heart defect; intelligence varies from lower levels of normal to severe retardation	as above	no cure; depends on level of intelligence but will probably need life-long care and protection
Children with emotional, adjustment or behavioural difficulties	unstable home life; physical, emotional or social deprivation	may be: a) obsessive b) disruptive c) solitary	child guidance (parent guidance); sometimes removal from home if severe deprivation	variable; some recover, others grow up to be deviants; may develop mental illness

THE GIFTED CHILD

A gifted child is more than just 'very bright'. Giftedness implies exceptional intellectual abilities, either of high intelligence, or in one particular sphere of activity – for instance music, ballet, art, sport. Less easily discernible, the special ability may be for creative thinking or innovation.

Identifying and recognising the gifted child

It is difficult to identify gifted young children, for several reasons.

The performance skills that are conventionally examinable have, on the whole, not yet been learned. We have, therefore, either to compare the child with his peers – a controversial and unfashionable pastime – or arrange for him to be tested by an educational psychologist. This course may produce an untrue picture of the young child, who may be affected by, for instance, hunger, or discomfort in a strange situation. Where testing can be carried out reliably, gifted children score approximately 140 or above intelligence quotient.

Gifted children come from all social classes and from parents with a wide range of intelligence.

In the nursery or the home, we may observe one or more of the following characteristics:

- Extreme liveliness, often associated with less need for sleep than usual.
- Early mobility, linked with curiosity.
- Advanced language development, and use of quite long and complex sentence constructions. Also frequent and searching questions, of the 'how' and 'why' variety. (Middle-class children may be deceptively advanced in their language development, showing evidence of encouragement and stimulation, rather than, necessarily, exceptionally high intelligence.)
- Advanced manipulative skills, often shown in problem-solving.

- Marked interest in topics usually associated with older children, e.g. makes of cars, stamp collecting, ornithology.
- Complicated imaginative games, with or often without props.
- Response to music – melody or rhythm – or marked artistic talent.
- Reading as young as two and a half or three. (Writing – of letters, words or figures – is seldom learned at such an early age; it is too tedious for a quick brain.)
- Exceptional performance in any area, e.g. detailed drawings, understanding of mathematical concepts.
- Complete concentration on the task in hand; perseverance.
- Initiative and originality.
- Marked independence.

Coping with a gifted child

Potential and performance can be two very different things. The child's gifts require recognition, understanding and skilful nurture. With these he can grow into a well-adjusted, happy individual who can contribute enormously to society – perhaps even change the course of history.

There may be problems and pitfalls. A toddler who is always on the go, exploring and investigating, particularly if he can find ingenious ways of reaching forbidden items, or 'escaping' from his place of safety, can exhaust his parents or nanny. It is worse if he cannot be relied on to settle down early to a good night's sleep. Adults may feel they are failing, or else may feel exasperated that, despite all their well-intentioned efforts, the child refuses to respond conventionally. Without reassurance and practical help, a mother may even fear for her own sanity, or her fitness to be safely alone with so demanding a creature. She must be helped to see that her child *is* different, and has different needs. Tranquillisers from her doctor, or supposed words of comfort about this being 'just a phase' that he will grow out of, are little help. What she does need is a partner and/or reliable child-minder to relieve the pressure sometimes in the day, and certainly during a long spell of disturbed nights. If there is an older child, he could be found a nursery or playgroup place. The toddler himself will need such extra outside stimulation at two or two-and-a-half; by the age of three, many typical nursery activities will be too babyish for him. Questions must be listened to and answered, interests followed, however tiring or trying this may be at times.

The child's 'differentness' may set him apart from his peers, whose company and interests hold little appeal for him. Yet older children will not accept him as an equal. At the playgroup or nursery he may evoke dislike because he appears superior, or else may try to organise the people there – including adults!

He must be helped to get along with his peer group, however uphill a struggle this is for the adults. Not only could failure here result in many years of miserable schooling for the child, but it could also instil anti-social attitudes for life.

His interests should be taken into account. He could be assigned an appropriate aspect of a group activity or project. For instance, if a model castle is being made out of junk material, perhaps he could research on vital facts and statistics for its construction and use. Freshly stimulating play material must frequently be presented to him. Home-made games, puzzles, etc., as well as improvised and borrowed materials, can supplement manufactured ones. New tasks can be set and lines of enquiry followed up, using basic materials such as sand and water.

At the same time as extending such a child's intellectual capacities, and working towards his social integration, the adult must recognise that the child's physical and emotional needs are as important as those of any other child. The stage these are at may even be characteristic of a younger child. For instance, his physical co-ordination may be poor. Parents, particularly, need help in being patient and acknowledging that his development may well be uneven. It may irritate them to watch a classic temper tantrum, staged after a narrow defeat at chess. It may also annoy them to find that common sense by no means always accompanies giftedness.

There are still some parents and teachers who regard gifted children as a nuisance, or even a threat. Some parents are ill-equipped to nurture their child's gifts. They may have little liking for music or mathematics themselves, or fear that their child is the 'wrong' sex to possess such a talent. They may play down their child's giftedness for any of the foregoing reasons, or else because they fear he will grow up conceited.

At infant school, the child may need different activities from the group, as he may work through things more quickly. There should be a wide and flexible range of activities available, responsive to the child's needs, in order to maintain his interest.

Where teachers cannot recognise, accept, or cater for the child's special needs, things can go wrong. Frustrated and bored, he may develop anti-school attitudes very early. He may become excessively withdrawn, or indulge in disruptive or aggressive behaviour. He may take on the role of the class clown. He may attempt to hide his giftedness in order to be accepted more freely by the group. He may need to attend the Child Guidance Clinic. Sadly, a few gifted people never find a satisfying role in society.

Joining with a group of older children to pursue his particular interest – for example playing an instrument – can ensure his active co-operation for at least a number of sessions per week. The Association for Gifted Children offers half-day activities and short courses.

Rushing him through the infant school curriculum only delays his boredom with school. Mentally challenging activities must be found for him, and here one can draw on the experience common to the group as a whole and let him go further. But he does require individual attention to 'extend' his powers and should not be expected to work on his own for long periods.

Some countries, including the USA and USSR capitalise on young children's strengths from an early age, by educating children with similar talents together. In Britain, most opportunities for generalised stimulation of particular talents are to be found in specific private schools.

Some educationalists believe that a 'hot house' atmosphere can be damaging to the child's total development; it has even been known for the gift itself to wither and die.

Wisely handled, a gifted child can bring great joy, indeed excitement, to all who know him.

EXERCISES

Investigation

1) Research the childhood and education of someone you know who is, or was, a 'genius'. This can be in any field of activity. How far do you think his/her gifts were nurtured by early experiences?

2) Find out what fund-raising activities are being carried out in your locality to support special care baby units.

Observation

Observe a child with learning difficulties coping within a normal school. In your evaluation, summarise the help he is being given. Is the arrangement working?

Project

1) Ask your tutor if it might be possible to invite into college the parent(s) of a child with one of the handicapping conditions listed on pages 202–10. Talk to them about the difficulties and rewards of bringing up their child. What attitudes have they met in other people? What provision and approaches have they found most helpful?

2) Find out about genetic counselling facilities in your area.

SUGGESTIONS FOR FURTHER READING

J. Bruner, M. Cole, B. Lloyd (ed.), *Learning Disabilities*, Fontana Books

Liz Thompson, *Bringing Up A Handicapped Child*, Thorsons Publishers Ltd

Vera Quin and Alan Macauslin, *Dyslexia*, Pelican Books

Barry McCormick, *Screening for Hearing Impairment in Young Children*, Croom Helm Ltd

Sundarq Lingam, David R. Harvey, *Manual of Child Development*, Churchill Livingstone

Joy Pollock, *Dyslexia – The Problem of Spelling*, Helen Arkell Dyslexia Centre

Michael Nolan, Ivan G. Tucker, *The Hearing Impaired Child and The Family*, Human Horizons Series Souvenir Press Ltd

Elizabeth Byrne, Cliff Cunningham, Patricia Sloper, *Families and Their Children with Down's Syndrome*, Routledge and Kegan Paul Ltd

Jane Carr, *Helping Your Handicapped Child*, Penguin Books

L. Pearson and G. Lindsay, *Special Needs in the Primary School*, NFER-Nelson Publishing Co Ltd

Wilfred K. Brennan, *Curriculum for Special Needs*, Open University

Wilfred K. Brennan, *Special Education Now*, Open University

Penny Low Deiner, *Resources for Teaching Young Children with Special Needs*, Harcourt Brace Jovanovich Inc

Richard W. Mills, *Observing Children in the Primary Classroom*, Unwin Hyman

12 Fact Sheets for parents who have children with special educational needs, available from The National Elfrida Rathbone Society, 11 Whitworth Street, Manchester

SOCIAL DEPRIVATION

The main cause of social deprivation is poverty and it has been estimated that about a fifth of the population of Great Britain live in poverty. This amounts to almost twelve million people and, as about two thirds of them are in families containing young children, it indicates that over three million children are without the necessities for a healthy life. Although it is almost unknown in Britain for a child to die of starvation, some of these children will die of diseases related to their poverty, and many others will grow up mentally and/or physically stunted by their environment.

The majority of poor families are in the lower socio-economic groups, that is classes D and E of the Registrar-General's classification. (See page 11.) It follows that the least well off in our society are the unskilled and the unemployed, and they are often referred to as 'the have nots' in comparison to 'the haves' and 'the have lots'.

Before discussing poverty in detail it is necessary to define it. Some people use the word to describe those whose income is equal to or below the level of social security since this level is meant to cover basic subsistence needs. Some say that 'a family is poor if it cannot afford to eat'. Others argue that social security payments only represent the amount and level of income the state is prepared to provide and therefore have little relationship to people's needs. Over the years various groups researching into the effects of poverty have concluded that when a person's income falls below one and a half times the level of social security payments then it is possible to identify and measure deprivation.

In 1983 a survey carried out for London Weekend Television called 'Breadline Britain' found widespread agreement amongst people from all social classes about the standards of life without which most people would feel deprived. These were basically:

- a roof over their head
- sufficient, appropriate food, and the means to cook it
- adequate heating in the living area of the home
- essential and adequate clothing suitable to the climate
- carpets, washing machine and refrigerator
- sufficient money to celebrate Christmas and children's birthdays.

Causes of poverty

Low pay. Four out of ten people living on an income below 140 per cent of social security payments were in families with at least one full-time wage earner. These figures were collated in 1981 and there is evidence to show that these numbers are increasing steadily now that minimum wage levels are being abandoned. In addition, trade union power to negotiate higher wages has been weakened due to high unemployment and falling membership. In many cases a family is better off if the 'wage earner' is unemployed because of the costs incurred in going to work e.g. tax, National Insurance, transport expenses and working clothes etc.

Unemployment. The problem of long-term unemployment may seem to be a recent phenomenon in this country, although students of history will be aware of the unemployment problem in the 1930s. In the past, being unskilled was no disadvantage and many children merely followed their parents into jobs. However, the economy now requires a smaller workforce which is highly skilled and computer literate. This should and could have been foreseen and planned for. Instead we have an increasing social problem which is creating a vicious cycle of deprivation to the detriment of the children of the poor.

Naturally, many of the long-term unemployed are the least able in our society, being under-educated and under-skilled. But some people have managed largely to overcome the difficulties of unemployment. Much depends on a person's ability, background and general outlook on life, and on the amount of redundancy pay they may receive. One advantage of unemployment may be that many fathers are able to spend more time with their children. Some parents have swapped roles and this can work well if the mother has a skill which enables her to earn a living. Others have set up businesses with their redundancy money.

Many people, however, find it difficult to cope with loss of work. Work gives people a purpose in life. It provides a goal and a discipline. Without that discipline many unemployed people become depressed and ill. The incidence of all types of illness is increased for unemployed people and their families. Some marriages break up under the stress. The debilitative effects of living in poverty may add to the possible feelings of worthlessness.

Single-parent families. Many single-parent families live in poverty because the head of the household is very often an unskilled woman who will either be living on social security or working in a part-time, poorly paid job. Often, she is caught in a trap – if she works full-time she needs a carer for her child but she is unable to earn enough to pay for adequate care, even if such care were easily available.

Disability and sickness. People who are suffering from chronic physical or mental illness, or are disabled are least able to obtain employment. In addition, they need a higher income because of their condition, e.g. they need a high standard of heating in their home because they are immobile and unable to keep warm by other means.

Homelessness

In the last few years there has been a steady increase in the number of families who do not have a permanent roof over their heads. For instance, in 1986 101 280 families containing children under the age of sixteen were known to be in this position. Approximately 6500 of them were living in bed and breakfast accommodation at the expense of housing authorities. The total number of homeless people is probably much higher than this and, contrary to popular belief, homelessness is seldom their own fault.

The main reason for so much homelessness in this country is the severe shortage of houses and flats available for rent due to various factors, such as:

- less council houses being built, resulting in longer waiting lists. In fact some 14 per cent of people on local housing authority waiting lists have been waiting for nine or more years!

- an enormous increase in the number of people buying their council houses due to recent legislation. This has further depleted the housing stock. Previously people who could afford to buy would move into the private sector thus leaving a vacant house for another tenant.

- an increase in longevity which has meant that more elderly tenants are still occupying their homes – often this might be a widow or widower in a three-bedroomed house, the family having grown up and moved away.

- a reduction in the number of flats and houses available to rent privately. This is thought to be due to Acts designed to protect tenants, making it less profitable to be a landlord.

The shortage of rented accommodation has meant that many more people have had to buy property, thus pushing up the prices. House prices in many areas, notably London and the South East, are now very often beyond the reach of many people.

Families liable to find themselves homeless include the following:

- Young parent(s) trying to set up an independent home.
- Divorced or separated parents trying to set up separate homes – even if there is a family house to be sold it seldom yields enough money to buy two more.

- Families on low incomes who have committed themselves to a large mortgage and are unable to keep up the payments – this is commonly due to unforeseen circumstances such as loss of employment. If the family qualifies for social security then only the interest on the mortgage will be paid. Most building societies will accept this for a short time, but after about six months will take steps to repossess the house.
- Parents in unsuitable rented accommodation, where the lease stipulates no children, being evicted when a baby arrives.
- Families living in 'unfit housing' which has been condemned.
- Families moving to a new area because of a job opportunity.
- Families whose home has been damaged by fire, flood or other disaster.
- Families returning to this country after living abroad.
- Families who have been living in 'tied' accommodation e.g. servicemen/women, farm-workers, caretakers etc.
- Persistent rent defaulters.

Help available. The Housing (Homeless Persons) Act 1977 places a legal duty on the local council to help the homeless and those threatened with homelessness, providing they fulfil certain conditions.

a) They must have local connections.
b) They must have a priority need:
  i)   dependent children
  ii) be pregnant
  iii) be vulnerable because of age, mental or physical illness or disability
  iv) have lost their home because of fire, flood or other disaster.
c) They must not have made themselves intentionally homeless.

This last proviso is decided by the housing authority and there is no appeal against this decision.

If the homelessness is deemed 'intentional' then the council must offer temporary accommodation for a 'reasonable' period of time to enable the person to find another home. The word 'reasonable' is open to interpretation and provision varies in different parts of the country.

When homelessness is unintentional the council must provide temporary shelter until it can provide a permanent home. Unfortunately such is the shortage of council housing that many families remain in temporary shelter for months, and sometimes years. Most temporary accommodation is 'bed and breakfast' in small guest houses and is open to much abuse. At best it is homely accommodation with people having the freedom to come and go as they please, but it can be far from homely. Often the rooms are very small bedrooms with as many beds as possible crammed into the space. There are no cooking or laundry facilities. Nor are there facilities for sterilising bottles, making up feeds, or bathing a small baby. The problem of lack of play space for older children becomes a nightmare for the parents. If the child has been attending nursery or playgroup, this will have been disrupted by the move. The child's whole life has been upset. In addition, adults in this situation feel alienated from other people and may become depressed and apathetic. The family is often expected to go out all day which creates problems especially if the weather is bad. Meals have to be eaten at cheap cafés or take-aways and the entire way of life is demoralising. Friends and relatives tend to blame the parents for their situation and hesitate to invite the family to spend the day in their home in case they outstay their welcome. This increases the adults' sense of isolation. Also many parents are apprehensive that their children will be 'taken into care' since they are unable to provide a home for them. This is very unlikely to happen but this fear often prevents them accepting help.

In many areas day centres are being set up for the homeless so that they can spend the day in shelter and buy a cheap meal. The children can have the space to play in safety, and their parents have some company and possibly some counselling. This, however, only relieves the problem. In the future more must be done to provide these families with permanent homes. The damage to children from being homeless is long lasting and the stress can destroy the family unit.

What is it like to be a child growing up in poverty?

A child born in poverty is more likely to:

- be premature
- be of low birth-weight
- be damaged at birth
- die at birth
- die in his first year, of infection
- die during his childhood
- have a reduced life expectancy during middle age
- suffer from congenital disease
- suffer a higher incidence of infection and illness throughout his life e.g. respiratory illnesses
- suffer from nutritional deficiencies such as anaemia
- be injured by accident at home or on the roads.

All of these things are preventable because so many are caused by environmental factors, which, with a little extra money, could be alleviated.

Life on a low income means:

- Poor housing – often damp and unheated.
- Poor diet – cheap food, too much bread and food containing sugar; less red meat containing iron; less fruit and vegetables containing vitamins because these are expensive.
- Inadequate clothing in bad weather.
- Lack of comfort in the home.
- Lack of stimulation – parents in this situation often become dispirited and depressed.
- Restricted ability to travel – no personal transport and public transport expensive and scarce.
- No holidays.
- Low self-esteem – feeling that you are on the losing end.

- Inability to get out of the situation leads to feelings of hopelessness.
- For parents, events like Christmas become a nightmare.

Children brought up in such a background are often said to be socially disadvantaged, although some parents seem able to compensate their children so that they do not suffer. Help from the extended family can sometimes make the crucial difference. It is also a fact that some children overcome severe disadvantages and grow up into mature, well-adjusted adults; whether this is due to their innate strength and ability or to other factors, we do not know.

However, let us focus on some ways in which children are frequently affected by a socially disadvantaged background:

a) Physical. Pregnant women in such circumstances tend to take less advantage of antenatal clinics and postnatal checks. This may partly be due to ignorance of services provided, or failure to see them as necessary unless something goes seriously wrong. (Many women do not welcome personal questions, for example about their smoking habits, which they regard as interference by 'authority' figures.)

Accessibility of clinics is not always ideal, and travel difficulties, coping with toddlers and buggies in lifts and so on, further deters attendance. Clinics are not seen as user-friendly.

As a result of poor diet and a generally low standard of living, the incidence of low birth-weight babies, and symptoms of failure to thrive in the early months are common.

Later the child's own poor diet and unsuitable sleeping arrangements may result in low grade health reflected by lack-lustre eyes, poor skin and hair, and general lack of vitality. There is often a poor standard of hygiene in the home so these children often appear grubby and their clothes may be smelly.

b) Intellectual. Mentally, such a child may be six months to one year behind normal development at the pre-school stage.

Being behind in language development, not necessarily in grammar and vocabulary but rather in verbal reasoning and other uses of language, and the confidence these can bring, will put the child further behind as he grows up. It is through such skills as monitoring our own behaviour, and obtaining and relaying information that we continue to grow as people.

He will be less likely to be able to read and do calculations well enough to cope with everyday needs.

Such deficiencies will seriously affect the child's academic achievements, and thus his life chances.

Parents are often too preoccupied with their own problems to give home support. They may also have bad memories of their own schooling, and see teachers as 'authority' figures. They may reinforce the child's disaffection from school, condone truanting and anti-school behaviour, and encourage the child to leave early and get a job. The only opportunities available are likely to be government schemes, or low paid, unskilled jobs with few prospects. Even if parents want to support their child in later schooling, financial need may determine that he leaves as soon as possible. Or parents may be easily dissuaded from letting a child stay on, if his performance does not seem to warrant this. Thus the cycle continues.

c) Social/Emotional. If he experienced little parenting skill as a baby and infant, the child may be unruly and aggressive, given to temper tantrums which his parents fail to control.

On the other hand, he may be withdrawn and unnaturally meek and compliant, seemingly incapable of showing initiative or spontaneity.

Either way, his self-esteem is probably at a very low ebb.

His behaviour may be less socially acceptable, which will make it harder for him to get on with others, or to become a fulfilled adult.

He is less likely than other children to be optimistic and constructive about the future.

Working with socially disadvantaged families

Trained nursery nurses are able to do a good deal in their different work settings to support families and ease burdens, especially in day nurseries, and now, increasingly, family centres. Nursery officers are often regarded as friends and as quite distinct from social services personnel.

It is up to all staff who work with young children, in every type of setting, to recognise the signs outlined in this chapter, and react appropriately.

Remember, it is not only inner city and urban areas which throw up problems of social disadvantage.

Helping parents

- Do not sit in judgement. It will help no one, least of all the child, if you side with him against his parents.

- Befriend the parents. Show empathy with their situation.

- Accept that attitudes, standards, and life styles may be very different from your own, and it is neither realistic nor desirable (nor possible) to change them.

- Listen to the parents' problems. Often, these will concern: depression, money and material problems, housing, health, care of the children, personal relationships, alcohol and drug related problems, and feelings of anxiety.
  Many of these problems may be due to a person's low self-esteem which limits his/her effectiveness both as a parent and as a partner. Also parents are often only too well aware of their limited skills which can make them defensive and even aggressive, especially if the nursery nurse appears to be able to cope with their child more effectively than they can.

- Practise complete confidentiality. If you need to get help for a parent, ask permission before you repeat some information to a third party.

- Notice improvements in the child's appearance/ behaviour etc. and tell parents.

- Act as a signpost to sources of help (merely providing a lot of leaflets will not suffice).
- Help in practical ways as far as possible, such as running a used-clothing stall, or introducing parents to self-help ventures like Gingerbread for single parents.
- Involve the parents in nursery/school life if they are willing. They will absorb a good deal about child management; for example, you can demonstrate how to forestall crying or temper tantrums, how to rely on verbal requests, and the importance of consistency. Parents will also see suitable play materials in use. In addition, they will feel supported, and refreshed by the break from home problems.
- Take every opportunity that arises to educate parents on health or child care matters, remembering to use a low-key, informal approach. Draw in expertise from the community if the parents desire it, for example a health visitor, or ear, nose and throat specialist to explain about operations for 'glue' ear. Nursery staff can often 'oil the wheels' to bring about helpful happenings of this kind, which also breaks down class and anti-authority attitudes.
- Encourage parents to befriend/support each other.

Helping children

- Show total acceptance and extra tolerance.
- Show warmth, care and friendship.
- Practise consistency, along with kind but firm handling.
- Do not try to override the child's cultural behaviour/attitudes with your own.
- Keep expectations realistic.
- Stress the positive. Praise and reward the child's smallest efforts and achievements, thus reinforcing desired behaviour.
- Relay 'good' behaviour and achievements to parents. Always use 'good' examples to begin a conversation, in order to sound positive.
- Encourage exchange of information about child's behaviour with parents (out of his earshot, naturally).
- Ensure provision of meals that are balanced and appropriate to cultural requirements.
- Notice the child's individual requirements, for example a daytime sleep, and try to supply them in a discreet way.
- Encourage language development, devoting considerable time, on a one-to-one basis. (See Chapter 12.)
- Provide a stimulating environment, and encourage his interaction with it.
- Encourage habits of concentration and perseverence.

EMOTIONAL DEPRIVATION

This is another form of disadvantage and is one that occurs right across social or class barriers.

It is a term applied to children who are denied affection by their early carer.

As we have mentioned in previous chapters, everybody needs one person's consistent care in infancy so that they can develop deep relationships. Without this foundation of care, many people grow up emotionally stunted. In most cases this care is provided by the natural mother in the process known as bonding. This is a complex process and consists of a response by the mother to the child's needs, eliciting a response from the baby, which in turn brings another response from the mother. The resulting interaction is essential for the child's mental and physical health. There is also evidence to suggest that it is necessary for all growth and development, including the brain, so would affect a child's eventual intelligence. Since the mother is the main carer in most cases, it follows that the chief reason for emotional deprivation is rejection by the natural mother. This could be because:

1. Initially the mother is unable to bond with her child due to her own problems, e.g. depression, low self-esteem, immaturity or because she, herself, was rejected as a child.
2. The child may be rejected because he is: unwanted, illegitimate, premature or ill (especially if separated from his mother directly after birth), handicapped, the 'wrong' sex, or difficult to manage (e.g. always crying, or difficult with feeds).

Other reasons for emotional deprivation include:

1. The father may reject his child by denying paternity.
2. The mother may desert her child because of marital problems.
3. The parent's social/business life style may prevent continuity of care.
4. There may be inadequate substitute care, such as unsuitable, or a succession of foster parent(s); a succession of carers – a new nanny every six months; reluctant step-parent(s).
5. An older child may be rejected because he does not fulfil the sometimes unrealistic expectations of his parents e.g. not as clever as siblings, 'wrong' colouring etc.

If rejection of a child is overt and unlikely to change, then the best solution for the child is to be removed and placed in foster care, which, if it is good, can fully compensate the child for what is lacking. Unfortunately, many cases of children who are emotionally deprived go unnoticed until the child is already damaged. Few parents are able to admit this is happening even if they are aware of it themselves, and it may not be apparent to outsiders.

A child who feels/knows himself to be unloved may be physically backward and grow more slowly than the normal child. This is mainly due to lack of encouragement and stimulation, but could also be due to poor feeding. In addition his general health may be poor. Lack of adult interest in his development will result in a poor self-image – because he is treated as being worthless, he will grow up to believe it. This can lead to problems of personality, communication, learning and ability to form personal relationships. Never having known unconditional love, he may be unable to give love to others. In extreme cases, this is thought to be the cause of psychopathic personality. The 'cycle of deprivation' means that such a child may grow up to become a parent whose children will suffer from the same emotional deprivation. To know such a child is a little like watching a damaged plant, one leaf of which never uncurls or faces the sunlight squarely.

Of course, autobiographies are full of real people whose lives contradict this depressing pattern. Interestingly, however, there often appears in these stories one adult figure who emotionally 'adopted' the youngster, saw his needs, recognised his potential, boosted his self-esteem, and possibly made the vital difference to his whole life. This figure may be a grandparent, an aunt or uncle, a teacher or even a neighbour. It is not an exaggeration to claim that nursery nurses must have played this role to many thousands of children, especially as nannies. Because the child is so young at the time, little is consciously remembered but the effect of experiencing acceptance, patience, tenderness, warmth, love, and a 'growing' environment for each child cannot be over-estimated.

Before we leave this subject, mention should be made of Dr John Bowlby who, in the 1950s, conducted and published his research concerning emotional deprivation of young children. He said that any break in the continuity of care could do irreparable damage to a child. His findings have since been modified, but the basic information remains and his work caused authorities to change their ideas about the desirability of large, impersonal orphanages for children in need of care. Nowadays children are much more likely to be fostered in a family setting. His work also highlighted the need for greater parental presence and support for sick children than hospital staff allowed at the time. On both these scores, we owe Dr Bowlby a great debt of gratitude.

CHILD ABUSE

All normal families have disputes, suffer accidents and punish their children for misdemeanours. But child abuse falls outside the normally accepted boundaries of adult behaviour.

It is not a new problem – it has existed for centuries with varying degrees of acceptance by different societies. The idea that government or society should intervene to protect children's rights is quite recent and may help to explain why, in Britain and many other countries, we appear to be seeing a tremendous upsurge in the number of cases. The exact number of children killed or injured is not known but it is estimated that in Britain between 3000 and 10 000 children are affected every year. The estimates for the number of deaths range from 100 to 1000 yearly.

There are four basic types of abuse, although they may sometimes overlap:

- Physical abuse (Non-accidental injury)
- Physical neglect
- Emotional abuse
- Sexual abuse.

It is very rare for child abuse to be confined to a single physical attack which most normal parents can understand and explain as an excessive response to an irritating incident. It is more likely to become a pattern of behaviour over a period of time and the longer it continues the more serious it becomes.

The underlying causes of child abuse are many and complex. It is unusual to find a straightforward reason for the abuse, such as one parent being mentally ill or psychopathic. It is much more common to find a multiplicity of causes ranging from the fact that the parents themselves were abused as children to the very low esteem in which most of these abusers hold themselves.

Child abuse is found in all classes of society but there are some common factors which occur in one or both parents:

- A disastrous childhood experience, e.g. poor parental models, neglect, deprivation, or ill-treatment.
- Low self-image – as a result of their own childhood experience of never pleasing anyone they often see themselves as worthless.
- Isolation – they grow up so fearful of rejection or criticism that they are unable to make friends or trust other people enough to ask for help.
- Unrealistic expectations of their children's development.
- A belief that children should always give them affection and gratitude.

A shallow relationship often exists between such parents because they are inadequate and their marriage may be held together by need and fear, rather than love.

Physical abuse

This is any injury deliberately inflicted that requires medical attention. At one time these children were known as 'battered babies' but now they are usually referred to as cases of non-accidental injury or concealed parental violence (CPV).

The commonest injury from this sort of violence is bruising, especially on the face, fractured skull or ribs, or cigarette burns. Bleeding into the brain is also found in some cases, where violent shaking has caused the jelly-like brain to bang violently against the hard skull. This sort of injury can lead to permanent damage, such as cerebral palsy or mental retardation.

Usually, the explanation of how the injury occurred is inadequate and the parental attitude may be bizarre.

Few people could fail to feel deep anger towards the parents when faced with a badly injured child, but evidence suggests that most of these parents love their child and are desperately in need of help. They are reacting to all the circumstances of their lives. Apart from unsatisfactory conditions and lack of money, many of the parents have acute problems of insecurity, inadequacy and possibly psychological damage during their own childhood. The isolation caused by some types of housing, especially high-rise flats and the separation from other members of the family, who in earlier times might have lived close at hand, and helped out in a crisis, also plays a part.

Many of the unfortunate, abused children have young parents who have the sort of background mentioned above, and in addition are living in poor housing and poverty. There is nothing new in this – in Britain there has always been an underprivileged section of the community. However, in earlier times that section tended to be set apart, socially and geographically, from the rest of the population. Nowadays, when shops, magazines and colour television reflect the comfortable life-style and enviable luxury of better-off people, those who are struggling with poverty realise the great disparities, and understandably resent them. It does not matter that the pictures they may see are grossly exaggerated; they merely emphasise to the less able members of our society their inadequacy, frustration and inability to compete. They feel they are failures in today's affluent society. And with the pressures they have to bear, it is natural for the parents to become short-tempered and irritable and their children become the nearest convenient targets for their anger. Often the mother is pregnant or has had a baby recently, so that she is not physically fit. She may be overwhelmed by all the responsibility and the worry.

Usually an abused child is a 'wanted' baby and when he is born is showered with affection. But he will be expected, in return, always to respond lovingly. The parents have little idea of a baby's abilities or of his needs, and are liable to make unrealistic demands for obedience and to have high expectations of his progress. When the baby is wakeful at night, refuses food or cries, it is interpreted as ingratitude and a rejection of the parents' love.

Sometimes it becomes apparent why one child in a family is being abused – he may have been a premature baby or had a difficult birth, so that there was early separation of mother and baby and bonding did not occur. Other typical abused babies are handicapped or they are those babies whose early days were marred by constant crying, possibly because of feeding problems or colic.

Physical neglect

Failure to provide the necessities of life for the child e.g. food, clothing, housing, supervision, etc. constitutes physical neglect. These families have a similar background to the previous group and may overlap. However, there are differences. Whilst most parents who ill-treat their children have a reasonable home, neglectful parents often live in dirty and chaotic homes which can be dangerous to the children. They seem to have little motivation or skills to effect any change in their lives and no idea of 'caring' for their children. They are often impulsive individuals who seek immediate gratification without regard to long-term consequences – they may be drug abusers or alcoholics. Besides having several children close together in age, they often keep large dogs, neglecting to feed any of them properly. The children are dirty, smelly and fail to thrive. More worrying still is the fact that they are often left unsupervised in the home whilst the parents go out. Not surprisingly, these children are frequently injured in accidents at home and on roads near their homes.

Emotional abuse

This may take the form of lack of affection, care, support and/or guidance; constant criticism; excessive, aggressive or unreasonable parental behaviour that places demands on a child to perform beyond his capability. Of all types of abuse, this is the most difficult to uncover and probably the most damaging in the long term. Bruises will heal and neglect can be rectified but emotional abuse is very hard to reverse.

Sexual abuse

This is the exploitation of a child under the age of seventeen for the sexual gratification of an adult. As a general rule, the term sexual abuse includes such activities as taking obscene and pornographic photographs and films, sexual exploitation, rape, incest, exhibitionism, and fondling of genitalia – in fact, any sexual activity between an adult and a child. Apart from incest which means the molester is a member of the family, the abuser could be a neighbour, baby sitter, or other non-related person.

The most commonly reported types of incest are father/daughter incest and incest involving the father figure. There are many more cases reported of girls being abused than boys. From the knowledge we have at present it appears that the most likely child to be abused is the eldest daughter from about the age of ten and often the abuser is a step-father or the mother's lover.

As well as having a common background with other types of parental abusers, there are certain characteristics of sexual abusers which seem to be common only to them. There may be marital problems which cause one spouse to seek physical affection from a child rather than the other spouse (a situation the 'denying' husband or wife may find acceptable). They are often isolated, lacking social and emotional contacts outside the home.

The adult male:
- is often very strict
- does not have any social activities outside the home
- is jealous and protective of the children
- does not have a criminal record
- usually confines his sexual activity to the home
- often initiates sexual contact with the child by first hugging and kissing which develops over a period of time into genital contact
- is often a stepfather.

The mother:
- is often aware of the sexual abuse but subconsciously denies it
- may prefer to keep sexual activity in the family as opposed to extra-marital affairs
- may feel that incest will relieve her from any wifely responsibility to sexual intercourse
- may be too scared to report it because the marriage could be destroyed
- often feels both guilty and jealous of the child.

Attempts to find a test which will prove conclusively that a child has been the victim of sexual abuse in the past, have so far been unsuccessful. The only way in which the abuse can be detected is to find semen in the child's vagina or rectum and match it up with the suspect. This means that the offence must be detected within a few hours of it taking place, which is rare. Usually, when suspicion arises and all the relevant facts are put together, it will all point to abuse and can be substantiated by the child's and parents' statements.

The following chart summarises some of the main facts concerning child abuse:

Physical indicators	*Behavioural indicators*
Physical abuse	
Unexplained bruises	Apprehensive when other children cry; wary of adults; frightened of parents; may be aggressive or withdrawn; may have an air of 'frozen watchfulness'; may report injury by parents
a) on lips and mouth, probably due to forced feeding with bottle	
b) on face i.e. black eyes, pinch or bite marks	
c) on body	
Bruises may appear to be of various ages, clustered in a regular pattern, or reflecting the shape of the article used to inflict them, e.g. belt, buckle	
Unexplained fractures:	
a) to skull, nose and face	
b) in various stages of healing	
c) multiple or spiral fractures, especially in very young babies	

Physical indicators	*Behavioural indicators*
Unexplained burns: a) cigarette burns on palms, back or buttocks b) reflecting the shape of the article used to inflict them, e.g. iron c) rope burns on arms, legs, neck or body d) immersion scalds e.g. sock-like or around buttocks Unexplained abrasions: a) to mouth, lips, gums and eyes b) to external genitalia c) bite marks	
Physical neglect Failure to thrive; underweight; poor hygiene; inadequate clothing; always hungry; often left alone in the home; untreated ailments such as sores, runny nose, chronic ear infection etc.; untreated developmental delay; frequent accidents	Begs or steals food; always tired – often falls asleep; 'accident prone'
Emotional abuse Poor physical development; failure to thrive; failure to grow; speech disorders	Excessive 'comfort' habits e.g. sucking, biting, rocking etc.; sleep difficulties; obsessional; has phobias; antisocial; destructive; aggressive or excessively compliant; may become inappropriately adult or very infantile; delay in mental and emotional development
Sexual abuse Difficulty in walking or sitting; torn, stained or bloody underwear; bruising and/or bleeding in vaginal or anal area; pain, swelling and/or itching in the genital area; cystitis; vaginal discharge; venereal disease	Unwilling to undress for gym; bizarre, sophisticated or unusual sexual knowledge or behaviour; poor relationship with other children; withdrawal or regressive behaviour

It is very important that all people working in child care should be vigilant about child abuse, but it is also important not to jump to conclusions. If child abuse is suspected then it is necessary to act very calmly and follow the correct procedures. The child must not be made to feel guilty by being questioned by all and sundry. Nor should he be pushed into being disloyal to his parents. If a child tells you about abuse, just listen and accept what he says. Any suspicions should be voiced privately to the head of the nursery or school and discussions should take place discreetly *out* of the child's hearing. Parents must be treated sensitively. Remember your professional responsibility to confidentiality.

Most authorities have a specific set of procedures laid down in a policy manual and these will be implemented by the Head. The usual procedure is as follows:

If there is a social worker involved with the family then he/she must be informed as well as the local social services department. The keeper of the social services department's 'child protection' register must be contacted to establish whether the family's name appears on it, so that all agencies can be alerted. Meanwhile, if the child is not already in a hospital accident department, he is taken to a hospital, general practitioner or clinical medical officer for a complete examination. The parents are interviewed and asked for an explanation of the child's condition so that their story can be checked against the injuries. It is usual to carry out a complete skeletal X-ray of the child to see if there are any healed broken bones as well as to check the extent of the present injury. If it is felt necessary, the child is either admitted to hospital or taken to a foster home under an emergency protection order. This order is granted by a court for eight days initially, but it can be extended by another seven days. As a safeguard, parents who were not present when the order was made, are able to challenge this decision after seventy-two hours.

A case conference is arranged to bring together professionals from all the different agencies involved with the family, to share information and to ensure consistency of approach. Through discussion at the case conference, all workers involved can decide upon a plan of action for future work with the family.

The case conference may decide:
a) to include the child and his siblings on the 'child protection' register
b) to appoint a case co-ordinator (or key worker) to co-ordinate all information and to work directly with the family
c) whether any legal proceedings should be taken to protect the child
d) what help could be offered to the family e.g. a day nursery place, domestic assistance etc.

The main aim is to protect the child and at the same time to change parental attitudes and improve the quality of the family life. Often the help given to parents is put into the form of a written contract, for example, the parents agree to attend a day centre with their children two days a week and the children will attend nursery on another two days, thus giving the parents some respite.

If legal proceedings are pursued, then any decision about the child's future will be made through the domestic courts. A guardian *ad litem* is appointed to represent the child's interests and the court may decide that the child should live at home under supervision or that he should go into a foster home. Progress is reviewed frequently and in cases where children are separated from parents great efforts are made to retain parental links. The aim is to return the child to his family eventually, if at all possible.

Obviously, prevention is the best cure for child abuse, but measures which would help most must come from society at large. Ensuring that good housing is available to all and the abolition of family poverty would solve many problems, because these two factors – unsatisfactory housing and a very low income – are often the last straw to inadequate parents. Educating young people so that they understand themselves, the role of parenthood and the needs of children may also help to prevent some of these cases.

In Britain progress has been made in identifying families whose children are at risk and offering early help and support. Research suggests that picking out mothers likely to react to stress with violence during the antenatal or early postnatal period may well be possible. These mothers could then be given extra help whenever stress is likely to occur. For example, a home help during the early weeks of a baby's life will enable the mother to care for and get to know her baby without the stress of coping with her home. Other help could be a day nursery place or nursery school place for the child for part of the day. In addition, if the parents have someone they can trust and to whom they can talk about their problems, it may act as a safety valve – health visitors, NSPCC officers and social workers can all fulfil this function. When families lived in a close community, a grandmother used to do this.

Many authorities have set up a lifeline for these parents, similar to that offered by the Samaritans, so that they can ask for help when things get too much for them.

Children must also be protected. Despite popular opinion, health visitors and social workers do not have right of entry into a home. If they suspect that a child is being ill-treated they must call the police and present the case to them before a warrant can be issued for the police to break in. Therefore it is important that anyone who suspects a child is being abused should report their suspicions either to the NSPCC or the police. They will investigate all calls.

Finally, everyone dealing with any form of child abuse must always bear in mind the possibility of there being a genuine reason for an injury.

Examples are:

- Bruising may be
  a) mongolian spot (see page 41)
  b) haemophilia
  c) purpura
  d) leukaemia
  e) scurvy.

- Failure to thrive may be caused by
  a) coeliac disease
  b) milk or other food allergy
  c) cystic fibrosis.

- Broken bones may be the result of
  a) brittle bone disease
  b) copper deficiency
  c) genuine accident.

EXERCISES

Investigation
If your placement is situated in an area of social disadvantage, talk to supervisors about the main problems for families with young children living in that area. Find out what other agencies/organisations operate locally to alleviate their difficulties.

Observation
Observe children playing in the home corner. What sort of insight does this give you into children's backgrounds?

Project
Discussion topic: Homelessness: should the State do more to help?

SUGGESTIONS FOR FURTHER READING

Peter Wedge and Juliet Essen, *Children in Adversity*, Pan Books Ltd
Robin Lenett and Bob Crane, *It's OK to Say No*, Thorsons Publishers Ltd
Lily Pincus and Christopher Dave, *Secrets in the Family*, Faber and Faber Ltd
Sherryll Kerns Kraizer, *The Safe Child Book*, Futura Publications
Janine Turner, *Behind Closed Doors*, Thorsons Publishers Ltd
Sue Rodmell and Alison Watt (ed.), *The Politics of Health Education, Raising the Issues*, Routledge & Kegan Paul Ltd
Bob Holman, *Putting Families First*, Macmillan Publishers Ltd
Nick Davidson and Peter Townsend (ed), 'The Black Report', *Inequalities in Health*, Penguin Books
Margaret Whitehead (ed.), 'The Health Divide', *Inequalities in Health*, Penguin Books
Peter Malpass (ed.), *The Housing Crisis*, Croom Helm Ltd
Lee Loveridge, *The Manufacture of Disadvantage*, Open University
Gill Gorell Barnes, *Working with Families*, Macmillan Publishers Ltd

19   Accidents and First Aid

PREVENTION

Accidents in the home or on the streets are among the commonest causes of death in young children under seven years of age. Every year out of every 100 000 children approximately ten will die as a result of an accident in their homes, seven will die because of road accidents and about 6000 children will require hospital treatment following an accident of some kind. Many, if not all, of these accidents could be prevented with forethought, and much physical and mental misery could be avoided.

Children in the birth to four years age group are most prone to home accidents, and there are several reasons for this:

- Children under four years lack experience and knowledge of what is dangerous and do not always understand verbal warnings.
- Children of this age are natural explorers – impelled by their own curiosity.
- Children put things in their mouths because this is how they explore and feel things.
- Children have a poor sense of taste.
- Children are vulnerable to adults' carelessness.
- Children copy adults' actions.
- Many adults under-estimate a child's reach and ability.

All adults in charge of children should examine the furniture and fittings in a child's surroundings and use their imaginations – and their knowledge of a child's ability – to detect potential hazards. Those hazards should then be tackled in some way. It is better to make the environment as safe as possible than to rely on saying 'No' or 'Don't touch'. Over-protection and constant warnings often cause children to become over-timid and unable to fend for themselves. As in all aspects of child-rearing, emphasis on the *positive* is always better than the negative.

Adults should themselves act safely at all times, especially when in charge of children, remembering that children will imitate their actions. For example, when crossing the road you should always use the proper crossing place, even if it means extra walking. Taking a chance and dashing across a road may be safe for an adult who can judge the speed of traffic, but could be fatal to a child who copies that action.

Good housekeeping and general tidiness will help to reduce accidents, and children should be taught to put away their toys and clothes. This habit is learned primarily by good example.

When buying furniture, equipment and toys think about safety and look for potential hazards. If possible buy articles which comply with the British Standards Institute specifications, a copy of which is usually available in public libraries. Manufacturers who comply with these standards may mark their goods 'BS' followed by a specific number and either a Kitemark or a Safety Mark. These articles include cots, carrycots, cot mattresses and pillows, baby walkers, prams, pushchairs, fireguards, highchairs and toys etc.

Children under seven should *never* be left alone in a house, not even for a minute when they are apparently safely asleep. There are many grieving parents who know, too late, how necessary this rule is. All dangers are multiplied many times when adults are absent.

We cannot discuss all eventualities here, but the following are some of the commonest accidents which happen to children (and in many cases cause their deaths) and routine preventive measures.

Cause	*Prevention*
Choking	
Baby left in pram or cot with bottle.	Babies should always be nursed when drinking from a bottle.
Baby vomits and inhales vomit.	Put baby on tummy or side to sleep, so that if he vomits he cannot inhale. Bring up baby's 'wind' before putting him down to sleep.
Child chokes on large piece of food.	Cut food into small pieces. Encourage child to chew properly. Never leave him alone when eating. Always make child sit down when eating – don't let him walk around.
Child inhales peanut.	Do not give young children peanuts.
Small beads or toys in baby's mouth.	Do not give very small toys. Check eyes, etc. on fluffy toys. Buy toys with BS safety mark. Pick up beads etc. from the floor.
Strangulation	
Tapes or string ties from equipment such as cot bumpers get tied around baby's neck.	Ensure that tapes are short; fasten firmly.
Suffocation	
Plastic bib flaps up over face – forms seal.	Do not use thin plastic bibs.
Plastic bag placed over head.	Destroy plastic bags when finished with. Never leave within reach of children.
Baby buries head in soft pillow.	Pillows are not necessary for a baby. Use 'safety' pillow made of foam rubber for older child.
Cat gets into baby's cot or pram – smothers baby.	Use a cat net. Discourage cats from getting on beds or entering bedrooms.
Child gets in refrigerator and closes door which cannot be opened from inside.	Remove doors from old refrigerators. Ensure refrigerator has magnetic catches on door which will open from inside.
Burns	
House on fire.	Never leave child alone in house.
Child plays with matches.	Keep matches away from children.
Portable heater tipped over.	Use fixed heater and fixed guard.
Clothes airing near fire ignite.	Do not leave clothes to air too close to fire; supervise it.
Cigarettes left burning.	Make sure cigarettes are out before discarding.
Child's clothes are set alight when he leans over fire.	Use a fixed guard on all fires. Use non-flammable materials for clothing. Do not put mirrors or children's possessions on mantelpiece.
Child plays with bonfire.	Never leave a bonfire unsupervised.
Child plays with live electric plug.	Disconnect plugs from kettles and irons, etc. when not in use. Use short and/or coiled flex.
Iron pulled from ironing board.	Never leave iron, ironing board in position if child alone in room.

Cause	Prevention

Scalds

Cause	Prevention
Hanging tablecloth pulled by child – hot tea pours on head.	Avoid use of tablecloth.
Child pulls saucepan handle – contents tip on child.	Use a guard for the cooker. Turn saucepan handles inward so that they do not overhang.
Adult drinks hot tea whilst nursing baby. Tea tips on child.	Always put baby down when drinking something hot.
Child climbs in bath containing very hot water.	Always put cold water in bath first.
Child burnt or scalded by hot water bottle.	Do not use boiling water. Use a cover on bottle. Check rubber bottles before each use for wear and tear.

Falls

Cause	Prevention
Baby left on bed, settee or table – falls off.	If you have to leave the baby for a moment, put him on the floor.
Baby falls in sit-in baby walker.	Always supervise baby. Do not use a walker upstairs.
Child falls from pram or cot.	Use safety harness in pram. Put child in a bed once he starts climbing rails of cot.
Child falls from top bunk bed.	Use a guard. Children under five should not sleep in top bunks.
Toddler falls from highchair or supermarket trolley.	Use a harness.
Toddler climbs and falls.	Give child somewhere safe to practise climbing under supervision, e.g. firmly-fixed low climbing frame with rubber mat or grass underneath. Teach child how to come downstairs backwards. Use a stair gate. Put ladders away when finished using. Make sure clothing and shoes are safe for climbing.
Child falls out of window.	Safety catches on all windows, or window guards. Do not put furniture under windows where child can climb.

Child falls or trips over:
    discarded toys;
    untied shoelaces;
    dressing-up clothes;
    loose carpet;
    rugs on slippery floors.
	Keep home tidy.
	Check shoelaces.
	Cut dressing-up clothes short.
	Fasten carpets securely.
	Do not polish under rugs.
	Ensure shoes are non-slip.

Drowning

Cause	Prevention
Falls in bath.	Never leave child alone in bath. Use non-slip mat in bath.
Falls in goldfish pond, swimming pool, paddling-pool, water butt.	Make sure these are guarded. Always supervise water play.

Cause	Prevention
Poisoning	
Child takes tablets prescribed for adult.	Keep tablets and medicines locked up. Take unused drugs back to chemist. Do not take tablets in front of children – they may think these are sweets and try to get one. Use child-resistant containers. Keep these things in cupboards with child-resistant locks.
Child drinks bleach, disinfectant, detergent or weedkiller.	Never put other liquids in lemonade bottles.
Child drinks alcohol.	Keep bottles locked up. Never leave glasses with dregs within reach of children.
Child sucks painted surface containing toxic substances.	Use lead-free paint on all surfaces.
Child eats berries or leaves from poisonous plants.	Remove these hazards from garden. Watch child when out on walks. Warn child.
Electric shock	
Child pokes something in plug.	Use safety dummy plugs and sockets with shuttered holes.
Bleeding	
Child plays with scissors, knives, pins, needles, razor blades, etc.	Keep all these away from children.
Toddler walking with drink in glass trips and breaks glass.	Make children sit down to drink. Use plastic cups.
Toddler falls against patio doors.	Use 'safety' glass or plastic safety film on the glass.
Other accidents	
Child gets out of house/garden and runs into road.	Use child-proof locks on doors and gates. Always supervise outdoor play.

Road safety

A great many children are killed or injured on quiet roads within a few hundred yards of home. So all roads must be considered dangerous to children under the age of seven years, and they should always be accompanied by an adult when away from their own home. The skills needed to cross a road must be acquired and practised. They do not come naturally. We all know from our work with children that their ability to concentrate is limited and they are easily distracted. They have no experience to fall back on when trying to judge speed and distance accurately. Words such as 'mind where you are going' and 'look out' mean nothing to a small child. In addition, their view of the road is limited by their size. They do not have the advantages of an adult, who can see over parked cars and can also be seen by drivers.

Training for road safety must be approached like any other learning process:

Protection from danger – keep doors and garden gates secure. Do not allow a child to play in the road.

Carers should always set a good example when crossing the road with a child

Hold his hand, or (preferably) use harness and reins when walking out. Use reflective bands on clothing and on pram wheels.

Talk to him about the road when you are out, pointing out features so that he becomes familiar with the language of road safety.

Show by example – always cross the road correctly and tell the child why you are doing this.

Repetition – teach the child the Green Cross Code as follows:
a) Find a safe place to cross, then stop.
b) Stand on the pavement near the kerb.
c) Look all round for traffic and listen.
d) If traffic is coming, let it pass. Look all round again.
e) When there is no traffic near, walk straight across the road.
f) Keep looking and listening for traffic while you cross. Repeat and use the code every time.

Gradual independence – let the child tell you and show you the Green Cross Code. Let him cross alone whilst you watch. Show him safe places to cross, with the lollipop lady, zebra or pelican crossings, subways, etc.

It is a good idea for children of three and over to join the Tufty Club organised by the Royal Society for the Prevention of Accidents. Details can be obtained from the Road Safety Officer employed by your local authority. The Road Safety Officer will also come and talk to groups of children and/or parents about road safety and provide many colourful posters.

See also: Safety in the car, page 239.

Fire

When fire occurs it can cause panic amongst adults as well as children, therefore it is best to be prepared in advance. Most institutions have an established fire drill and practices are carried out at random intervals to test procedures. You should know what is expected of you and proceed in a calm manner so that the children will follow your example. If you are in a private home, make sure you know all the exits and try to plan ahead what to do in the event of fire. It is a sensible precaution to keep a coil of rope in an upstairs room as a last means of escape.

Your first duty is to get your children out of the building to a place of safety quickly, however small the fire. Do not delay – it is not your job to fight the fire. But you should raise the alarm and close doors and windows as you go out, because air circulation helps to fan the flames. Remember that smoke and fumes can be as lethal as actual flames.

Should you be trapped in a room, close all doors and stand by a window so that you can be seen from outside and wait for help. Usually the fire brigade will be there within minutes of an alarm, so do not throw children out or jump unless the fire is overwhelming you.

Kidnapping and assault

It is a sad reflection on modern life to have to teach children to be wary of adults, but children *are* at risk of being taken from their parents or guardians. Apart from one parent snatching a child from the other in custody cases, there are complete strangers who snatch and ill-treat children. Children must be taught never to go with strangers and to say no if they do not want to be touched. School and nursery staff should know parents of children by sight and not allow a child to be taken from the premises by an unknown person. They should beware of strangers loitering around the school. Children under the age of seven should not be allowed to play outside unsupervised.

FIRST AID

All accidents, however trivial, are accompanied by some degree of shock, and most children are very frightened when they are hurt. Fear increases shock,

so it is important that the adult in charge should keep calm and appear to be in control, even if she is quaking underneath. A hurt, frightened child needs comfort and support and this is also the treatment for shock.

Sit or lie the patient down, hold his hand or cuddle him and tell him it is going to be all right. This must be the *first* action, whatever the injury and fortunately most parents and nursery nurses do this instinctively. It is no use expecting a small child to report accurately on what happened, as he will not be able to tell you properly. Use your own observation and make a quick examination whilst you are comforting him. Is he pale or flushed? Is he bleeding? Is one of his limbs at an unnatural angle?

Potentially fatal conditions

The main purpose of a first-aider is to save life, so it follows that any condition threatening life must be dealt with first. There are four main causes of death following an injury:
1. shock – treat with comfort, reassurance and rest;
2. bleeding – treat by raising the affected part and by putting pressure on the bleeding point;
3. asphyxia – treat by using mouth-to-mouth resuscitation;
4. heart stops – treat by giving heart massage (this applies *only* to a trained first-aider).

In nurseries and schools there should always be someone available who is trained in first aid, because if a child needs mouth-to-mouth resuscitation or heart massage it must be started within four minutes to be effective. All these conditions need medical aid urgently, so send for an ambulance immediately – don't waste time.

Other conditions

The other purposes of first aid are to prevent the injury becoming worse and to aid recovery. Often the best way is to do nothing apart from treating shock and sending for an ambulance. Too much interference can sometimes make the injury worse.

Unconsciousness (for any reason). If the child does not respond to his name, he is unconscious. Extend head by raising back of neck.

1. Check whether he is breathing – put your ear to his mouth and listen.

If he is breathing:

2. Turn him almost on to his tummy with his head on one side. This is known as the recovery position and it prevents his airway being blocked, either by his tongue falling to the back of his mouth or by the child's own saliva or vomit collecting in the back of his throat. Stay with him to support him and keep him in this position. Talk to him gently, because he may be able to hear you. (Hearing is the last sense to be lost in unconsciousness.)
3. Send for medical aid.

If he is not breathing:

2. Start mouth-to-mouth resuscitation.
3. Send for medical aid.

A blow on the head.

1. Comfort child.
2. Cold compress (cottonwool squeezed in very cold water) can be put over injured part.
3. Allow child to rest but watch his condition.
4. Inform parents.
5. Medical aid is needed if any of the following conditions is present:
   i)   any unconsciousness, even if only momentary;
   ii) vomiting;
   iii) confusion.

Fainting. Put child in the recovery position and observe as with any unconscious person.

Cuts and wounds. Large gaping cuts or wounds which bleed a lot will need hospital treatment.

1. Stop bleeding:
   i) Raise the injured part.
   ii) Place a pad over the wound and apply firm pressure. If the wound is gaping, press edges together before applying pad. The only exception to this is a head wound where you suspect that there may be a fracture under the wound. In this case press edges of wound together only.

2. Apply a dry, sterile pad and bandage firmly – if blood comes through this dressing, add another pad and bandage.
3. If a foreign body is present in the wound, leave it alone unless it is easily removed. It is rare for a wound to bleed heavily if a foreign body is present, because it acts as a plug. In this case leave it alone and cover loosely with a sterile dressing.
4. Get medical aid.

Small cuts and wounds, grazes and scratches which do not require medical attention should be treated in the following way:

1. Wash well with soap and water.
2. Dry and leave exposed to the air.
3. It may be necessary to apply a dressing for psychological reasons, but this should only be temporary and should allow air to circulate. Wounds heal much better when exposed to air. If the child is playing in a sandpit or mud, etc., then a temporary dressing may be needed to protect the wound from contamination.

Antiseptics and antiseptic cream should *never* be used in first aid work. This is in accordance with modern views and practice.

Cat and dog bites. Treat as any small cut or wound. Refer to medical aid.

Insect stings.

1. Remove sting if present.
2. Treat as any small cut or wound.
3. Medical aid is needed if sting is in the neck or face area, or if there is excessive swelling.

NB: When treating any break in the skin, the first-aider should enquire whether the patient is protected against tetanus. If he is not, then the patient or his parents should be advised to seek medical aid. Most children under five will have protection, because it is included in the routine immunisations. If the older child had a 'booster' immunisation before entering school, then he also is protected.

Nose bleed.

1. Sit child down with head slightly forward.
2. If child will co-operate, make him blow his nose in order to remove clots and mucus.

3. Pinch the nose just below the bony prominence for three minutes (by the clock). This should control the bleeding.
4. Sponge the child's hands and face and remove bloodstained clothing as quickly as possible.
5. Encourage child to sit quietly and try to avoid blowing his nose for the next hour.

Bruises.   These are due to bleeding under the skin and this is controlled by the increasing pressure of the skin, so that no first aid is necessary. However, a cold compress can be applied and the injured part elevated. If bruising is extensive, suspect further injury underneath and get medical aid.

Squashed fingers.   Treat as for bruising.

Fractures, dislocations and sprains.   Usually these are preceded by a fall, blow or twist. There is immediate pain and there may be swelling. Movement will be painful and difficult. No first-aider is qualified to differentiate between a sprain and a fracture so all these injuries should be treated as a fracture.
1. Keep patient still.
2. Call an ambulance.

Burns and scalds.
1. Reduce heat immediately by immersing the affected part in slowly-running cold water for ten minutes – do not remove clothing or burst blisters.
2. Cover with a sterile cloth and bandage.
3. Medical aid will be necessary if blisters or a reddened area larger than a 10p piece are present.

Poisoning.
1. If patient is unconscious and breathing – place in the recovery position.
2. If patient is conscious – give nothing to drink unless poison is corrosive, when sips of milk or water can be given. DO NOT MAKE CHILD VOMIT.
3. Get medical aid immediately.
4. Save any tablets, liquids, containers and vomit so that the poison can be identified.

Foreign bodies.
a) lodged in eye:
   i) sand or dust – can be lifted from white of eye with a piece of moistened cottonwool;
   ii) if embedded – apply sterile eye pad and get medical aid;
   iii) if corrosive – wash continuously with water until medical aid arrives.
b) lodged in ear or nose: do not attempt to remove foreign body. Get medical aid.
c) lodged in throat: hold child head downwards and slap sharply between shoulder blades, or try to hook foreign body out with fingers. Mouth-to-mouth resuscitation is necessary if breathing stops.
d) splinters – remove with sterilised needle; treat as any wound.

Mouth-to-mouth resuscitation

All adults in charge of children should learn how to perform mouth-to-mouth resuscitation by practising on a dummy. The method used is as follows:
1. Tip the child's head right back by placing one hand under the back of the neck and the other on the forehead. This will give a clear airway and may be all he needs to enable him to start breathing. Check before proceeding.
2. Keeping your hand under the neck to maintain position, pinch the nostrils with the other hand.
3. Take a breath in and then, covering the child's mouth with your own to make a seal, breathe into the child. Watch the child's chest rise.
4. Remove the mouth and take another breath.
5. Repeat this action about twenty times a minute.
6. If the chest does not rise, the airway must be blocked, so check for any obstruction before continuing.

First aid box

The Health and Safety (First Aid) Regulations 1981 provide guidance on the provision of first aid boxes as follows:
1. Boxes or other containers should be clearly marked with a white cross on a green background.

2. They should contain only the following items:
    a) card giving general first aid guidance;
    b) individually wrapped, sterile adhesive dressings;
    c) sterile eye pads with attachment;
    d) triangular bandages;
    e) safety pins;
    f) a selection of individual sterile medicated wound dressings, to include standard dressings Nos. 8, 9, 13 and 14 BPC and ambulance dressings Nos. 1 and 3 BPC (amounts according to number of employees).
3. Soap and water and disposable drying material should be available. If not, sterile water in 300 ml containers.

Useful additions which can be kept near the official box are:
crêpe bandage; tweezers; needle in a cork; pad and pencil; large piece of clean linen; scissors; first aid book.

Keeping a record

Always remember to make a note of all the details of the injury and treatment given as soon as possible, because it is so easy to forget details. Be sure to date and time your note, as you may be asked about the incident at any time in the future. In nurseries and schools there will be an official accident book for this purpose so make sure you know where it is kept. Always report accidents to the head of the school or nursery. Parents should also be informed, and if the child needs to go to hospital try to get one of the parents to accompany him, not only because it comforts the child, but also because the hospital authorities may need to know the child's medical background and obtain consent for the child's treatment. In an emergency this may not be possible and in this case the head of the nursery or school can act *in loco parentis* (in place of the parent). She should know who the child's general practitioner is so that he can be contacted if necessary.

If a child arrives at nursery or school with an injury such as bruising, do remember the possibility of child abuse. If possible, detain the mother and ask for an explanation. Do this in a discreet and tactful way, because children do have accidents and parents feel very guilty, even if it is not their fault. Any suspicions should be reported to the head of the school or nursery, out of the child's hearing. Arrangements are then made for a complete medical examination to check for other injuries.

EXERCISES

Investigation
What does the first aid box in your practical placement contain? Where is the accident book kept? Talk to the person in charge about the frequency and nature of accidents.

Observation
If the situation arises, observe a qualified member of staff at placement administering first aid to a child.

In your evaluation, suggest what you consider to be the most important aspect of her care.

Project
Plan a health education project for school age (five to seven) children on the subject of road safety.

State what you hope to achieve, how the children will participate, and how your project might have longer-term effects.

Here are a few ideas to get you started:
crossing the road safely,
the role of the lollipop man/woman,
different types of traffic.

SUGGESTIONS FOR FURTHER READING

British Red Cross Society, *Practical First Aid*
Robin Lenett and Bob Crane, *It's OK to Say No*, Thorsons Publishers Ltd
Sherryll Kerns Kraizer, *The Safe Child Book*, Futura Publications

20 Travelling with Children

We believe that children today should grow up as part of the family, and part of the world in which they are going to live. However, the broadening influence of travel is more to the benefit of older children and adults; young children prefer the continuity and comfort of home and, for the under-sevens generally, as far as holidays are concerned, they will be happier on a local beach than in Majorca. However, parents' needs must be considered too, and often desperation for sunshine or a complete change is felt by the mother or father and must take precedence over small children's requirements. The child need not suffer. In fact he may have a wonderful time, and the whole family benefits.

Apart from holidays, there will be other circumstances when children have to travel – for instance to accompany a father who is in the armed forces or doing other work abroad.

All travel with children needs to be planned in advance. The longer and more ambitious the journey is, the more thought and preparation will be involved.

Modes of travel will depend on time available, finance, preference of adults, and circumstances. It

may happen – for instance, in an emergency or after a sudden change of plan – that a journey must be undertaken at quite short notice. This makes it doubly important for a nursery nurse who intends to become a nanny to know what preparations are advisable before setting out, and the difficulties that could arise. 'Nanny' is often put in sole charge of a child or two; she may even be taken on expressly to look after them while travelling.

We shall deal with specific types of travel and the needs of the different age groups in this chapter. Some general advice applies in every case, however. Try to arrange the journey so that there is the least possible disturbance to the child's routine, and, if possible, so that he has some familiar things around him during the journey, and when he arrives. Try to adopt a calm and confident attitude towards the event yourself. Tension, flustered or fussy behaviour on your part will be sensed by the child and make the journey miserable for both of you. Plan to be self-sufficient; you *may* receive offers of help, but do not count on it!

If you are going abroad, you will need to obtain information from your doctor or travel agent about health matters such as immunisation, vaccination and standards of hygiene at your destination. Any immunisation should be carried out some time before the journey. You will need to know whether the milk and water will be safe to drink and whether the baby's milk will be obtainable.

It may be necessary to take stocks of dried milk and a means of purifying water to make up the milk, as well as sterilising equipment for the baby's feeds. Water sterilising tablets can be purchased in any good chemist or alternatively some means of boiling water, such as a picnic stove will serve the purpose. If the child is on solid food, you need to know if the local food will be suitable; if not, you may have to take stocks of tinned food. The position will be rather different if the purpose of the journey is to take up long-term residence, in which case the baby will gradually have to get accustomed to local food. Whether suitable food and drink is available will also depend on whether the place where you will be staying is to be a hotel or private home.

For some destinations, where medical and hygiene standards are suspect, it is wise to take a kit containing sterilised syringes and needles, and suturing equipment as a safeguard against contracting AIDS from contaminated needles. Such a kit can be obtained from the London School of Hygiene and Tropical Medicine, as well as advice about the various immunisations recommended for different countries.

Medical insurance is essential, especially when travelling outside Europe, because children are likely to be ill and the cost of medical care is expensive. Some countries, such as New Zealand, have reciprocal rights to health care. In Europe, it is necessary to produce form E111 to obtain state-assisted medical aid. This form can be obtained from your local DSS office before you leave the country.

TRAVELLING WITH A YOUNG BABY (UP TO TEN MONTHS)

With a small baby, travelling is fairly simple and straightforward. The only real burden – literally! – is the amount of luggage required, which is out of all proportion to the size of the infant.

As well as minimum disturbance to routine, minimum handling will also benefit the baby. A pram which can be divided into a carrycot and wheels is invaluable here, as the baby can 'stay put' whenever and however he is being moved about.

When planning for his needs, bear in mind that unexpected delays are possible. His food should stay the same, and no changes should be made as the journey draws near. Bottles can either be made up as wanted, or made in advance and refrigerated before being packed in an insulated bag to keep cold. If the baby is being weaned, however, he should become used to tins or jars of baby food *before* the journey. Most babies will accept these foods at room temperature, but the jar can be stood in hot water if preferred. It is safest to feed straight from the jar or tin, and throw away any uneaten remains.

List of baby's requirements
either:
several sterilised bottles with teat and screw-on cap
vacuum flask of hot boiled water
milk powder and scoop

or
sterilised bottles containing teat and feed made cold in insulated bag
vacuum flask of hot water (for heating bottle to correct temperature when ready)
container to stand bottle in

also
rusks for older baby
bottle containing cool boiled water
jars or tins of food, tin opener, plastic spoon
bag containing baby's toilet requisites (excellent plastic 'duffle' bags, with space for talc, etc., and a separate zipped pocket for soiled nappies, can be bought in baby shops)
disposable nappies
plastic pants, if needed
spare set of clothing, including jumper or cardigan
2 damp flannels or 'wet wipes'
tissues
familiar toy

clothing should be in several thin layers so that it can easily be adjusted according to temperature.

Emergency sterilising of a bottle can be carried out by cleaning it and then filling it to overflowing with boiling water – obtainable in cafés and restaurants where tea-making urns are used.

Requirements for stay at destination.   These will be dictated by your knowledge of the situation, but you will certainly need sterilising equipment. You will need to find out whether the cows who supply the local milk are tuberculin tested, and whether the milk has been pasteurised. If the quality of the local milk is suspect you should use powdered milk instead. As a general rule, boil all water and milk before use for the under two year old.

Useful additions, depending on destination and climate:

sun hat
insect repellant
insect net for cot or pram
rehydration sachets in case of diarrhoea
sun-tan lotion suitable for a baby.

TRAVELLING WITH A CHILD (FROM TEN MONTHS TO TWO YEARS)

This can be the most difficult age, because toddlers dislike change. If they become tired or miserable, they regress in behaviour and need to be treated like babies. When wide awake and in good spirits they want to be active, independent, noisy and self-assertive.

More than ever, the principle of trying to stay within their routine is important. If the child is used to a nap in the morning, afternoon or both, then means must be found for this. A combined pram and carrycot will still be useful at this stage; although a pushchair is easier to manoeuvre, a pram is a comfortable and familiar place for the child to sleep, and at other times, is useful for holding luggage.

Meals should be light and plain – the sort of food he normally has at home. No extra sweets or snacks should be given, but a drink of cool water or unsweetened fruit juice and an apple, might be a good idea from time to time.

If the child is using a potty, then his own familiar one should be taken along. Familiar toys are just as important.

Requirements
bottles as for baby, if child still has bottle feeds
toilet articles as for baby
several spare pairs of pants
spare jumper
potty
familiar toys
plastic sheet or tablecloth (useful for beds and
    underneath feeding chairs)
apples
drinking water and/or fresh fruit juice
harness with reins.

Requirements for use at destination:
insect repellant
rehydration sachets in case of diarrhoea
sun hat
sun-tan lotion
calamine lotion in case of sunburn.

TRAVELLING WITH AN OLDER CHILD (UP TO SEVEN YEARS)

At this age, the child can understand a little of what is in store, if you talk with him beforehand about the journey and look at suitable children's books about travel. A child of six or seven may well enjoy looking at a simple map or travel brochures.

If possible, the journey should be broken up by stops for stretching legs, going to the toilet and perhaps having picnics, etc. If this is not possible, or even in between stops, the child will need a good deal of amusing if he is not to become restless or bored. Give him his own bag or case containing favourite toys, books and drawing materials. Perhaps a comic or two may be bought specially for this journey, adding to the sense of occasion. The adult in charge should be careful to space out any little treats of this kind to break the tedium.

A damp flannel or 'wet wipes', and spare jumper and pants are still a wise precaution. A harness and reins are still useful for the under four-year-olds.

At this age the child will enjoy chatting to an interested adult and commenting on all his new and exciting experiences. There are also many simple games which two can play, while just sitting quietly – for instance, 'I spy' and an easy version of 'twenty questions'. If you can see the scenery from the window you can soon think up more 'spotting' games.

Backward facing car seat for babies

METHODS OF TRANSPORT

A car journey is probably the commonest and least stressful way to travel with children, because most children are used to car travel. Luggage is easier to manage, timing can be arranged to suit the travellers (during the night can be quite convenient) and you are not dependent on outside factors, except traffic and weather conditions.

A *baby* can stay in a carrycot on the back seat, anchored by a safety strap, or sit in a backward facing chair especially designed to be fastened by the seatbelt on the front passenger seat.

A *toddler* should sit in his own car seat, safely strapped in the back.

Older children should always sit in the back restrained by safety straps. A booster cushion can be used to elevate the child so that he can see out of the window, and to make an adult seat belt safe for him to use. If there is more than one child, an adult should sit with them (probably between, to prevent squabbling) and organise a few games. You will not have to worry about annoying strangers, so singing games are ideal, with your own adaptations, if you like.

Cassettes can also be used to entertain children – often a favourite story will prove very popular, or familiar songs which the children can sing. However, children must understand that squealing and horseplay are not allowed, as they can distract the driver and be dangerous. Keeping several children happy on a long journey can be quite demanding. For this reason there should always be in addition to the driver another adult looking after the children. If the two can take turns with the driving, so much the better. The journey should be broken up into spells of approximately two hours, but stopping places will need to be carefully chosen for safety. Adequate ventilation will make conditions more pleasant, and children's car locks should, of course, be present on the doors.

Useful things to take include some plain biscuits, boiled sweets, and cold non-fizzy drinks. If any of the children have a tendency to travel sickness, consult the doctor in advance to obtain a suitable anti-sickness pill or medicine.

Travelling by train can be a novelty and quite exciting to a small child. It is better to book in advance to avoid last-minute panics, and also to travel mid-week and avoid the rush hours. If the journey is very long, overnight travel may be a good idea and sleepers can be booked. The corridor allows people to stretch their legs and visit the toilet and will help to break the monotony. A meal or snack on the train can also be exciting for a toddler or older child, and is probably easier than taking a packed meal.

Travelling by coach.   There will be little chance to get at your luggage, or to move around or go to the toilet during coach journeys. There will not be much space for belongings and toys; activities, too, will be limited. But you will have a good vantage point to watch the passing scenery and there will probably be plenty to interest a young child.

Travelling by ship.   It is as well to ask in advance exactly what provision there will be for a baby or toddler, especially for meals and washing. On a long journey, a nursery kitchen is available for making up feeds, while any special food or milk can be ordered in advance if sufficient time is allowed. There will be facilities for the adult to do washing, and most probably a laundry with nappy service. This service, and buying disposable nappies on board, will, of course, involve some expense. There is usually a special early evening meal for toddlers, and stewards will act as a baby alarm so that adults can eat together later. On a large liner there will also be a crèche and trained nursery nurses, but such facilities may be crowded, depending on demand. A cot will be provided, but a pram will be useful for going on deck.

Travelling by air.   This has the advantage of getting you to your destination quickly, and many airlines are extremely helpful to adults with babies and children, provided they are informed in advance. For airline purposes, all children under two years of age are called babies, and are allowed to travel at 10 per cent of the adult fare. No seat is provided, but on request the accompanying adult(s) will be given a bulkhead seat, which allows plenty of leg room as there are no passengers in front. A 'skycot' is also provided. This is a small cot suspended from the bulkhead. The baby has no luggage allowance, but all his travel needs are free of charge, and usually this is generously interpreted. On most aircraft, at least one toilet contains a flap-down changing table for baby's use.

A baby under one year will travel happily under these conditions, but if the child is a lively, active toddler between one and two it could well be worth considering whether to pay the child's fare of 50 per cent so that he may have a seat of his own, and a normal luggage allowance and normal meals.

If you let the airline know beforehand they will probably allow an adult who is travelling with young children to board the plane first, and they will provide help to settle the children in their seats. On take-off some children may be frightened at the extra noise and strange sensation. They should be told about this before the actual flight, if they are of an age to understand. The ears tend to pop because of changing pressure. This can be eased by swallowing, or for a baby a drink of diluted fruit juice from a bottle will help. Air travel is very dehydrating, so give frequent drinks throughout the journey.

Many airports have nurseries where changing and feeding can be done conveniently and in privacy.

NURSERY AND SCHOOL VISITS

Nursery nurses working in day care and nurseries will appreciate the stimulation that comes from visits – outings undertaken for their own sake. Apart from the obvious benefits of fresh air and exercise, and a welcome break from normal routine, a visit offers valuable opportunities to broaden children's horizons. A city child, for instance, can see life on a farm; another child may perhaps travel on a train for the first time. Excellent incidental teaching can easily arise from such topics as road safety, conservation of the countryside, kindness to animals, dealing sensibly with litter, respecting property, and showing appreciation. There are bound to be many talking points which will later lead on to follow-up activities and books.

Sometimes a visit like this just happens spontaneously, inspired by a lovely day, or perhaps the arrival of an interesting ship at a nearby dock, or workmen at a local building site. At other times, a visit will be organised well in advance, needing arrangements about transport, packed meals, etc. As a general rule, the younger the children, the shorter and less ambitious should be the outing, particularly the travelling time.

In every case, the permission of the head of the establishment is required, and also, of course, the permission of the parents. Qualified staff must *always* be included, even if the outing is to be very local and low-key. Care must be taken that domestic and other arrangements at the nursery are not disturbed, and that all the staff concerned with the children are kept informed about the plans.

Adequate adult supervision must be provided – preferably not more than four children to one adult and fewer than this if the children are very young. Parents can often be invited; they will need to be reliable people who will understand what the staff hope the children will gain from the outing and co-operate with them. Accompanying babies and toddlers can be a mixed blessing, depending on the tolerance level of staff! But a mother with her hands full with a baby or buggy will not be able to give the same degree of supervision as unencumbered parents. Badges with the name of the school are a good idea, and each child must be clear about whose group he is in.

The children can be told a little of what is to happen. For example, if they are going to the zoo, a few animal songs or poems can be introduced. However, one of the benefits of an outing is the freshness and directness of impact that the experience will make on the children, so do not overdo the preparatory talk.

Where an outing involves travel, take along spare clothes, damp flannels, plastic bags, first aid kit and other 'accident' provision. If a coach is being hired, it is best to make enquiries from several firms about prices, as these can vary considerably, and cost should be kept as low as possible, so as not to embarrass any parents. It is also wise to find out about parking facilities at your destination, picnic sites, and alternative arrangements in case of wet weather. Admission charges to public places are

A visit to an urban farm

usually reduced for parties of children, and sometimes waived altogether.

During the visit, the children must be closely supervised, and number of children studying any one aspect of the place you are visiting should be kept very small. In this way there will be enough viewing space, opportunities to answer questions and take up comments, and there will be less chance of children getting over-excited. Provide for regular visits to the toilet, and a comfortable break for a meal, if you are having one. Keep a careful eye on the picnics that individual children have brought, as these can vary from a huge feast to almost nothing. For this reason, many nurseries and schools like their kitchen to provide a standardised picnic for everyone. You should, in any case, have previously discouraged the bringing of sweets and sticky foodstuffs, and also glass bottles and tumblers. Arrangements about spending money should also have been made clear in advance. If children are allowed to bring money it is wise to stipulate a small maximum sum, and allow only one fixed time for spending it. Money easily gets lost, causes jealousy, and encourages children to dart off in the direction of an ice-cream van, or disappear into a shop, causing delays to one's schedule, worry to the adults, and possibly breaking up the group.

The adults should see that periods of walking are alternated with resting and periods of concentration and listening alternated with periods of vigorous exercise. Otherwise the children will become overtired, fractious or bored.

An increasing number of places like leisure parks, museums or locomotive centres offer worksheets, or trail guides, which successfully engage the participation of children who can read and write. Some also offer other forms of active participation, e.g. dressing up facilities, or guides who are dressed up as nineteenth-century farmworkers, or Roundheads. All such approaches have done a great deal to make history come alive for children, and offer an exciting and memorable day.

If the visit is a success, and visits usually are, most children will want to talk eagerly about it to others when they return, or during the next few days. While enthusiasm lasts, this is a good time to make a display of their mementos on a related subject – for instance castles – while sometimes a group or class 'book' is made. Each child should be encouraged – but not forced – to contribute. A display of this nature frequently attracts much interest from parents and affords a valuable opportunity for friendly contacts and conversation. This is a way of showing appreciation for parents' co-operation over outings, and probably ensures it also for next time.

'TREAT' OUTINGS FROM HOME

Many families prefer outings to parties for the birthday child; usually they involve less preparation, commotion, and clearing up afterwards.

There are plenty of possibilities, to suit all pockets. At the more costly end of the market, there are theatres such as 'Polka' in Wimbledon, which perform plays by both puppets and 'live' actors for children of all (clearly specified) ages. They also offer party accommodation, catering and cake production facilities. Many burger bars also offer a room 'upstairs' where children can enjoy a partified version of their fast food operation.

Less costly might be a bus or train ride (a rare experience for many children) to a picnic site, or, depending on the age of the children, a session at a nearby leisure centre, swimming pool, or 'gym tots'. Often the most successful outings are also the cheapest. Given reasonable weather, the local park has much to offer.

In all cases, success is more likely if a few common sense guidelines are followed:

- If you are a nanny in this situation, absolutely everything you do must either follow the parents' wishes, or have their agreement.
- Inform parents of other children exactly what you propose to do, including the timing, and any contribution to costs involved.
- Have a wet weather plan to fall back on, if applicable.

- Enlist enough adult help. This is absolutely essential with very young children, or if you are going somewhere requiring extra supervision, such as swimming baths.
- Choose a picnic site free from hazards, and demarcate it in some way to prevent children wandering off.
- Have a clear plan in your head about
  a) timing – it is better to end with the children still asking for more, rather than let it drag on with whining, quarrels and bad temper
  b) organisation – it is better to have too many activities planned, and not need to use them all, rather than have to ask desperately if anyone has any more ideas, when things may quickly deteriorate.
- Be decisive about, for example, ice-creams in the interval, and stick to what you decide.
- If a picnic meal is involved, it is a good idea to pack each child's meal separately, in something like a shoe box, complete with serviette, drink and plate; this has the added advantage that each child can carry his own.
- Deliver each child safely home or be back promptly for collection by carers.

'Treat' outings do not have to be limited to birthdays. Boxing Day, for example, can be a good time to get some fresh air and exercise with small children who may be irritating over-fed adults. A 'nature treasure hunt' can be laid on – children can be asked to find and collect in plastic bags: something shiny, something prickly, something that has once been alive etc. A simple meal can be offered afterwards: children over five might like to make their own open sandwiches from a selection of 'goodies' almost certainly available.

EXERCISES

Investigation
Study some air and sea travel brochures to find out what provision is offered for babies and young children. Comment on your findings. What other measures might be a good idea?

Observation
Observe a child (not accompanying you) on a bus or train during a journey of not less than fifteen minutes. What attracts the child's interest?

In your evaluation, suggest how enjoyable or otherwise the journey was for this child. Could anything have been managed differently to heighten the enjoyment/value of the experience?

Project
Plan a day's outing to the seaside with two children of five and seven. List:
destination and reasons for choice,
preparation,
organisation/activities,
use of public facilities,
eating arrangements,
how you hope the children will benefit.

SUGGESTIONS FOR FURTHER READING

Richard Dawood, *Travellers Health, How to Stay Healthy Abroad*, Oxford University Press
Susan Grossman, *Have Kids, Will Travel*, Croom Helm Ltd
Baby Travel, St Johns Wood Press

Leaflets:
Protect Your Child in the Car, (HMSO)
Before You Go, (DSS)
While You're Away, (DSS)

USEFUL ADDRESS

London School of Hygiene and Tropical Medicine, Keppel Street, London WC1 E7BR.

21 The Government and the Welfare State

Britain is a parliamentary democracy, which broadly means that all adults have a voice in government, either directly or through their elected representatives. Therefore it is very necessary for everyone to understand how the parliamentary system works.

Although the Queen, as monarch, is the constitutional Head of State, her powers are limited and the actual business of policy-making and government is carried out by the House of Commons and the House of Lords. Political power is held largely by the House of Commons although the House of Lords – whose members include hereditary peers, bishops, the law lords and various worthy people who have been made 'life peers' in recognition of their ability or their service to the country – may suggest amendments to proposed laws or even slow down their passage. In the Commons each Member of Parliament (MP) has been elected to represent the interests of the people living in his or her area (or constituency). The country is divided into more than six hundred constituencies and every person over the age of eighteen, who is on the electoral roll, is eligible to vote for a representative in a general election, held at least every five years.

Most potential MPs belong to specific political parties, though some choose to be independent. When an election is announced, each party publishes a manifesto setting out the policy it will follow if it comes to power. Leaflets are delivered to voters' homes on behalf of the various candidates, describing their particular policies and aims. Meetings are held in each constituency so that candidates may explain their party's standpoint and try to gain votes, and vigorous campaigns are run in all the media. After the general election the leader of the party with the largest number of elected members is invited by the Queen to become her Prime Minister and to form a government. The second largest party becomes the official Opposition.

Its role is to offer constructive criticism of government policy and to hold itself in readiness as a possible alternative government.

Proposals for new laws are brought before the two houses in the form of Bills. After discussion and debate they are put to the vote and, if passed by a majority in both houses, become Acts of Parliament and are entered in the statute book. Statutes are the country's written laws.

An important duty of the Prime Minister is to appoint other ministers to take charge of government departments such as the Department of Health, the Department of Social Security, the Department of the Environment, the Ministry of Agriculture, Fisheries and Food, etc. These ministers must be members either of the House of Commons or the House of Lords. Each government department is staffed by permanent civil servants whose job is to implement the various Acts of Parliament.

Central government also passes on some of its functions to local government, which makes local by-laws, provides essential services, including policing and the local courts. Local government comprises local authorities, which may be county, city, or urban district councils and consist of councillors who are elected in local polls, which are similar to national polls. The local authorities employ professional administrators and officers who organise such local services as education, social services, environmental health, housing, highways and town and country planning. To finance these operations rates are collected from local house-holders and businesses, and each local authority also receives a grant from central government. In 1990 rates were replaced by a community charge, payable by everyone aged eighteen and over.

The national income needed for the whole range of government activities, and for MPs' salaries, etc. is raised from taxes, which include direct taxation such as income tax and motor vehicle tax and indirect taxation – for example, value added tax, duties on alcoholic drinks and tobacco and customs duties.

This very simplified description of how Britain is governed serves to emphasise the following points:

1. Our right to vote gives us some small influence on our government and, as responsible citizens, we should use our votes to try to elect the best possible Parliament and local authority.
2. None of the services we get from the government is free. We all pay directly or indirectly for these services. It is true that some people pay more than others and that some people need to make greater use of the services but that is the hallmark of civilisation – the strong should help look after the weak.
3. We are governed by our consent, which means that people must respect and obey the laws in order for our parliamentary system to function.

The most far-reaching Acts of Parliament in modern times have been those which formed the foundations for the Welfare State. Although in the past, attempts were made to aid people in distress, especially poor families with young children, the Welfare State that exists in Britain today did not come into being until after the Second World War. Before the war many people felt that if a family was destitute it must be its own fault. They argued that if help was too readily available then families on very low incomes would only take advantage of it and would not try to help themselves. However, it was eventually realised that poverty could arise from events beyond a person's control. Therefore help given at the right time and in the right amount could prevent unfortunate families from sinking irrevocably into destitution, and give them the hope and the means to keep on trying.

Much of the assistance available to poor people before the war was given by charitable institutions and by kindly, well-meaning individuals, so the degree of help varied widely from area to area. But in

1942 Sir William Beveridge produced a report recommending a comprehensive national insurance system and the formation of a Health Service. In his report he described the five evils which lay in the path of a better society – want, disease, ignorance, squalor and idleness. He said that all members of a society should be free from these evils.

This concept marked the final stage of development of the social and health services started at the beginning of the century. The report was followed by several Acts of Parliament which laid the foundations of the services we enjoy today:

1944 *The Education Act* (took effect from 5 April 1945)
This provided for free education from a statutory five to fifteen years (later, sixteen) according to age, ability and aptitude, in a system of public education organised as a continuous process in three stages – primary, secondary and higher (for those who wished to go on beyond fifteen). Until this time free education had been largely elementary and from five to fourteen years only.

1945 *The Family Allowances Act*
This provided an allowance for each child in a family, other than the first child. The allowance is now called child benefit and all the children of a family are now entitled to it.

1946 *The National Health Service Act* (took effect from 5 July 1948)
This provided free medical care for all, whether they paid contributions or not. From 1951 charges were made for dental treatment, prescriptions, spectacles and some appliances, although children and some special categories of patient are exempt.

1946 *The National Insurance Act* (took effect from 5 July 1948)
This scheme paid certain financial benefits in return for fixed weekly contributions from employed persons and their employers – for example, unemployment benefit and sickness benefit.

1948 *The National Assistance Act* (took effect from 5 July 1948)
This provided financial assistance for those whose needs were not met by National Insurance or any other source. It also provided residential accommodation for the aged, infirm and homeless. These arrangements are now known as social security benefits.

1948 *The Children Act*
This Act was designed 'to make further provision for the care and welfare, up to the age of eighteen years and, in certain cases, for further periods, of boys and girls when they are without parents . . .'

Since 1950 many more Acts of Parliament have been passed which have modified and changed the provisions of the original acts, in an attempt to make good any deficiencies and to ensure that the various provisions and services continue to meet the changing needs of British society.

Today, the following services are available to everyone who lives in Britain:

1. Health. The main changes which have occurred since the 1948 Act are these:
1967 *The Family Planning Act*
This made contraceptive advice freely available to all. Previously this was (officially) confined to women with medical problems. This has since been amended so that all family planning aids are free, either from family planning clinics or the family doctor (GP).

1968 District nurses were allowed to treat people on Health Premises, thus paving the way for the health centre treatment room.

1968 *The Abortion Act*
This made the induction of abortion legal under certain conditions.

1973 *Reorganisation of the Health Service*.
Originally the Health Service was divided into Hospital Services and General Practitioner Services, each with their own management, and Community Services which were managed by the local authority. With the reorganisation all three sections were unified and came under the management of Regional Boards, which were divided into Area Health Authorities. These authorities were subdivided into districts which were in turn subdivided into units. With this organisation came the growth of health centres, which had been proposed in the 1948 Act but were slow to develop. The reason for

their growth was the new concept of a primary health care team working together to achieve the optimum health of the community they serve. A team consisted of a general practitioner (family doctor), health visitor, midwife and district nurse. It was obviously better for them to work from the same premises. Previously the general practitioner had worked independently, and there had often been an overlap with the work of other disciplines.

Regional health authorities

A second reorganisation was accomplished in 1982–3, aimed at reducing the number of administrators and making the service more efficient. The Area Health Authority tier of management was abolished, and the country was divided among regional health authorities. Each region was sub-divided into several small district health authorities. Each district consists of approximately ten smaller management units. The composition of each unit varies in different districts, but might typically comprise one hospital and a group of community workers, such as health visitors or, in some districts, all the community services may be in one unit.

General practitioner (GP)

Everyone can register with a general practitioner and receive free medical treatment, except where prescription charges are applicable. GPs must produce a prospectus of services provided. They must also offer medicals and preventive services.

Primary health team

In most areas the GP is part of a primary health team usually working from a health centre and providing many services:
a) health visitors – who visit all families, especially those with children under five years of age, to advise on health matters including the prevention of illness
b) midwives – who care for mothers before, during and after the birth of their babies; community midwives are mostly concerned with antenatal clinics and classes and also visit mothers and babies at home after discharge from hospital until the baby is ten to fourteen days old
c) home nurses – who care for sick people in their own homes at the request of hospitals and general practitioners
d) child health clinics
e) immunisation clinics
f) antenatal and postnatal clinics
g) antenatal classes for parents
h) family planning clinics
i) a treatment room staffed by qualified nurses
j) well person clinic.

Other optional services could include physiotherapy, speech therapy, dental services, hearing assessments, social workers, abortion counselling service, infertility clinics, etc., although many of these are also available in the local hospital.

Free drugs and medicine on prescription from a doctor

These are provided for:
a) children under sixteen years of age
b) children under nineteen years of age, in full-time education
c) pregnant women
d) mothers of children under one year of age
e) people suffering from certain medical conditions
f) women over sixty years of age
g) men over sixty-five years of age
h) people receiving war or Ministry of Defence disablement pensions who need prescriptions for their disability
i) people on either income support or family credit
j) people on very low incomes.

All other people pay a flat charge for prescriptions. If a person needs prescriptions often but is not eligible for free prescriptions, it is possible to buy a pre-payment certificate to cover four or twelve months' prescriptions for a reduced price.

Dental care

Everyone can register with a dentist and have their teeth inspected and treated regularly.
This is free for:
a) children under eighteen years of age (except dentures and bridges if the child is working)
b) children up to nineteen years of age, in full-time education
c) pregnant women

d) mothers of children under one year of age. Charges are reduced for people on income support or family credit and those on very low incomes.

Other people pay a reduced cost up to a fixed` maximum.

Ophthalmic services

Eye tests and prescriptions for glasses are provided at a reduced cost. NHS vouchers towards the cost of glasses are given to the following:

Full cost to

a) children under sixteen years of age

b) children under nineteen years of age, if in full-time education

c) people on either income support or family credit.

Part cost to

a) people on very low incomes

b) people who need glasses having at least one exceptionally powerful or complex lens.

Free hospital services

These include: general, children's, orthopaedic, eye, maternity, and mental hospitals; the services of consultants, registrars, housemen (doctors), nurses, physiotherapists, radiologists, occupational health therapists and medical social workers; in-patient and out-patient treatment; ambulance service and VD clinics.

Help with the cost of travel to and from hospital is given to:

a) people on income support or family credit

b) people on a war or Ministry of Defence disability pension who are being treated in an NHS hospital for their disability

c) people on very low incomes.

School health service

This provides the services of:

a) school doctor – school medical inspection

b) health visitor/school nurse – hygiene inspections, hearing and vision tests, etc.

c) dentist – dental inspections

d) audiometrician – hearing tests

e) ophthalmic services – eye test and provision of spectacles

f) nutritionist – advice on diets

g) chiropodist – foot clinics

h) speech therapist – speech clinics

i) family welfare visitors

j) family guidance service.

2. Social services. The 1948 Children Act was administered by Children's Officers from the Children's Department of the local authority. In 1970, following the Seebohm Report, the Local Authority Social Services Act required local authorities to set up a Social Services Committee and to appoint a Director of Social Services and a staff of social workers. The present Department of Social Services is an amalgamation of the existing Children's Department and departments for welfare services to the elderly, handicapped and mentally disordered. The duties required of it are:

a) provision of social workers to work with individuals and families needing help with personal problems

b) child care under the various Acts of Parliament, e.g., Children Acts, Children and Young Persons Acts, Nursery and Childminder Regulations and the Adoption Acts (see below)

c) welfare services for the elderly, the handicapped, the chronically sick and those suffering from a mental disorder

d) provision of residential accommodation for the elderly and disabled

e) provision of home helps and meals-on-wheels for people in need

f) delegation of any or all of these responsibilities to a voluntary organisation with subsequent support, for example, WRVS meals-on-wheels service run with a grant from Department of Social Services.

Under the Child Care Acts social workers:

a) supervise children in day nurseries and play-groups

b) supervise children in private foster homes

c) work with families in trouble; try to prevent a break-up leading to children being taken into 'care'; they do this by giving guidance to parents and involving other agencies and methods will vary from area to area

d) if child abuse is suspected, investigate and convene case conferences with other workers involved, such as health visitor, probation officer, police and NSPCC officers, to pool knowledge and make the best plan of action for the family

e) keep a central child protection register of children known to be at risk of abuse

f) arrange and supervise adoptions

g) take children into care when parents are unable to look after them, either temporarily or permanently

h) take children into care when subject to a court order, usually because the child needs care and protection because of an offence committed (or likely to be committed) against him or because the child himself has committed an offence

i) accommodate and maintain children in care and look after their interests; 'care' may be with friends, relatives, foster parents or in a community home or voluntary home.

3. Education.

a) nursery schools/classes
b) primary schools
c) secondary schools
d) special schools for handicapped children
e) hospital schools
f) home teachers
g) evening classes
h) colleges of further education
i) colleges of higher education
j) polytechnics
k) universities.

Staff

Teachers and lecturers; nursery nurses; ancillary helpers, school inspectors, school welfare officers.

Subsidies and grants

a) free school meals for children in families receiving income support

b) help towards school fares and school uniform for families on income support

c) uniform grants

d) fares paid for primary school children if they live more than 3.2 km (2 miles) from their school

e) fares paid for secondary and further education students if they live more than 4.8 km (3 miles) from school or college

f) grants for further and higher education

g) transport to and from school for handicapped children

h) educational maintenance allowance

i) school health service
j) student grants.

4. Finance.   In 1986 a new Social Security Act was passed in an attempt to simplify social security payments which had grown up haphazardly since the National Assistance Act in 1948. This Act took effect in April 1988 and has proved to be difficult to implement. Some people have gained from the changes in benefits but many more have lost out and it appears that the worst sufferers are the families with young children which the original Acts were designed to protect. It may be that modifications will have to be made in the future.

Social security is now known as income support and family income supplement (FIS) is now family credit.

The system is still based on three different kinds of benefit:

- x – those dependent on payment of National Insurance contributions in the past

- y – those based on assessment of present income and/or savings (means tested)

- z – those dependent on the claimant meeting certain conditions.

The benefits listed below are marked x, y or z accordingly.

Child benefit (z): a weekly amount payable to mothers for each dependant child from birth until the time of leaving school.

This is the only benefit which is universal. All others depend on a person's circumstances, as follows:

a) Poor

Family Credit (z): a weekly allowance paid to a family, one of whose parents is employed for at least twenty-four hours a week, on a very low income.

Housing benefit (y): help may be given with the payment of rent and rates to people on family credit, income support, or very low incomes.

b) Unemployed

Unemployment benefit (x): a weekly payment for

fifty-two weeks for the unemployed person, with extra payments for dependants.
or
Income support (y): a weekly payment for people who have insufficient means of support.

Housing benefit (y): help with rent and rates or 50 per cent of interest on a mortgage for the first sixteen weeks followed by 100 per cent.

Training allowance (y): paid if a person attends a training course.

Interview travel expenses: paid to cover the cost of attending an interview when looking for work.

Job start allowance: an allowance paid to enable an unemployed person to cover the cost of starting a new job and having to work for a week or a month before being paid.

c) Sick or disabled
Statutory sick pay, SSP (x): paid by the employer for up to twenty-eight weeks in a spell of sickness, after the first four days of illness.

Sickness benefit (x): if a person is unable to claim SSP then sickness benefit is paid after the first four days of illness for up to twenty-eight weeks.

Invalidity benefit (x): after twenty-eight weeks on sick pay or benefit, a person who is still ill can claim this benefit.

Severe disablement benefit (z): if a person has been incapable of work because of illness or disability for twenty-eight weeks or more he/she can claim this benefit.

War disablement pension (z): a pension for people disabled by war injuries.

Industrial injuries disablement benefit (z): this is for people who are disabled by an accident at work or an industrial disease.

Industrial injury compensation (z): an employer must pay compensation to a person injured at work.

Mobility allowance (z): if a person between the ages of five and sixty-five years is unable, or virtually unable to walk, he can claim this monthly allowance to enable him to be more mobile e.g. help towards buying a car.

Attendance allowance (z): a weekly sum for adults and children over two years of age who are severely disabled, and need to be looked after for more than six months. There are two rates, one for daytime care and the other for night-time care.

Criminal injuries compensation (z): this can be claimed by innocent people who are injured during the commitment of a crime.

d) Looking after a disabled person
Invalid care allowance (z): a weekly payment for someone who spends at least thirty-five hours a week looking after a person receiving attendance allowance.

Home responsibilities protection (z): if someone cares for a disabled person who is receiving attendance allowance they can get National Insurance contributions credited towards their retirement pension.

e) Pregnant
Statutory maternity pay, SMP (z): this is paid by an employer for eighteen weeks. Thirteen out of the eighteen weeks must start six weeks before the expected date of birth but the other five weeks may be taken either before or after this period. The following conditions must be satisfied:
a) the pregnant woman must have worked continuously for her employer for six months by the time she is six months pregnant
b) she must have earned enough to pay National Insurance for the last eight weeks of that time
c) she must carry on working until the twenty-sixth week of pregnancy.

The amount varies according to the length of time she has worked for her employer.

Maternity allowance (x): this is similar to SMP and is paid to self-employed women and those who are unemployed but have worked and paid National Insurance for at least six months of the year ending when they are six months pregnant.

Maternity payment (z): women who are receiving family credit or income support can claim this lump sum to help with the cost of providing the necessities for the baby.

f) Single parents
One parent benefit (z): an extra payment paid with child benefit to the first child only in a single parent family.

g) Widowed
Widow's payment (x): a tax-free lump sum paid to widows provided:
a) she was under sixty years of age when her husband died
b) her husband was not drawing retirement pension when he died.

Widowed mother's allowance (z): a basic allowance plus extra for each child, paid to widows who have a child or are pregnant when their husband died.

Widow's pension (z): a woman who is over forty-five years of age when her husband dies can claim this allowance.

h) Guardians
Guardian's allowance (z): if a person takes over the care of an orphan he/she can claim this allowance.

i) Retired
Retirement pension (x): men over the age of sixty-five and women over the age of sixty years who have worked and paid National Insurance contributions can claim a weekly pension. Husbands whose wives have not worked can claim extra for them as dependants. Income support, to supplement this, can be claimed providing savings do not exceed a certain level.

j) Redundant
People who are made redundant can claim a redundancy payment.

The Social Fund
This fund can be divided into two parts.

The first part provides for maternity expenses and funeral payments for people who are living on family credit or income support providing they do not have savings of more than £500.

The second part provides interest-free loans to people in urgent need, thus replacing the old system of single payments in the form of a grant. Each social security office is allowed a set amount every year to be used for this purpose. Borrowers must prove their need and repayments are deducted from their benefits over a fairly short period.

5. Housing. Local housing authorities are responsible for:
a) the provision and maintenance of council houses, to rent, for people who need homes
b) the sale of council houses to occupiers
c) the provision of accommodation for homeless families
d) encouragement and help to housing associations who provide cost-rent houses and flats, and co-operative or co-ownership housing
e) the provision of mortgages to home-buyers who cannot get loans from other sources
f) the provision of grants and loans to home-owners to improve and modernise their houses
g) rent rebate scheme for people on low incomes
h) the provision of specially adapted homes for the disabled.

6. Environmental health. Environmental health inspectors are responsible for:
a) provision of clean air, water and food
b) noise abatement
c) pest control
d) removal of rubbish and sewage
e) inspection of housing and condemning of unfit houses.

7. Other services in the community.
a) Legal services
Free legal aid   This is means-tested, so that the amount granted will depend on a person's income.

Law centres   These exist in some areas to provide free legal advice.

Guardians ad litem   Independent social workers who are appointed to represent children involved in court actions, e.g. in cases of adoption or child abuse.

Probation officers   Social workers, attached to courts, who work with criminal offenders. They also undertake reconciliation work in cases of broken marriage.

b) Public services

Free library   Provided by local authorities.

Police

Fire brigade

Citizens Advice Bureaux   A general advisory service which helps people, especially those with legal, matrimonial or housing problems.

School crossing patrols   By an Act of Parliament of 1954, a school crossing patrol can stop traffic if the patrol-person is wearing a uniform or emblem approved by the Secretary of State.

8. Voluntary services.   There are many of these and they vary from area to area. Some examples are:
Branches of the Women's Royal Voluntary Service often help families in need, by providing second-hand items of clothing, etc.

The British Red Cross Society operates a loan service of walking-aids, wheelchairs, bed-pans, and other nursing equipment.

EXERCISES

Investigation
How have state benefits etc. changed in recent years?

Discuss with tutors and fellow students the nature of these changes, and the philosophy behind them.

Observation
If possible, watch a video about the work of a voluntary organisation which exists to help families and children.

How does their approach differ from help offered by the state?

Project
Work out a weekly budget for a young family, where both parents are unemployed, who have a child of five and a baby of nine months, on the understanding that they are collecting the benefits to which they are entitled. What should be their priorities? Will they have enough money to cover these?

SUGGESTIONS FOR FURTHER READING

Winifred Huntly, *Personal & Community Health*, Baillière Tindall

Phyllis Willmott, *The Consumers' Guide to the British Social Services* (Pelican Original), Penguin Books Ltd

Brian Meredith Davies, *Community Health & Social Services*, English Universities Press Ltd

DSS leaflets from social security offices

N. J. Smith, *A Brief Guide to Social Legislation*, Methuen & Co Ltd

A. E. Leeding, *Child Care Manual for Social Workers*, Butterworth & Co Ltd

P. J. North, *People in Society*, Longman Group Ltd

Beth Lakhani, Jan Luba, Anna Ravitz, Jim Read, Penny Wood, *National Welfare Benefits Handbook*, Child Poverty Action Group

Pat Thane, *The Foundations of the Welfare State*, Longman Group Ltd

Martin Rathfeld, *How to Claim State Benefits*, Northcote House Publishers Ltd

22

Provision for the Early Years

There are really three main issues underlying the demand for provision for the under-fives:

1. It is generally accepted, following a great deal of research, that this is a crucial period in children's development, and requires input by experts if a child's full potential is to be realised.

2. Crowded urban living, isolated rural living, families of only one or two children, the breakdown of extended family systems and, frequently, of the nuclear family itself, have all resulted in the under-fives lacking safe play space, companions, and sufficient caring adults. Parents, especially single parents, can feel unsupported and unrelieved in their parenting role, to the extent that they become tense, irritable and depressed, which will affect their children.

3. Equal opportunities for women, maternity rights, the high cost of living, colossal mortgages, and the threat of redundancy or unemployment for their partners, have resulted in increasing numbers of mothers deciding to work full or part-time.

Unlike most European countries, Britain's level of provision for the early years is inadequate to meet demand. Only some 23 per cent of under-fives are in nursery school, mostly on a part-time basis. Nursery education is not a statutory branch of education, and is usually the first victim of cuts in times of national or local stringency. 20 per cent of under-fives are in reception classes of infant or first schools, which do not always have adequate play provision or quota of suitably trained adults. Approximately 40–45 per cent of under-fives attend playgroup part time. Day nurseries are for social priority cases only. Child-minders are negotiated privately.

In addition, there is an artificial boundary between what is seen as day care and what is seen as education.

For the parent who works full time and who does not have a partner or relative staying at home, either a child-minder or a nanny is the only realistic and sufficiently flexible solution. Both of these will account for a high proportion of the parent's wage packet.

The overall picture, then, is piecemeal.

By the time children are assessed in school tests at age seven, they will have experienced many different influences and opportunities in their lives thus far. Much depends on where they live. Some will have attended several different establishments on different days or at different times.

As will be seen from the following table, provision by agencies is fragmented due to different agencies controlling different branches, sometimes even on the same premises. Lack of co-ordination, and cohesion, unnecessary expense and duplication can easily give rise to friction, frustration and resentment.

It seems curious that, while in the horticultural world no-one questions the wisdom of growing seedlings in nourishing compost or pricking them out when they are ready, in the field of early childhood provision, the deliverers of the services are constantly being asked to justify and prove what they are doing and why, merely in order to be allowed to continue.

To a certain extent, pre-school workers are still tagged with a cosy image of a 'mother hen' figure, 'keeping children happy'. It is time that this image was replaced by that of clear-headed professionals, who can confidently explain what their service has to offer, and can invite society to come and see their work. Such a professional approach would help to raise the status of pre-school workers, which might lead to greater enlightenment and rationalisation by governments and authorities of what is provided.

An overview of current pre-school provision in Britain follows, in an attempt to clarify the confusing scene. In each case, we have tried to give factual information about clients and services, as well as convey the essential aims and atmosphere of each type of provision. We have also highlighted the part played by nursery nurses, and indicated career structure, where applicable. Readers will be aware

that parental involvement is an integral and essential element of every service.

Many of these establishments and roles will be familiar to nursery nurses from their practical work.

The information that follows may help readers to make decisions about where their career aspirations may lead them.

Provision for children in the early years in Britain	Authority responsible
Public sector	
Day nurseries	Social services
Family centres	department
Registered child-minders	
Sponsored child-minders	
Residential care	
Hospitals	District health
Hospital playgroups	authority
Nursery schools	Local education
Nursery classes	authority
Combined nursery centres	
Infant schools	
Special schools and units	
Private sector	
Private day nurseries	Registration, approval,
Private nursery schools	liaison, and
Crèches	consultation required
Playgroups	with local social
Opportunity groups	services department
Mother and toddler groups	
Playbuses	
Adoption	
Private nannies	
Voluntary sector	
Local community support schemes	Registered charities, e.g. Barnardos, Save
Day care	the Children, NSPCC,
Preventive work	Children's Society
Residential care	

DAY NURSERIES

Since the last war, when many day nurseries were opened to cater for the children of mothers doing war work, expansion has been confined to areas of social deprivation, such as inner cities or large housing estates.

A day nursery is staffed by an officer-in-charge (NNEB and/or RGN, CQSW, or CSS trained), two or three deputies, a senior nursery officer, and nursery officers on a ratio of one to four children. All these staff will have been NNEB trained, but there is increasing pressure for staff who seek greater responsibility to take further social work training. As the nature of day nursery work changes and evolves, initial training requirements may also be reviewed.

Several domestic staff will also be employed, as children can be offered breakfast, lunch and tea (free or at minimal cost), and of course there is a good deal of laundry and cleaning involved.

The children are divided into family groups of six to eleven children, covering the total age span, which can be a few weeks to five years old. New, purpose-built nurseries are designed to accommodate this pattern of grouping, but many nurseries are still housed in large, old private houses which lend themselves to such use, apart from the inconvenience of many stairs and attendant fire risks. A babies' and toddlers' room is sometimes included, but children under nine months are accepted only in exceptional circumstances.

Some children may stay at the nursery for several years; others remain only weeks or months during a temporary domestic crisis.

Day nurseries open from 8.00 a.m. until about 5.30 p.m., although few children are likely to stay there for the whole day. They close only for statutory holidays and a few other specified days. Some children attend part time, and there is a good deal of flexibility to meet the families' needs.

Most clients are referred by social workers, health visitors or doctors. Family breakdown, debt, serious and psychiatric illness, death, eviction, involvement with drugs or alcohol, depressive and suicidal tendencies, incidence of non-accidental injury, immaturity, poverty, handicap, sub-standard housing, imprisonment, are some of the problems experienced by parents, causing severe strain on families and small children. Each family's needs will be reviewed regularly.

A good day nursery offers excellent physical care, including medical support and developmental checks, and the services of such professionals as social workers, teachers of the deaf, speech therapists, health visitors and educational psychologists. This aspect makes it a good monitoring service of children's health and development.

A good nursery also offers stability, security and linguistic and cognitive stimulation, any of which may be noticeably missing from children's lives.

Funding by social services makes it an expensive form of care, but in the sense that it is preventative, relieving strain sufficiently to keep families together and to keep children out of residential care, it is an effective one.

With children having such disrupted backgrounds, some difficult behaviour is inevitable, which can give rise to yet another unfavourable environment for the children. However, it is the aim of staff to create an atmosphere of unconditional acceptance and affection like that offered by a good home, and many children respond positively.

Increasingly, day nursery staff are committed to working with families, of whom the majority will be mothers. Methods include parent groups, individual programmes, home visits, and acting as 'signposts' to further forms of help such as contraception or housing.

Parents are invited to six-monthly reviews of children where progress, any problems and future plans are discussed, and where parents' voices are genuinely listened to. Parents are also invited to doctor's visits.

If a child is taken into care, parents can have their access visits in a day nursery.

Parents are treated with respect, friendliness and honesty, never rejection. Sometimes the honesty can lead to anger but usually parents acknowledge that staff are working for their child's good. Some parents require a good deal of individual time and attention, and appear unaware of the demands of a roomful of children as a whole. At times like this, a good nursery officer will try to remember that the parent may be at the end of his/her tether, after a long wait and frustrating treatment at a DSS office.

Some parents will have had figures of authority such as the police or social workers 'on their back' since they were children themselves. They may have been so burdened with their own concerns that real bonding with their children has never taken place. Most will have poor self-esteem. Women may have a poor image of men if they have been abused or abandoned by them. Men may experience inner conflict if their partners work and they do not.

Day nursery staff have to be good listeners; they must try not to judge their clients' lives by their own standards. They must always be available in times of crisis. Any progress made should be given support, encouragement, and reinforcement by praise.

To work in a day nursery requires a high degree of maturity, sensitivity and resilience.

FAMILY CENTRES

A further step in carrying out social work *with* rather than *to* families, while integrating services offered to them, has developed in the form of family centres.

The first one was opened in Bath in 1970, and there are now about 300 in the UK.

They vary greatly, according to local needs and which agency funds and controls them. This is usually the social services or education department, but may be a health authority, voluntary body, or partnership of two of these.

A family centre might give a high profile to second language work, basic adult education, or closer integration between local Asian and white communities, for example. Where a family centre is funded by the local education authority and held on a school campus, there will be strong emphasis on the child's transition from one department to another, and the 'whole school' approach. Some centres have residential accommodation, and can work with teenagers towards rehabilitating a family as a unit.

An example of a successfully functioning family centre is provided in the following description of a centre in Avon.

The Centre was set up by Barnardos in response to a need identified by the social services department. Initial funding was provided by Barnardos, and by the DSS 'Under-Fives Initiative'; the latter contribution was subsequently replaced by social services' finance. The location is a 1950's housing estate on the outskirts of Bristol, and accommodation is a small three-storey building which was previously three 'hard-to-let' flats. The aim of the Centre is, 'through partnership with parents, to facilitate opportunities for growth and development for parents and under-fives, and where appropriate prevent the reception into care of young children'.

Before the Centre opened, staff undertook a detailed assessment of need by interviewing 100 families in the neighbourhood, and gaining the views of professionals working in the area. As a result, a varied programme has been devised which recognises the multiple factors which encourage or impede the development of children and their families.

There is a project leader, four full-time and three part-time project staff, and a project secretary. Parents participate in, and influence, the running of the Centre through a Parents' Council which is attended by representatives of each Centre activity.

These are the services and activities offered:

- A twice weekly 'drop in' for parents and children under five. Parents chat and drink coffee while children play under the supervision of play workers.

- Welfare rights afternoon. This includes advice on benefits, housing and financial problems. Parents are encouraged to do their own negotiations, work towards solutions and develop self confidence.
- Confidential family work. Counselling is offered on relationship difficulties, problems with children etc.
- A weekly family group day helps parents who are going through a particularly difficult time caring for their children.
- Activities groups. These vary with demand, and have included painting a mural, knitting and sewing, reading and writing, and cookery. Particularly popular were movement sessions, which helped parents and children to establish control and tenderness through positive physical contact.
- Self-help groups. Again, these evolve from local needs. They have included a group for women whose partners are in prison, groups for parents of handicapped children, and a group for single parents.
- Parents' courses. These are ten-week courses for parents to learn more about how children develop, to gain ideas about meeting their play needs, and to learn about local resources for young families.
- Outings for families, particularly in the school holidays.
- Low-priced holidays by the sea in the Centre's own caravan.
- Tenants' and community groups. These have been successful in getting action over residents' local problems, such as security measures in flats, frequently flooded areas and pavement repairs.
- A development worker who helps set up and support mother and toddler groups in nearby localities.
- A part-time high-rise resource worker who promotes groups for families with young children in high-rise flats.
- Link visitors. Parents already using the Centre encourage parents who are hesitant to attend and also follow up newcomers who have not returned to the Centre.

- Coin-operated telephone and launderette facilities are both much appreciated in an area of high vandalism.
- The premises are also used for other purposes such as meetings of groups of low-rise flat dwellers, women on probation and access visits for children and parents separated from each other.

The staff see the work of the Centre as preventative and supportive. They believe families can play a vital role in helping and supporting one another. Some Centre users may be young and/or unsupported parents who lack effective role models: support and care for them may enable and improve their parenting.

Another development along family centre lines within the same county has been the setting up of a purpose-built Pre-school Resource Centre. Again, the aim is to offer a wide range of services to families in a particular area and to make these as flexible as possible.

As well as day care, services here include a mother and toddler group, home visits, parents' groups, sessions on parenting skills and a toy and information service. An outreach group currently operates in a nearby area for children unable to reach the Resource Centre. Other developments will include support by staff to other child carers in the area, such as playgroups, child-minders and foster parents, holiday schemes for older children and wider community work. Inter-agency liaison is vital for the Centre's way of working, which is essentially one of exploring and responding to local needs.

This Centre represents the social services department's willingness to support with finance the idea of working with whole families. Yet the emphasis is very much on the child: all help offered must directly or indirectly benefit the child. Staff ask for a clear commitment from parents and expect to work with them whilst the child is attending, either on an individual basis or in a group setting.

CHILD-MINDERS

Anyone who is paid to look after an unrelated child for more than two hours a day is a child-minder, and must conform with regulations as amended in the Nurseries and Child-minders Regulations Act of 1968.

Child-minders are the most widespread source of full day care for children of working parents. There are some 60 000 registered child-minders in the UK, caring for more than 140 000 under-fives. They offer very flexible care, some offering part-time care to more than one set of children, to fit in with parents' part-time jobs. This can involve very complex and overlapping arrangements.

Because there are usually not more than three children around, including the minder's own, much one-to-one attention is possible. Children can enjoy an intimate, relaxed atmosphere. They can participate in everyday happenings such as cooking, shopping, preparing food and counting socks into a washing machine. Children are taken out to local parks and to attend mother and toddler group or playgroup.

It is important that parents visit several minders before choosing the one with a lifestyle and attitude to child care which suits them, and that there is a well-planned settling-in period for the child to have a chance to adjust. Parents and minders need to communicate fully and regularly about the child's development.

Sometimes a suitable minder will live quite near the child's home, thus avoiding a long journey, and other community links and friendships can be maintained. Provided the parent can overcome possible feelings of jealousy at the close relationship her child will form with the minder, close friendships can develop: older children can continue to go to the minder after school.

On registration, a social services officer and, in some areas, a fire officer will visit the home, and look at questions of safety and hygiene. There are rigorous checks with the police on the criminal record of all adult members of the child-minder's household. Enquiries will also be made about her own and her family's health, her previous child care experience, and to establish that this person really does like small children. Sometimes a reference from a health visitor will be obtained.

The minder will be visited from time to time, and may also participate in local facilities such as a toy library or loan of first aid kits, safety equipment and items such as a double buggy.

Working in your own home with small children is an occupation that brings little credit and low financial rewards. Often one half to two thirds of what is earned has to be spent on running costs – food, play equipment, outings, extra heating and power, laundry, wear and tear, and replacements in the home. Child-minders are often eager to go on courses, take Open University and GCSE child development courses, for which they have to pay themselves. A few areas are beginning to offer subsidised or free courses, while many child-minders' groups organise their own courses based on recognised pack materials, with input from social services workers.

Child-minders are, in general, a most committed group of people who enjoyed being parents themselves and wish to continue this role. They usually have a variety of educational and employment experience behind them. Child-minders used to have a poor image in the eyes of the public, but this is becoming increasingly unfair and untrue.

The emergence of the National Childminding Association (NCMA) has encouraged the setting up of local support groups and published information leaflets on such topics as rates of pay, holidays, sickness and absence. It also produces registers and record forms, and offers a comprehensive insurance policy to give public liability cover in the event of injury of a child. The NCMA encourages clear definition of the business side, including a proper contract (see opposite) which should be reviewed at least once a year, in order to minimise misunderstandings and enable good relationships to build up.

CONTRACT/AGREEMENT BETWEEN PARENTS AND REGISTERED CHILDMINDER

Two copies of this form should be completed and signed.
One copy to be kept by the parent(s), one copy by the
childminder.

NAME OF CHILDMINDER: _____   NAME OF CHILD: _____

ADDRESS: _____   ADDRESS: _____

_____   _____

TELEPHONE: _____   _____

REGISTERED BY: _____   TELEPHONE: _____
               Social Services Department

NAME OF PARENT RESPONSIBLE FOR PAYMENT: _____

DATE THE CHILDMINDING ARRANGEMENT IS TO START: _____

HOURS: From _____ am/pm   To _____ am/pm

DAYS: _____

MEALS TO BE PROVIDED: _____

FEES:		
Weekly	£ _____	per week
Hourly	£ _____	per hour
Daily (maximum 8 hours)	£ _____	per day
Overtime (after _____ pm)	£ _____	per hour
Unsocial hours (before 8 am or after 6 pm)	£ _____	per hour
Occasional minding	£ _____	per hour
Weekends or Statutory Public Holidays	£ _____	per hour

CHARGES FOR ABSENCE:

Due to child's or parent's sickness	£ _____
Due to childminder's sickness	£ _____
Parent(s)' occasional days off	£ _____
Parent(s)' annual holidays (_____ wks/yr)	£ _____
Childminder's annual holidays (_____ wks/yr)	£ _____
On Statutory Public Holidays	£ _____

PAY DAY: _____ in advance.

NOTICE REQUIRED OF HOLIDAYS (on both sides) _____

NOTICE REQUIRED OF TERMINATION OF THIS CONTRACT _____ WEEKS OR FULL FEE IN LIEU OF NOTICE
(this applies to both minder and parent).

PARENTS TO PROVIDE: _____

PLAYGROUP FEES TO BE PAID BY: _____

CHILDMINDER CAN TAKE CHILD ON OUTINGS: _____

ANY SPECIAL ARRANGEMENTS: _____

This agreement is subject to review every _____ months. Date of next review _____

SIGNED: _____ (parent)   Date: _____

SIGNED: _____ (childminder)   Date: _____

Please note that childminders cannot normally undertake the care of sick children.

Although it is illegal to mind children without registration or insurance, it is not illegal to use such a minder, and many parents do not realise the risks or implications.

Sponsored child-minders

These are experienced minders known by local social services personnel to have the special skills and personal qualities required to care for very young or withdrawn children who would otherwise go into a day nursery group or remain at home in a very stressed family situation which might lead to family breakdown and the child going into residential care. Social services pay the sponsored child-minder for minding such children. This is seldom more than the local 'going rate' for ordinary child-minding, a state of affairs which seems grossly unfair when one considers the heavy responsibility sponsored minders carry, and the sensitivity and maturity required.

Many of the parents of these children are very young: with this arrangement, they see a role model of a mother in her own home. The care is unlikely to stop or change suddenly as only committed, reliable people take on this role. Help is there at weekends in time of crisis and the minder often gets involved with the whole family. The young mother with few parenting skills is more likely to learn willingly from another mother than a professional, who may make her feel inadequate or threatened.

Many nursery nurses have taken on this role very successfully, often when they have small children of their own.

RESIDENTIAL CARE

Residential care can take the form of a community school or residential home but for the small child, caring will be done by foster-parents in their own homes. Foster-parents are recruited, prepared, supported and paid by social services departments.

There are often many powerful and difficult emotions surrounding the fostering of a child. He may feel angry, confused or abandoned, and he should be allowed to show these feelings. The natural parents may appear aggressive, critical or inadequate; they find it hard to accept that someone else is coping efficiently with their child, where they, for whatever reason, have failed. Foster-parents are dedicated, tolerant and understanding, but may be sorely tried when, for the child, the 'honeymoon' period of stable home life is over, and he may test how naughty he can be yet still retain his foster-parents' affection and regard. He will need consistent handling, lots of praise, and never to be threatened with rejection. He may have to go to a different school, which is another unsettling experience. Visits from natural parents may further unsettle him. His social worker will try to stay closely in touch with all concerned, encouraging links of all kinds, however difficult and painful, including links between natural siblings. The keeping of a 'Life Story' book is thought to be a helpful pastime which boosts self-esteem. A thread of continuity is maintained with the aid of photographs, letters, and written accounts.

Reviews will be held frequently, to evaluate the child's progress and the family's circumstances and feelings. All the information entrusted to, or learned by, the foster-parents about the natural parents and their circumstances and past lives, must be treated with the utmost confidentiality.

Foster-parenting allowances are paid by cheque in arrears and cover normal maintenance, clothing, holiday and pocket-money payments. Christmas and birthday money will be in addition.

There is a great shortage of foster-parents for children who are 'difficult to place,' such as teenagers, who are often moody, temperamental, disaffected from school and society in general. Such normal characteristics (for teenagers) may have been aggravated by unhappy experiences and perhaps trouble with the law.

Mature nursery nurses, with experience of handling children of all kinds, often make ideal foster-parents.

It may not be a career as such, but is an eminently worthwhile occupation. As one nursery nurse expressed it, 'It's really satisfying, being a grow bag.'

HOSPITALS

Many sick children are kept in hospitals today for only very short stays. The reasons are partly financial and partly psychological, based on what we know about the harm that can be caused when children are separated from their families. Even with seriously ill children, parents can be taught to administer drugs and carry out treatment, so that the child can spend as much time as possible at home. When they are well enough, school-age children will be encouraged to attend their normal school and retain normal links.

The unrestricted access to children in hospital and encouragement of parents to help with care has also greatly changed the experience of hospitalised children.

Many hospitals run a playgroup and schooling is provided for all school-age children.

Some health authorities employ nursery nurses to work with babies and children in hospital. They are to be found in maternity wards, special care wards, ear, nose and throat wards, and children's hospitals. With babies, they will help with changing, feeding and general duties, as well as supporting and helping the mothers with breast-feeding and bathing. With older children, nursery nurses may be employed at night in a general surveillance capacity, or during the day to offer companionship, play and educational opportunities. Some hospitals employ nursery nurses as play leaders or play workers. To organise play therapy, they would need to take a further training course.

Nursery nurses may have close contact with the children's parents and siblings. Some run play sessions for visiting siblings, to enable parents to stay with sick children as much as possible.

Sometimes nursery nurses are involved in admis-sions procedures, where small children are gently introduced and familiarised with the surroundings and procedures before coming for treatment.

Despite the valuable work they do, nursery nurses are not being replaced in hospital jobs in many instances. The reasons given for this are financial cut-backs, the need for expertise in high technology and the idea that handling by few people enhances bonding by mother and baby.

NURSERY SCHOOLS

Rachel and Margaret McMillan, working in the slums of Bradford and Deptford in the early twentieth century, pioneered the idea of nursery schools in this country. Theirs was rescue work, focusing on the poor health and limited world of these small children and their families. It soon came to be seen as a gateway to much wider experience and a preparation for later schooling.

Demands for more nursery schools have been made continuously since then, but governments have adopted a stop–go policy. Nursery schools are expensive and the short term gains they bestow are difficult to prove. Some research has even denied that there are any short term gains. However, more recent and extensive research has shown that children who benefit from a good nursery school education grow up to be better socially adjusted, less involved with crime, more self-regulating, and more ambitious yet realistic in their career aspirations than other children.

Nursery schools are not a statutory part of the education system but are administered as part of the state primary system. They are housed in separate buildings, with their own headteacher, and are staffed by teachers and nursery nurses. A school might comprise of two or three classes of approximately twenty-five three to four or five-year-olds (depending on the age of infant school entry in the area).

Nursery school hours will be approximately 8.45 a.m. to 3.30 p.m., with normal school holidays.

A midday meal is available for those who require it. Attendance can be full time, but in the main it is part time, to benefit the maximum number of children. Nursery schools often have long waiting lists, and many referrals from health visitors and social workers, who may pick up the fact that a child's language development is delayed, or that he has no safe play space. Headteachers have the difficult task of maintaining a balance of children with and without problems, and a spread of birthdays, so that each class always retains a nucleus of settled children to aid those coming in. The ethnic make-up of the school naturally reflects the population of the locality.

Nursery schools provide an attractive play and discovery environment, where children investigate and absorb a whole range of new experiences in the company of others. This alone could be called education in its broadest sense. But with the interaction of skilled adults, they learn how to knit together, define and interpret their first-hand experiences – they are learning how to learn.

There will be a relaxed but predictable pattern to the day, including a balance of free play and quiet or group times. There will be much free movement around the room, and the adults will always be at hand to guide, explain, restrain, extend, and apply 'tender, loving care' as needed.

The degree of structure to the play activities will vary from one school to another (see Chapter 16).

All good nursery school programmes enable the child to find his own way through the activities on offer, discreetly encouraged by the adult's sound developmental knowledge.

Nursery schools invite much parental involvement and provide parental support. The sensitive adult will build on a knowledge of each family to supply a child's individual needs: one child may have no opportunity to run around freely and make a noise, another may do little else and need encouraging to sit down and concentrate on small motor skill activities.

Nursery nurses will carry out programmes as planned by the class teacher, supporting and complementing his/her work all the time, as well as contributing their own ideas. A nursery nurse will often be expected to supervise toilet and washing procedures, but will also take regular small groups for a whole range of activities.

Nursery nurses will be involved in keeping records of the children's developing skills, will attend staff meetings and reviews of children's progress and the success of programmes, and will be included in staff training days.

People working in schools often tend to stay there for many years. This means that openings for newly qualified nursery nurses are few. Obtaining supply work to cover maternity leave can often be a way in. In some areas there is a register of nursery nurses who are available for work of this kind.

There is no nationally recognised structure for career promotion for nursery nurses in schools, a situation that trade unions and others have been addressing for many years.

NURSERY CLASSES

These are attached to infant schools, and are administered by the infant or primary school headteacher, although the teacher of the nursery class or unit often enjoys a degree of autonomy. The hours, curriculum, and programmes are all very similar to those of nursery schools.

Most nursery education expansion has been in the form of creating a nursery class within an infant school. The declining birth rate has made this possible, and financial stringency made it a more economical development than building a new school.

The main advantages of a nursery class are that the children experience less change and interruption in their schooling. They feel part of a larger unit. They can 'taste' what it is like to be in 'the infants' through such activities as PE in the hall, festivals and special occasions.

Staff can assess each child individually to judge when he is ready to be transferred.

COMBINED NURSERY CENTRES

The first combined nursery centre was opened in Coventry in 1971 in response to a general demand for a more co-ordinated approach to services for the under-fives. Since then, another thirty-nine have opened, situated mainly in, or near, large housing estates from London to the North West.

These centres, though very different from one another in many ways, offer an integrated service to children from birth to five years, combining day care and education in one setting. They are open, effectively, all year round between the hours of 8.00 a.m. and 6.00 p.m., and parents are offered flexibility in the hours their child attends; these hours may be changed during the child's years or months of attendance. Centres also offer facilities and support to families in the vicinity. Most are jointly funded and managed by education and social services departments. Sometimes this results in ludicrous situations such as half the buildings' windows being cleaned! The staff comprises of trained teachers and nursery nurses. Some children pay for attendance but most pay only for a midday meal.

There are close links between the centres and local health visitors, social workers, and other people providing services to families. Education home visitors operate from centres as their base.

Parental involvement is essential to effective functioning. A key worker is often attached to a newly admitted child and family. Ideas such as the provision of drop-in centres, special parents' rooms where they can smoke, toy libraries and recent innovations like a 'Well Woman' clinic have been initiated and sustained successfully. Obstacles to parental involvement are that, in areas of employment opportunities, parents take advantage of the nursery centre's long hours which enable them to return to work. Because of their locality in social priority areas, parents are often weighed down with personal problems which need help before they can give their minds to constructive occupations. Many parents also value the respite given from caring for their children, and do not always wish to spend this time at the nursery.

The disadvantage to children of combined nursery centres is that they may meet a very large number of other children in a day. Sometimes open-plan buildings and the resultant noise level feels threatening to them.

Staff who work at a centre need to be very committed, and highly flexible. They also need plenty of stamina, as holidays have to be staggered throughout the year. Few centres close for more than odd days together. Therefore staff are very often reduced, and the situation where the centre closes, is given a good spring clean, and everyone comes back refreshed together, does not arise. There can be cause for resentment at the disparity of salaries among staff who effectively do the same job.

Because of their ill-defined position and status, centres can feel they lack recognition. Visits from Department of Education and Science inspectors may be rare, and employment of probationary teachers may not be permitted. Staff need all the support and recognition they can get for their work with families who are socially disadvantaged.

INFANT SCHOOLS

Many local education authorities accept children into infant schools soon after they are four years old.

Infant schools are part of the state school system; all children must attend after age five unless approved home teaching arrangements have been negotiated with the local education authority.

Intake at a school will represent the whole cross-section of children and families throughout that area. Parents have some degree of choice as to which school their child attends.

Infant schools are often housed separately from junior schools, with their own headteacher, or they may be part of a 'junior mixed infant' primary school, with one overall head teacher. Class sizes vary from fifteen to over thirty children.

Infant schools are staffed by trained teachers, with minimum ancillary help. Headteachers are forever bemoaning the fact that they are not allowed to employ more nursery nurses, especially for reception classes, where, in areas where children are admitted at age four, extra individual help is desperately needed. In an attempt to cater for the four-year-olds, this reception class idea has been revived. Numbers are kept low, and a nurturing ambience is created. Five and six-year-olds are often to be found in parallel classes, while 'top infants' may be grouped separately as preparation for junior school.

The work of the infant school is dealt with more fully in Chapter 14. Suffice it to say here that the investigative, discovery and problem-solving approach underpins much of what goes on. But there will be perceptible growth in children's ability to abstract information and knowledge, to sort, organise and understand, and to apply and present their work by more formalised methods (literacy and numeracy skills).

In schools that are able to justify the employment of a nursery nurse his/her role will be to assist teachers in carrying out their programmes, administer 'tender loving care', take groups for creative activities and sometimes carry out first aid procedures. Nursery nurses are sometimes employed to give specialised help to a child with a handicap who attends normal school. One nursery nurse frequently has to service several classes, offering different activities on different days. These posts are generally advertised as 'general assistants', for which, technically, an untrained person can be appointed. Pay is very low: some nursery nurses fulfil this role but have to work on Saturdays or during holidays as well, in order to make ends meet. There is no career structure for nursery nurses in infant schools.

SCHOOLS FOR CHILDREN WITH SPECIAL NEEDS

These schools exist within the state education system for children with a variety of physical or mental handicapping conditions, or behavioural disorders. Complete integration of such children within mainstream schools is not always possible or desired by the parents.

The schools are usually staffed by specially trained teachers, and assistants who are often trained nursery nurses. In enlightened schools, the role of teacher and nursery nurse is virtually interchangeable. Sadly, the pay structure does not reflect the importance of the nursery nurse in this position.

The age range of children may be from three to eleven or even sixteen. Nursery nurses usually find themselves working with the younger children, although older children with a mental handicap, for example, have much in common with younger children and require similar skills of management. The ratio of adults to children is, of necessity, low – around one to eight.

Every child will be helped towards developing his full potential in skill building. Staff will set and strive towards individually set goals or targets. Social goals may be to raise the level of child interaction; self-help goals may concern dressing skills; intellectual goals may concern puzzle completion; physical goals may involve something as simple as picking an object up from the floor without toppling over.

The nursery nurse will play an important part in working with individual children, helping them to plan, record and report on what they achieve. Nursery nurses also help to create a close relationship with parents. Often a 'diary' is passed to and fro which records the child's progress, achievements and difficulties. This is especially valuable if the child is brought to school and taken home by special transport, so that staff only get to meet parents when they themselves are on transport duty or at social events.

There are many professionals with whom staff will need to co-operate, such as speech therapists, physiotherapists, teachers of the deaf or sight impaired, educational psychologists, school nurses or social workers.

Social and communication skills are given high

priority, as these will determine how well each child copes with later life and overcomes his basic disabilities. With this in mind, many nursery nurses go on training courses themselves, for example to learn Maketon (based on British Sign Language), or to learn how to help disabled children ride horses, swim and trampoline. It is also possible to attend courses about the Derbyshire Language Scheme (a method of assessing and helping language impaired children) or a particular condition such as autism.

Nursery nurses may develop new talents themselves by helping organise events such as school concerts, special outings or a school magazine. Goodwill and fundraising by the community often brings exciting contact with visitors, even celebrities.

The role is often physically demanding, and may include intimate caring tasks such as changing children's colostomy bags or helping to manage calipers and wheelchairs. Adults working in special schools need to be strong, positive, cheerful, resilient, caring and sensitive without becoming over involved emotionally: some children's conditions may deteriorate unavoidably or end in death. Job satisfaction is very different from that of a nursery nurse working in a 'normal' school, but it is very real and rewarding.

Some special schools are residential, where clearly, the adults will be responsible for more physical and nurturant care. Special units may be attached to existing primary schools, for example for language-impaired or partially hearing children. Then there are assessment units, where differing kinds of developmental delay and handicapping conditions are studied and monitored, and decisions are taken about each child's educational and general needs.

In some areas, peripatetic nursery nurses are employed by local social services departments to visit pre-school children with special needs and offer support, help, liaison over day care places, and monitor ongoing difficult or sensitive situations. Such a nursery nurse may offer the Portage scheme, which is an early intervention programme for young children with special educational needs. It comprises versatile materials which parents will be helped to use with their child, and record progress.

PRIVATE DAY NURSERIES

There has been a proliferation of these in recent years in response to demand and inadequate state provision, and the incompatibility of playgroup hours of attendance with employment of parents.

They are set up in individuals' private houses and offer their services to any parents who can afford to pay for their children to attend. Many accept children under age two; some accept babies from six weeks. They are often to be found in districts where there is little other provision and opportunities exist for better-paid women's jobs. Therefore they are often situated in pleasant residential districts and country towns.

Premises and facilities must be inspected and approved by social services personnel, a fire prevention officer and an environmental health officer. If the person in charge has neither NNEB nor RGN qualifications, one person on the staff must be qualified. The ratio of adults to children is one to six, higher if the intake includes children under three. The keeping of records is compulsory, and the nursery will be visited regularly by social services staff and health visitors.

Fees will be fixed by the proprietor, and clear arrangements made about paying in advance, holidays, absences etc. Charges have to cover all overheads, staff wages and children's meals – often two or three of these in a day. Length of day will vary according to parents' needs, and there is some flexibility. Nurseries usually stay open most of the year.

The service offered is good day care and pre-school stimulation. Groups are kept small and there is usually a relaxed homely atmosphere.

The increase in numbers of private day nurseries has created many jobs for newly-qualified nursery nurses, who find fulfilment in meeting these children's needs.

It is the dream of many nursery nurses to open their own nursery, and there are countless examples of people who have turned this dream into successful reality, often persevering through endless red tape and frustrating delays.

PRIVATE NURSERY SCHOOLS

Much of the above information applies equally to these establishments, except that there is no legal requirement for staff qualification. With the orientation towards early schooling, however, it is usual to find that the proprietor is a trained teacher or nursery nurse, or employs at least one teacher, full or part time.

Hours will be more like those of an ordinary school. Holidays will vary from one establishment to another.

The age of children will usually be two and a half to five years, and ratio of adults to children is one to eight.

Besides monitoring by fire prevention and environmental health personnel, private nursery schools will also be visited from time to time by local education authority inspectors and advisers.

A good private nursery school will offer opportunities similar to a state nursery school. Staff sometimes have to tread a wary path between keeping their paying clients happy, and not acceding to expectations of very early headway in the three Rs as their basic priority.

Many independent preparatory and senior schools have a kindergarten and infant department, for which the fees will be relatively high.

CRÈCHES AND WORKPLACE NURSERIES

This French word, meaning cradle, is still used to describe a private nursery in a factory, shop or other workplace. It is a child-minding facility for children of employees, or in some cases, students, trainees, or customers. It may be a 'one-off' arrangement, e.g. for a day conference, or permanently offered day care.

Crèches which open for more than two hours per day while parents are not on the premises must be registered with the Dept. of Social Services. Officers will check out the qualification of the leader, suitability of other staff, and the premises for space, safety, equipment, and other requirements similar to those of Day Nursery. Ratio of staff to children is one to four unless all children are over age three, in which case it can be one to six.

This arrangement can mean a shorter day for a child than if he were taken to a child-minder or day nursery, and the parent is close at hand in case of an emergency. However, children may miss out on the neighbourhood links and friends.

The idea has been slow to catch on in Britain. If crèches were more widely offered in hospitals, for example, it might have done much to alleviate the chronic shortage of trained nurses, largely caused by wastage of nurses who have families and do not return to work. With 'high-tech', there are now fewer factories which traditionally used to employ women to do mechanical jobs, thus there are fewer concentrations of women workers. Currently there are signs of an increase in the provision of workplace nurseries at banks, insurance firms and hospitals. Government encouragement of working women has included tax incentives for participants. In times of unemployment, however, these have little impact.

To work in a crèche is very tiring; demands fluctuate, clients are frequently changing. Shop crèches have the added disadvantage of serving a constantly changing clientèle of strangers, having to cope with unpredictable demand, and parents' return being delayed. However, they do perform a useful service for the customers, especially in these days of out-of-town shopping and huge precincts. They can eliminate much boredom from the child's life, and harrassment between parent and child. Some shops dealing in baby and child commodities have a small indoor adventure playground for customers' children.

PLAYGROUPS

Since the 1960s, the Playgroup movement has grown and flourished in the UK, in response to the lack of safe play space and companionship opportunities available to pre-school children. Today, about 45 per cent (roughly half a million) of British children attend a playgroup, usually twice or three times a week for half a day.

There is a national organisational structure which co-ordinates, oversees and supports individual playgroups. The Pre-school Playgroup Association (PPA) operates at both grass-roots and national level. It receives government funding, a proportion of this going to each of the eleven regions in England and Wales.

Individual playgroups are funded in various ways. Parents pay for each session their child attends, but most groups also receive local authority help, perhaps in the form of rent-free premises or the means to buy equipment in bulk.

Most playgroups are run by parents, although some are run by the NSPCC, Barnardos or Children's Society.

Children attending are mainly aged three and four, although some two-year-olds are accepted, and some children remain until they are five, if that is the local age for school entry. Mothers of children under three are legally required to stay with their children. Playgroups are held in private houses, halls, schools and community centres. Numbers may vary between six and twenty-four children. The ratio of adults to children is one to eight, plus a supervisor. There will be parent helpers, sometimes on a rota basis, or permanently.

Play provision will vary depending on premises, space, equipment and finances available. A high standard is always aimed at, incorporating messy creative opportunities, energetic physical activities, and play to develop concentration and fine manipulative skills. All groups offer children the chance to mix socially and be gradually weaned away from dependence on parents.

Fees are kept as low as overheads permit so as not to exclude any child. In some areas, a child's place at playgroup may be paid for by the social services department.

The PPA offers a structured range of training courses for helpers, dealing mainly with child development and child management, and also the business skills necessary to run an efficient group. It also circulates newsletters, organises conferences, events, exhibitions, and sales of children's books, play equipment and raw materials.

Playgroups should not be regarded as nursery schooling 'on the cheap'. They are a remarkable form of self-help, where parents come together to enable their children to extend their learning experiences beyond their own homes.

Playgroups have many links with local communities through fundraising events and through their willingness to assist secondary schools with pupils' work experience. Older people are also welcomed into many groups, and supply the grandparent figure – kind, patient, able to listen – that is often missing from children's lives. Lonely, unsupported parents and those new to the area are also offered the chance to get involved and make friends. The atmosphere is kept relaxed and informal; far-reaching commitments will not be asked of parents.

Playgroups are responsive to local needs. Groups have been formed in conjunction with one-parent projects, Asian Link workers and Afro-Caribbean parents.

Many helpers have found new enthusiasms and whole new careers through the Playgroup movement. Trained teachers and nursery nurses have derived great satisfaction from the devoted service they give to playgroups during the years when they have chosen not to return to full-time work. Such experience can enhance career development, although it is not comparable with a job in terms of financial rewards.

Working in a playgroup demands a low-key, friendly approach to parents, without whose involvement the group will not be a success. It also demands a high degree of flexibility and stamina, particularly when it comes to packing away in a cupboard a whole half-full of equipment, in readiness for the aerobics class or Brownie pack which share the same premises.

OPPORTUNITY GROUPS

These are playgroups to cater for children with handicaps. Non-handicapped siblings can also attend. The ratio of adults to children is high and the age range is from birth to age five.

Parents sometimes stay and help with the group, or may be relieved to have a little time to themselves. They also gain from contact with other parents of handicapped children as they can feel very isolated, and from the chance to meet professional workers who visit these groups to diagnose and counsel.

Opportunity groups may be organised by the PPA or voluntary agencies.

HOSPITAL PLAYGROUPS

These may be organised by the hospital or by Save the Children and are held in play areas in the wards. Numbers fluctuate according to patient numbers. Visiting siblings can often join in.

MOTHER AND TODDLER GROUPS

These groups offer play space and opportunities to children at a stage when they are often particularly exhausting, demanding, and unused to socialising.

Sometimes they are offshoots of a playgroup, or they can be set up by health visitors at health centres, by church organisations, or by teachers at secondary schools or colleges (where the toddlers can be usefully observed and helped by their child development students).

Parents are committed to staying with their children, and derive much support and companionship from this contact, while their children, under supervision, learn their first lessons in mixing and coping outside their own home.

There is considerable flexibility in the age range accepted; for example a mother will be welcome to bring her new baby along with her eighteen-month-old child.

They are sometimes self-help groups, requested and set up by parents, or they may be initiated by others who see a local need and who will, perhaps, work with any parents who may be low on parenting skills.

PLAYBUSES

A playbus is a second-hand double-decker bus which has been refitted as a mobile play space.

The attractive and Pied Piper-like spectacle of playbuses can often be seen around Britain's major cities and elsewhere. Sometimes they are initiated by the PPA, or community schemes. Funding differs from one to another, but playbuses attract finance and practical help from local authorities and commerce. The pay-off for local firms is the spectacular advertising these vehicles can carry.

There is a National Playbus Association, and each playbus has its own committee.

Great ingenuity is exercised in the way playbuses are refurbished, adapted and set out for a variety of activities.

The original idea of playbuses was to set up playgroups in areas where there were none. Staff (often students, or people on community schemes) then worked with parents who became involved in the group they set up and helped to oversee the establishment of permanent playgroups.

This is still happening, but playbuses now also have many other functions. They attend a variety of public social gatherings and provide crèche/recreational facilities for children. Puppet shows can be given on one level of the bus. 'On the spot' painting competitions can be arranged. Some playbuses have regular dates with schools for children with special needs, where they provide fun, novelty and fresh stimulus.

The playbus idea, being essentially both mobile and flexible, is highly responsive to changing community needs.

ADOPTION

Adoption of babies by childless couples is less common than it used to be. Such a couple is likely to try conceiving by means of artificial insemination, or implanting of a fertilised ovum, before recourse to adoption. There is a great shortage of babies available for adoption because of widespread contraception and the possibility of abortion.

Adopting parents have to be well under forty years of age, and considered to be suitable and responsible by the agency concerned. They may have to wait as long as two years before a baby becomes available. It is easier to adopt an older child or a child who may have proved 'difficult to place'.

Since adopted children are clearly so much wanted, there is every chance that, provided adoption takes place early in their lives, the arrangement will be highly successful.

In the past, adoption agencies tried to 'match' children and parents for colouring, intelligence and background. This was obviously to minimise embarrassment and disappointment, but today it is thought to be a mistake. After all, natural parents cannot predict exactly what their children's hair colour or intelligence quotient will be!

Before an adoption can be approved, the couple's home will be visited by a social worker to see that adequate standards of cleanliness, space, economic security, etc. are assured. But most important will be the couple's own relationship, and attitude towards the forthcoming child. Adopting a child to rescue an ailing marriage would bring happiness to no-one. One enthusiastic and one reluctant partner could also bode trouble. In some circumstances, single people are also allowed to adopt.

Adopting parents will need to discuss their views on how to tell the child he is adopted, and also explore how they will react if he later wishes to trace his natural parents, which he is legally able to do.

It is generally thought advisable for a child to grow up knowing he was 'chosen', so that there is never an awful moment of revelation. For some adopted children, the story of, for example, how parents first saw him in his hospital cot and fell in love with him on the spot, *knowing* he was the right one for them, can become their favourite story and a guarantee of strong feelings of security and ownership.

Adoption of step-children is very widespread today. It can be seen as a sign of good intentions, acceptance, shouldering of new responsibilities, and a break with a less than happy past for the parents. However, the child's feelings also need to be considered. Maybe he does not want to cut off from not only a parent, but also possibly an extended family. The child will lose the right to inheritance and maintenance which may not matter at this time, but could be critical if financial circumstances deteriorate, or both natural remaining parent and step-parent die before the child.

A sort of legal 'half-way house' is custodianship, which entails control by the custodial parents in matters of daily living, but not the foregoing of inheritance rights by the child, nor the right to take him abroad to live, nor to change his name.

PRIVATE NANNIES

During the nineteenth century, and later, English nannies became a byword for propriety, hygiene, discretion, and firm handling tempered by love. A nanny might stay with 'her' middle or upper-class children for many years, and was often closer to them than their parents, maybe even remaining with the family after the children had grown up.

Changed social conditions today have meant that nannies are more commonly employed by mothers who are also professional or business people, or are public figures. Few houses today can offer 'staff quarters' which the nanny of old would have enjoyed, and so some nannies may lack privacy or time off. Living as one of the family is quite common, and so are nannies employed on a day-time basis. A nanny may be required for a year or so only, or else she may choose to move on. She may be offered chances of travel abroad. Each nanny position is unique. A nanny works in triangular interaction with the parents and the child or children. How successfully she handles this situation will depend on her maturity, skills, diplomacy, sensitivity, good humour and staying power.

Her employers' expectations of her will be influenced by their experience of previous nannies, and possibly those of their own childhood, their knowledge – or lack of it – about her training course, the age difference between them and the nanny, and their views on child-rearing practices, such as toilet training and discipline.

These matters, and many others, should be discussed at an interview, and explored further if there is to be a trial weekend before the nursery nurse accepts the job. Salary and salary review, duties, hours, sickness arrangements, use of a car and insurance of car and driver, freedom to entertain friends (perhaps other nannies with their charges), National Insurance, tax responsibilities and contributions, weekends off, a trial period are all areas to be discussed, many of which can be written into the contract. Some parents are less than enthusiastic about having a contract, as they feel it reduces flexibility, but nursery nurses should insist on having one as a safeguard. (See the example on page 272.) This is particularly true of a residential post because hours of work are so elastic, and it is very difficult for a nursery nurse to complain if this might lead to her losing her 'home'. Both sides need to be flexible, but both also need safeguards. Employers can exploit their position, but nannies may also take advantage of theirs, for example by adding a Monday to a weekend off. If conditions of service are clearly spelt out in a contract, it reduces resentments and misunderstandings, and gives both sides something tangible to refer to. A three-month trial period is wise: one month does not allow for the residential

The image of the nanny has changed over the years

nanny to overcome homesickness. If a starting salary cannot be agreed upon, the nanny may be willing to come down to the level being offered, given assurance of a rise at the end of a trial period.

The services of a nanny agency are frequently sought by today's prospective nannies. The cost of such a service lies entirely with the employers, so there are clear advantages for the employee. A standardised contract will be insisted upon, including clear statements about household duties, hours and time off. It will save the nursery nurse the cost of telephone calls, letters, and possibly travelling to interviews. The agency will have vetted the family, and will try to match employer and employee, aided by their knowledge and an outsider's perception of both parties.

Agencies come and go with alarming frequency, but a longstanding reputation is not necessarily a guarantee of a good experience. Personal recom-

mendation is the best guide. A nursery nurse can apply to several agencies, and pursue the one she likes best. Application forms can be an indication of a reputable and efficient organisation or the reverse.

It is advisable for the nanny, once employed, to take out personal insurance for professional negligence, then she will be covered for damage to property or children.

The nanny should be prepared for feelings of loneliness and homesickness at first, lack of professional support and guidance (as enjoyed by new nursery nurses at day nursery, for example), the constraints of twenty-four hour care and the charge of a sick child, both of which may be completely new to her. She should also expect a process of adjusting to living under the roof of another family, one which may be different from her own in every way, socially

PARTICULARS OF EMPLOYMENT FOR NANNIES PLACED THROUGH MEMBER AGENCIES OF THE FEDERATION OF PERSONNEL SERVICES

INTRODUCTION
It is important that all contracts of employment operate on the basis of goodwill between the parties involved, and where resident employment is concerned, it is also important that both parties accept a degree of flexibility in the contract. However, to confirm the conditions of your engagement we set out below the details of employment as required by legislation.

NAME AND ADDRESS OF EMPLOYER _____
_____
NAME OF EMPLOYEE _____
DATE OF ISSUE OF THIS CONTRACT _____
DATE OF COMMENCEMENT OF EMPLOYMENT _____
PREVIOUS SERVICE (IF ANY) COUNTING TOWARDS CONTINUOUS EMPLOYMENT (1)
_____ JOB TITLE _____

REMUNERATION	Your salary is £_____ (2) per annum payable *weekly/calendar monthly in arrears. Tax and National Insurance are to be deducted from this sum. There will be a salary review once/twice a year on _____ (3).
PROBATIONARY PERIOD	The employee will be employed for a probationary period of _____ (4).
HOURS OF WORK	Employment in a private household is such that it is very difficult to define hours of work and free time. However, you will be allowed _____ (5) free days per week and _____ (5) free weekends per month, from _____ (6) to _____. These hours of work can only be changed by mutual agreement. In addition, the employee will be allowed _____ (7) weeks holiday in each year. In the first or final year of service, the employee will be entitled to holidays on a pro rata basis. Paid compensation is not normally given for holidays not actually taken. Holidays may only be carried into the next year with the express permission of the employer. The employee will be free on all bank holidays, or will receive a day off in lieu, by agreement.
SICKNESS	The employer will pay sick benefit for the first eight weeks of sickness in any year, at the rates stipulated by the Government. Your qualifying days for Statutory Sick Pay will be Monday to Friday. In addition, the employer will make up the sickness benefit payable under the Statutory Sick Pay scheme to the normal level of your salary for the first four weeks of sickness for staff who have been employed for more than thirteen weeks, but less than one year, and for the first eight weeks of sickness for staff who have been employed for more than one year. The employer is covered under his 'Employers and Public Liability' policy against claims for injuries.
TERMINATION	In the first four weeks of employment one week's notice is required on either side. After four weeks continuous service either the employee or the employer may terminate this contract by giving four weeks' notice.
CONFIDENTIALITY	It is a condition of employment that now and at all times in the future, the employee keeps secret the affairs and concerns of the household and its transactions and business.
PENSIONS	The employer does not run a pension scheme.
GRIEVANCES	If the employee has any grievances against the employer he/she has the right to go direct to _____.

(continued)

DISCIPLINE   Reasons which might give rise for the need for disciplinary measures include the following:
a) causing a disruptive influence in the household
b) job incompetence
c) unsatisfactory standard of dress or appearance
d) conduct during or outside working hours prejudicial to the interest or reputation of the employer
e) unreliability in time-keeping or attendance
f) failure to comply with instructions and procedure.

In the event of the need to take disciplinary action, the procedure will be:
Firstly - oral warning
Secondly - written warning
Thirdly - dismissal.

Reasons which might give rise to summary dismissal include the following:
a) theft   b) drunkenness.

———————————————————————   ———————————————————————
           Signed by Employer   Signed by Employee

FOOTNOTES:
1. Insert details where applicable.   2. Insert salary.   3. Insert date or dates.
4. Insert probation period. This is usually one month.   5. Insert number of free days/weekends.
6. Insert period over weekend when nanny will be free.   7. Insert number of weeks holiday a year.   *Delete where applicable.

An example of a contract of employment for a nanny

and culturally. If this family has not employed a nanny before, it will take a little while for the complementary roles of mother and nanny to evolve and establish themselves to the satisfaction of both.

If there is not enough discussion and explanation and too little attempt to 'match' the nanny and family at an early stage, misunderstandings and disappointment may creep in, perhaps with resentment on both sides. The nanny may feel an intruder, or the parents may feel alienated from their child. The mother may not have thought through the idea of sharing the children's love with a nanny, and what this may mean in practice. The nanny may feel that she is exploited and her skills and training are not being used to the full. A bad atmosphere may build up, creating tension, confusion and unhappiness for the child. The nanny may resign sooner than she intended, leaving in her wake a disturbed child and a disgruntled employer. This sequence of events does nothing to raise the reputation and status of nursery nursing.

Many nursery nurses, however, enter this work well prepared, with a mature, sensible attitude. They enjoy the process of widening their horizons, stay with 'their' families as long as is appropriate, and

remain life-long friends. A good nanny offers her charges above all companionship, stability, stimulation and affection.

With her knowledge of child development, and sensitivity to children's needs, a nanny should be prepared to work really hard to make each job a success and to stay with the family a reasonable length of time. She should think long and hard before she succumbs to the temptation of, for example, a few extra pounds a week offered by another employer and weigh this against 'her' children's well-being.

The private sector is a growth area for jobs. If newly qualified nursery nurses are prepared to move away from their home town/area, there are jobs for all. You have only to look at the situations vacant pages of magazines such as *Nursery World* and *The Lady* for proof of this encouraging fact.

VOLUNTARY SECTOR

Space does not permit a full description of the work being done by voluntary sector agencies. This in no sense reflects an assessment of the contribution made by them.

The personal concern, close relationships, and freedom from red tape and officialdom which often characterises voluntary schemes are often exactly what is most needed by the families they are serving. A volunteer visitor working for Bristol's Home Plus – one such home-support scheme – aptly summed up this approach when she said, 'We aim to be good next-door neighbours to our clients; it's just that we happen not to live next door'.

As indicated on page 254, many of the services offered by the voluntary sector are also offered by state or private agencies. Therefore the delivery will be very similar.

To go into more detail about case work by, for instance, NSPCC child protection teams, is to enter the realms of social work, which is beyond the scope of this book. Leaflets and information about voluntary organisations (which are constantly evolving and meeting new needs in imaginative ways) are usually obtainable from their headquarters.

PARENTS AS PARTNERS

Readers must be well aware by now that parental involvement has been a thread running right through this chapter.

Perhaps, in summary, we can make some general observations.

It has long been appreciated, and research in the last thirty years has borne this out, that parents and nursery or school staff must all pull in the same direction. They must agree on the approaches used, so that the child may derive maximum benefit from the establishment he is attending, with its rich store of materials, opportunities and trained personnel. Any divisions of loyalties because of disagreements, lack of respect, misunderstandings or aloofness will adversely affect the child's progress and well-being.

The involvement of parents in nursery or school life varies tremendously, according to people and circumstances. But it ought to begin, in the case of an oldest child in the family, when the parent comes to discuss the child's admission. A warm, accepting and welcoming tone must be set. Many parents still have feelings of unease, even failure, dating back to their own schooling. In the case of admission to day nursery, they may feel they have failed as parents, or reveal hostility, defensiveness or indifference towards 'authority'. Ways must be found to break down this 'them and us' mentality.

Preliminary visits to the establishment by the child, before he begins regular attendance, are now common. They are a widely accepted way of minimising the pain of separation from the parents and the strangeness of the surroundings, and they also help the parents to feel reassured and part of the establishment.

In due course parents may find themselves invited to take part in activities such as sewing, with or for the children; fund raising; cooking either just for fun, or as part of the preparations for a special occasion. At infant school, parents may run a National Savings Bank, lending library or book club; repair books or equipment; help with the provision and laundering of dressing-up clothes or clothes for a play or festival; help to run a parent group or more formal association; help with sports, PE, swimming, outings, chess, or cycling. Where parents listen to abler children read aloud it gives the teacher more time to focus attention on the less able.

Special occasions such as Diwali, Christmas and musical or dramatic productions are always well attended by parents. Parents will also be asked to attend open days or evenings, and visits by specialists of services to children such as speech therapists, where this is appropriate.

Parents who are willing to share a special talent such as playing the guitar, or who have a job that would appeal to children, such as farming or pottery-making, are much appreciated.

Fathers are often specially welcome because of the male figure missing from many children's lives.

If parents from a minority ethnic group are hesitant about getting involved in local affairs, the school can be a useful focal point of the community. Home language or community language work often takes place in schools (see pages 132–3), and this is a practical example of the sharing of skills and cultures, to everyone's advantage.

Some nursery establishments run a home visiting scheme, where younger siblings of nursery children are introduced by teachers to worthwhile play and language activities, often based on improvised materials. Such visits enhance good relationships between staff and homes, and afford valuable insights for all concerned into the home atmosphere, patterns of child rearing, and nursery approaches. Spontaneous visiting may also occur when a child is taken ill at school, or when staff are concerned about a child's unexplained absence.

Some day nurseries have official parent and child placements, which gives the parent the chance to be there regularly, absorb the nursery atmosphere and see how it is run. Sometimes a member of staff works with a parent on a one-to-one basis, helping with parenting and homemaking skills. Either can be of positive value to a very young or unsupported mother. Learning something useful and 'neutral', such as cookery, is often the first step in a parent being ready to become more involved in parenting.

With most parental involvement schemes, a low-key, small beginnings, informal approach is best. Most parents dislike being organised, making far-reaching commitments, being patronised, or being made to feel that they are being 'got at' or 'done good to'.

The most successful and longest running semi-formal parent organisation that the authors know is held at an almost inaccessible nursery school in a depressed industrial area. Here, the headteacher, who had suggested the club, faded into the background as soon as the parents were willing to run it themselves and decide on the speakers and activities *they* wanted. How to make an Indian curry, and how to carry out home repairs, were examples of their early choices. The headteacher remains on the best of terms with the parents, and conveys to them all kinds of useful information about dental hygiene and road safety, for example, through strategic placing of displays and casual chats. Toddlers are welcomed into the school and are allowed to join older siblings. The group flourishes and declines over the years, as parents' needs change, but always it is the parents who set the pace.

Many schools, throughout the school attendance age range, operate what they call an open door policy towards parents.

The activity of parent-governors on school governing bodies has, in recent years, also contributed to closer links between home and school, and parents' participation in policy making.

Where there is a good relationship between home and school, not only do children perform happily and well, but the activity generated can be a real focal point in a community, a source of help, companionship and support between parents, and a springboard for further self-help ideas.

THE NURSERY NURSE'S ROLE

This chapter ends by focusing on the nursery nurse, her professional responsibilities, and her place in the work team.

Her first responsibility is to the child or children with whom she works, and to their families. But she is also responsible and answerable to her employer.

In private work, she will be dealing direct with that employer. In public sector work, authority lies with her headteacher or officer-in-charge. To them, she owes punctuality, reliability, co-operation, conscientiousness and loyalty. If she is seriously at odds with her superior over measures concerning children's well-being, she must privately, and as dispassionately as possible, voice her views to the person in charge. Trivial day-to-day sources of irritation should be played down as much as possible in the interest of maintaining a good working relationship and relaxed atmosphere. Tensions and sulks will quickly be conveyed to children and be manifested in their behaviour.

Confidentiality

A vital feature of a nursery nurse's professionalism is confidentiality. She will find herself, in almost every job, privy to highly personal information about the backgrounds of her children. Newcomers to this position can find the temptation to share a 'tasty' piece of gossip or scandal irresistible. In doing so, they may betray the trust placed by parents in the nursery or school, and perhaps undo years of patient work spent in establishing good relations. They may also be instrumental in the stigmatising or ostracising of a child or family. Instead of an improvement in the situation, which is the aim of the nursery staff, there may be a worsening of it. Other families will be deterred from confiding or trusting in the nursery staff.

Styles of management

Nursery nurses will meet many different styles of management in their places of work. Some managers make most policies and decisions themselves and expect their staff to carry them out; this is an authoritarian or autocratic style, and is now generally out of favour. Other managers prefer issues to be debated by staff, and agreed by majority decisions – a democratic approach to management.

The ultimate responsibility for the functioning of any establishment and the outcome of policies pursued and activities undertaken, rests with the manager, be they headteacher, playgroup supervisor or officer-in-charge.

The manager is accountable for the safety and well-being of all those children, the management of budget and other monies, such as funds raised to buy extra amenities,and for the just treatment of children and their families. It is a heavy responsibility and nursery nurse students who find certain constraints frustrating, such as not being allowed to take children to the local shop or library unaccompanied by qualified staff, would do well to remember some horrific accidents that occurred on school trips in recent years: if anything were to go wrong, the manager would be answerable in a court of law, as well as having to live with the inevitable guilt and distress for the rest of his/her life.

Where a sizable staff in an establishment consists predominantly of nursery nurses/officers (as in a large day nursery), there will be levels of seniority. There

may be designated responsibilities, for example the overseeing of student training. Working parties may be set up to look at specific areas of activity and suggest new approaches, for example in working with parents, or record keeping – an increasingly important task.

Teamwork

Nursery nursing is a multi-disciplinary field of activity, which gives it special breadth, interest and variety. But it demands flexibility and sensitivity to changing situations. In an ideal setting, there is no set hierarchy, but each member representing different disciplines within the same team gives of her best as she sees fit, and acknowledges and reacts to the special contributions made by others.

As an example, a nursery nurse working in a children's hospital ward may play a valuable role in providing companionship, play activities and general understanding support to the children. She may be asked to run a crèche for the young children of visiting parents. Through her well-trained eyes and ears she will be quick to observe changes in children's physical or emotional well-being. She will share this information with the nurses who are there to carry out treatment as prescribed by doctors and consultants. She may also work alongside and complement hospital school teachers, the play therapist and possibly the medical social worker if there are problems at home. Both her role, and her interaction with others, make her an important member of a smoothly running team.

Managing the present and looking to the future

Nursery nursing can be physically exhausting and emotionally draining. 'Switching off' from work concerns when off-duty is never completely possible, especially when one is dealing with tragic or deeply worrying circumstances. Anyone who found this easy would surely be insufficiently sensitive to do the job well. But it must be remembered that a haggard, overwrought exhausted nursery nurse is no good to anybody.

Besides functioning as well as she can from day-to-day, the nursery nurse has a responsibility to think of her future, and take every possible opportunity to continue her professional development.

The availability and quality of in-service courses open to her varies greatly from one area to another. In some localities, social services departments offer an encouraging range of in-service training courses for their staff. Some local education authorities mount in-service days organised by nursery/infant inspectors or advisers, especially for nursery nurses working in schools.

An increasing number of colleges offer the Certificate in Post Qualifying Studies (CPQS) for nursery nurses with at least two years' experience. This certificate, comprises six units, with a degree of choice about the length of time over which it is possible to study. Many holders of the CPQS have moved on to more challenging and responsible jobs, although so far few authorities have recognised it for incremental purposes (salary increase).

Nursery officers in the day nursery field may study for their Certificate in Social Work (CSS) while still employed, or, more rarely, obtain permission to study as a full-time student for a Certificate for Qualified Social Workers (CQSW). As the nature of day nursery and family centre work evolves in response to changing social problems, especially child abuse, so the character of specific training courses is changing.

Under NVQ (National Vocational Qualification) child care students will achieve a certain level of competence, and will be able to build on their initial qualifications in such ways and at such time as is appropriate for each individual and to further their careers.

The days when people trained for a particular job and counted on remaining in that same job all their lives are surely gone forever.

Trade unions and professional organisations

Many people are afraid of trade unions because they do not understand their purpose, which is to serve and protect their members. Unions should be the servants, not the masters, of their members; they can strive and negotiate for better conditions of work, pay and status. A union can only be effective if its members unite and co-operate. By belonging to a union, nursery nurses have the right to be directly involved in furthering and improving their conditions of service and, consequently, their careers. Membership of a trade union also affords legal protection and support; a union will represent members at grievance and disciplinary hearings. Situations where this might be necessary might concern accidental damage to property, or injury to children.

There are several trade unions to which nursery nurses can belong. These are:

National Union of Public Employees (NUPE),
National and Local Government Officers Association (NALGO),
Managerial, Administrative, Technical and Supervisory Association (MATSA) (this is the white collar section of the General, Municipal, Boilermakers' and Allied Trades Union),
Association of Clerical, Technical and Supervisory Staff (ACTSS) (this is a branch of the Transport and General Workers' Union, TGWU),
Confederation of Health Service Employees (COHSE),
Professional Association of Nursery Nurses (PANN).

All, in their various ways, are striving to improve the conditions of service, pay, career structure, and status of nursery nurses. It is up to each nursery nurse to decide which is the right one for him or her: much will depend on local activity and membership. In recent years, some unions have staged days of action in various parts of the country in support of different sectors of the profession and there have been a few encouraging local outcomes.

PANN is alone in opposing strike action, but it is also the only union founded specifically for nursery nurses. Because it is not affiliated to the Trades Union Congress (TUC), it has no power to negotiate at local authority level, but is active in negotiating on behalf of individual members in their work-places.

A list of trade unions' addresses is included at the end of this chapter.

Professional associations have slightly different aims in that, although they strive to influence conditions of service etc. at many levels, their main functions are to offer their members support, in-service training, a sharing of current research findings and good practice, and a forum for debate and consultation.

The associations to which nursery nurses may belong are:

The National Association of Nursery and Family Care, National Association of Certificated Nursery Nurses, British Association of Early Childhood Education, National Children's Bureau.

In addition, there are many local associations, formed and maintained in ways that meet local needs. They often strive to bring together people from a variety of disciplines, who have in common the well-being of young children.

EXERCISES

Investigation
1) Imagine that you are a single father with a three-year-old child and you want to stay in full-time employment. Find out what child care facilities would be open to you in your locality. Compare the costs, advantages and disadvantages of each.

2) Write to a children's charitable organisation and find out what services they offer. If a number of students write to different organisations, it could lead to a discussion about which one you might like to support at a future sponsored or fund-raising event.

Observation
If possible, arrange a visit to a playgroup. Do a series of 'snapshot' observations recording what each child is doing, at three twenty-minute intervals. In your evaluation, state what functions you think this play group is providing for these children.

Project
Imagine that you are going to open your own private day nursery. Devise a leaflet/brochure in which you briefly describe the aims and philosophy of the nursery, and also give potential clients necessary information about the way it will be run. (Remember you are trying to *attract* customers!) You may also like to plan a site for the nursery in a locality you know, and discuss reasons for your choice with fellow students.

SUGGESTIONS FOR FURTHER READING

Jerome Bruner, *Under Five in Britain,* Oxford Pre-School Project

Lesley Garner, *How to Survive as a Working Mother,* Penguin Books

Joyce Lucas and Ann Henderson, *Pre-School Playgroups,* Allen and Unwin Ltd

Penelope Leach, *Who Cares?,* Penguin Books

Frances Kemper Alston, *Caring For Other People's Children,* University Press, Baltimore

National Children's Bureau, *Working with Parents: A Training Resource Pack*

Jim Docking, *Primary Schools and Parents,* Hodder & Stoughton

Jennie Laishley, *Working with Young Children,* Hodder & Stoughton

Mike Sullivan, *Bright Ideas Management Books: Parents and Schools,* Scholastic Publications Ltd

Linda Mort and Janet Morris, *Bright Ideas for the Early Years: Getting Started,* Scholastic Publications Ltd

LIST OF ADDRESSES

Association for All Speech Impaired Children (AFASIC)
347 Central Market, Smithfield, London EC1A 19NH

Association for Children's Play and Recreation
Britannia House, Great Charles Street, Birmingham B3

Association of Clerical, Technical and Supervisory Staff (ACTSS)
Transport House, Smith Square, London SW1P 3JB

British Agencies for Adoption and Fostering (BAAF)
11 Southwark Street, London SE1 1RQ

British Association of Early Childhood Education (BAECE)
111 City View House, 436 Bethnall Green Road, London E2 9QY

Building Students Association
3 Savile Row, London W1X 1AF

Child Accident Prevention Trust
28 Portland Place, London W1X 14DE

Campaign for Single Homeless People (CHAR)
5–15 Cromer Street, London WC1H 8LS

Confederation of Health Service Employees (COHSE)
Glen House, High Street, Banstead, Surrey SM7 2LH

Child Poverty Action Group
4th floor, 1–5 Bath Street, London EC1P 9PY

Cruse
Cruse House, 126 Sheen Road, Richmond, Surrey SU9 1UR

Families Need Fathers
BM Families, London WC1N 3XX

Family Action Information and Rescue (FAIR)
BCM Box 3535, PO Box 12 London WC1N 3XX

Family Rights Group (FRG)
6–9 Manor Gardens, Holloway Road, London N7 6LA

Family Welfare Association (FWA)
501–505 Kingsland Road, London E8 4AU

Gingerbread
35 Wellington Street, London WC2E 7BN

Invalid Children's Aid Association
126 Buckingham Palace Road, London SW1W 9SB

Managerial Administrative, Supervisory Association (MASA)
Thorn House, Ruxley Ridge, Claygate, Esher, Surrey KT10 0TL

National Association for The Welfare of Children in Hospital (NAWCH)
Argyle House, 29–31 Euston Road, London NW1 2SD

National Association for Certificated Nursery Nurses
162 Langdale Road, Thornton Heath, Surrey CR4 7PR

National and Local Government Officers' Association (NALGO)
1 Mabledon Place, London WC1H 9AJ

National Childminding Association
8 Masons Hill, Bromley, Kent BR2 9EY

National Children's Bureau
8 Wakely Street, London EC1V 7QE

National Council for One Parent Families
255 Kentish Town Road, London NW5 2LX

National Council for Special Education
1 Wood Street, Stratford-upon-Avon, Warwickshire CV37 6WE

National Council for Travelling People
c/o Sister Mary Gallagher, Sister Mercy Convent, Balling, County Mayo, Republic of Ireland

National Foster Care Association (NFCA)
Francis House, Francis Street, Victoria, London SW1 1DE

National Toy Libraries Association
68 Churchway, London NW1 1LT

National Union of Public Employees (NUPE)
Civic House, 20 Grand Depot Road, Woolwich, London SE18 6SF

Pre-School Playgroups Association (PPA)
61–63 Kings Cross Road, London WC1X 9LL

Parent to Parent Information on Adoption Service (PPIAS)
The Laurels, Lower Baddington, Daventry, Northants NN11 6YB

Professional Association for Nursery Nurses (PANN)
99 Friar Gate, Denby DE1 1EZ

The Law Society
113 Chancery Lane, London WC2A 1PL

Womens' Aid Federation
P.O. Box 31, Bristol BS99 7WS

Index

Acknowledgements

We should like to express our thanks to all our friends and colleagues who have helped in the preparation of this book.

Jack Ashton, Gill Bassett and Westminster Nannies, Dorothy Broadbent, Juliet Burcombe, Cherry Brain, Jill Brown, Karen Burton, Maud Carpenter, Anne Chilcott, Dorothy Clark, Gwen Cussans, Gill Davies, Doreen Deal, Sue Griffin and NCMA, Karen Gwinell, Peter Heaslip, Catherine Hodgson and Bristol Social Services, Pat Holmes and the West Midlands Education Authority Service for Travelling Children, Anne Jarrold, Libby Lee, Ann Lewis, Elizabeth Lloyd, Pam Marcus, Caroline Martin, Christine Menzies, Jane Nelson-Smith, and the Bristol Children's Hospital, The Open University, Jean Parker, Wendy Parslow, Gillian Pugh and the National Children's Bureau, Cindi Potter, Nora Quas and Bristol Home Plus, Maureen Rees, Keith Ripley, Joan Sharp, Mavis Simpson, Pat Smail, Tony Staunton, Christine Stone and the Fulford Road staff, Judy Watts and People Projects, Virginia Watson, Kay Williams, Mary Williams, Sheila Windsor, John Windsor and Isobel Worley.

The authors and publishers would also like to thank the following for permission to reproduce photographs and other illustrations:

Castlemead Publications, p. 113; Clarks Shoes Limited, p. 82; Lupe Cunha, pp. 90, 106; Gina Glover/Photo Co-op, p. 269; Sally and Richard Greenhill, pp. 10, 33, 44, 48, 75, 110, 115, 119, 125, 137, 139, 147, 152, 158, 165, 179, 195, 241; Hulton Picture Company, p. 271 (right); The Mansell Collection, p. 174; National Childminding Association, p. 259 (NB At the time of going to press, the NCMA contract form was under review. To obtain copies of the revised forms, see address on page 279.); RoSPA, p. 231; Janine Wiedel, p. 271 (left).